LEARNING ENGINEERING TOOLKIT

Evidence-Based Practices from the Learning Sciences, Instructional Design, and Beyond

Edited by Jim Goodell
with Janet Kolodner

Foreword by Chris Dede, Harvard University
Preface by Bror Saxberg

Contributions from Avron Barr, Michelle Barrett, Erin S. Barry, Laura Casey, Jesse Chuang, Scotty D. Craig, Erin Czerwinski, Brandt Dargue, Diana Delgado, Tanvi Domadia, Scott W. Greenwald, Andrew J. Hampton, Daniel Jacobs, Aaron Kessler, Dina Kurzweil, Jodi Lis, Prasad Ram, Brandt Redd, Steve Ritter, Sae Schatz, Jordan Richard Schoenherr, Robert Sottilare, Khanh-Phuong Thai, Richard Tong, and JJ Walcutt

Routledge
Taylor & Francis Group
NEW YORK AND LONDON

Accolades

"I am so impressed with how clearly and methodically this book has laid out the main tenets of the field and provided both practical examples and inspiring stories to bring the principles to life. I think this will be an immensely useful resource."

– **Joseph South, PhD**, Chief Learning Officer, International Society for Technology in Education, and former director of the Office of Educational Technology at the US Department of Education

"Popularized by MOOCs and the move to online learning during the pandemic, learning engineering is an emerging field that will become a standard discipline within universities in the years to come. Where science is the understanding of nature and engineering is the use of science in service of humanity, learning engineering incorporates learning science and cognitive science-based strategies to improve student outcomes. The *Toolkit* is an essential resource for understanding this field and a playbook for leveraging learning engineering."

– **Anant Agarwal, PhD**, Chief Open Education Officer at 2U and Founder of edX

"Great advancements in learning can come from a multi-disciplinary approach that recognizes the value of different professions and mindsets."

– **Angela L. Hernandez, EdD**, Lead Skills Architect, Western Governors University

"The outstanding authors of this text answered most of my uncertainties about the new learning engineering approach. The chapters in this well-written book clearly describe the questions that need to be addressed when designing learning experiences for all ages and contexts. It then provides tools that can be used to provide answers and generate new questions. Readers who might be concerned about whether 'engineering' can be applied to human learning will be impressed with the scope of the chapters and the examples provided.

I was especially attracted to the emphasis on supporting diverse learners and on making ethical decisions as well as the tools suggested for scaling small but successful efforts. The approach described in this book is our best hope for drawing together the many professional fields and specializations that attempt to create effective learning experiences in all areas. The authors clearly intend to adopt the best of what we've learned from past research in related areas while developing tools that fill the gaps in those areas. I intend to use the book as an introductory text for my undergraduate instructional design and educational psychology students."

– **Richard E. Clark, EdD**, Emeritus Professor of Educational Psychology and Technology, University of Southern California

"This new *Toolkit* brings together complementary, diverse, and fresh perspectives on learning and development in our rapidly changing world. I can see it forming an invaluable handbook for learning and development professionals, or curious organisational leaders interested in the science and engineering of effective learning at scale."

– **Julian Stodd**, author and founder of Sea Salt Learning

Accolades (Continued)

"I have talked with many CEOs of EdTech companies and chief learning officers over the past few years. All of them have asked, 'what is learning engineering and how do we do it?' I have wanted to have a handbook I could hand them and their teams to be able to better mature their systems for designing and improving learning. Well, here it is! Full of theory, process, methods, tools, and above all, examples, stories, and extremely practical tips. This book has everything a learning team needs to begin applying learning engineering. And no wonder: It was written by a truly cross-disciplinary, cross-industry, cross-functional, and truly boundary spanning team. This book will sit next to my computer—well worn and marked through—as I guide teams in building impactful learning experiences."

– **David Porcaro**, VP of Learning and Innovation at General Assembly and former Director of Learning Engineering at the Chan Zuckerberg Initiative

"The *Learning Engineering Toolkit* effectively introduces the foundations of this emerging field and then provides a plethora of tools, strategies, and relevant examples that help the reader clearly see what this might look like in practice. There are many valuable concepts here for learning scientists, data scientists, software engineers, and leaders of organizations who are seeking a systematic approach to actively designing and building interventions to improve learner outcomes. This book presents a compelling case for learning engineering as a distinct field and topic to which any future-thinking education professional should be paying attention."

– **Chris Millet**, Senior Director of Learning Design for the Penn State World Campus, Pennsylvania State University

"The references and storytelling bring new insights, a fresh perspective and wonderful synthesis."

– **Jim Flanagan**, Chief Operating and Strategy Officer, International Society for Technology in Education

"This book is an essential toolkit for learning and development professionals. It's a comprehensive roadmap for the new way of learning and working."

– **Amy A. Titus, EdD**, Human Capital Managing Director, Deloitte Consulting

"The *Learning Engineering Toolkit* offers a path to revolutionize how we experience learning at school and work—by codifying the development and delivery of learning as a data-driven, continuous design process. In the true spirit of human-centered design, learning engineering integrates the power of diverse scientific disciplines, mixed-methods data collection, and a bias for action through constant iteration and co-production with learners. Research is design, and design is research. By building evidence into every step of the learning design and delivery process, learning engineering can ensure learners engage fully, learn deeply, and perform optimally."

– **Sydney Heimbrock, PhD**, Chief Industry Advisor for Government, Qualtrics

Cover image created by Sae Schatz using Adobe Stock #245704448 by pickup

First published 2023
by Routledge
605 Third Avenue, New York, NY 10158

and by Routledge
4 Park Square, Milton Park, Abingdon, Oxon, OX14 4RN

Routledge is an imprint of the Taylor & Francis Group, an informa business

Library of Congress Cataloging-in-Publication Data
A catalog record for this title has been requested

ISBN: 9781032208503 (hbk)
ISBN: 9781032232829 (pbk)
ISBN: 9781003276579 (ebk)

DOI: 10.4324/9781003276579

Editing assistance, visual design, and typesetting (in Acumin Variable Concept, Calibri, Consolas, Ink Free, Market Pr, Nimbus Sans, P22 Cezanne Pro, Source Serif Variable, Times New Roman, and Wingdings) by Sae Schatz.

Publisher's Note: This book has been prepared from camera-ready copy provided by the editor.

CONTENTS

Contributors, Reviewers, Interviewees

In addition to the twenty-nine authors this book couldn't have been possible without countless others who participated in interviews or learning engineering groups, contributed key ideas, reviewed drafts of chapters, or helped with the publishing process. Some people listed here are named in stories used in the book and others played behind-the-scenes roles. And the community that influenced this book goes beyond those named here. Thank you, all!

AUTHORS

Avron Barr
Michelle Barrett
Erin S. Barry
Laura Casey
Jesse Chuang
Scotty D. Craig
Erin Czerwinski
Brandt Dargue
Chris Dede
Diana Delgado
Tanvi Domadia
Jim Goodell
Scott W. Greenwald
Andrew J. Hampton
Daniel Jacobs
Aaron Kessler
Janet Kolodner
Dina Kurzweil
Jodi Lis
Prasad Ram
Brandt Redd
Steve Ritter
Bror Saxberg
Sae Schatz
Jordan Richard Schoenherr
Robert Sottilare
Khanh-Phuong Thai
Richard Tong
JJ Walcutt

OTHER CONTRIBUTORS

Vincent Alevin
Anthony Altieri
Maria Andersen
Mart Aro
Brenda Bannan
Michelle Beasley
Peter Berking
Sujata Bhatt
Norman Bier
Shelly Blake-Plock
Chris Blakesley
Mitch Bonnett
Bill Brandon
Chelsea Chandler
Alexandria Clapp
Donald Clark
Richard Clark
Nicola Cleveland
Ted Courtney
Francisco Crespi
Richard Culatta
Alisha Dakon
Meghan Edwards
Sarah Ensor
Charles Fadel
Cameron Fadjo
Stephen Fancsali
Jim Flanagan
Marie Franetovic
Shane Gallagher
Kirti Garg
Kumar Garg
Patrick Getchell
Ian Gibson
John Gillmore
Christian Glahn
Amos Glenn
Barish Golland
Abigail Goodell
Benjamin Goodell
Patti Goodell
Sunil Gunderia
Shawn Hammack
Sherri Hartzell
Cristina Heffernan
Neil Heffernan
Angela L. Hernandez
Davinia Hernandez-Leo

Kelli Hill
Michael Horn
Nick Howe
Simon Hsu
Shakir Hussain
Michael Jay
Edward Jennings
Bill Jerome
Andy Johnson
Alisha Kadon
David Kelly
Whitney Kilgore
Lissa Klueter
Ken Koedinger
Chad Lane
Kim Larson
Lisa Larson
Mark Lee
Hao Li
Eddie Lin
Marsha Lovett
Laura Lukes
Linda Macaulay
Susan Magdziarz
Greg Maki
Emily Marasco
Karen Marcellas
Andrew McCallister
Brendan Meeder
Christopher Millet
Lee Mitchell
Piotr Mitros
Tom Moher
Erin Mote
John Murray
Alan Mustafa
Katie Nicksic
Amy Ogan
Jenna Olsen
Elizabeth Owen
Kevin Owens
Bozena Pajak
Jim Paradiso
Martina Pavelko
Jenessa Peterson
Oliver Pincus
David Porcaro
Mark Potter
Stephanie Pounds
Mike Preble
Andrew Scott Pyle
Thomas Reeves
Jess Resig
Robby Robson
Jeremy Roschelle
Todd Rose
Meagan Rothschild
Anindya Roy
Nicholas Runco
Henry Ryng
Ali Sadakon
Michael Sandbothe
Rebecca Scales
Richard Scheines
Daniel Schwartz
Burr Settles
Eric Shepherd
Aaron Silvers
Kimbery Sinnott
Joseph South
Jess Stahl
Nick Stanley
Adam Sullivan
William Sullivan, Jr.
Candace Thille
Allyssa Thompson
Laura Thompson
Kristin Torrence
Lauren Totino
Eric Tucker
Rachel Van Campenhout
Tom VanderArk
Todd Vanek
Ellen Wagner
Lynn Wietecha
Craig Wiggins
David Wiley
Beverly Woolf
Fred Yan
Michael Yudelson
Leonora Zefi
Carrie Zierath
Participants in IEEE ICICLE
Participants in the Learning Engineering Google Group

Editorial oversight by Janet Kolodner.

Special thanks to Benjamin Goodell for countless hours of copyediting, compilation, facilitation, and ghostwriting some stories based on interview transcripts. And special thanks to the Quality Information Partners team for supporting this project and copyediting.

Foreword

The pandemic is a terrible human tragedy, but it has silver linings, as illustrated in this series of innovation stories: silverliningforlearning.org. This Toolkit describes one of the opportunities that forced remote instruction has created: large-scale engineering of learning. Potentially, we now have sufficient students and enough streams of multi-dimensional data to personalize each learner's experience: time, path, pace, place, choice, and voice. It's disappointing that many institutions are not recognizing this opportunity. Campus services that support continuous evidence-based innovation in face-to-face instruction have typically not created a learning engineering infrastructure in the rapid and chaotic transition to remote teaching. Nor have they conducted professional development on how instructors might take advantage of personalization to each student, which is a powerful way of empowering marginalized and underrepresented populations to realize their full potential.

Although this failure to implement learning engineering is disappointing, it's clear that the pandemic is not going away anytime soon, and we are far from some stable "new normal." Over the next few years of online and HyFlex teaching, we can apply the strategies, heuristics, and insights in this Toolkit. If engineering learning at scale is realized, not only will many students and instructors benefit, but also we will gain many new insights about the nature of learning itself.

Chris Dede
Harvard University

Preface

by Bror Saxberg

This book is a terrific source of insights, tools, and frameworks for *learning engineering*. That term is not a new one—it was used by Herb Simon back in the late 1960s to describe what university faculty members ought to be like when they are teaching—but the fundamental importance of the idea seemed to disappear over decades. This book does much to make clear why it's a valuable practice, and how to do it.

Learning engineering is about the design of learning solutions in the real world. This means, at its best, working with and within the constraints of communities and learners, focused on clearly defined actions we want learners to become able to decide and do, grounded in the sciences of learning and development, being guided by (but not limited to) research and practice that has come before, and generating and using high-quality evidence to problem-solve and iterate from an initial solution to better solutions over time.

Like many engineering initiatives (civil engineering, chemical engineering, electrical engineering, and even medicine has an engineering flavor to it), learning engineering is inherently multidisciplinary. While cognitive psychology and education research have important insights to offer, as this book points out, so does data science, computer science, motivational psychology, ethics, and more. This is inherently a complex undertaking if you want to do it well.

It's worth the complexity, and worth doing it well. First, ignoring the complexity doesn't make it go away: You may wish that all learners master writing the same way, from the same experiences and examples, but that does not make it so, inconveniently and unfortunately. There have been many well-meaning but unsuccessful efforts to "solve education" by scaling tools that worked in one context, with one type of learner, with the hope that "surely this will work for all kids," only for schools, students, teachers, and parents to discover it's not that easy.

Engaging with the complexity is especially worthwhile now, in a context of rapid change in tools, expertise, and best practices for organizations. If we can get a deep and clear understanding of what top performers decide and do (both consciously and nonconsciously) and how that changes over time, we will have insights on how key people's decisions and tasks should change—and how the associated learning environments must change too. The real value of improving the median performance of high-value, high-volume, high-variance decision-makers in an organization (project managers in a construction firm, teachers/faculty/trainers in a learning environment, nurses in a health care setting, and so on) to get closer to that of top performers is often substantial.

Becoming good at learning engineering also allows an organization to take advantage of the substantial familiarity of existing employees with the organization's history, mission, purpose, and stakeholders. If you try to "fire and hire" your way to improved skills within an organization, the increasingly rapid pace of expertise change means you are having to replace key decision-makers faster and faster. Unfortunately, the deep mastery of relationships, mission, and context takes time (years, often) to master, so rapid turnover works against you. Reliably changing what your own people decide and do instead of changing out your people gives you the best of both worlds.

This approach also pays dividends for people's careers. As our working lives become longer, we can build more expertise. It does not have to be in the same field as we start out with: Research suggests it takes about ten years of intense half-time effort to build to world-class expertise in many domains. If our working lives now stretch out for four, five, even six decades, think of the combinatoric possibilities: For example, you might start out becoming an expert gardener, then shift to becoming an expert at business, then add robotics to your list: You are now the perfect person to set up a world-class robotic gardening company (especially if you add expertise in law to deal with inevitable lawsuits). The combinatorics are very helpful: If you take hundreds of different kinds of expertise, cross these together to create multi-domain experts, far from becoming irrelevant to the future, people become uniquely qualified to innovate in the many new niches unlocked.

What does it take to do great learning engineering?

As mentioned above, and discussed in the book, a first step is deeply and clearly understanding what you are trying to get people to decide and do, perhaps by understanding what top performers decide and do (both consciously and unconsciously), with techniques like cognitive task analysis.

It is important to recognize that top performers are usually not narrow domain experts: They are often also expert at communication, prioritization, organizing teams, motivation, and more, which are often not taught to mastery within conventional training programs in school or in the workplace. Real value accrues to organizations that recognize this and whose experts then master these additional areas.

Tied closely to defining what we need people to become able to decide and do is to develop sources of evidence about their ability to decide and do these things. Following the evidence-centered design approach from the science of learning measurement, the key is to accept the multi-dimensionality of the evidence-gathering process: Instead of one perfect measure of a skill or capacity, think deeply about what many instantiations and consequences of a complex skill should occur, and then instrument many sources of evidence to look for these consequences. Yes, this creates a complex picture—but the consequences of skill acquisition are a complex picture in the real world.

In addition, it's critically important to be aware how different contexts for learning and performance mean differences in the learning environments. Unlike certain medical problems where the treatment depends almost exclusively on what bug you have, or what narrow deficit you have, almost everything about successful learning depends on various contexts: What have you already mastered related to the new skills? What other things have you mastered or are you deeply familiar with that could be drawn on to start learning new complex skills (limiting the cognitive load)? What issues of motivation, including identity, are already cemented in your mind before starting a round of learning, which may either help your progress, or provide an additional challenge to be worked through? While important to draw on research and experience from other settings, this means it is especially important to use inclusive and equitable design processes, co-creating as closely as possible with the people who will be doing the learning and the teaching, so as not to miss critical elements of context that could help you or create unexpected challenges.

Often, too, not enough attention is paid to the training of the other adults in the learning environment. Many professional development experiences are dreaded by teachers and trainers for good reason: They often do not reflect the application of learning and development science principles, or a rich understanding of the training/learning context, to train teachers and trainers for their work with students. This runs the risk of creating incoherent learning environments for students, as some of their experiences (for example, technology-enhanced ones) may reflect one approach to learning, while other experiences (mediated by adults) may reflect a different approach. It makes sense to design professional development for teachers/trainers at the same time as you design new learning environments for students/trainees, and use the same principles of evidence-grounded and context-aware learning design, working closely with students and their teachers, to create complete, coherent, and continuously improving learning environments.

That last point is worth repeating: Expect to iterate. With any complex innovation project, even as you do your best to create a high-functioning first draft, you should expect things to not go as expected for many different reasons. That means before you start, think ahead to what might go wrong and try to instrument what might be at risk. This way when failure occurs (and it usually will), you have a rich set of data to narrow in on exactly where in a complex set of interlocking processes and conditions the problem(s) might be. The mantra must be, *Celebrate success, but instrument for failure!*

This book provides guidance for all these ideas. Authored by a wealth of experts from many different disciplines with a wide range of experiences, you will find all kinds of wisdom through many different lenses to help your projects be successful. The book is filled with examples of learning engineering in practice—it celebrates learning engineering as something enacted in the world, not a theory. The language and purpose is overwhelmingly practical, suited to giving good guidance to many different kinds of readers. And it includes a range of stories about many different kinds of learning engineers tackling different challenges in the world.

As our need to change what we decide and do to follow the changing nature of expertise increases, becoming better at learning engineering allows our organizations and individuals to continue to grow, add value, and be motivated over their entire lives. This book provides a terrific toolkit to help expand the repertoire of methods to achieve extraordinary outcomes for people that can continue to improve over time. ★

INTRODUCTION

SECTION INCLUDES "HOW TO USE THIS BOOK"
+ EXPLAINS LEARNING ENGINEERING

START HERE

INTRODUCTION

How do I use this book?

by Jim Goodell

If you want to get the most out of this book, there is one thing that matters more than any technique or rule. Unless you have this one thing, a thousand techniques and strategies for learning and development will have little value. And if you do have this one thing, then we think you can achieve great things with the insights and tools in this book. Do you have a deep desire to help people learn? Do you have a driving desire to help people reach their full potential and enjoy the new opportunities that learning will bring to their lives? You do? Congratulations!

Whatever your specific motivation—making the world a better place, being a part of something bigger than yourself, improving the success of the work you do, helping more people learn about what matters most to you, opening up your own career opportunities and achieving personal success, or creating new opportunities for success and fulfillment for traditionally disadvantaged people, or all of the above—that deep desire to help people learn is essential to get the most out of this book.

Picture yourself, in whatever role you play or will play, being part of something bigger than yourself, achieving great success, and being a valued key contributor to the learning experiences and conditions for learning that help people achieve unprecedented success. Imagine breakthroughs in learning that are exponentially better than what you see in today's classrooms, training facilities, or online and blended learning environments. Constantly remind yourself how important these breakthroughs in learning are to you and how mastery of the concepts and use of the tools in this book will lead to the richer, more fulfilled future for yourself and for others.

[1]

The introduction section is designed to cover the big ideas and set the context for the rest of the book. The "What is Learning Engineering?" chapter is supported by stories of real people doing learning engineering. Stories have proven effective at making ideas stick. We suggest you start by reading through the introduction section quickly at first to get the big picture and then reread it, stopping frequently to compare these concepts to your current approaches and notions of learning engineering. Even though your circumstances may be different from those of the people and organizations in the stories, you can look for ideas that you can transfer to your situation. Think about how the ideas might apply to you. What kinds of changes in your own thinking and practices, or the practices of your organization, would be needed to realize the potential of these learning engineering approaches? As you work through the book, consider how to apply what you're learning to your own professional development in the field of learning engineering.

[2]

Although we suggest a sequential read through the introduction section, you may want to randomly access other parts of the book, read some chapters out of order depending on your background knowledge and interests to suit your learning, and later reference different parts as you apply the tools to real learning engineering contexts. Some of the stories interwoven throughout the book build on one another, but the benefit of your self-directed active learning will override the value of reading the stories in sequential order, and they will make sense either way. So, feel free to follow the order in the book or jump around. Do whatever works for you.

The sequential book format is not ideal for all kinds of learning and certainly not how you would use a toolkit, so we recommend adapting it to your needs at different stages of learning and application. You can think of this book as content in a learner-centered adaptive learning system, but you need to provide the intelligence to adapt the system. We've only provided some imperfect tools to help you fit some new ideas into what you already know, assess what you're learning, and adjust what you do next to make it work best for you at any point in the process. Selectively use the parts of this book, at appropriate times, to augment your own intelligence and performance as a learning engineering professional.

[3]

This volume is meant to offer a kit of practical tools that can be applied to learning engineering. You can use the tools section in chapters eight through nineteen as you engage with each step of the learning engineering process. The section also includes tools and recommended practices that may be broadly applied across the learning engineering process including learning engineering as a team, Lean-Agile development, software and technology standards, learner motivation, design patterns for learning, and ethical decision-making.

Tools have no value unless they are put to work. So, look for every opportunity to use the tools in this book. Experiment with different tools and approaches in your own work. What tools work best for what kinds of challenges? Reflect on what tools worked well and why. How might small changes in how you do your work result in products that better support learners and learning? The more you apply the concepts and strategies, the more you will fix them into your long-term memory and cause them to become valuable habits of mind and practice.

[4]

This toolkit, just like any learning engineering solution, is intended to be iteratively improved based on data about learner/user experiences. Please give us feedback on your experiences with the book and how we might improve it in future revisions or through supplemental services or resources. Send comments and suggestions by email to:

learning.engineering.toolkit@gmail.com

Please note that we (the editor and authors) will not be able to respond personally to every comment or suggestion—*but we'll try!* ★

SCIENCE AT SCALE

INTRODUCTION

What is learning engineering?

by Jim Goodell

Many people are uncomfortable when the words *learning* and *engineering* are used together. Online discussion threads on the topic of learning engineering prompted strong reactions. One comment compared learning to the weather—a complex outcome of social, cultural, and economic conditions that cannot be engineered (or engineered for). Someone else correctly pointed out that learning is what a learner does, not something done to the learner.

Learning is a human process, and "engineering" sounds too mechanical or industrial. The "art" of teaching sounds more natural. When talking about creating solutions for learning, isn't "design" a better term? The words *learning engineering* justifiably raise concerns and questions, especially for professionals who care deeply about human learning at all levels. In the following pages, we define learning engineering—it's engineering *for* learning. Learning engineers don't engineer learning any more than civil engineers engineer civilians. Just as civil engineers create and maintain physical infrastructure *for the benefit* of civilians, learning engineering creates solutions *for the benefit* of learners and learning.

People from diverse fields of practice have wondered, is *learning engineering* just a new label on what we already do? Is it possible for a teacher, instructional designer, learning scientist, data scientist, or instructional system designer to *do* learning engineering? If it's different from what people already do, how is it different?

Through the following pages, we hope to answer those questions and make the case for learning engineering as a professional practice that complements related professional practices and fields of study. We offer stories about teams of professionals doing learning engineering—whether they call it learning engineering or use a different name. In practice, however, what most education, training, and learning analytics professionals do daily only partially overlaps with the practice of learning engineering. Learning engineering is often concerned with solving problems that teachers, curriculum designers, and textbook publishers are not usually asked to solve.

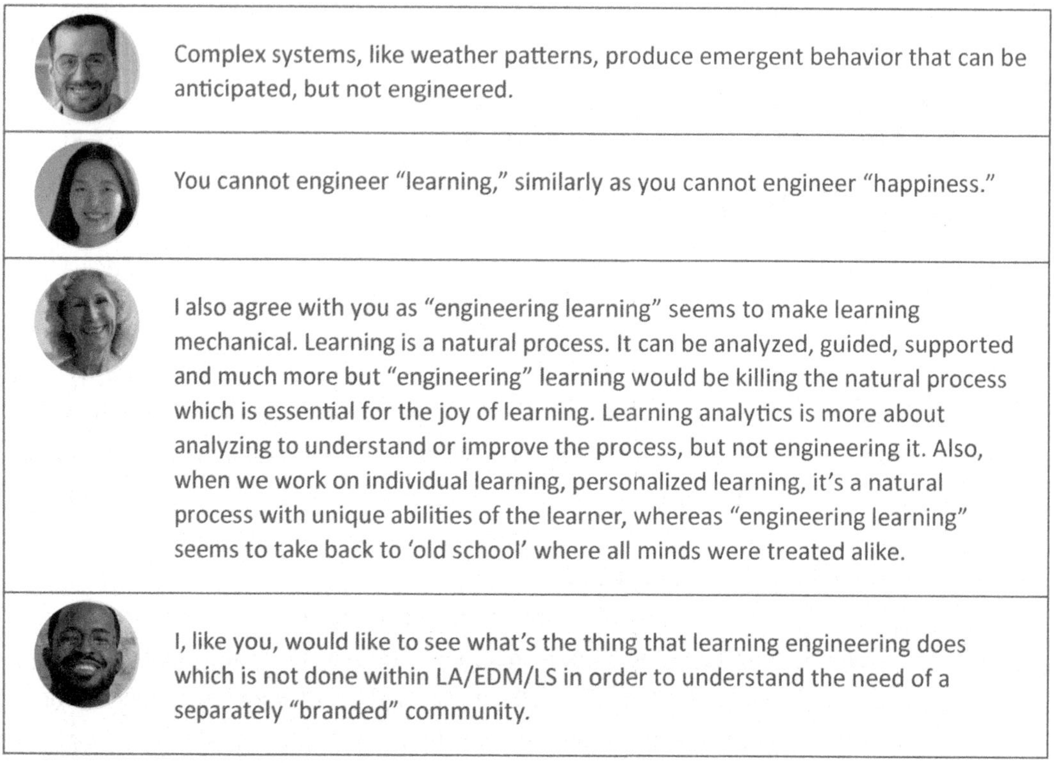

FIGURE 0.1. Discussion thread about learning engineering (adapted from real discussion)

This book offers learning and e-learning professionals opportunities to improve their work with additional engineering tools, techniques, and mindsets (without changing the name of what they do). And it offers foundational knowledge and tools for those wishing to practice as learning engineers.

[1]

In 1928, Scottish scientist Alexander Fleming discovered penicillin. The discovery was a scientific breakthrough that saved countless lives during and since World War II. The 1945 Nobel Prize in Physiology or Medicine was awarded to Fleming and two Oxford University scientists who made progress in making concentrated penicillin and proved the effects of the drug. However, the Nobel Prize–winning scientists never developed the ability to produce the drug at scale. The Oxford team found that it was impossible to produce in sufficient quantities in their laboratory.

In 1941, mounting deaths from World War II battle wounds prompted these British scientists to reach out for help from the United States. The Rockefeller Foundation in New York arranged for Howard Florey and Norman G. Heatley to travel in July 1941 to meet with Charles Thorn, the US Department of Agriculture's chief mycologist. As a result of that trip, thirty-nine separate drug laboratories began producing penicillin. The United States entered the war later that year when the Japanese bombed the American fleet in Pearl Harbor, Hawaii.

But by June 1942, the US labs had only enough penicillin available to treat about ten patients. The urgency of lives being lost in the war meant that production of penicillin needed to move out of the laboratory and into mass-production. This was no longer just a scientific endeavor; it required engineering.

The goals of science and engineering are different. The goal of science is to discover the truth about the world as it is. The goal of engineering is to create scalable solutions to problems using science as one tool in that endeavor. Like engineers, scientists use data to find the truth. They are concerned about reliability of the data and what the data reveal about general principles by which we understand our universe. Outlier data are often ignored by scientists as noise. Engineers are often concerned about outlier data. For example, scientists may be interested in better understanding the physics of flight. An engineering team, on the other hand, might want to know exactly what outlier conditions cause one specific airplane design to crash and for what reason. Scalable designs require manufacturing tolerances for parts that eliminate outlier failures.

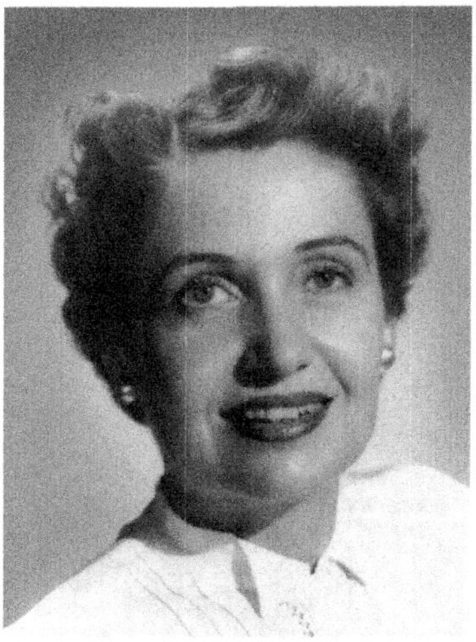

FIGURE 0.2.
Margaret Hutchinson Rousseau

Credit: Walter P. Reuther Library, Archives of Labor and Urban Affairs, Wayne State University

Margaret Hutchinson Rousseau was the first woman to earn a PhD in chemical engineering from MIT and the first woman to be accepted as a member of the American Institute of Chemical Engineers. She oversaw the design of production plants for strategically important materials during the war, including synthetic rubber and penicillin.

Pfizer scientist Jasper H. Kane suggested using a deep-tank fermentation, a method Pfizer had used to produce vitamin C. On September 20, 1942, Pfizer purchased the old Rubel Ice Plant on Marcy Avenue in Brooklyn, NY.[1] It had the refrigeration equipment needed and was equipped with fourteen 7,500-gallon tanks. Dr. Rousseau worked with a multidisciplinary team to turn the Rubel Ice Plant building into the first deep-tank penicillin fermentation commercial plant. In March 1943, the plant began producing penicillin.

The process started with a sterile culture of the penicillin mold grown in three-liter flasks, then in two-hundred-gallon seed tanks, and finally in one of the fourteen 7,500-gallon tanks. Then the drug needed to be extracted from the broth, purified, bottled, frozen, and dehydrated. Large quantities of the broth needed to be produced because 10,000 parts broth only contained four parts of the drug.[2]

By May 1943, deep-tank fermentation produced 400 million units of penicillin. In July 1943, the United States War Production Board supported a plan for mass distribution of penicillin stocks to Allied troops fighting in Europe. Hutchinson's engineered process and those developed by other engineers such as G. Raymond Rettew made it possible for the United States to produce 2.3 million doses in time for the invasion of Normandy in the spring of 1944 and over 646 billion units per year by June 1945. This engineered process is credited with helping to win the war.

This story is a victory for both science and engineering.

To scale innovations for broad use in education and training also requires both science and engineering. Learning scientists discover what works in human learning, and learning engineering teams develop production models for scaled impact. Learning engineering aims to optimize specific learning solutions to understand under what conditions and with what learners a current design is optimal or not, and to develop and test alternative more robust, or more refined, solutions that are more scalable. Just like with the discovery and production of penicillin, great advancements in learning can come from a multidisciplinary approach that recognizes the value of different professions and mindsets.

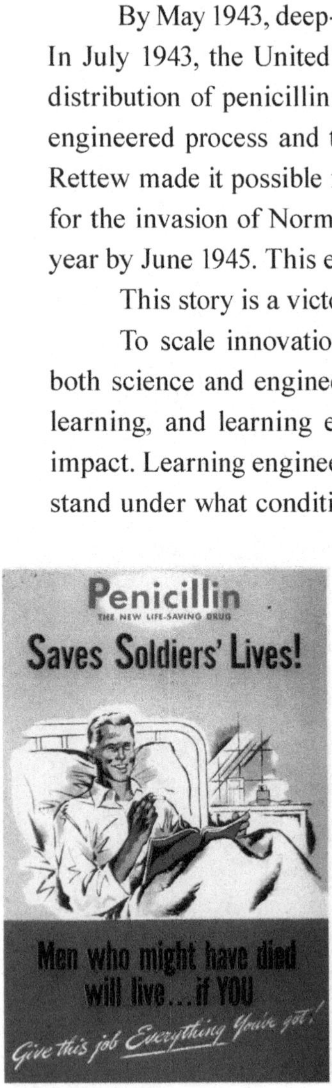

FIGURE 0.3. World War II poster, "Penicillin Saves Soldiers' Lives!"

[2]

If you want to learn about learning engineering, a good place to start is Pittsburgh, Pennsylvania. What was once the steel-making capital of the world is also arguably the birthplace of, and a focal point for, the emerging field of learning engineering.

More than fifty years ago, Herb Simon, a Carnegie Mellon University Professor, coined the term "learning engineering."[3] Simon, a Nobel Laureate, was instrumental in launching departments at the Pittsburgh-based university that continues to be a world leader in cognitive and learning sciences, learning technologies, and the application of the sciences to optimize human learning.

Pittsburgh is also home to the Pittsburgh Science of Learning Center (a.k.a. LearnLab) managed by Carnegie Mellon University and the University of Pittsburgh, and it's the home of spin-off businesses developing some of the world's most innovative platforms and solutions for learning.

FIGURE 0.4.
Herbert A. Simon
CC-BY-SA by Richard Rappaport

While the theoretical idea of learning engineering is over fifty years old, the formal definition of learning engineering as a professional practice is still emerging. However, in the pages that follow you'll read about teams in Pittsburgh and elsewhere developing exemplary solutions using learning engineering practices. Their stories paint a picture of what it means to do learning engineering as a professional practice.

[3]

In 2018, IEEE—the organization that developed the standards behind WiFi and Bluetooth—established the Industry Connections / Industry Consortium on Learning Engineering (ICICLE). The group was established to help define and advance the profession of learning engineering. Participants in ICICLE include experts from fields of learning sciences, instructional design, learning technology, psychometrics (an area of study concerned with measurement of knowledge, abilities, attitudes, and personality traits), learning analytics, user experience design, and other fields.

Some of the leaders influencing the work of ICICLE have ties to the roots of learning engineering. People like Ken Koedinger at Carnegie Mellon University can draw their academic lineage back to Herb Simon, the visionary who coined the term learning engineering. With ICICLE, Ken co-led the Curriculum Special Interest Group with Mark Lee. That group began the development of a formal definition of learning engineering.

Establishing a clear and concise definition was not easy. Just like today, some people felt uncomfortable with the words *learning* and *engineering* being used together. Others wondered if learning engineering was unique enough, or if it was just a new label for what they already do. The participants debated what makes learning engineering unique based on a first draft by Ken, Mark, and Janet Kolodner. Before establishing a concise definition, Ken's group merged with the learning engineering Competencies and Credentials Special Interest Group led by Jim Goodell and Michael Jay. The combined groups came to consensus on a definition that was adopted by ICICLE. That definition is as follows:

Learning engineering is a process and practice that . . .

1. applies the learning sciences,
2. using human-centered engineering design methodologies, and
3. data-informed decision-making

. . . to support learners and their development.

The products of learning engineering are the conditions and experiences under which people can achieve great learning outcomes.

Just like with the discovery and production of penicillin, great advancements in learning can come from a multidisciplinary approach that recognizes the value of different professions and mindsets. In 2018 and 2019, Janet Kolodner was leading ICICLE's Design for Learning group. Janet is a superstar in the world of the learning sciences, having been the founding editor in chief of *The Journal of the Learning Sciences,* a founding executive officer of the International Society of the Learning Sciences (ISLS), and a founding program officer of the Cyberlearning and Future Learning Technologies program of the National Science Foundation (now called RETTL). While leading the ICICLE Design for Learning group, Janet helped launch a master's degree program in learning engineering at Boston College.

Janet's group helped develop the idea that learning engineering is often a team sport. They recognized the wealth of knowledge and talent in well-developed fields of learning experience design. They explored the knowledge, skills, and mindsets that were needed for those who design learning experiences and learning systems. Then they developed a conceptual model for the kinds of professionals who might work with designers to solve learning engineering problems.

For the 2019 ICICLE Conference, they gave input into a flower diagram with petals representing the professional fields that might be part of solving a learning engineering problem. Figure 0.5 is a later iteration of that diagram based on input from the ICICLE community.

In the closing session of that conference, Chris Dede observed that "Learning engineering is more of a verb than a noun." (Chris Dede is the Timothy E. Wirth professor in learning technologies at Harvard Graduate School of Education and editor of *Learning Engineering for Online Education*[4] and *The 60-Year Curriculum.*[5])

For some challenges, an individual learning engineer with expertise in multiple disciplines might be sufficient. But usually, the big problems to be solved through learning engineering exceed any one person's ability. Consider this description of a learning engineer from the Educause Learning Initiative's resource, *7 Things You Should Know About Learning Engineering:*

> Learning engineers typically have broad knowledge of engineering processes as well as of learning science, computer science, and data science. In addition to understanding instructional design, artificial intelligence and machine learning, pedagogy, and andragogy, they offer skills in systems and user experience design, product testing, and the development of policies, regulations, and standards. They leverage those skills to create learning experiences, courses, and curricula; define educational competencies and assessment standards; and use research and data to improve teaching and learning.[6]

It's extremely rare for any one person to have expertise in all of these areas. Organizations have found it difficult to recruit candidates with such a breadth of competencies.[7] Indeed, it is probably appropriate to refine the Educause definition by making it a definition of a "learning engineering team" as much as that of an individual learning engineer.

Given the multidisciplinary expertise needed on a learning engineering team, we envision multiple paths to learning engineering talent development. For example, a person may start with a credential in instructional design or software engineering and add to that foundation understanding of how people learn. He/she/they may add to their knowledge and skills by engaging in formal coursework, learning from others on the team, or participating in workshops put on by other professionals. Everyone on the learning engineering team doesn't need to know everything, they just need to know enough to communicate with the other experts on the team. (See Chapter 10, Tools for Teaming.)

As important as talent development for the individuals who will contribute to a learning engineering team is the development of the team culture, organizational processes, and a shared vocabulary.

We've observed learning engineering as a team *process* that builds on professional specialties within the engineering team as a coordinated effort rooted in a shared understanding and vocabulary. Also, we've observed that the application of learning engineering generally falls into at least three categories:

1. Learning engineer as *consultant* (e.g., teaming with an instructor)
2. Learning engineer as a *member of a team* designing learning experiences, platforms, resources, or other solutions as a contributor or as the lead learning engineer that coordinates across the various other specialists and sets the direction for the work to be done
3. *Multiple learning engineering professionals*—having a base set of common competencies and shared vocabularies for the practice of learning engineering while having different roles and areas of expertise

Different professional practices, work processes, and team dynamics apply to each kind of team. In teams with multiple learning engineers, the work may be organized by smaller role-based teams that influence decisions about different aspects of the iterative design.

While we've observed learning engineering being done by teams of people who are not called learning engineers, we've also observed an emergence of a distinct professional discipline and job title. These engineers have specific competencies and mindsets and a specific role in the learning engineering process, just as a civil engineer has a specific role in the building of a bridge. Chapter 4, Learning Engineering is Engineering, covers some perspectives on engineering professions. Other chapters include stories in contexts where "learning engineer" is identified as a job title.

[4]

Located in the culturally diverse East Liberty neighborhood of Pittsburgh's East End is the headquarters for Duolingo, home of the team behind the award-winning language learning platform. It's no coincidence that the team is located just two miles from the Carnegie Mellon University campus where Herb Simon coined the term learning engineering. It's one of several learning technology companies with roots in CMU's Human-Computer Interaction Institute, derived from its Departments of Psychology and Computer Science. The company was founded by Carnegie Mellon University professor Luis von Ahn and his graduate student Severin Hacker.[8]

On a chilly Friday in November, Mark Lee and Jim Goodell met with Burr

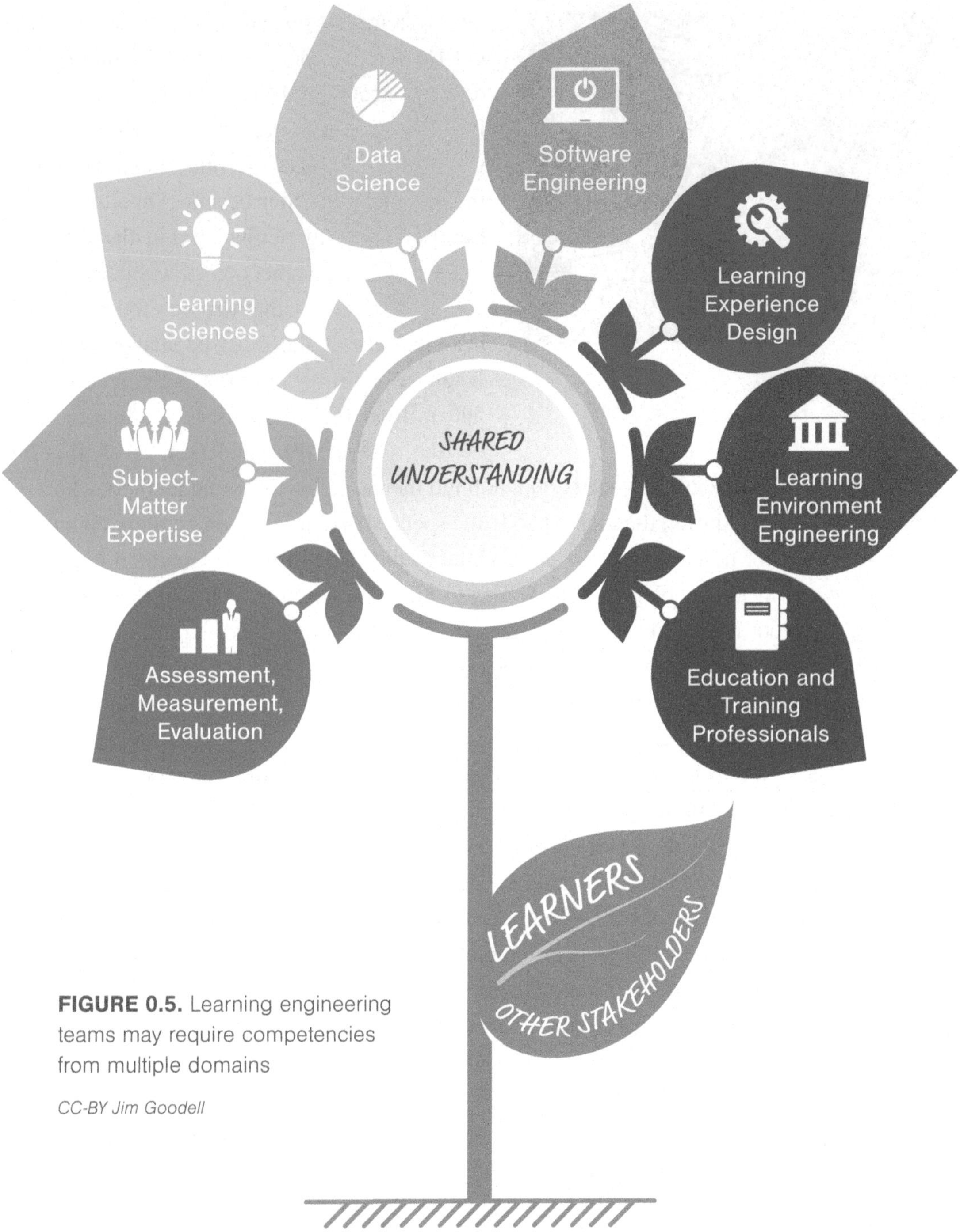

FIGURE 0.5. Learning engineering teams may require competencies from multiple domains

★ IMPORTANT DIAGRAM

FIGURE 0.6. Bozena Pajak and Burr Settles at Duolingo

Settles, a former postdoc at Carnegie Mellon University who now leads Duolingo's research group, and his colleague Bozena Pajak, a linguist and learning engineer who at the time had the title Staff Learning Scientist and later became Director of Learning and Curriculum. From the outside of the inconspicuous gray building, you wouldn't know that this was the world headquarters of the most popular mobile language learning platform, serving over 500 million registered users. (Influenced by the COVID-19 pandemic, over the month of March 2020, new users on Duolingo increased by 101% and learners who joined Duolingo during the global pandemic spent 13% more time on Duolingo than was typical for new users in the past.[9]) One of the ways in which Duolingo is innovative is in its use of game mechanics to motivate learners. "One of the tricks is figuring out how to marry things that are pedagogically sound with things that are reinforcing motivators," Burr told us. To figure these things out, they use engineering techniques rooted in scientific research. "We run controlled experiments for almost everything we change," he said.[10]

This kind of testing and iterative improvement is a common practice among practitioners of learning engineering whether the product is an app, course content, or changes to a learning environment.

For every design decision that the Duolingo team makes, they have to consider multiple metrics of success. Those metrics include measures of learning, measures of user engagement, and how user interactions impact the company's bottom line. They know that to continue to provide free language learning to millions of people around the world they need to stay in business. This means that every decision is a balance between these metrics. If they can improve one metric without hurting the others, they do it.

The team at Duolingo improves its products through its own scientific research while applying the scientific discoveries of others. For example, they know from prior learning sciences research that when learning new words, the best time to practice is when you are on the verge of forgetting.

"Our approach is based on the spacing effect: the finding that short practices spaced out over time is better for learning than 'cramming.' A related finding is the lag effect: You can learn even better if you gradually increase the spacing between practices. These ideas go back to 1885, when German psychologist Hermann Ebbinghaus pioneered the concept of the forgetting curve."[11]

The science of learning is informed by what we know about how the mind works. These sciences include:[12]

- **Neuroscience:** Biological studies of the nervous system and brain
- **Cognitive psychology:** Study of the human mind through behaviors
- **Learning sciences:** Study of learning in realistic settings
- **Education research:** Models and interventions at the classroom+ level
- **And others**: As well as many other disciplines, such as developmental psychology, social psychology, and anthropology[13]

Learning engineering is informed by the combination of what each of these research traditions has to offer. Learning engineering also can benefit from research in areas of cognitive and social psychology such as behavioral economics (the study of psychology as it relates to economic decision-making) that can help us in understanding learner motivation and engagement. Emerging opportunities in learning engineering take advantage of biomedical research and development for innovations, such as devices that monitor learner attention levels using EEG (electroencephalogram) sensors that monitor brain waves. Finally, learning engineering is increasingly the application of data science—an interdisciplinary field that uses scientific methods, processes, algorithms and systems to extract knowledge and insights from data. It has been called the "fourth paradigm for scientific exploration."[14]

Some of these sciences are relatively new. Neuroscience was first recognized as a unique academic discipline in the 1950s and 1960s,[15] cognitive science was established in the mid-1970s,[16] and learning sciences emerged in the 1990s.[17] And yet the pace of discovery has accelerated with the help of innovations like functional magnetic resonance imaging (fMRI) and genomic mapping of the brain.[18]

Learning science findings applicable to learning engineering include cognitive, noncognitive, and motivational aspects of learning. Environmental and noncognitive physiological factors are also considered, such as physical health and safety, relationships, and social contexts.

Learning engineers are concerned not only with how the brain works in general, for the average person, but also understanding and empathizing with the uniqueness of each learner. In *The End of Average,* Harvard Professor Todd Rose showed that no one is an "average size." The size of a person can be measured on multiple dimensions (height, weight, shoulders, reach, chest, torso, waist, hips, legs).

To understand a person's learning and talent development requires measuring many more dimensions than those physical attributes of size.

> Just about any meaningful human characteristic—especially talent—consists of multiple dimensions. The problem is that when trying to measure talent, we frequently resort to the average, reducing our jagged talent to a single dimension like the score on a standardized test or grades or a job performance ranking. But when we succumb to this kind of one-dimensional thinking, we end up in deep trouble.[19]

Two students could get the exact same set of questions wrong on a test, but for different reasons. Promoting robust learning requires addressing those multiple reasons. Learning engineers ask the *why* questions to determine the multi-dimensional reasons that individuals might or might not master a learning objective under various conditions. With insights into possible root-causes, they create and test solutions that might overcome those problems.

Good learning engineers have a deep understanding of how the human brain learns and develops: "Because trying to reengineer learning without being versed in the basics of learning is like trying to improve brain surgery without knowing much about the brain."[20]

[5]

An engineering design methodology particularly suited to learning engineering is called **human-centered design**, a problem-solving process that begins with empathetically understanding a challenge that people face and then iteratively developing and discovering a best fit solution for a given person or group to meet a specific need within a specific context.

Human-centered design existed as a practice long before it was formalized and given a name. In 1894, Will Kellogg used human-centered design to invent a breakfast cereal.[21] His older brother John Harvey Kellogg was a medical doctor and director of a hospital in Battle Creek, Michigan. Will, a former broom salesman, moved to Battle Creek to help his brother at the hospital. They had empathy for the patients who were struggling to eat toast in the hospital setting. John was a nutritionist and concerned about the digestibility of his patient's foods. They wanted to offer an alternative. With this need in mind, Will experimented with a pot of boiled wheat that he had left out overnight. He rolled it out and baked it. The crispy flakes were the first of many iterations over several years to perfect the process. He gave it to

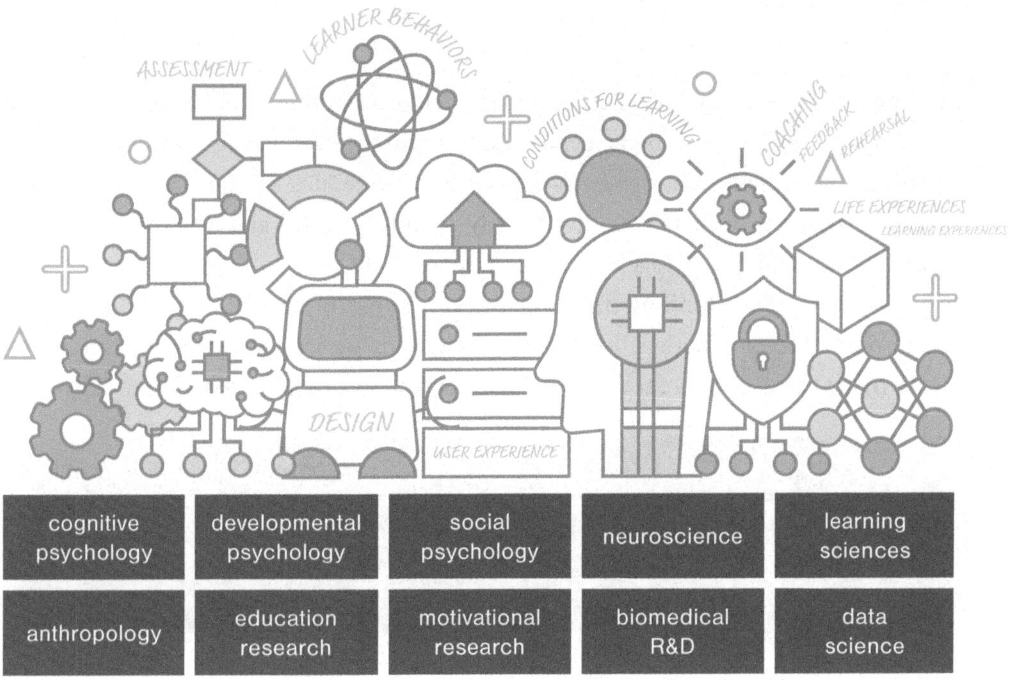

FIGURE 0.7. Sciences of learning are a foundation for learning engineering

CC-BY Jim Goodell, 2021

his brother's patients, confirmed the flakes were easier to eat, and got their feedback with each iteration. He eventually used corn and invented corn flakes.

Today human-centered design is used to better match product designs to the needs of the people who will use them. The process is being used to design everything from software user experiences to entire school districts.[22] The process has been formalized as an international standard (ISO 9241-210) for developing interactive technology, but the concepts are the same even when applied to non-technical problems. With user-centered design:[23]

1. Designs use an explicit understanding of users, tasks, and environments
2. Users are involved throughout design and development
3. The design is driven and refined by user-centered evaluation
4. The process is iterative
5. The design addresses the whole user experience
6. The design team includes multidisciplinary skills and perspectives

In the case of learning engineering and instructional design, the human-centered design challenge is for a set of people to learn something. Principles and practices of engineering help further define how the work of developing and improving learning solutions gets done. Learning engineering combines design methodologies with data-driven processes and principles of engineering—such as engineering control theory—not typically found in traditional design practices, to iterate closer and closer to a best fit solution.

Deeply understanding the people who will use or benefit from the solution is an important idea, whether that solution is a piece of software or something lower tech, like a breakfast cereal or, as we discuss below, a new kind of donkey cart.

> Learning engineering is more of a verb than a noun.
> – *Chris Dede*

[6]

The Duolingo team develops software, but technology isn't the only product of learning engineering. It could be a low-tech learning resource, an improved process, a physical environment; anything designed to provide learning experiences and conditions for learning that work; anything developed to solve a learning problem. Technology is just one of the tools in the learning engineering toolkit. Sometimes the needed solution is low tech.

Shelly Blake-Plock was the founding chair of ICICLE. Shelly is a technical genius and the founder and CEO of Yet Analytics, a company that specializes in data analysis in support of human learning. But he will be the first to tell you that learning engineering is not about the technology, it's about problem solving in support of learning. He saw this firsthand when he visited the West African country of Gambia.

The problem to be solved was student access to local schools. "In a concerted effort to reduce inequity, the government abolished school fees and increased the number of communities that have schools within three kilometers from 83 percent in 2013 to 95 percent in 2018," according to a story posted to the World Bank website.[24] However, nearly 30 percent of school-aged children still didn't attend classes. A problem was that a three kilometer walk to school was too far for three- to eight-year-old students. Parents were concerned about their children's safety over the long distances.

The problem was framed by the context of poorly developed or nonexistent roads. "Donkeys, a common means of transport in The Gambia, were a natural, yet innovative, choice," according to the World Bank article, "and different communities across the country were enthusiastic about the idea." Donkey carts were engineered to carry ten young children each and could be driven by an older student.

A key strategy in any engineering design is iterative improvement. The low-tech donkey cart solution used an iterative process. "An initial pilot revealed that while the original carts were an effective means to transport children to school, these were too heavy and needed to be redesigned. As a result, a lighter 2.0 model of the cart was launched in 2015. Built with locally sourced materials, the revamped carts handle more easily, have a seat for each child, and incorporate important safety features such as a gate and easy-to-grab handles." For more on learning engineering that's helping people in underdeveloped countries see Chapter 3 for a story about a team developing a mobile app for people in another West African country, Ghana.

When Herb Simon first coined the term learning engineering over a half century ago, the tools of the trade available now didn't yet exist. Key learning sciences concepts had yet to be discovered. The most advanced learning technology outside of academia might have been the rudimentary screen-less flight simulators being used by the military and commercial airlines to train pilots.[25] For academic classrooms, state-of-the-art technology was the chalkboard, the textbook, overhead projectors, and the mimeograph machine.

Today, teams of learning engineers have rich sets of learning sciences and technology tools that can be applied toward realization of Herb Simon's vision for learning engineering. These tools include ubiquitous internet-connected devices, sophisticated software substrates and development tools, artificial intelligence, virtual and augmented reality, project-based and collaborative pedagogies, and online and blended learning modalities. (See Chapter 14, Software and Technology Standards as Tools.)

Among the most powerful tools in the learning engineer's toolbox is the ability to collect and use data to iteratively improve the learning design and iteratively improve the solution for any given learner.

[7]

In 1998, Carnegie Mellon University spun off Carnegie Learning, Inc. to support scaled adoption of cognitive tutors, the kind of intelligent tutoring system developed through the university's research. Carnegie Learning's MATHia offers one-on-one tutoring in mathematics covering content for grades 6, 7, 8, Algebra I, Geometry, and Algebra II. The intelligent tutoring software presents problems for students to solve; it provides feedback to students as they are working through problems based on answers given and other data. According to their website, the software "monitors the status of the student's knowledge on a moment-by-moment basis and tailors course material, based on these continual assessments." The twenty-two-year-old company merged with New Mountain Learning in 2018.

While Carnegie Learning doesn't use the label "learning engineer," they're doing learning engineering as a "team sport," bringing together groups of specialists to solve problems. A cognitive science team, a data and research team, an instructional design team and everyone developing and maintaining the product as a whole might be called the "learning engineering team." They often bring together people from the various groups to have "data jams." When the data scientists discover a case where the data are telling them that something is not working for a subset of students, they call a team meeting in which everyone works together to find the root cause of the problem and suggest possible solutions.

Groups that participate in "data jams" don't all need to understand data science, but "they certainly need to basically understand how to think about data," Steve Ritter told Jodi Lis, Mark Lee, and Jim Goodell when they visited Carnegie Learning's Pittsburgh headquarters in 2018.

Ritter's team builds tools to support the non-data-scientists on the team. "They use the tools to try to figure out how to improve instruction, and we use the tools to figure out what this data means," he said, "is there a better way to sort the world, to figure out what's really going on?"

Michael Sandbothe, the lead programmer on data tools at the time, worked to make it so the end users need the least amount of high-level data science skills. "You don't need a PhD in statistics to use the tool," he said. Stephen Fancsali, a research scientist on the team, might find an inconsistency in the data but does not know what's happening. Why are students able to answer one mathematics problem but not able to answer one just like it? The instructional design teams, former mathematics teachers, and other content experts have insights that the data scientist might not have. They might say, "Here's what's really happening, the students are confused about this." These kinds of insights become hypotheses that the research team can test against the data. More insights from Carnegie Learning and others on data-informed decisions are available in Chapter 6.

Continuously examining the data to discover how to make a product or solution better for learning is a key part of the learning engineering process. The method for deciding what data to collect and how it will be collected is called "instrumentation," and is covered in Chapter 5.

[8]

If you use Duolingo to learn a new language, the app can predict your future. After you've been introduced to a new word and had some practice with it, the app can predict whether or not you will have forgotten it at some point in the future. To predict the future, it doesn't use a crystal ball, it uses data and a scientific discovery made more than a century ago.

In 1879, German psychologist Hermann Ebbinghaus was curious about how memory worked. He created experiments to test how well he could recall new words. He knew that he would be influenced by prior knowledge if he used real words, so he created a list of nonsense syllables composed of three letters (a consonant on each end and a vowel in the middle). He eliminated syllables that sounded like or were parts of real words (for example, BOL or PED, respectively). Then he tested himself by randomly looking at a sequence of cards with the nonsense syllables, writing them in a notebook, and then trying to recall the list.[26]

In 1885, he published findings about the learning curve, how fast people learn new facts, and the forgetting curve, how fast people forget what they've learned.[27] His discoveries about the forgetting curve are the basis of Duolingo's ability to predict your future.

Additional research over the last century has led to a more complete scientific understanding about the **spacing effect**,[28] the finding that people are more likely to remember something if they spread out the learning over time rather than cramming by trying to learn it all at once. In the case of learning a new language, newly introduced and more difficult words should be reviewed more frequently, and older or less difficult words should be reviewed less frequently.

Another phenomenon, the lag effect, is that people commit information to long-term memory better if the time between study or practice increases gradually. Yet other research showed that the best time for people to practice is right before they're about to forget something. **Spaced repetition models** try to figure out when the best times are to review or practice specific facts or skills.[29]

Duolingo's Burr Settles and a former Duolingo employee, Brendan Meeder, who later moved to Uber's Advanced Technologies Group, developed a "trainable spaced repetition model." It's software that uses data and artificial intelligence to learn the best time to have people practice specific words in a new language that they're learning. This model used by Duolingo isn't the first of the so-called forgetting functions, but it's a new approach that uses modern machine learning techniques. It takes in data about a student's practice history (when they practiced and whether or not they remembered correctly) and data that helps the machine learning algorithm know how difficult a word is to memorize compared to other words. More insights from Duolingo are found throughout this book.

Like Margaret Hutchinson Rousseau and the engineering team at Pfizer, they took a scientific discovery and engineered a solution that helps hundreds of millions of people. Using data and a century-old scientific discovery, Duolingo can personalize and optimize your learning of a new language—by predicting your future, for example, knowing when you're likely to forget a word. ★

- Learning engineers and learning engineering teams apply the learning sciences using engineering design processes and data-informed decision-making to create the conditions for optimal learning.
- Engineering is different from science. Learning scientists discover what works in human learning. Learning engineers aim to optimize particular learning experiences, test different options, and build scalable solutions.
- Learning engineering is often a team process that brings together professionals from different fields, including the learning sciences, assessment, learning experience design, software engineering, and data science. Team members don't need to be experts in all areas.
- Technology is a tool that can help scale the implementation of learning experiences. It also enables data-informed decision-making. However, learning solutions don't necessarily require advanced technology.
- Learning engineers design learning experiences, but that's not all they do. They also address the contexts and conditions that lead to great learning. These might include the architecture of physical or virtual learning environments, social structures, learners' mindsets, and habits of practice as well as more obvious targets, such as curriculum design, educational technology development, and learning analytics.
- Learning engineers don't design for the "average" student; they engineer adaptations and variations to fit real people and sometimes even individual learners' needs.
- Data instrumentation and analysis are critical to learning engineering. They inform an iterative process of creation, implementation, and investigation. Data can help optimize learning activities and feedback, such as Duolingo's trainable spaced repetition model.
- Learning engineers keep in mind the science of how people learn and how people are motivated to learn.
- Learning engineering takes a systemic view of learners' broad experiences, including the life experiences that impact their learning.

WHAT IS LEARNING ENGINEERING?

KEY POINTS

Endnotes

1 Sharkey, John, Donald Clark, Anne O'Brien, and Yorke Rhodes. "History of the New York Section Committee: 2008 Annual Report." www.newyorkacs.org/reports/NYACSReport2008/pfizerlandmark.html

2 Ginsberg, Judah. *Development of Deep Tank Fermentation Commemorative Booklet*. Pfizer Inc., 2008. www.acs.org/content/dam/acsorg/education/whatischemistry/landmarks/penicillin/development-of-deep-tank-fermentation-commemorative-booklet.pdf

3 Simon, Herbert A. "Job of a college president." *Educational Record 48,* no. 1 (1967): 68–78.

4 Dede, Christopher J., John Richards, and Bror Saxberg, eds. *Learning Engineering for Online Education: Theoretical Contexts and Design-Based Examples.* New York: Routledge, 2018.

5 Dede, Christopher J., and John Richards. *The 60-Year Curriculum: New Models for Lifelong Learning in the Digital Economy.* New York: Routledge, 2020.

6 Educause. *7 Things You Should Know About Learning Engineering.* Philadelphia, PA: Educause, 2018. https://library.educause.edu/-/media/files/library/2018/9/eli7160.pdf

7 Mitchell Bonnett, comments made during meeting of the IEEE Learning Technology Standards Committee Meeting in Alexandria, VA, August 27, 2018.

8 Wikipedia. "Duolingo." Last modified December 9, 2021. https://en.wikipedia.org/wiki/Duolingo

9 Blanco, Cindy. "Changes in Duolingo Usage During the COVID-19 Pandemic." *Duolingo Blog,* April 8, 2020. https://blog.duolingo.com/changes-in-duolingo-usage-during-the-covid-19-pandemic

10 Goodell, Jim, Mark Lee, and Jodi Lis. "What We Discovered at the Roots of Learning Engineering." In *Proceedings of the 2019 Conference on Learning Engineering, Arlington, VA, 2019.* New York: IEEE. https://sagroups.ieee.org/icicle/wp-content/uploads/sites/148/2020/07/ICICLE_Proceedings_Learning-Engineering.pdf

11 Settles, Burr. "How We Learn How You Learn." *Duolingo Blog,* March 16, 2020. https://blog.duolingo.com/how-we-learn-how-you-learn

12 Willcox, Karen E., Sanjay Sarma, and Philip H. Lippel. *Online Education: A Catalyst for Higher Education Reforms.* Cambridge: MIT, 2016. https://oepi.mit.edu/files/2016/09/MIT-Online-Education-Policy-Initiative-April-2016.pdf

Fusco, Judi, Jeremy Roschelle, and Pati Ruiz. "What is Learning Sciences and Why Does It Matter?" *Digital Promise Blog,* March 10, 2020. https://digitalpromise.org/2020/03/10/what-is-learning-sciences-and-why-does-it-matter

13 National Academies of Sciences, Engineering, and Medicine. *How People Learn II: Learners, Contexts, and Cultures.* National Academies Press, 2018. https://doi.org/10.17226/24783

14 Hey, Tony, Stewart Tansley, and Kristin Tolle, eds. *The Fourth Paradigm: Data-Intensive Scientific Discovery.* United States: Microsoft Research, 2009. www.microsoft.com/en-us/research/wp-content/uploads/2009/10/Fourth_Paradigm.pdf

15 Wikipedia, "History of Neuroscience." Last modified November 4, 2021. https://en.wikipedia.org/wiki/History_of_neuroscience

16 Thagard, Paul. "Cognitive Science." In *Stanford Encyclopedia of Philosophy.* Stanford, CA: Stanford University, 2018. https://plato.stanford.edu/entries/cognitive-science

17 Kolodner, Janet L. "The Journal of the Learning Sciences: Effecting Changes in Education." *The Journal of the Learning Sciences* 1, no. 1 (1991): 1–6. https://doi.org/10.1207/s15327809jls0101_1

18 "Allen Brain Map." *Allen Institute for Brain Science,* 2021. http://portal.brain-map.org

19 Rose, Todd. *The End of Average: How We Succeed in a World That Values Sameness.* New York: HarperOne, 2016.

20 Hess, Frederick M., and Bror Saxberg. *Breakthrough Leadership in the Digital Age: Using Learning Science to Reboot Schooling.* Thousand Oaks, CA: Corwin, 2014.

21 Thomsen, Dave. "Why Human-Centered Design Matters." *Wired (Insights),* December 2013. www.wired.com/insights/2013/12/human-centered-design-matters

22 "How Can Design Advance Learning and Education?" *IDEO,* 2021. www.ideo.com/question/how-can-design-advance-education

23 Travis, David. "ISO 13407 Is Dead. Long Live ISO 9241-210!" *Userfocus (Article),* June 6, 2011. www.userfocus.co.uk/articles/iso-13407-is-dead.html

24 Grimsland, Alison M. "How Donkey 'School Buses' Benefit Early Grade Children in the Gambia." *World Bank Blogs,* May 29, 2018. https://blogs.worldbank.org/education/how-donkey-school-buses-benefit-early-grade-children-gambia

25 "Lufthansa Full Flight Simulators." *ProFlight.* www.proflight.com/en

26 Wikipedia. "Hermann Ebbinghaus." Last modified December 2, 2021. https://en.wikipedia.org/wiki/Hermann_Ebbinghaus

27 "Ebbinghaus, Hermann." In *Encyclopedia.com.* Last modified August 13, 2018. www.encyclopedia.com/people/medicine/psychology-and-psychiatry-biographies/hermann-ebbinghaus

28 Ebbinghaus, Hermann. *Memory: A Contribution to Experimental Psychology.* Translated by Henry A. Ruger and Clara E. Bussenius. New York: Teachers College, Columbia University, 2013. http://psychclassics.yorku.ca/Ebbinghaus/index.htm

29 Tabibian, Behzad, Utkarsh Upadhyay, Abir De, Ali Zarezade, Bernhard Schölkopf, and Manuel Gomez-Rodriguez. "Enhancing Human Learning via Spaced Repetition Optimization." In *Proceedings of the National Academy of Sciences 116,* no. 10 (2019): 3988–3993. https://doi.org/10.1073/pnas.1815156116

FOUNDATIONS

ESSENTIAL CONCEPTS IN LEARNING ENGINEERING

PROCESS

CHAPTER 1

Learning Engineering is a Process

by Aaron Kessler, Scotty D. Craig, Jim Goodell, Dina Kurzweil, and Scott W. Greenwald

Learning engineering is a **process** and practice that applies the learning sciences using human-centered engineering design methodologies and data-informed decision-making to support learners and their development.

A process is a series of actions or steps taken in order to achieve a particular end.

A process has:

1. inputs
2. process steps
3. outputs

Baking chocolate chip cookies is a process defined by a recipe. It has inputs (the ingredients), action steps (directions), and outputs (the cookies). Baking one batch of cookies is a project. The recipe defines a repeatable process that may be iteratively adjusted and improved.

Learning engineering is also a repeatable process intended to iteratively design, test, adjust, and improve conditions for learning. It starts with a challenge. The scale of that challenge could be small and focused, such as the need to prepare students for a class of difficult problems on a high-stakes test (see Chapter 6), the scale may be the design of a global learning platform serving education in a whole variety of disciplines for millions of students (Chapter 4), or the scale could be of any size in between. The nature of the challenge could be about teaching adults to adopt healthy behaviors (Chapter 3) or motivating middle school students to engage in more productive learning behaviors (Chapter 6). It could be about tactical training for teams of soldiers (Chapter 5) or ethical training for medical professionals or any other learning context (Chapter 7).

True stories featured throughout this book demonstrate the wide variety of challenges addressed with the learning engineering process, such as the following:

- Optimizing learner experiences on a global language learning platform (Introduction, Chapter 5, and Chapter 6)
- Getting kids to where they'll be learning in West Africa (Introduction)
- Designing curricula and professional development and scaling a new learning technology for broad use (Introduction and Chapter 6)
- Developing software for a collaborative VR experience to help learners understand a complex scientific concept (Chapter 1)
- Designing numeracy games for two- to three-year-olds (Chapter 3)
- Designing for low literacy users and in humanitarian settings (Chapter 3)
- Engineering a global learning platform serving 3,000 university-level courses to about thirty-three million students (Chapter 4)
- Providing the right level and frequency of feedback (Chapter 4)
- Designing sensors for learning analytics for military training (Chapter 5)
- Designing game-based learning for four- and five-year-olds (Chapter 5)
- Developing a platform for collecting learning analytics from game-based learning (Chapter 5)
- Discovering with a multidisciplinary team why results from a formative assessment delivered immediately following online instruction yield a poor pass rate (Chapter 6)
- Designing simulated training for medical professionals (Chapter 7)

Additional examples are provided as visions for the future of learning engineering (Chapter 19) and in supplementary case studies. As the contexts and needs for learning change, the learning engineering process has the potential to address future challenges that we cannot imagine today.

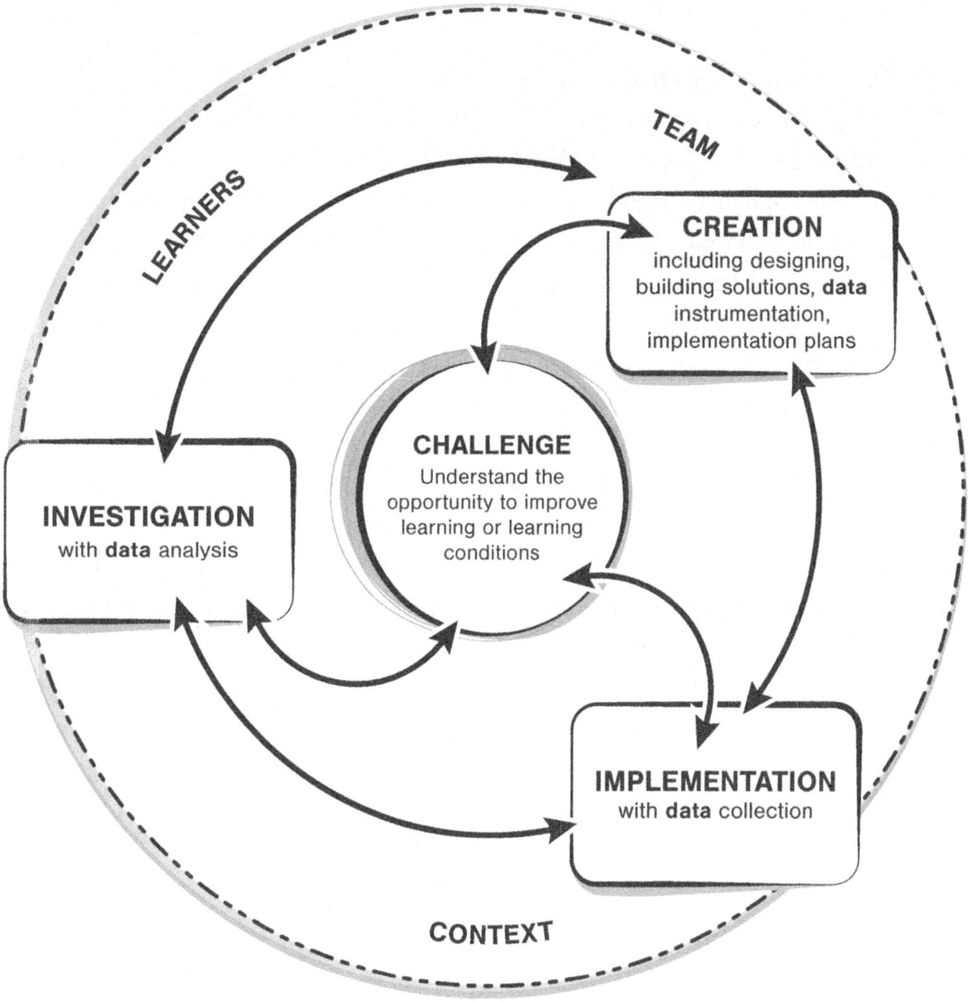

FIGURE 1.1. The learning engineering process

CC-BY Aaron Kessler

[1]

In 2020, Aaron Kessler of MIT's Open Learning led development of a draft learning engineering process model with the Design for Learning Special Interest Group of the IEEE Industry Connections / Industry Consortium on Learning Engineering (ICICLE). This chapter presents the next iteration of that model that considers the parts concurrently as a cycle, with a challenge at the center. The chapter also provides a concrete example of how the process was used at MIT to develop a VR learning experience called the Electrostatic Playground.

Figure 1.1 shows a high-level view of the process. It starts with a challenge (an opportunity to create or improve learning conditions) and follows with investigation, creation, and implementation of a solution. The exact order and specific work to be done will vary based on the nature and scale of the challenge and other factors. However, the learning engineering process always involves multiple iterations, and it always uses data to inform decisions.

The outcomes that can be achieved by engaging in this process are broad. Therefore, the model is designed to work across a multitude of settings, levels of education and training, kinds of challenges, and groups of people. The specific process will vary based on the challenge, learner context, team context, available resources, and other factors. Specific processes used by a large team may be different from or the same as those used by a small team, and the process for developing a simulation may be different from the process for designing a project-based learning experience.

In this chapter, we use the example of a learning solution developed at MIT. This is just one example; the other examples throughout the rest of the book offer other kinds of challenges that can be addressed by using the learning engineering process. Despite these differences, the core of the process represented in Figure 1.1 is seen throughout these examples and can help those hoping to engage in learning engineering to organize their work in purposeful ways.

[2]

Challenge

Learning engineering always begins with a challenge or problem associated with learners and learning. The inputs required to identify the challenge can come from many different sources. For example, a new challenge may come to light based on data from a previous cycle of the learning engineering process. The challenge may be a changed environment or business process that requires new learning for people in the workforce. Challenges can be noticed as new learners join a community with different needs requiring changes to the status quo. The opportunity to improve learning might address a topic known to be challenging within a field or domain of teaching and learning.

Regardless of how the challenge is illuminated, understanding the challenge (or the problem you are trying to solve) includes understanding the learning objectives, the learner(s), and the conditions that will hinder or help learners reach the

Electrostatic Playground Challenge

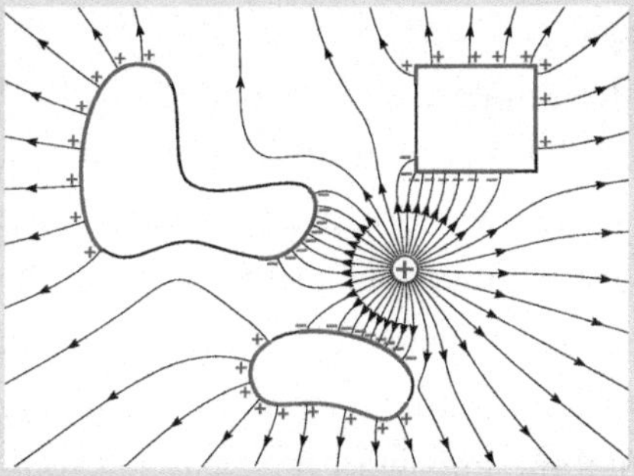

FIGURE 1.2. Two-dimensional electrostatics diagram

Electrostatics is the branch of physics concerned with electric charges at rest, and it is typically covered in the introductory physics curriculum. Many students lack familiarity with the concepts since they are difficult to directly observe or visualize in the real world. Within electrostatics, Gauss' Law is one of the most challenging topics, largely because it is fundamentally 3D, and therefore difficult to imagine or to capture in 2D whiteboard sketches. A further consequence of this is that it impedes instructors and learners from jointly attending to interactions (for example, sharing experiences of asking questions or checking for understanding) around the phenomena. One potential solution to this problem is to use 3D representations in a digital environment, using, for example, VR.

The Electrostatic Playground project set out to provide students opportunities to engage with electrostatic representations in a VR environment. In this project the main challenge to be addressed in the learning engineering process was to get students to collaboratively engage with electrostatics representations in ways that produced key insights about basic principles of physics.

targeted goal. As in other engineering disciplines, learning engineering does not start with a solution looking for a problem, rather the key to the process is to thoroughly understand the challenge before seeking solutions.

The Electrostatic Playground project is small compared to some projects. It focuses on a limited set of learning objectives for introductory physics students in a specific university course with access to VR equipment. Regardless of the size of the work, defining the challenge to be addressed is central to the work. (Chapter 8 offers tools for understanding the challenge.) It is also critical to realize that challenges are not static or self-contained, in fact, it is highly likely that to address a challenge you must address a set of sub-challenges. If the primary challenge is to develop a learning experience, sub-challenges include the need to develop instrumentation and plan implementation along with sub-challenges related to developing and iteratively improving the learning objects themselves. New sub-challenges will arise as the process is followed, for example, testing a prototype may identify new problems to be solved to fully address the primary challenge.

In the case of the Electrostatic Playground example, a sub-challenge involved the limited ways the typical VR system logged data about user activity; often a single "eye in the sky" structure is used (like a single video camera looking down on the action instead of separate cameras showing all points of view). Because the project was concerned with collaboration between participants, data limitations had to be addressed to investigate potential collaborative learning experiences. Lacking such data would limit opportunities to understand the impact of the designed solution and hinder future rounds of improvement. These multiple levels and types of challenges are often the hallmark of work that can be addressed using the learning engineering process.

[3]

Challenges to be solved using the learning engineering process do not occur in black boxes, instead they are situated within specific contexts. The context circle (dotted line in the learning engineering model diagram) encompasses the defined challenge and the entire process and is intended to be an outer bound for two main contextualized groups, learners and the learning engineering team.

Learners

Learning is situated. This means that learners in different situations, with different resources, learning conditions, and backgrounds will interact with each other and with resources very differently. This will lead to different learning experiences and outcomes. The learning context includes:

- People (learners, teachers, tutors, other learners, and others supporting)
- Environment(s) (virtual or physical)
- Learner backgrounds and prior knowledge
- Cultural norms for learners' home, community, and learning community
- Available tools
- Everything about the population of learners and potential learning conditions that may help or hinder the learning

The stories in Chapter 3 highlight the stark differences in learner contexts that must be considered when developing solutions to learning engineering challenges. For example, developing effective online learning activities for two- to three-year-old

Electrostatic Playground: Learner Context

The learners were first-year introductory physics students who were well versed in using mathematical formulas to represent and solve physics problems in a stepwise process. However, most had minimal prior experience engaging with visualizations or representations of electrostatics-based phenomena to develop more conceptual understandings. The project partially aimed to address this by having students engage with the content and other students in a VR environment. In this course students work on problem sets throughout the semester with the same group of two or three students, and many opted to sign up for the VR session with these partners. This meant that the students were accustomed to communicating and problem solving with their VR session compatriots. Thus, the work associated with learning community norms was something established in the traditional class work and was able to be leveraged in the context of the VR setting. Finally, the VR environment was constrained to focus only on a small set of learning goals, meaning learners engaged with the proposed VR implementation would not be exploring other physics phenomena at the same time.

children is very different from designing activities for four- and five-year-olds and completely different from designing simulated hospital settings for helping medical students learn new procedures. These, in turn, are quite different from educating low literacy learners in developing nations. Also see Chapter 2, Learning Engineering Applies the Learning Sciences, for insights on how people learn and the science applicable to contextual conditions for learning.

Team

Challenges that must be solved using the learning engineering process are highly complex and often require a team of people in order to develop appropriate solutions. Learning engineering teams bring together specialists in the realms of education, technology, and training to address a challenge.

Large teams may use different processes or the same ones used by small teams. The value of these teams does not lie entirely in their current individual abilities, but also in the team's ability to grow, develop together, and address the complex challenge collaboratively. A shared disposition toward growth and improvement, when combined with the shared knowledge of the team, makes the solving of learning engineering challenges possible. This team-oriented approach is recognized as a

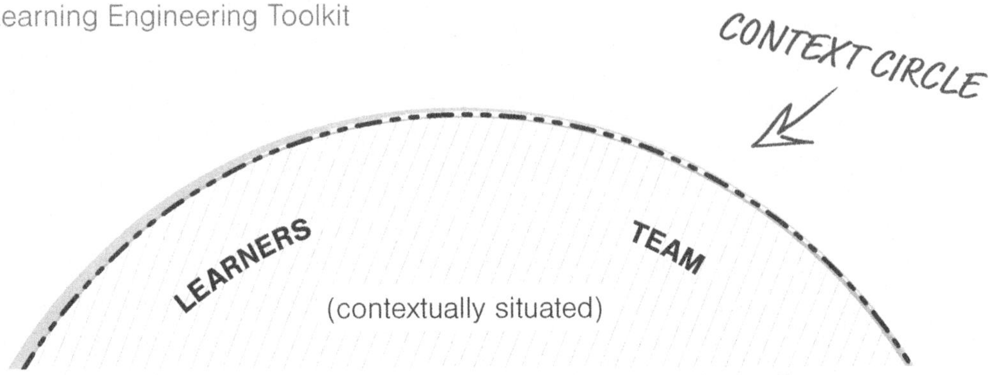

FIGURE 1.3. Learning engineering process detail: learners, teams, and context

common practice for the development of e-learning in the corporate training domain.

Learning engineering as a team process builds on professional specialties within the engineering team through a coordinated effort rooted in a shared understanding and vocabulary. The learning engineering flower graphic (Figure 0.5 on page 13) shows professional domains that might be required to address a learning engineering challenge. The professionals on the team require some shared understanding of the challenge and enough understanding about the other domains to effectively communicate as a team. (See Chapter 10, Tools for Teaming, for more discussion on learning engineering teams.) Learners and other stakeholders might also be considered part of the team.

Context

The context circle is meant to be a reminder to those engaging in the learning engineering process that these two groups, learners and the learning engineering team, are situated in contexts that will have norms, expectations, affordances, and limitations that will need to be taken into account as work on the central challenge is carried out.

[4]

Creation

Moving to the outer portion of the process from the central challenge is not a one-size-fits-all proposition. Depending on some of the contextual factors discussed above, a team working to address a challenge may be able to begin their work in any

Electrostatic Playground: Team Context

The Electrostatic Playground project was initiated and led by a research scientist in human-computer interaction with a focus on learning sciences and a prior background in mathematics and physics. The project scope grew to involve a team that included subject-matter experts, VR systems developers, and educational researchers. The subject matter experts contributed on three levels:

(a) suggesting technical (software implementation) approaches,

(b) suggesting component user experiences (tools and corresponding visualizations), and

(c) providing guidance on scaffolding for curriculum alignment (narrative segments and corresponding exploratory activities).

The primary subject-matter expert was an instructor familiar with simulation techniques (relevant here because a simulation-based, exploratory experience is being designed) who could therefore contribute on all three levels. Three other course instructors also contributed to the last two areas (b and c). Six teaching assistants were recruited to participate just in category (c), first by holding live office hours in the multiuser VR space, and after gaining experience with that, structuring recorded narratives with suggested activities that aligned specifically with elements of the course curriculum. All of the subject matter experts were responsible for implementing the learning environment with students.

The VR systems developers, including the project lead and two software engineers, handled the detailed user experience design and software implementation, including the physics simulation (with guidance from the primary subject matter expert), building the environment, creating usable data structures, conducting user testing, and supporting the final implementation with students. During the process they were able to contribute original component user experiences, which could then be validated and integrated by the instructors.

Finally, the educational researchers (a senior learning scientist and an undergraduate intern) were responsible for providing feedback on how the data collected during the implementation could be analyzed, engaging in reflection on results in connection with stated goals of the work, and connecting data outputs with potential changes to the user experience and scaffolded curriculum for the next round of implementation.

Electrostatic Playground: Creation

Early on, the team identified the topics of electric flux and Gauss' Law as good matches for the technology. They're topics that students have difficulty with (and therefore would represent an opportunity for clear benefit), and the relevant conceptual constructs are particularly 3D in nature (difficult to explain in 2D and requiring 3D mental manipulations).

On this basis, the learning engineering team discussed how they could leverage the affordances of VR to encourage joint collaboration among students as they explored field lines and Gaussian surfaces. This collective team structure allowed for the concurrent development of the learning experience and VR system to capture students' actions and attention in ways that could inform iterative improvement later in the cycle.

After an initial round of development with the subject-matter experts describing critical features that students should attend to, the developers coded those ideas into a usable form in the system, and then a series of user tests was conducted. Graduate students, staff, and other subject-matter experts were asked to engage with the system while designers, developers, and a researcher observed.

The initial design, which included both technology and interaction design elements, was meant to be a sandbox where learners would be introduced to the tools available in the system and allowed to freely explore features and relationships among objects. This system was piloted in a live tutorial setting, with teaching assistants instructing one or two students directly in the environment without a specific script or lesson plan. Beyond the observation of the test, data were collected in the form of a playable recording that could replay the session in 3D, either immersively (in VR) or non-immersively (on a desktop PC).

Two key actions resulted from this user test. First, across the team everyone agreed that a series of short instructor-led prompts, to partially guide and get learners started in the exploring and noticing of critical features, needed to be created by the subject-matter experts. The resulting explanatory components of the learning experience took the form of mini-lectures recorded by an instructor within the VR system and played back by the learners as they begin each learning segment. These mini-lectures would end with the prompt, "Now it's your turn," from the instructor, indicating that the learners should begin exploring the interactive elements. This explanatory-exploratory structure was repeated with several cycles of consecutive prompts before learners were given a final opportunity to engage in free exploration of the environment.

Second, the learning engineering team noted that the third-person perspective associated with the session recordings made it difficult to observe when and where learners were exhibiting joint attention to objects. As a result, the developers recommended adjusting the VR system to allow for spatial recording. This technique allows viewers to adopt any perspective, but for the purposes of efficiently seeing what each learner was attending to, the first-person perspective was the most advantageous.

This decision to instrument the system to capture the learning experiences from each student's perspective would later turn out to be incredibly valuable in understanding when and how learners had *aha!* moments. Had the team not been working collaboratively and concurrently on these parts of the process, it's likely that the process would have, at best, been extended, and given the nature of the questions and ideas raised in the collaborative meetings, the resulting VR experience may have looked very different.

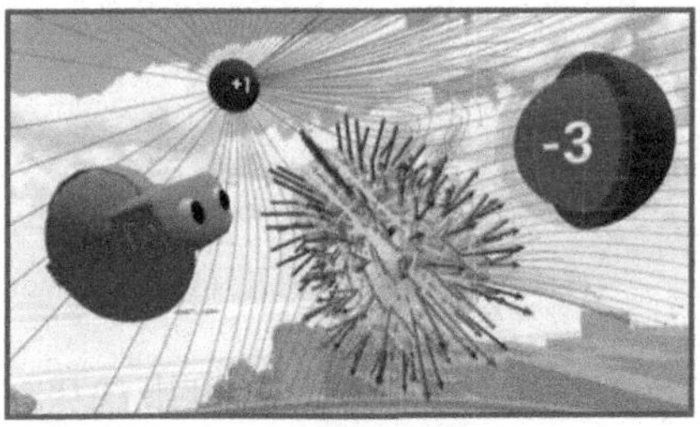

FIGURE 1.4. Playback from the Electrostatic Playground VR

one of the outer action steps of the process. For the purposes of this chapter, we start with the creation step; however, teams might begin with implementation and or investigation depending on the challenge established at the beginning of the process and the context in which they are working.

The creation portion of the process contains several key mini and iterative cycles of the learning engineering process that include designing, developing, instrumenting, and user testing potential solutions. Remember that these are happening simultaneously. For example, a simple paper prototype (creation) may be tested (implementation) with a small focus group to collect initial data for checking suitability of a design (investigation).

A key feature of the creation portion of the process is that the mini-processes should be considered concurrently rather than sequentially. This concurrent work requires the person or people working to solve the challenge to engage in the work of creation in cycles that take into account:

1. What's known from the learning sciences literature that can inform the designed solution (Chapter 2)
2. Human-centered and engineering practices to improve initial design into a viable solution that will function as intended in the contextualized operating conditions (Chapter 3 and Chapter 4)
3. How data related to targeted learning can be collected and analyzed (Chapter 5 and Chapter 6), both to support learning and as feedback for refining the solution
4. How values and ethics are embedded within the design and implementation process (Chapter 7)

In many current settings, especially within education technology companies, each of these sets of mini-processes is completed independently. For example, a designer creates a set of specs that are handed to the development team, who builds a solution that is handed off to the implementation team, who collects data and hands it off to the data scientist, and so on. The Electro VR example provides a view into how the learning engineering process can bring these sometimes disparate mini-processes together into a Lean-Agile or concurrent, and potentially more coherent, creation process. (See also Chapter 11, Lean-Agile Development Tools.)

[5]

Implementation

Once a potential solution to the learning engineering challenge has been created, the process shifts to focus on implementation. As discussed earlier in the chapter, the context of the learners and how they will be supported in their specific environment must be initially considered as you define the challenge, and implementation planning must be part of the concurrent work done in the creation phase. The implementation phase of the learning engineering process involves having real learners in real contexts engage with the output from the creation stage. Implementation is not limited to full release or full-scale implementation of a product or solution.

Note that the Electrostatic Playground context allowed for a comparatively straightforward implementation: Subject-matter experts, who were also the instructors of the course in which the system was implemented, along with their teaching assistants for the course, who were also the user testers, enacted the instructional plan and facilitated the VR experience. This may or may not be the case for other learning engineering contexts.

When an implementation is more wide-ranging, usually later in the iterative

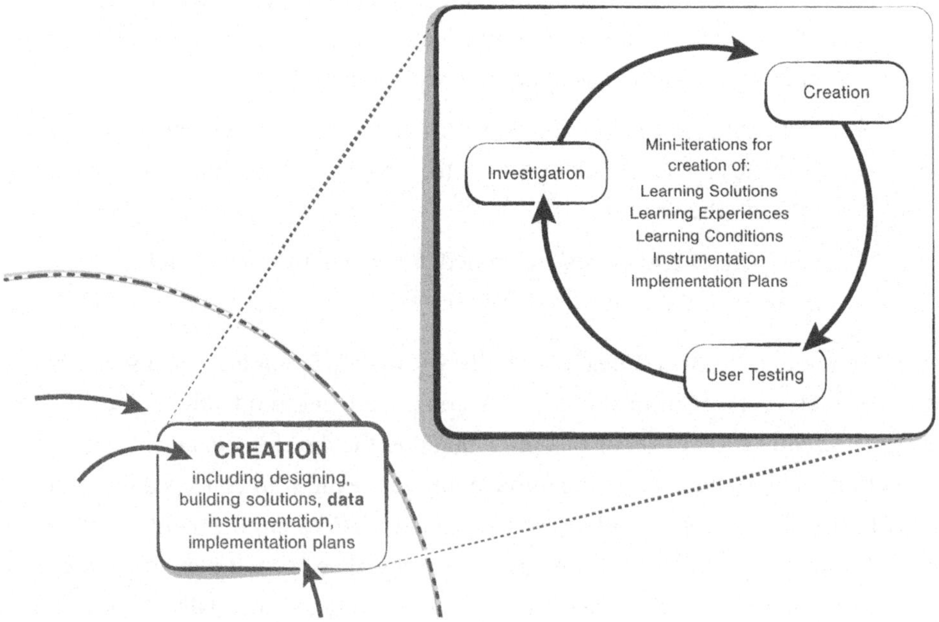

FIGURE 1.5. Learning engineering process detail: the creation cycle

process, it is often fraught with difficulties and complexity. Even at a slightly larger scale there can be complexity. For example, in a project that implemented robotics-based proportional reasoning tutoring systems, implementation and testing was done across just three different school settings with three different educators.[1] Each educator operationalized and enacted the system in a different way, leading to mixed results. Much of the complexity came from differences in the specific learning goals that each of the educators hoped to address. Implementation and testing generally become more complex in each iteration as venues and teachers or facilitators are added, requiring more focus on details of implementations and their similarities to and differences from what was expected as more variation is added. In fact, understanding how systems are implemented and the impacts of such work could be a separate learning engineering challenge that must be addressed. (See Chapter 16, Implementation Tools.) Thus, the work of understanding and accounting for the implementation during the creation (or improvement) phase of the process is critical.

Electrostatic Playground: Implementation

The first implementation involved a group of first-year physics students engaging with the system as part of their coursework. Ultimately twenty-three students participated in what the instructor called an optional part of the course that could help reinforce their understanding of electric flux and Gauss's Law. The implementation took place shortly before final exams. The students who participated in some cases had already understood the concepts well when they were initially introduced, while other students were hoping to understand these concepts more fully the second time around. Using the explanatory-exploratory structure described above, student groups engaged with each of the three learning segments and the final open-ended exploration time. The total time to complete the experience lasted around an hour, and no group went over one hour and fifteen minutes in the environment.

[6]

Investigation

Having implemented the solution and collected data, the work of processing, analyzing, and interpreting the outcome can be done. In some instances, this part of the process might begin as soon as the very first learners are done engaging with the created experience or system; in other instances, hundreds of learners will need to finish work before this part of the process can begin. Much of the analysis process will be dependent on the knowledge and skills of the team members engaged in the work. In most instances the use of qualitative, quantitative, and mixed-method approaches to data analysis are likely appropriate and each analysis will have different timelines for when actionable interpretations can be produced back to the larger team. (See Chapters 5 and 6 for more details of how data instrumentation and analysis apply to learning engineering.)

In some instances, the results can feed directly back to the implementation group to support learner engagement, while in others the results will inform the next round of design and improvement of the experience or system, and in yet other instances the results will show positive outcomes for the challenge while highlighting other challenges within the same context. It's also important to note that sometimes the results are inconclusive, unclear, or simply more data are needed to verify results. In these instances, the learning engineering team may decide to rerun the implementation without making any changes. In some instances, the team may make small adjustments based on results but keep the system mostly the same to implement with more learners or just in a new context that they believe the already designed solution will work.

[7]

Completing the Loop

Completing a loop of the learning engineering process means feeding what was learned back into other parts of the cycle to improve the work continually and iteratively. The learning engineering process is intended to allow people or teams continually and purposefully to address complex learning challenges in ways that are informed by results and improve over time. Such iterative attention to detail is critical in designing learning solutions that work as intended for the many different situations in which a solution will be implemented.

While the learning engineering process is intended to be a way to focus on the central challenge, it is likely foolish to think that only one challenge will need to be worked on at a time, especially in business or large-scale settings. Although the people and teams working on an individual learning engineering process should be highly integrated and focused on the central challenge, the reality of most settings is that a "single challenge" will be connected with or nested within dozens of

Electrostatic Playground: Data Story

Data from each of the learner sessions were captured using an approach that was fully integrated with the software. During sessions, the system captured audio from the microphone of each participant (integrated with the headset) and logged all activity within the interactive environment, including the movement of the headsets and controllers and controller-based object interactions. Using the corresponding data logs, the system could play back the entire session either in VR or on a 2D screen, including audio, for further analysis.

While the data allowed for recordings of the sessions to be played back from the perspective of each participant, the learning engineering team found it difficult to encode the data. It was challenging keep track of each participant's actions and also complicated to structure the data in a way that would allow for exploration from both single participant and multiple participant (i.e., **joint attention**) perspectives. Further, no existing data coding platform allowed for easy coding of such recording data structures (mostly due to file format limitations). As such, the learning engineering team needed to address the issue of coding the data in a manageable and useful way. The VR system developers were tasked with creating an interface that allowed the data coder to watch the playback of the session from the first-person perspective of a participant while at the same time visualizing the session from the complementary perspective of a third person or seeing another adjustable point of view that allowed the coder to understand the wider context.

Having addressed the challenges related to coding the sessions, the next step in the mixed method approach was to create a codebook. The new first-person playback system allowed for the data coders to play back each session from the point of view of each learner and code time intervals for events like object attention, attention to the other participant, joint attention to an object, and attention to the recorded lecture. The head VR developer, with the assistance of a researcher and an intern, coded segments together to iteratively identify a set of codes that could be used to obtain good inter-rater reliability. Finally, with an established codebook in hand, the researcher and intern coded each session from the perspective of each individual participant with nested connections to coded activities of other participants who were in the VR environment simultaneously.

One of the primary emergent results from the codebook development was the identification of *aha!* moments. These moments were defined by a participant verbalizing a clear understanding or breakthrough as evidenced by an *aha!* exclamation or statement of excitement around noticing or demonstrating something. Having the data coded within the platform allowed for programmatic analysis of the data, including seeking patterns of joint attention and exploration in connection with *aha!* moments. The discovery of these *aha!* moments represented a critical step toward understanding that the created solution had demonstrated a potential for addressing the stated challenge of encouraging collaborative exploration of electrostatics principles.

other challenges that may need to be simultaneously addressed in order to produce a viable result for learners. For example, in the case of Electrostatic Playground, there was a broad challenge to make electrostatics concepts more accessible and a narrower challenge to make the data easier to label. Complex challenges call for engineering mindsets, systems thinking, and modular design. In the same way, the learning engineering process is both iterative and nested. (See Chapter 4, Learning Engineering is Engineering.)

Regardless of the number of nested challenges or difficulty associated with addressing these, each part of the process continues to center and apply the learning sciences using human-centered engineering design methodologies and data-informed decision-making to support learners and their development. Ultimately, the learning engineering process allows the team to focus their attention on the challenge at hand, while the context reminds them of how this challenge can be situated within other work being done to support learners in the context that binds their work. ★

Electrostatic Playground: Closing the Loop

Two key actions became clear based on the results of the implementation and discussions among the learning engineering team. First, while the *aha!* results were promising, the overall small number of learners who engaged with the system in the first round dictated that another round of implementation should be carried out before conclusions related to effectiveness could be made. Second, while this initial data suggested strong connections between joint object attention and *aha!* moments, the learning engineering team, especially the subject-matter experts, noted a need for more purposeful data related to content learning gains of participants. This need would require additional instrumentation to collect pre-post assessments of electrostatics situated within the overall physics course structure. With these two outputs from the initial learning engineering process clarified, the next round of implementation was scheduled for the following term with the implementation of the VR system enacted as it was in the previous cycle to ensure comparability across the data.

Endnote

1 Kessler, Aaron, Melissa Boston, and Mary Kay Stein. "Exploring How Teachers Support Students' Mathematical Learning in Computer-Directed Learning Environments." *Information and Learning Sciences 121,* no. 1/2 (2019): 52–78. https://doi.org/10.1108/ILS-07-2019-0075

- A process defines how work is done. Processes have inputs, process steps, and outputs.
- The learning engineering process can be generalized: it starts with understanding the challenge within a context, and then it includes cycles of creation, implementation, and investigation.
- The process is iterative and includes multiple passes.
- Challenges that need to be solved using the learning engineering process are often complex and require a multifaceted learning engineering team to address them.
- The learning engineering process starts by understanding the challenge in context, but after that, the next steps may vary. Different teams will have different journeys through it, depending on their challenge and its contextual factors. The challenge may call for creation of a new learning experience, adjustments to the implementation of an existing learning solution, or additional data analyses as part of the investigation phase.
- Learning engineering processes used by a large team may be different from those used by a small one, and the processes for developing one kind of experience (for example, a training simulation) may be different from those used for designing a different activity (such as a secondary school curriculum).
- Learning engineering challenges, as well as the processes used to address them, often have sub-challenges or require sub-processes that need to be considered concurrently.
- Processing, analyzing, and interpreting the data from an implementation of a learning experience is necessary to inform the next iterative cycle of the learning engineering process.

Learning Engineering is a Process

KEY POINTS

UNDERSTAND

CHAPTER 2

Learning Engineering Applies the Learning Sciences

by Jim Goodell, Janet Kolodner, and Aaron Kessler

Learning engineering is a process and practice that **applies the learning sciences** using human-centered engineering design methodologies and data-informed decision-making to support learners and their development.

In 1928, Alexander Fleming discovered the miracle drug penicillin. That scientific discovery had limited value to humanity until, more than a decade later, the chemical engineers at Pfizer developed a process to make penicillin available to the masses. The medical breakthrough took both scientific discovery *and* innovations in engineering to produce the drug at scale.

In 1967, the father of learning engineering Herb Simon wrote, "learning is a complex psychological process, and it would be naïve to think that anyone can design an effective learning environment and an effective program of learning experiences for students without a mastery of what is known, scientifically and practically, about that process."[1]

While the twenty-first century has been called the "golden age for brain research," many learning science discoveries have yet to be applied at scale. Formalizing the tools and practices of learning engineering as a profession might create the opportunity for us to move from the "golden age for brain research" to the "golden age for human learning."

This chapter examines some key concepts from the learning sciences. It includes closely related concepts about learning and the human *mind* (a conceptual model

FIGURE 2.1. A simple conception of up and down

of how people think and learn) and concepts related to the *brain* (the physical and chemical aspects of the human nervous system that enable thought and learning). Some concepts apply to both the mind and the brain, even if just one of those words is used. Of course, this chapter only scratches the surface of what's known about how people learn. It's intended as a primer for those with backgrounds in other fields but who are entering the world of learning engineering, perhaps as part of a multidisciplinary team. It might also be a refresher for some with prior knowledge of the learning sciences.

[1]

Let's start with a fictitious story as we unpack how learning works. Mia is four years old, and her brother Kai is three. They're naturally curious and always learning. They learn by observing the world around them. They learn through play. They learn from interactions with their parents and other adults. They've both learned some basic notions of quantity. Mia learned from her mom how to count ten blocks. Kai so far can count to three, and Mia is helping him as they play with blocks. They're also exposed to educational media such as *PBS Kids* and recent iterations of the preschool classic *Sesame Street*.

Mia and Kai have imperfect understandings of the world. They observed how gravity works by dropping food from their highchairs and then by falling down when trying to walk. They assume that the world is flat and that things and people can fall down. Their concept of gravity is something like the idea shown in Figure 2.1.

Both have learned how to recognize a circle, and Mia understands that a circle is round. So, when someone tells Mia that the world is round, she fits

FIGURE 2.2. "Round" earth conception

this new information as best she can into what she already knows. Combining the concepts of *down* and *round* might look like the idea in Figure 2.2.

It's actually quite complex to come to the understand that *down* depends on where you are on earth, and cognitive scientists and educational psychologists have done much research to learn how to help children who are having difficulty grasping that idea.[2] It won't be until years later that Mia understands the concept of a spherical earth or the force of gravity, even as imperfectly conceptualized in Figure 2.3.

But it's not only children who have to make sense of new ideas and concepts, and it's not only children who have difficulty grasping the complexities and nuances of new concepts. Adults, as well, are continually adjusting our **mental models** (or "schemas" or "internal models") to refine our understandings of concepts and to accommodate new discoveries. For example, learning engineering professionals need to be life-long learners who make it their business to always be up to date on what's known about how people learn—continuously updating their understanding so that they can design the most effective learning experiences and conditions.

Indeed, gaining **expertise** is the process of constantly reworking one's mental models. The more varied experiences someone has had with some idea, the more chance that person has had to add complexity and nuance to their mental models. We recognize someone as an expert when they've organized and filled their mental models so well that they can figure things out faster than others and when they can use their mental models to figure out things others can't. We'll explore expertise in more detail later in this chapter; for now, the important thing to recognize is that becoming an expert requires more than just memorizing more facts. Experts think differently than novices because they've developed better mental models. As learners move from novice to expert, they are continuously reconstructing their understanding, reorganizing knowledge into categories, and connecting new ideas to previously learned concepts.

Throughout this chapter we'll follow Mia and Kai as they develop a deeper understanding

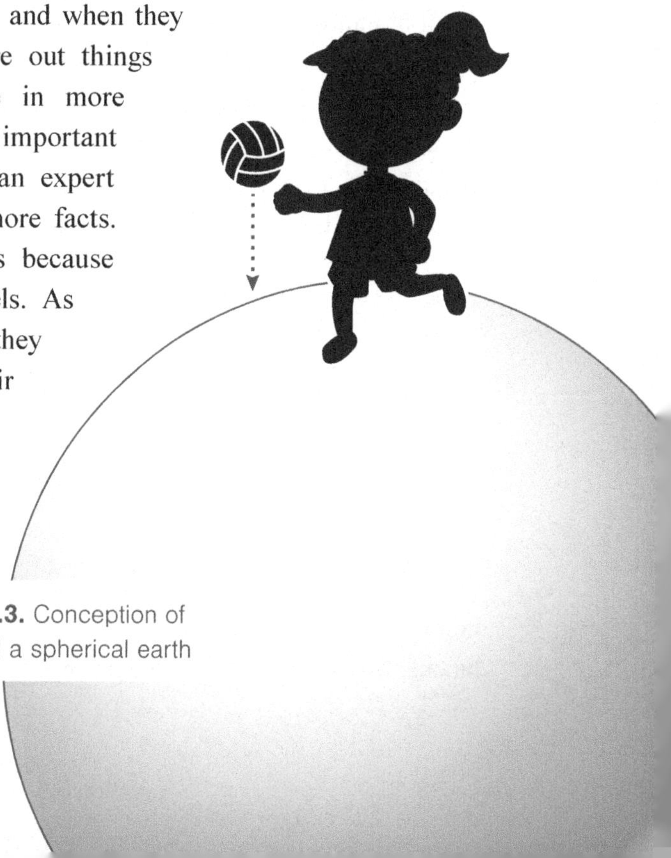

FIGURE 2.3. Conception of gravity and a spherical earth

of the world in which they live by perfecting their mental models through formal and informal learning experiences.

[2]

> EXPERTS DON'T JUST KNOW MORE. THEY KNOW DIFFERENTLY.

Novice learners, in any new domain, start with an incomplete and imperfect understanding. Learning and practice build new connections and replace others, gradually improving their understanding and ways of organizing the concepts.

As Mia enters elementary school, she has a foundational understanding about how addition works based on her background knowledge about quantity derived from, for example, her time spent playing with blocks. She understands the concepts of *more* and *less.* Counting sets of blocks may have also helped her build an understanding of the concept of multiplication, and that puts her at an advantage over children who try to learn multiplication as simply a set of facts. Mia has a deeper understanding of the concept of multiplication, which builds a foundation for more advanced mathematics learning. In contrast, a child who only memorizes a script of multiplication tables probably won't have the necessary conceptual understanding needed to move on to more advanced topics.

Despite Mia's early experiences with basic arithmetic, her mental model is imperfect, and it'll be challenged later in elementary school when learning new concepts such as negative numbers. For example, she understands that taking away two blocks from three blocks leaves one block.

But she's confused by a subtraction problem that would result in a negative number:

She thinks, *you can't take away three—because there's only two!* Negative numbers don't make sense when your mental model is based entirely on counting blocks. Mia will experience **cognitive dissonance** when a new concept contradicts her existing understanding of the world. "Cognitive dissonance refers to a situation involving conflicting attitudes, beliefs, or behaviors. This produces a feeling of mental discomfort leading to an alteration in one of the attitudes, beliefs, or behaviors to reduce the discomfort and restore balance."[3]

Mia's fourth- or fifth-grade teacher will need to help her transform and refine her existing concept of *quantity* into a more sophisticated form that includes negative numbers. Cognitive scientists would say this is refining an imperfect mental model of how the universe works so that it's more accurate and consistent with new experiences.[4] As this description implies, the idea of mental models recognizes that people construct small-scale internal models of the world and of their places in it.[5] Old ideas can combine with new ones to improve upon a naïve or imperfect understanding or ability.[6] No one can know all things, so we do our best to create those internal representations and then fill in the gaps to make sense of what we already know or eventually learn. Children learning the concept of negative values must, in a sense, build in their mind an improved internal model so they can better understand how quantity works in the real world. As they adjust their mental models, new connections are formed in the structures of the brain. In the case of learning to add and subtract, the new mental model must eventually work for both positive and negative quantities.

How can we help learners develop better mental models? One way is by helping them recognize a connection to something else they've already learned or experienced. For instance, Mia had a mental model of fractional quantities from when she baked snickerdoodle cookies with her grandma and measured a half cup of flour. That experience helped her when it was time to learn fractions. Before learning about negative numbers Mia had played "store" and acted out not allowing her brother Kai to buy a plastic food item because he didn't have enough money. She told him he needed to "go to work" and earn two more dollars, and then he would have enough. She understood that money is used to buy things and that a person can only buy something if they have enough money. She modeled in play with her brother what she had observed from the adults in her life, who had to go to work to earn more money.

If the teacher picks up on this tangible example rooted in Mia's prior conception of the world, then it's a short way from there to making the connection to negative numbers (as useful for expressing how much more of something, like money, that someone needs). Another student in her class may also have played store but in a less sophisticated way that didn't get into figuring out the difference between how much more someone needs to buy something. For that student, the prior knowledge

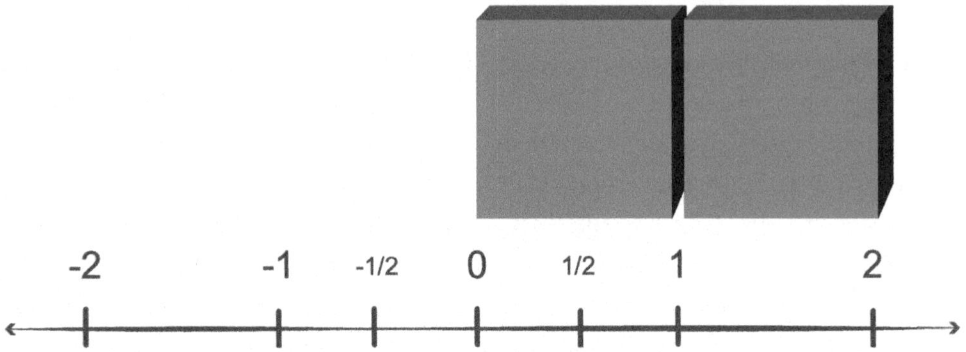

FIGURE 2.4. The child exposed to a number line is given a new mental model allowing negative numbers and fractional quantities to make sense alongside prior knowledge of whole number quantities

gained from play may not be a sufficient anchor for the new concept. As we'll explore later in this chapter, developmental factors also affect this. A learner may not be developmentally ready to grasp a new concept.

Teachers may also help Mia and her classmates expand their mental models by using a number line as shown in Figure 2.4 (above). First the positive side of a number line is used to help children understand whole numbers and fractional quantities. Later the negative side is used to introduce the concept of negative numbers. The number line introduces fractional quantities and then negative numbers in a way that makes sense alongside well-established concepts of positive whole number quantities from playing with and counting blocks. With the number line model, addition and subtraction of positive integers still works, but children can begin to grasp more advanced concepts like negative numbers and fractions.

[3]

Cognitive science defines categories of learning processes. Each can lead to different kinds of knowledge changes and, ultimately, to robust learning outcomes. Cognitive learning categories include:[7]

- Understanding and sense making
- Induction and refinement
- Memory and fluency building

Across all of the categories, an important component for learning is **constructive feedback**. Feedback gives learners information about the quality of their ideas and performance that they can use to make adjustments, and effective feedback is specific, understandable, timely, non-threatening, and actionable.

In the 1940s, Dutch chess master and psychologist Adriaan de Groot wanted to find out why world-class chess masters outperformed their challengers. He showed world-class masters and less experienced—but still extremely good—players examples of chess games and asked them to think aloud as they chose the moves they would make. "DeGroot's hypothesis was that the chess masters would be more likely than the non-masters to (a) think through all the possibilities before making a move and (b) think through all the possible countermoves of the opponent for every move considered."[8] He was wrong.

His research found that the world-class experts were able to recognize patterns of information that the extremely good players couldn't see. More recent research has discovered that information is organized differently in an expert's brain and chunked together in ways that allow them to solve problems. "DeGroot concluded that the knowledge acquired over tens of thousands of hours of chess playing enabled chess masters to out-play their opponents. Specifically, masters were more likely to recognize meaningful chess configurations and realize the strategic implications of these situations; this recognition allowed them to consider sets of possible moves that were superior to others."

In his best-selling book *Outliers: The Story of Success,* Malcolm Gladwell popularized the idea that those who are the best in the world—at everything from music to computer programming—have probably spent ten-thousand hours practicing and developing their abilities.[9] He makes a case that the 1960s rock band, The Beatles, had ten-thousand hours of deliberate practice before becoming worldwide superstars. There's nothing scientific about the number "ten thousand," but there is science behind the idea that to become highly skilled in any profession requires deliberate practice with feedback. Of course, there are those who have practiced music, a sport, or chess for more than ten-thousand hours and haven't become superstar musicians, Olympic athletes, or world champion chess players. Some of the differences may be influenced by innate abilities or disabilities relevant to the given domain. For example, it's harder for someone under six feet tall to become an NBA basketball player when competing against others over seven feet tall. (Although players like Isaiah Thomas, at five feet and nine inches, show that sometimes shorter people *can* train their body and mind to become among the best in the world!)

Very often it's not inherited ability or disability that keeps the novice musician, basketball player, or mathematician from becoming an expert. Moving toward expertise can be held back by a lack of foundational knowledge, lack of interest, faulty mindsets about what's possible, lack of a sufficient level of focus or intensity of deliberate practice, or lack of the right formative feedback.

A person must learn the basics before attempting to learn the advanced concepts in most knowledge domains, and they also must develop connections with:

1. the *contexts and practices* in the world in which the knowledge is intended to apply,
2. *core concepts* that serve to organize and make sense of the knowledge, and
3. the *representations and ways of communicating used by experts* in the domain.[10]

Early introduction of these connections can build bridges to higher levels of learning and ultimately to transfer of learning. **Transfer** is one of the characteristics of expertise; it's the ability to extend knowledge, reapplying it to new contexts or new kinds of problems. Transfer involves a variety of steps, including recognizing the potential fit, figuring out the correspondences, making the mapping, and adapting the *old* into the *new*. This is easier or harder depending on **reflection** done in earlier situations, the specifics of existing mental models, and the connections among those mental models.

[4]

Fredrick Reif was a physics teacher at the University of California who shifted his interest from research in physics to research on thinking and learning in complex domains. He joined Carnegie Mellon University in 1969. His 2008 book, *Applying Cognitive Science to Education,* was dedicated to the memory of his friend and colleague, the father of learning engineering, Herb Simon. In the book, Reif advocated for "a truly scientific approach to education" that strives to better understand "the underlying human thought processes and knowledge required for good performance" in particular domains. "Such an approach would then deliberately exploit an understanding of these underlying mechanisms to help students learn."

Technological advances in the way we study and explore the brain have discovered that "the brain is a dynamic organ, shaped to a great extent by experience—by what a living being does and has done."[11]

We now know that neural pathways in the brain are continuously being formed based on life experiences. Learning organizes and reorganizes your brain, changing its physical structure. This and other breakthrough findings direct us to think differently about teaching and learning, about the structures and culture of current systems, and about the practices and processes of education and training.

How Your Brain is Wired

The "wiring" of your brain is shaped by experiences that determine both the behavior of individual brain cells (neurons) and the network of connections among them. Figure 2.5 shows the structure of a neuron.[12]

You can think of a neuron as the basic wiring of the brain, with inputs controlling outputs. Like how an electrical circuit for a light may have a switch (input) that controls whether the light is on or off, each neuron may have inputs in the form of chemical stimuli from the nervous system that result in output conditions. If you turn on a light switch (the input) something happens at the output, the light bulb illuminates as shown in Figure 2.6.

A slightly more complex circuit has two double-pole switches controlling one light, like when there's one light switch at the top of a set of stairs and one at the bottom. If the light is off, switching the position of either of the switches will turn it on.

An electrical circuit with multiple switches is a helpful mental model for beginning to understand the underlying principles of the neuroscience of learning. Each neuron is wired to react to a combination of inputs. A certain set of inputs, in the form of chemical or electrical messages, will trigger the neuron to "turn on" outputs. Through experiences and effort, learners' brains change. Learning builds new connections and changes how individual neurons respond to stimuli. This "rewiring" improves the memory recall and capability of the brain.

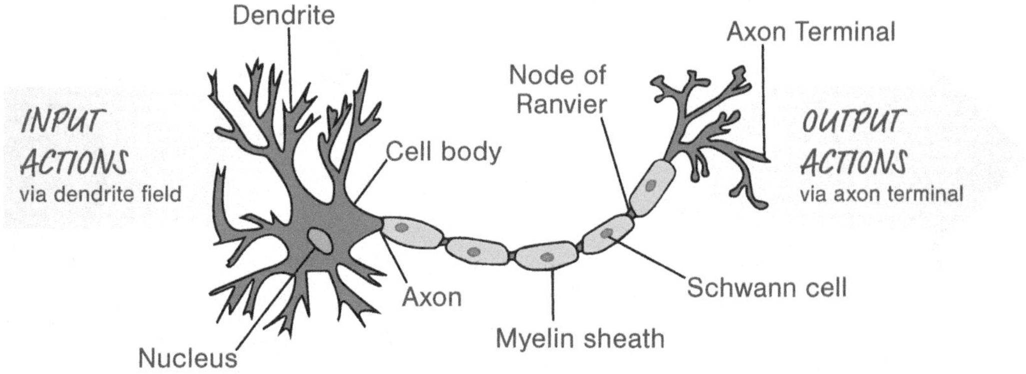

FIGURE 2.5. Function of a neuron

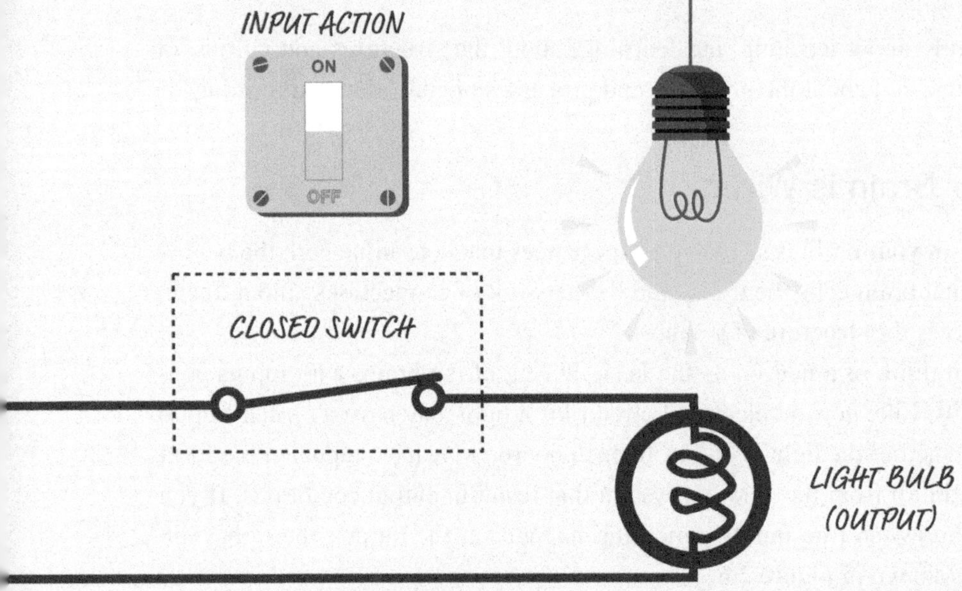

FIGURE 2.6. A simple single switch circuit: Closing the switch turns on the light

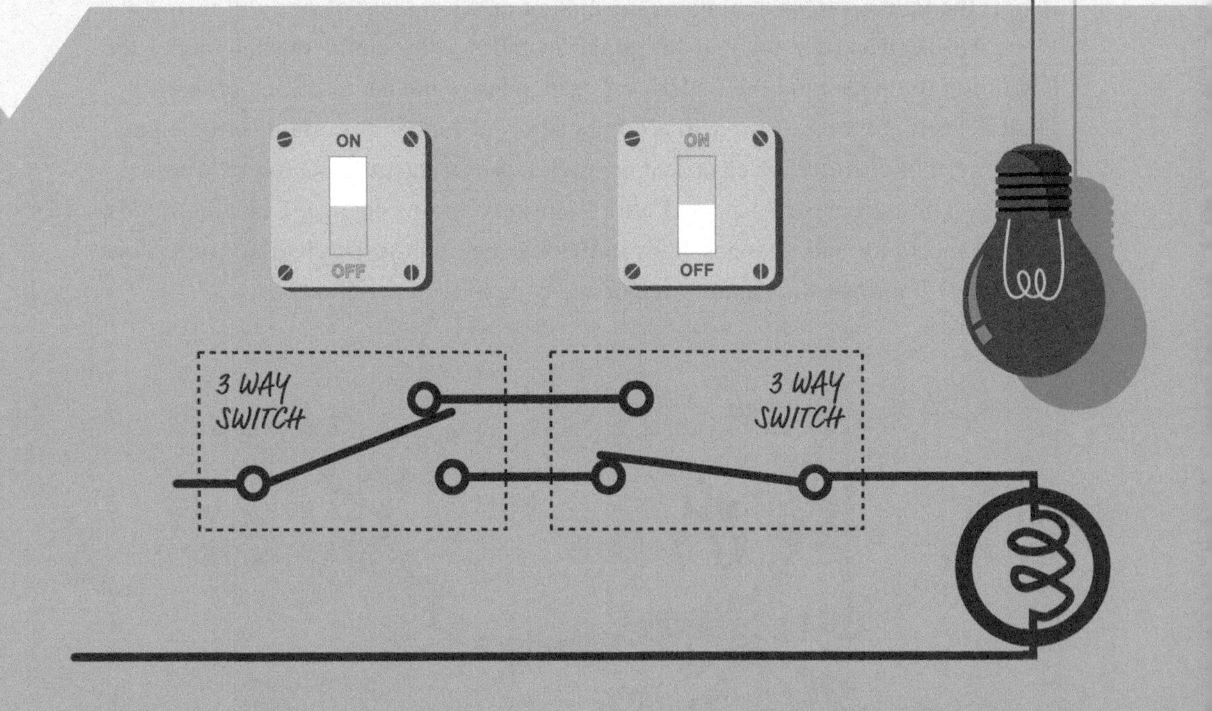

FIGURE 2.7. Three-way switch: Changing the position of either changes the light's state

You don't need to be a neuroscientist to do learning engineering, but it's essential to have some basic notions about how people learn. For example, with the knowledge that learning experiences make structural changes to the brain, learning engineering teams can approach their problem solving unconstrained by old notions that human brains are fixed in structure and capacity. As Channa Cook-Harvey, senior researcher at the Learning Policy Institute, explains:

> The brain and the development of intelligences and capacities are plastic and malleable. The brain develops over the entire lifespan as a function of experiences that activate neural pathways which permit new kinds of thinking and performance. The kinds of experience matter greatly. Relationships also matter greatly for learning.[13]

There is no learning from scratch. Learning is an active process in which a learner constructs meaning by mapping new information onto prior knowledge. As we experience life, our minds try to fit new information into what we already know about the world. Learning works best when we have the background knowledge that helps us make sense of the new information. Learning doesn't work well if the prerequisite knowledge on which to anchor the new knowledge is missing.

FIXED BRAIN NOTION	PLASTIC BRAIN NOTION
Some people are intelligent, some are not	A person can learn (almost) anything with the right conditions, experiences, and will
Fixed curriculum (variable outcomes)	Adaptive learning experiences (fixed objectives)
Fixed pace (some will get it others never will anyway)	Get prerequisite "structure" in place before moving on
Instructor led	Student centered
Uses primarily established pedagogy and andragogy	Considers all approaches, conditions and experiences that might lead to the desired learning objectives

FIGURE 2.8. Comparison of fixed brain vs. plastic brain notions

We used the example of a light switch to introduce the concept of how a neuron works because we assumed some readers wouldn't have prior knowledge of neurons or brain chemistry but that all readers would have experience with light switches. (Ideally, we would have assessed your prior knowledge, left out concepts that you didn't need to learn, and left in just enough for you to anchor new knowledge to existing knowledge. But the book format is limiting. It doesn't adapt and personalize the learning experience to optimize your learning outcomes.)

The wiring of a light switch is only an imperfect model of how a neuron works. A neuroscientist reading this might object to the analogy and point out the ways in which such a simple and concrete model is wrong. Similarly, a cognitive scientist may feel that the cognitive science concepts presented later in this chapter are over-simplified. Novice learners, in any new domain, start with incomplete and imperfect understanding.

[5]

In our fictitious story about Mia and Kai we examined an example of how shallow conceptual understanding of quantity, from counting blocks and playing store, can be enriched by helping learners expand and refine their mental models. We've looked at a shallow conceptual model for how the brain works, building new connections based on existing structures. This notion of "building on what exists" is foundational, and it's a concept shared by neuroscience and cognitive science.

In the early twentieth century, Soviet psychologist Lev Vygotsky theorized that people learn best within the **zone of proximal development**—that sweet spot just beyond what a person can do on their own but not beyond what they can do with help.[14] That is, learning tends to work best when learners are challenged beyond their current levels of development by just the right amount. As a person learns, the zone moves, and they can engage in more advanced learning.

In other words, productive learning requires that learning activities are

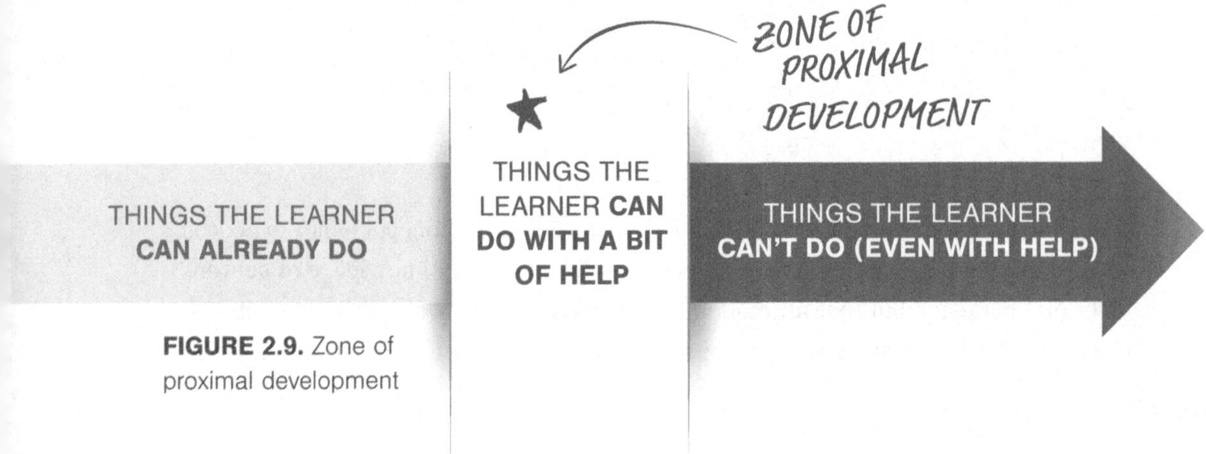

FIGURE 2.9. Zone of proximal development

continually at the proper level of difficulty. Tasks that are too difficult are frustrating and impossible to connect with prior knowledge, and tasks that are too easy have no challenge in them and often result in boredom. In between these two extremes lies what cognitive scientists call "**desirable difficulty**."

When activities remain at the desirable level, learners have the opportunity to experience **flow**. Psychologist Mihaly Csikszentmihalyi called flow an optimal condition that "can result in deep learning and high levels of personal and work satisfaction."[15] Said another way, the right level of challenge keeps learners engaged and focused.

One way to help learners find the right level of desirable difficulty is to provide the proper scaffolding. **Scaffolding** creates support while recognizing a learner's roles in their own learning process.* Scaffolding provides the structure they need to successfully engage in, and learn from, more complex tasks than they could otherwise handle. Scaffolding includes hints, prompts, conceptual frameworks (like advance organizers), process support, focus support, and strategic guidance. The goal is to provide just enough support to make tasks achievable without losing useful complexity or context.

Most adults are already familiar with scaffolding. Parents often scaffold learning for their infants in ways similar to those used by effective educators.[16] For example, they may:

- arrange the environment to promote learning,
- give cues to guide understanding about how to behave in new situations,
- use labels to classify objects and events,
- frame or model language and behavior,
- help the child connect a new situation to a more familiar one,
- interest the child in the task,
- reduce the number of steps required to solve a problem,
- maintain pursuit of a goal by directing activity and motivational feedback,
- control frustration and risk, or
- demonstrate an idealized version of the act to be performed.

The list above gives examples of supporting knowledge and skill as well as frustration and motivation. Some scaffolding focuses on cognition, such as making

---

* *A popular misconception is that the function of education is to pour information into the learner's mind. The truth is that learning takes focused effort on the part of the learner. Learning doesn't happen without some level of effort or attention.*

a task easier for a learner. Other scaffolding can focus on, for example, drawing a learner into a task, sequencing steps for desirable challenge, or creating structure to help a learner reach their objectives.

Not only must a learner be an active participant for effective learning, what a learner thinks about themselves—and about learning—makes a difference. Helping learners understand that many aspects of successful learning, such as strategy and effort, are under their own control fosters a sense of **self-efficacy**. And a related concept for learning engineering is **learner agency**, the "methodological development of both the capacity and the freedom of learners to exercise choice regarding what is to be learned and to co-create how that learning is to take place."[17] Learner agency assumes that learners have some role in:

- Setting goals
- Initiating action toward those goals
- Reflecting on and regulate progress toward those goals

Like many aspects of learning engineering, there are trade-offs in balancing the benefits of learner agency with the agency of education and training providers. Later in the chapter we will explore the importance of cultural contexts for learning, including the role of a safe environment and nurturing relationships. When learners feel safe, they're more likely to see failure as an opportunity to find out what they still need to learn and adjust learning strategies; that is, learners are more likely to persevere.

[6]

Let's fast-forward in the lives of our fictional learners Mia and Kai. Mia is entering middle school, and Kai is in elementary school. Mia is an 'A' student and an avid reader. She loves reading mysteries, and her favorite subject is mathematics.

Kai has had some difficulty in the early grades. The policy and culture of the school tends to support a teach-to-the-middle approach; it doesn't optimize the learning experiences based on the learner variability, and Kai isn't an average student. His abilities and disabilities don't fit the teach-to-the-middle approach. He takes longer to do writing assignments and is a slow reader. He developed faster than his peers in other areas such as executive function, deeper understanding of mathematics concepts, and critical thinking, but the grading system didn't reflect those abilities. **Executive function** is the group of complex mental processes and cognitive abilities needed for goal-directed behavior.[18]

For Kai, it was frustrating every time the teacher said, "time's up; turn in your assignment," when he was half finished, but he struggled through it for several years, doing just well enough to get average grades.

By fifth grade, he was at risk of needing to repeat the year. He was struggling with reading, writing, and memorizing math facts. Until then, he was able to fumble along, eking out passing grades in the mold of group instruction. However, one incident in fifth grade brought the disconnection between the instructional model and Kai's learner differences to a head. The teacher wrote on the board several columns of facts for the class to transcribe and then, presuming the class was done with the first column, erased it to write more facts. Kai wasn't finished with the first column. The teacher noticed this time that Kai was frustrated and struggling—not lazy.

Kai was diagnosed with a learning disability and given some extra help with reading. Still, most of the time he was stuck in the fixed-pace and non-differentiated group instructional model.

One bright spot in this part of Kai's life was playing chess. It was something he could feel good about. His uncle taught him the basics of the game, and he was able to beat his sister Mia most of the time, even though she was a year older and "smarter" (meaning she did much better in school). For Kai, chess was challenging but not frustrating.

[7]

Learning is dependent on cognitive capacities such as attention, executive function, working memory, and processing skills. Cognitive science research on grandmaster chess players and other experts helps us understand how the expert brain can do things faster and easier than novices. It also helps us understand how novices can become experts. The difference between a novice and an expert brain has a lot to do with how each uses two kinds of memory:

- **Short-term, working memory** is slower, error prone, more deliberate, has limited retention, requires greater mental effort, and is the place where new learning starts.
- **Long-term memory** has long retention, is efficient, operates automatically (without effort), and when trained error-free; it's what experts use to do complex tasks effortlessly.

Both kinds of memory are used to make sense of new information. Experts, however, have been able to rewire their brains over time so that long-term memory can make sense of, and act on, even very complex information without consciously thinking about it.

Renowned psychologist Daniel Kahneman in *Thinking, Fast and Slow* describes two systems that drive the way we think. System 1 that uses long-term memory is fast, intuitive, and emotional. System 2 is slower, more deliberate, more logical, lazier, and easily distracted.[19]

SENSORY MEMORY	WORKING MEMORY (SYSTEM 2)	LONG-TERM MEMORY (SYSTEM 1)
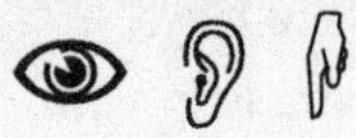 Combining senses, e.g., audio and visual, aids memory	• Short retention • Verbal, conscious • About 5 things at once • Slow • Error prone • Highly flexible • Can generate new insights • More discriminating	• Long retention • Nonverbal, not conscious • Highly parallel • Fast • Error-free recall (with training) • Rigid (decisions must "fit") • Biased (doesn't challenge what seems to "fit")

FIGURE 2.10. General comparison of memory types

Figure 2.10 illustrates the relationship among working memory, long-term memory, and sensory memory. **Sensory memory** is very short-term retention of impressions of sensory information such as seeing an image or hearing a sound. That sensory information may be passed easily to working memory (conscious memory) if used for immediate processing. With effort (practice, study) a learner may move information from working memory to long-term memory. This multi-store or modal model of memory was first proposed by Atkinson and Shiffrin in 1968.[20]

A novice chess player uses System 2 and working memory to try to think about the consequences of each move, two or three moves out. This is hard work. It creates what cognitive scientists call cognitive load. On the other hand, using System 1, an expert chess player can recognize patterns automatically and with far less cognitive load. This pattern recognition gives the expert a kind of intuition to sense the level of risk and opportunity of a given move.

Working memory—where new learning starts—has limited capacity and requires greater mental effort. **Cognitive load** is the effort used in working memory. In some cases, a heavy cognitive load can impede learning. **Cognitive load theory** suggests that learning experiences should be designed so that they don't overload working memory.

Another kind of cognitive load has to do with the number of sensory inputs a person has to process at a single moment. It's more difficult to think and learn in a chaotic and distracting environment or when too much information is presented for processing at once. A novice chess player sees the position and rank of up to thirty-two pieces on the sixty-four squares of the board as separate inputs. The expert has learned to see patterns that *chunk* information to be processed as fewer sensory inputs.

Building expertise takes deliberate practice with feedback. Newly learned skills or knowledge are generally forgotten over time if not reinforced with practice and applied. Even if the goal were only to pass a test, cognitive science has found that short practices spaced out over time are better for learning than cramming. Spaced learning or the spacing effect and related findings about the lag time in between practice sessions (lag effect) helps inform mathematical models for optimizing the amount and frequency of practice a learner needs to gain and retain knowledge.

> The **spacing effect** is the observation that people tend to remember things more effectively if they use spaced repetition practice (short study periods spread out over time) as opposed to massed practice (for example, cramming). The phenomenon was first documented by Ebbinghaus (1885), using himself as a subject in several experiments to memorize verbal utterances. In one study, after a day of cramming, he could accurately recite twelve-syllable sequences (of gibberish, apparently). However, he could achieve comparable results with half as many practices spread out over three days.
>
> The **lag effect**[21] is the related observation that people learn even better if the spacing between practices gradually increases. For example, a learning schedule might begin with review sessions a few seconds apart, then minutes, then hours, days, months, and so on, with each successive review stretching out over a longer and longer time interval.[22]

Different kinds of learning, such as learning a word in a new language versus learning how to solve a kind of mathematical problem, may have different optimum practice schedules. The best time to practice is when you're on the verge of forgetting, but that time may be different for every new word you're trying to learn or every step in a procedural process. A learner can't possibly keep track of when they're on the verge of forgetting every possible thing they want to retain, so learning engineers develop solutions that use **formative assessments** to help keep track and schedule practice for them.

Building expertise is about making new mental models, and spaced learning is about making what you know more accessible; *retrieval practice* combines the two. After many hours of practice, the expert brain is *conditionalized* to recognize and respond[23] effortlessly.[24] The expert mind also has developed more sophisticated mental models for addressing novel problems. The chess master recognizes a pattern and knows what to do based on the patterns wired into long-term memory. This quick retrieval of relevant information from long-term memory is effortless, not necessarily faster; experts might take longer to answer a question because they want to fully understand a problem. The same kind of process applies to learning to read, learning to code, or becoming a star athlete.

> Learning high-level chess can be compared to learning to read. A first grader works hard at recognizing individual letters and assembling them into syllables and words, but a good adult reader perceives entire clauses. An expert reader has also acquired the ability to assemble familiar elements in a new pattern and can quickly "recognize" and correctly pronounce a word that she has never seen before. In chess, recurrent patterns of interacting pieces play the role of letters, and a chess position is a long word or sentence.[25]

At the most basic level, learning engineering is about facilitating this overall learning process—helping a learner move from novice to a greater level of expertise for any given skill, knowledge, or ability.

[8]

Carnegie Mellon University professor Ken Koedinger is an inventor of intelligent tutoring software for mathematics, founder of the Pittsburgh Science of Learning Center known as LearnLab, and co-founder of Carnegie Learning, Inc.[26] His work builds from John Anderson's ACT-R theory of cognition (adaptive control of thought–rational), a theory for simulating and understanding human cognition. Anderson's theory, in turn, builds from the work of Allen Newell and Herbert Simon, who received the Association for Computing Machinery's A. M. Turing Award in 1975 for contributions to artificial intelligence and the psychology of human cognition.

Influenced by generations of thought leaders at the roots of learning engineering, Ken developed the **Knowledge-Learning-Instruction (KLI) Framework**[27] with Albert Corbett and Charles Perfetti. It helps people apply cognitive science research to practice. (See Figure 2.11.)

A **learning sciences framework** like KLI organizes discrete facts from the learning sciences into a model that can be practically applied in the design of learning experiences and solutions. It recognizes that we can't know exactly what thought process is going on inside a learner's head. However, we can build an approximate model of what a person knows and how they think by measuring how they respond to specific prompts. The more precisely we can define what a learner knows, the better we can measure their strengths, weaknesses, specific knowledge, and skill gaps. With that and other data, we can infer what conditions and experiences might help that learner fill those gaps.

One of the authors interviewed Ken in his office at the Human Computer Interaction Institute in Newell-Simon Hall on the Carnegie Mellon University campus. (The building was named after Herb Simon and his colleague Allen Newell, both pioneers in artificial intelligence and the psychology of human cognition.)

"From my experience," Ken said, "you can't just take the science and apply it. There are a lot of decisions I'm making for which science provides me little to

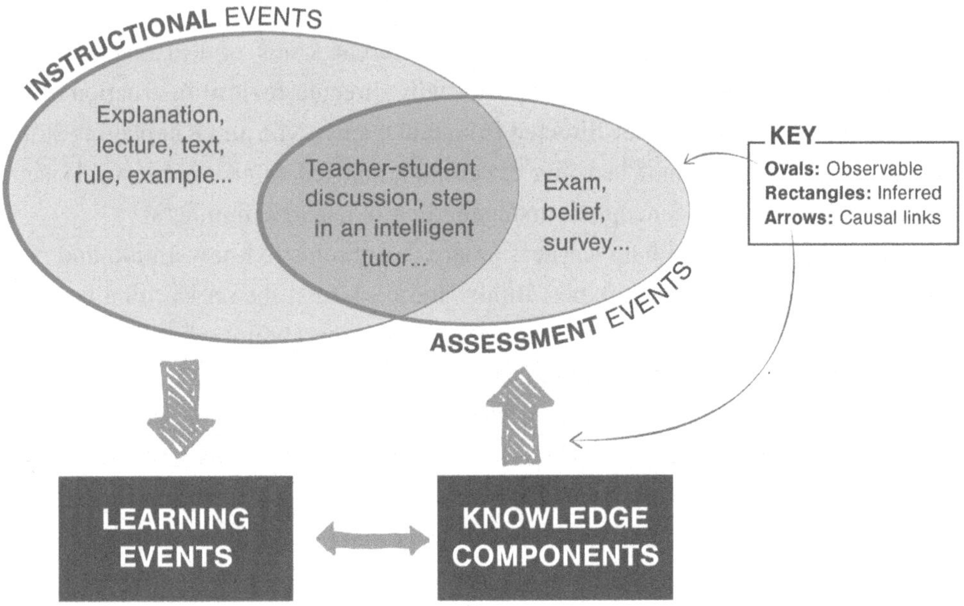

FIGURE 2.11. The KLI Framework defines observable instructional and assessment events, and unobservable learning events. Knowledge components are the competencies that cause learner performances, which can be observed/measured with assessment events.

no guidance. So that led me to believe, well, maybe I can do some of my own little studies on these and then other times we'll just guess. And then, when we had the opportunity to test whether those guesses worked, maybe 50 percent of the time—maybe—they did."

The KLI Framework defines observable **instructional** and **assessment events** as well as unobservable **learning events**. Performances observed and measured with assessment events tell us something about a person's learning.

Instructional events are changes in the learning environment or learner experiences intended to cause learning events. Sometimes an assessment event is an instructional event, such as with formative assessments where the learning measures are instrumented into the learning experience, for example, tracking what a learner does during an online simulation or instrumented classroom activity. Other times, an assessment event is just an assessment.

KLI identifies three broad classes of learning events:

1. memory and fluency processes,
2. induction and refinement processes, and
3. understanding and sense-making processes.

Different learning events call for different kinds of learning experiences. Learning experiences can include externally directed **formal** instructional and assessment events or learner-directed **informal** events. Mia and Kai playing store was an observable informal learning experience that led to an unobservable learning event (Mia gaining conceptual understanding of negative numbers).

If the goal is to help learners rewire their brains to know, think, and perform closer to the way that an expert thinks and performs, then a learning engineering challenge is to understand what's going on inside expert brains when they demonstrate a complex skill or ability. What facts do they use? What mental strategies do they employ? What does mastery look like? It turns out this is a big challenge because experts often can't tell you why they know something or how they get something done. Experts conditionalize their mental processing to be automatic. Expertise is often wired so deeply into long-term memory (the System 1 brain) that to the expert it may seem like intuition. *They just know the answer!*

Another problem is that experts tend to forget how their brains worked as novices. Ken Koedinger and his learning scientist colleagues call this the **expert blind spot** in which "advanced content knowledge without well-developed knowledge of the learning and teaching of novices can lead to expert-based views of curricula that are at odds with the learning process." Their research showed that "people with greater expertise tend to make assumptions about what novices know that turn out to be in conflict with students' actual performance and developmental propensities."[28]

The learning sciences community that discovered challenges such as the expert blind spot also developed processes for unpacking expertise and understanding what competencies learners must develop on the path toward it. Here, a **competency** defines any skill, knowledge, ability, attitude, habit of practice, or disposition that a person can possess. Broadly defined, it's any learning outcome.

Learning engineering can take advantage of methodologies developed by learning scientists to unpack competency definitions to an atomic level. This allows us to develop finely grained assessment items and learning supports based on the set of competencies that make up complex tasks. This level of specificity makes it possible to use observable instructional and assessment events to infer learning events (unobservable changes in a learner's brain that impact performance).

In KLI, an atomic competency definition is called a **knowledge component**. Competency definitions can be defined at a higher level of granularity for assessing complex tasks that involve coordination or synthesis of many knowledge components. However, best practices for formative assessment call for unpacking that competency definition into its parts and designing assessment items or performance tasks with scaffolding, such as hints, that also measure those more granular components. If a learner doesn't succeed with a complex learning task, the more granular items can be used to discover the root cause of the failure, for example, which knowledge components need further development and support.

Competency definitions used for purposes such as job descriptions or academic standards are necessarily defined broadly and leave room for interpretation. For example, an academic standard for mathematics specifies that a student should be able to "solve word problems involving addition and subtraction of fractions referring to the same whole, including cases of unlike denominators." A job description may include the requirement that the candidate has "knowledge of arithmetic, algebra, geometry, calculus, statistics, and their applications."[29]

Learning engineering calls for competency definitions with data-justified specificity, meaning we want to be able to prove that the competency is at the atomic level with data. A common mistake is to assume a competency definition addresses a single measurable skill when it represents two or more skills that need to be further unpacked to be reliably taught or assessed.

To get to well-defined competency definitions with data-justified specificity we can employ two sets of approaches:

1. The first approach is a systematic process to understand the cognitive elements of a more broadly defined competency. One such methodology is called **cognitive task analysis**.
2. The second tool is a data analytics methodology using student learning data to either validate or discover the human errors inevitably in the initial version of a set of competency definitions.

Learning engineers assume that the first draft of a set of competency definitions won't be perfect. Data expose those imperfections and allow us to iteratively fix competency assumptions as well as fix any learning activities and assessment items that were designed to teach or assess based on those flawed competency definitions. A story in Chapter 6 covers **learning curve analysis**, one data analytics method used to check assumptions about data-justified specificity.

[9]

Our fictitious characters Mia and Kai are now in college. Mia is studying cybersecurity, a good fit for her, inspired by her love for mystery novels and proficiency in mathematics.

Kai realized sometime along the way that he didn't fit the mold of school but he could learn to be successful academically. Sometimes that involved figuring out for himself a mental workaround, such as on-the-fly calculating a math fact that he hadn't memorized or visualizing a problem in a different way for deeper understanding rather than just using the rote method presented by a teacher or textbook. Although he struggled with reading as a child, his reading fluency grew with practice, and motivated by natural curiosity, he grew to love reading. He learned to love history, especially figuring out what circumstances affect other circumstances. He reads history well, now, because he has enough understanding of factors that might affect other factors to draw inferences as he reads. He had to spend a lot of time working on developing that competency.

By developing his **metacognitive strategies**—that is, actively reflecting on and adapting his own mental processes—Kai was able to overcome what was diagnosed as a learning disability when he was younger. In fact, he's found that his learning differences and metacognitive strategies often put him at an advantage over his peers. He excels in some areas, such as chess and other strategy games.

While Kai had to overcome some differences that didn't fit the mold of school, some apparent learning struggles that children have early on when compared to peers may be due to normal development. Children progress developmentally at different paces. If you plan to develop learning solutions for specific age groups, it's helpful to understand something about how the brain develops and functions at different stages of life, from birth through late adulthood. Figure 2.12 shows stages of brain development over the course of human life.

We previously discussed how the brain is wired and how learning, in a sense, rewires your brain. **Neuroplasticity**, also known as brain plasticity or neural plasticity, is the ability of the brain to change throughout an individual's life.[30] At the single cell level, synaptic plasticity[31] refers to changes in the connections between neurons, whereas non-synaptic plasticity[32] refers to changes in their intrinsic excitability, for example, how responsive they are to the chemical signals they receive.[33] The structure of the brain can change throughout life but may be more "plastic" during developmental periods from prenatal to early 20s. For more detailed explanations of what researchers have discovered about changes that occur with age and learning across the life span, see *How People Learn II.*[34]

[10]

As an adult, Mia is a cybersecurity expert for the Institute for Defense Analyses, an American nonprofit corporation that helps the US government address national security issues. Part of her success is that in addition to being a subject-matter expert, she's an expert life-long learner. Like many professions in the twenty-first century, Mia's job requirements for what she has to know and be able to do change continually.

Learning works best when the learner has "learned how to learn" and takes an active role in the learning process. Learning how to learn includes developing knowledge about learning strategies and practicing skills that apply those strategies. It also involves developing productive mindsets (what the learner thinks about learning) and dispositions, including habits of practice. People can learn to become **expert learners**. As an adult, Kai is an expert learner and historian working as a strategy analyst for governments and corporations.

Learning to learn often involves so-called **noncognitive factors**. A report by the University of Chicago Consortium on Chicago School Research identified five noncognitive factors:[35]

<table>
<tr>
<td>The PRENATAL brain develops new neurons, synapses, and myelinated axons at an astounding rate. At birth it has more structural elements than it needs.</td>
<td>The brain increases fourfold during PRESCHOOL YEARS and by age six is about 90% of adult brain volume. Synaptic connections (gray matter) and myelination of nerve fibers (white matter) dramatically increase. Growth and synaptic pruning are shaped by experiences.</td>
<td>Explosive growth continues AGE SIX TO ADOLESCENCE offset by synaptic pruning. The structure of the brain is shaped by experiences.</td>
<td>Growth and pruning continues from ADOLESCENCE TO EARLY ADULTHOOD. The brain reaches a size of about 86 billion neurons and 84 billion non-neuron cells.</td>
<td>The ADULT BRAIN continue to add and maintain synapses and generate myelin in response to new learning. As the adult learner acquires new knowledge, regions of the cortex develop specialization of function known as experience-dependent learning.</td>
<td>LATE ADULTHOOD is associated with declines in memory, speed of cognitive processing and ability to learn new information. However, it is associated with increased skill in solving social dilemmas.</td>
</tr>
<tr>
<td colspan="4">Synaptic Pruning (birth to mid-to-late twenties)—use it or lose it! During this period the brain lets some synapse connections die off while adding and strengthening others. Synapses continually used are retained, those that are not used are eliminated. Both axon (transmitter) and dendrite (receiver) completely decay and die off. This sculpting of the brain improves the networking capacity of the brain and is associated with a heightened ability to learn. Some of the most significant "brain remodeling" happens during adolescence from pruning and the laying down of myelin sheaths that make the transfer of information about 3,000 times faster for those connections. Through practice the learner's brain lays down myelin to enable a skill.</td>
<td colspan="2">Effects of aging on the brain: The outer layer of the brain (cortex) starts to thin after age forty. It is not clear if this means a decrease in brain tissue or is the result of some other factor such as lower hydration. It does, however, seem to correspond to the start of cognitive decline often observed in older adults. Older adults are more likely to remember the important implications of an event while younger learners will likely remember more details about the event. Conditions such as life satisfaction and having strong social networks can reduce the speed of age-related cognitive decline.</td>
</tr>
</table>

FIGURE 2.12. Life-long brain development

Sources: (a) Siegel, D. J. "Dr. Dan Siegel - BRAINSTORM: Brain Remodeling, Pruning and Myelin." November 8, 2013. Video, https://youtu.be/s_MJg5zofOo. (b) Siegel, D. J." Pruning, Myelination, and the Remodeling Adolescent Brain." Psychology Today, February 4, 2014. (c) How People Learn II. (ibid.) (d) O'Rourke, M., Gasperini, R., & Young, K. M. (2014). Adult Myelination: Wrapping up Neuronal Plasticity. Neural Regeneration Research, 9(13), 1261–1264. https://doi.org/10.4103/1673-5374.137571.

1. Academic Behaviors
   Going to class, doing homework, organizing, participating, studying
2. Academic Perseverance
   Grit, tenacity, delayed gratification, self-discipline, self-control
3. Academic Mindsets
   I belong in this academic community. My ability and competence grow with my effort. I can succeed at this. This work has value for me.
4. Learning Strategies
   Study skills, metacognition, self-regulated learning, goal-setting
5. Social Skills
   Interpersonal skills, empathy, cooperation, assertion, and responsibility

These factors point to learning-to-learn competencies that can be developed in and by learners. Learning engineering teams should keep in mind that productive mindsets and behaviors can be reinforced or undermined by their designs. Helping learners understand that many aspects of successful learning, such as strategy and effort, are under their own control fosters agency to learn. A productive mindset may be encouraged by giving process-focused feedback in an environment that treats mistakes as an opportunity to reflect and learn.

Not only is it important what the learner thinks about learning in general. It's also important how the learner thinks about their own learning while learning. **Metacognition** is thinking about one's own thinking; it's where learners actively reflect on activities and their own mental processes.

Metacognition in learning includes knowledge of one's own learning strengths and weaknesses as well as the demands of the learning at hand. It also includes self-regulation—the ability to correct errors when appropriate and the ability to reflect on one's own learning.[36] Learners need insight into their own learning before they can effectively plan or self-regulate.

Metacognition is often a learned behavior; it doesn't come naturally to everyone. Learners may not be aware of their own internal dialogue or how important it is for the learning process unless explicitly taught to attend to it. Like other learned behaviors, that internal dialogue is influenced by culture and previous experiences, and the type of self-monitoring that's most productive will vary by academic or professional discipline.

Scaffolded metacognition as learners are learning may prompt them to reflect on or articulate what and how they're learning. *Did I already know that? How would*

I explain that to someone else? Does it conflict with what I thought I knew or thought I could do? How well do I know this? How well do I know how to do this? On what parts of this do I need help or more practice?

> An emphasis on metacognition must accompany instruction in each of the disciplines because the type of monitoring required will vary. In history, for example, the student might be asking himself, "who wrote this document, and how does that affect the interpretation of events," whereas in physics the student might be monitoring her understanding of the underlying physical principle at work.[37]

When designing learning experiences, it's equally important to understand subject-matter experts' internal dialogue and to model that thinking for novices. Such domain-specific thinking supports domain-specific **chunking** (sorting and grouping of knowledge into long-term memory). Learning engineering teams can bundle a learning experience with metacognitive coaching and modeling, such as contextually appropriate conceptual frameworks and reflective exercises. This can help learners recognize and evaluate their own conceptualizations or practices.

In August 2020, Laura Fries, Ji Li Son, Karen Givvin, and James Stigler published the paper "Practicing Connections: A Framework to Guide Instructional Design for Developing Understanding in Complex Domains." Based on what research suggests about how experts are able to organize and connect chunks of knowledge, they suggest a practical framework for helping learners practice connections:

> The building blocks of this transferable knowledge, sometimes referred to as schemas [or mental models], emphasizes the connections between abstract relations (such as hierarchies, embedded categories, and functional systems) rather than lists of discrete facts and procedures. For example, expert physicists' schemas for a range of problems situations are organized by fundamental relationships [for example, the relationship of work to energy] rather than by superficial surface-level details specific to problem contexts. Experts also have fewer and more interconnected schemas.

To help learners think more like experts, the authors suggest incorporating features of scaffolding and instruction that explicitly prompt learners to build connections between a domain's core concepts, key representations of those concepts, and the contexts and practices in the world, for example, how physics is used in the real world by physicist and engineers.

[11]

Mia and Kai each had individual experiences that led to their own learning as well as shared experiences and cultural influences that likely had some common impact on those unique journeys. Every experience that a learner has influences their brain and their ability to learn new things. At a macro level, the culture in which the learner is situated can also impact learning—in positive and negative ways. **Culture** refers to the shared beliefs, social forms, and material traits of a racial, religious, family, or other social group; and the integrated pattern of human knowledge, belief, and behavior that depends upon the capacity for learning and transmitting knowledge to succeeding generations.[38]

> Learning does not happen in the same way for all people because cultural influences pervade development from the beginning of life. – *How People Learn II*[39]

The bottom line is that people bring a set of beliefs, behaviors, motivators, feelings, prior knowledge, prior misconceptions, and mindsets to every new learning experience, and these are influenced by the experiences formed in the communities in which they live. People can compartmentalize their cultural identities, adopting more than one set of cultural norms. For example, a student may reflect one set of behavioral habits and beliefs when in a school or work setting and a different set at home. However, while this tendency to compartmentalize may be helpful to counteract negative external influences on learning, it can also hinder the transfer of learning to new contexts.

Learning takes place within a social context. Even independent learning where a learner isn't interacting with another person is influenced by social and cultural expectations. Remember, there's no learning from scratch. Mia's understanding of elementary school mathematics was shaped by her prior experiences of playing with blocks and playing store.

> An individual's development is affected by the environment in which she lives—including not only the family and other close relationships and circumstances but also the larger contexts in which families and communities are situated.[40]

In addition to culture, the contextual conditions during learning experiences matter. Disruptions, such as forced remote learning in 2020 due to the COVID-19 pandemic, can have positive impacts for some learners and negative impacts for others. Learning engineering includes creating conditions that promote learning. That goes beyond just creating instructional materials. Some learning engineering challenges involve creating an appropriate culture and context of learning within an institution, organization, or school.

- Does the learner feel safe?
- Is the learner hungry, too cold, too hot, sick, stressed?
- Is the environment distracting?

The conditions don't need to be perfect, and the environment doesn't need to be comfortable for people to learn. Air conditioning and three meals a day aren't prerequisites. However, a person experiencing severe hyperthermia or malnutrition probably will need some food and a lower body temperature before doing any productive learning.

Similarly, while stress is a necessary and important factor in human development, chronically high levels of stress, without buffering, derail healthy brain development and impact school and work performance.[41] In the wake of the September 11, 2001 attacks on the United States, Pamela Cantor co-authored a study that found more New York City school children were traumatized by their experience of growing up in poverty than by what they had witnessed on that terrifying day. Her organization, Turnaround for Children, applies learning science to help schools counter such negative influences. According to Cantor, "It's impossible to feel curious, for example, while also feeling threatened." The good news, she says, is that science also tells us that the brain is malleable and given the right environment, children and adults can learn the skills and mindsets for success in learning and in life.

[12]

The **learner model** is a dynamically updated profile of the learner used for diagnosis, feedback, coaching, and prescription of learning activities. In one-on-one tutoring, the tutor mentally constructs a learner model based on observations and interactions with the student. Data-driven learner modeling in adaptive instructional systems similarly uses student interaction data to build explanatory models of a learner's cognition, metacognition, and motivation. No matter the time in their life, this type of adaptive data-driven support could have provided both Mia and Kai with the types of feedback and learning experiences that would have better supported their individual and collective learning journeys.

Teachers, tutors, learning coaches, and adaptive learning systems can provide good guidance and feedback when they understand where a learner is on the pathway toward mastery, what misconceptions they have, and where there is room for improvement. The right kind of observation and measurement gives the visibility needed to optimize feedback.

> **Data-driven learner modeling** is "use of student interaction data to build explanatory models of elements of learning (e.g., cognition, metacognition, motivation) that can be used to drive instructional decision-making toward better student learning."[42]

A learner model includes not only information about a learner's progress but insights into the learner's thinking, knowledge gaps, and misconceptions. A study of middle school physical science teachers found "that teachers who know their students' most common misconceptions are more likely to increase their students' science knowledge than teachers who do not."[43]

Likewise, learning experiences can be engineered to approximate what's going on inside the learner's mind and respond accordingly. Platforms like Duolingo use data about the difficulty of a task in combination with learner model data to predict the likelihood of a learner answering the next prompt correctly.

Gaining visibility into learner mastery and misconceptions often is achieved through formative performance assessments. A best practice is to embed continual measurement of learning within learning activities rather than present assessments as separate events. Great teachers, tutors, and intelligent tutoring systems first determine if the learner's response indicates mastery of a competency, and then if not mastered, they use follow-up assessment items or metacognitive activities to unpack the misconception or imperfection in the learner's thinking. With this information the tutor or system can provide the right kind of feedback and follow-on learning activities.

To reach this granular level of understanding—this level of visibility into learners' thinking—requires well-defined competency definitions and a well-defined knowledge base of what can go wrong for learners in mastering each competency.

It's not enough to know if a learner understands or can do something. We also want to know how well they can use their competence to address new kinds of problems (transfer) and how well they've retained their competence for long-term use. We also want to know what barriers exist, blocking the way to mastery, and what possible strategies might overcome those obstacles. Similarly, because part of the journey from novice toward some level of expertise involves the learner's ability to think about their own thinking (and to regulate their own learning), learner models can also contain estimates of learners' metacognitive skills, mindsets, motivations, attitudes, and anything else that impacts learning.

[13]

In summary, the learning sciences form the bedrock of learning engineering. They guide its theories and practices and provide an initial blueprint for designing learning experiences. But as important as the learning sciences are, remember the lesson from the story of penicillin discussed in the introduction: it takes more than scientific discovery to produce innovation at scale.

> Efforts to design effective learning environments and activities cannot be based solely on scientifically validated theories of learning: theoretical advances are often too slow in coming, too blunt, and too idealistic. Engineering and other design-based approaches use faster methods of testing innovation. Design-based approaches are goal directed and contextualized and often employ frequent, formative assessments as part of iterative design-implement-evaluate-redesign methods. This allows for highly responsive, evidence-based course corrections so that it is possible to realign solutions to suit local constraints and to resolve on-the-fly decisions that are underspecified by prevailing scientific models.[44]

Engineers look at everything as a system, and while the learning sciences provide the basis for learning engineering, alone they're not sufficient. Read on, to learn more about how the learning sciences join with the other sub-disciplines of learning engineering to create a complete system. ★

- Many learning science discoveries aren't yet applied at scale.
- People build mental models (also called schemas), which are internal representations of the world. Expertise is the process of continually improving these and connecting different mental models together.
- There is no learning from scratch. All learning builds on prior knowledge and experiences, and these are influenced by culture and context.
- Learning is different for everyone, and different topics and developmental levels call for different kinds of learning activities.
- Optimal learning takes place when the difficulty level is just right. By adding scaffolding (like hints), learners can complete activities they couldn't otherwise. That's when some of the best learning takes place.
- Cognitive factors, such as executive function and metacognition, affect learning. Executive function is related to working memory—or System 2, the more deliberate kind of memory.
- Using working memory takes effort. It creates cognitive load. Too much cognitive load can interfere with learning.
- Over time, experts learn to rely more on the mental models stored in their long-term memory—System 1, the faster, automatic memory.
- Knowledge, skill, dispositions, habits of practice, and even intelligence are trainable to a significant and meaningful degree.
- You can learn to be an expert learner.
- Metacognition refers to "thinking about thinking." Metacognitive skills, like self-regulation, can be learned, and it greatly improves learning outcomes.
- We can't see inside learners' heads to know if they're learning, but we can build learner models from assessments, which let us infer those unobservable learning events. These models can be "built" in a teacher's mind or via data-driven computational methods.
- Learning is different for everyone.

Learning Engineering Applies the Learning Sciences

KEY POINTS

Endnotes

1 Simon, Herbert A. "Job of a College President." *Educational Record 48,* no. 1 (1967): 68–78.

2 Duschl, Richard A. *Taking Science to School: Learning and Teaching Science in Grades K-8.* Washington, DC: The National Academies Press, 2007. https://doi.org/10.17226/11625

3 McLeod, Saul. "Cognitive Dissonance." Simply Psychology. February 05, 2018. www.simplypsychology.org/cognitive-dissonance.html

4 Maskiewicz, April Cordero and Jennifer Evarts Lineback. "Misconceptions Are 'So Yesterday!'" *CBE Life Sciences Education,* 2013. www.ncbi.nlm.nih.gov/pmc/articles/PMC3763002

5 Johnson-Laird, PN. "The History of Mental Models." In *Psychology of Reasoning: Theoretical and Historical Perspectives,* edited by Ken Manktelow and Man Cheung Chung, 179–212. London: Psychology Press, 2004. https://doi.org/10.4324/9780203506936

6 Smith, John P., Andrea A. diSessa, and Jeremy Roschelle. "Misconceptions Reconceived: A Constructivist Analysis of Knowledge in Transition." *The Journal of the Learning Sciences 3,* no. 2 (1993): 115–63. www.jstor.org/stable/1466679

7 Koedinger, Kenneth R., Albert T. Corbett, and Charles Perfetti. "The Knowledge-Learning-Instruction Framework: Bridging the Science-Practice Chasm to Enhance Robust Student Learning." *Cognitive Science 36* (2012) 757–798. https://doi.org/10.1111/j.1551-6709.2012.01245.x

8 Bransford, John D., Ann L. Brown, M. Suzanne Donovan, and James W. Pellegrino, eds. *How People Learn: Brain, Mind, Experience, and School.* Washington, DC: National Academy Press, 2003, 32. https://doi.org/10.17226/9853

9 Gladwell, Malcolm. "Complexity and the Ten-Thousand-Hour Rule." *The New Yorker,* August 21, 2013. www.newyorker.com/sports/sporting-scene/complexity-and-the-ten-thousand-hour-rule

10 Fries, Laura, Ji Y. Son, Karen B. Givvin, and James W. Stigler. "Practicing Connections: A Framework to Guide Instructional Design for Developing Understanding in Complex Domains." *Educational Psychology Review 33,* no. 2 (2020): 739–762. https://doi.org/10.1007/s10648-020-09561-x

11 Bransford et al., *How People Learn,* 115.

12 Adapted from Wikipedia, "Neuron," last modified August 7, 2011, https://commons.wikimedia.org/wiki/File:Neuron.jpg, and from US National Institutes of Health, "Nerve Tissue," https://training.seer.cancer.gov/anatomy/nervous/tissue.html.

13 Cook-Harvey, Channa. "The Science of Learning and Development and Its Implications for Transforming K-12 Education." International Association for K-12 Online Learning. Aurora Institute. May 2018. www.inacol.org/wp-content/uploads/2018/05/iNACOL-Leadership-Webinar-May-2018.pdf

14 In *Mind in Society,* Vygotsky defined the Zone of Proximal Development as "the distance between the actual development level as determined by independent problem solving and the level of potential development as determined through problem solving under adult guidance or in collaboration with more capable peer" (p. 86).

Vygotsky, Lev Semenovich, and Michael Cole. *Mind in Society: Development of Higher Psychological Processes.* Cambridge, MA: Harvard University Press, 1978.

As quoted from Shabani, Karim, Mohamad Khatib, and Saman Ebadi. "Vygotsky's Zone of Proximal Development: Instructional Implications and Teachers' Professional Development." *English Language Teaching 3,* no. 4 (2010): 237–248. https://files.eric.ed.gov/fulltext/EJ1081990.pdf

15 "Flow (Csíkszentmihályi)." *Learning Theories.* February 4, 2017. www.learning-theories.com/flow-csikszentmihalyi.html

16 Bransford et al., *How People Learn,* 104.

17 Poon, Jennifer Davis. "Part 1: What Do You Mean When You Say 'Student Agency?'" *Education Reimagined,* September 11, 2018. https://education-reimagined.org/what-do-you-mean-when-you-say-student-agency

18 Merriam-Webster. "Executive Function." Accessed November 27, 2021. www.merriam-webster.com/dictionary/executive%20function

19 Kahneman, Daniel. *Thinking, Fast and Slow.* New York: Farrar, Straus and Giroux, 2011, 20.

20 McLeod, Saul. "Multi-Store Model of Memory." Simply Psychology. January 1, 1970. www.simplypsychology.org/multi-store.html

21 Melton, Arthur W. "The Situation with Respect to the Spacing of Repetitions and Memory." *Journal of Verbal Learning and Verbal Behavior 9,* no. 5 (1970): 596–606.

22 Settles, Burr, and Brendan Meeder. 2016. "A Trainable Spaced Repetition Model for Language Learning." In *Proceedings of the 54th Annual Meeting of the Association for Computational Linguistics, Berlin, Germany, August 7–12, 2016,* 1848–1858. Stroudsburg, PA: Association for Computational Linguistics. https://aclanthology.org/P16-1174.pdf

23 IGI Global. "What is Conditional Knowledge." Accessed December 29, 2017. www.igi-global.com/dictionary/conditional-knowledge/5277

24 Bransford et al., *How People Learn,* 44–49.

25 Kahneman, *Thinking, Fast and Slow,* 238.

26 "Timeline of Cognitive Tutor History." Cognitive Tutor Authoring Tools: Timeline of Cognitive Tutor History. Carnegie Mellon University. Last modified 2015. http://ctat.pact.cs.cmu.edu/index.php?id=timeline

27 Koedinger, Corbett, and Perfetti, "The Knowledge-Learning-Instruction Framework."

28 Kessler, Aaron, Melissa Boston, and Mary Kay Stein. "Exploring How Teachers Support Students' Mathematical Learning in Computer-Directed Learning Environments." *Information and Learning Sciences 121,* no. 1/2 (2019): 52–78. https://doi.org/10.1108/ILS-07-2019-0075

29 "15-1132.00 - Software Developers, Applications." O*NET OnLine. US Department of Labor. www.onetonline.org/link/summary/15-1132.00

30 Goodell, Jim and Janet Kolodner. "Learning Sciences: Concepts for Learning Engineering." Prototype Card Deck Prepared for the IEEE ICICLE 2019 Conference on Learning Engineering. https://drive.google.com/file/d/13XqSu3BMMHWd0_pRut7cuoijG6vK1pHC/view

See also: Goodell, Jim and Janet Kolodner. "Learning Science Cards." In *Proceedings of the 2019 Conference on Learning Engineering, Washington, DC, May 20–23, 2019.* http://sagroups.ieee.org/icicle/wp-content/uploads/sites/148/2020/07/ICICLE_Proceedings_Learning-Engineering.pdf

31 Wikipedia. "Synaptic Plasticity." Last modified September 21, 2021. https://en.wikipedia.org/wiki/Synaptic_plasticity

32 Wikipedia. "Non-Synaptic Plasticity." Last modified November 16, 2011. https://en.wikipedia.org/wiki/Non-synaptic_plasticity

33 Wikipedia. "Neuroplasticity." Last modified December 8, 2021. https://en.wikipedia.org/wiki/Neuroplasticity

34 National Academies of Sciences, Engineering, and Medicine. *How People Learn II: Learners, Contexts, and Cultures.* Washington, DC: National Academies Press, 2018. https://doi.org/10.17226/24783

35 Farrington, Camille A., Melissa Roderick, Elaine Allensworth, Jenny Nagaoka, Tasha Seneca Keyes, David W. Johnson, and Nicole O. Beechum. 2012. *Teaching Adolescents to Become Learners: The Role of Noncognitive Factors in Shaping School Performance: A Critical Literature Review. Consortium on Chicago School Research.* Chicago, IL: The Chicago University Consortium on Chicago School Research. https://files.eric.ed.gov/fulltext/ED542543.pdf

36 Bransford et al., *How People Learn,* 97.

37 Bransford et al., *How People Learn,* 21.

38 "Culture." Merriam-Webster. Accessed November 18, 2021. www.merriam-webster.com/dictionary/culture

39 National Academies, *How People Learn II*, 22.

40 National Academies, *How People Learn II*, 21.

41 "The Science." Turnaround for Children. May 3, 2018. https://turnaroundusa.org/what-we-do/the-science

42 Koedinger, Kenneth R., Elizabeth A. McLaughlin, and John C. Stamper. "Data-Driven Learner Modeling to Understand and Improve Online Learning: MOOCs and Technology to Advance Learning and Learning Research." *Ubiquity,* May (2014): 1–13. https://doi.org/10.1145/2591682

43 Sadler, Philip M., and Gerhard Sonnert. "Understanding Misconceptions: Teaching and Learning in Middle School Physical Science." *American Educator.* September 27, 2016. www.aft.org/ae/spring2016/sadler-and-sonnert

44 Sawyer, R. Keith, ed. 2014. *The Cambridge Handbook of the Learning Sciences.* Cambridge University Press, 23. https://doi.org/10.1017/CBO9781139519526

45 Closing quotation from Hess, Frederick M. and Bror Saxberg. *Breakthrough Leadership in the Digital Age: Using Learning Science to Reboot Schooling.* Thousand Oaks, CA: Corwin Press, 2013, 32.

Trying to reengineer learning without being versed in the basics of learning is like trying to improve brain surgery without knowing much about the brain.

– *Breakthrough Leadership in the Digital Age*[45]

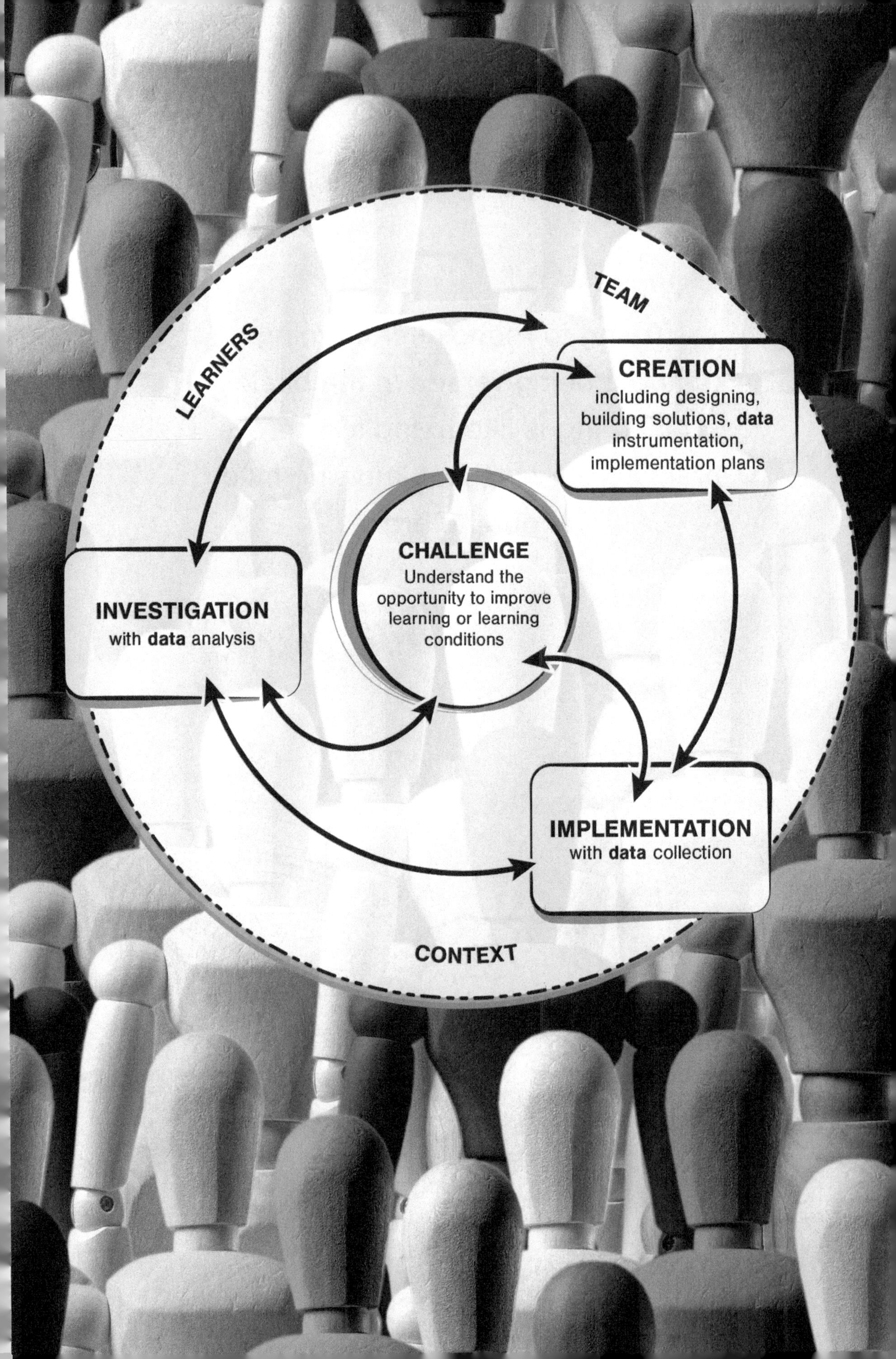
TEAM
LEARNERS
CREATION
including designing, building solutions, data instrumentation, implementation plans
CHALLENGE
Understand the opportunity to improve learning or learning conditions
INVESTIGATION
with data analysis
IMPLEMENTATION
with data collection
CONTEXT

CHAPTER 3

Learning Engineering is Human-Centered

by Khanh-Phuong Thai, Scotty D. Craig, Jim Goodell, Jodi Lis, Jordan Richard Schoenherr, and Janet Kolodner

Learning engineering is a process and practice that applies the learning sciences using **human-centered engineering design methodologies** and data-informed decision-making to support learners and their development.

What's "human-centered" within learning engineering?

Human-centered engineering design means designing from the perspective of humans who will be interacting with implemented designs.[1] Learning engineers design from the perspective of the learners who will engage with designed products:

- What will keep learners engaged and motivated over time?
- What support do they need to learn well?
- How can those supports be provided in ways that simultaneously support learners' mental model building along with maintaining their interest, motivation, and engagement and also foster positive attitudes, emotions, and identity development?

These are only some of the questions that must be answered to produce effective and engaging designs that result in engaged and productive learning.

Establishing deep connections with targeted learners can be difficult. Chapter 2 lays out some of the complexities of how people develop understanding of concepts and flexible capabilities, and it describes many of the different cognitive, social, emotional, cultural, and other factors that affect learning. We know that learning is not simply "tea steeping." That is, we can't assume that learners will simply acquire knowledge over time as they listen to lectures, work on problem sets, and engage in other learning activities. When learning engineers design for learners and their learning, they must consider the knowledge, values, beliefs, life experiences, and strategies learners bring with them into the learning environment and the difficulties inherent in making the inferences necessary for deep understanding and competency development. We need to use that understanding to design in ways that invite learners in, keep them wanting to participate, and support their learning.

The learning engineering process (as outlined in Chapter 1) starts with understanding the challenge or problem to be solved and the context in which learning will take place. Investigation is needed before beginning to design in order to come to know learners' interests, capabilities, developmental stages, probable prior knowledge, everyday experiences, beliefs, support needs, sometimes their living conditions, and perhaps other things about them. Investigation also needs to include knowing those same things about the facilitators or teachers who will aid the learning process as well as the opportunities and constraints presented by the learning context itself (for example, the kinds of physical venues learning will take place in and the capabilities and beliefs of people who are available to learners in those contexts). Similarly, the investigation should also examine the capabilities and constraints imposed by the variety of solution stakeholders (for example, the organizations offering the learning experiences, the people and organizations available to participate in design, budget, and due dates). This knowledge, learned through the initial investigation, defines the challenge, and it's used continuously during design, including when:

- Developing potential designs and pieces of designs
- Critiquing potential designs and refining them
- Deciding between possible designs and design choices
- Choosing participants for testing designs
- Designing assessments, evaluation approaches, and instruments

This is done best in conjunction with stakeholders, including learners, teachers or other facilitators, those who set policy, and representatives of community organizations that may be involved in the designed solution.

The learning engineering process includes design as a part of the creation phase, which itself includes ideation as well as refining, critiquing, culling, and choosing among ideas. This, too, is a human-centered process and requires working closely with a variety of stakeholders, many of the same ones who collaborate in understanding the challenge. Stakeholders who have experienced the challenges being addressed have valuable insights.

Coming to understand the challenge is an iterative process. Designers do their best to learn early in the process, but as ideas are developed, design teams must learn more before making setting requirements. If relevant stakeholders are engaged with the design team, they often can provide answers to questions that were not addressed earlier in the process.

Testing also must be driven in a human-centered way. The learning engineering team must identify subgroups of the targeted population who should be included in testing, indicators of progress toward targeted goals, and how to measure progress. Here, too, stakeholder experience and understanding can help professional learning engineers identify indicators and procedures for measurement.

To accomplish all of this, the learning engineering process borrows from many methodologies, including human-centered design,[2] design thinking,[3] universal design for learning,[4] learning experience design,[5] design-based research,[6] and engineering design.[7] At its core, the best designs for learning are informed by predictions about how learners will interact and function within a designed learning environment. They're iteratively tested for efficacy, and data are collected about learners and elements of their learning environment. (More specifics about bringing a learner-centered approach to testing through data instrumentation and analysis can be found in Chapters 5 and 6.) What's learned from those data is used to refine designs and design elements.

In the rest of this chapter, we'll explore various human-centered approaches that inform learning engineering. Then we'll present narratives of three learning engineering design efforts and how each group addressed challenges inherent in designing effective learning experiences for their targeted learners.

[1]

A Human-Centered Approach to Learning Engineering

Human-centered design requires at least the following six activities:[8]

1. Observation, consulting the appropriate research literature, and interviews to understand the target end users and their environment.
2. Ideation, coming up with options for addressing the challenge, focuses on designing toward what's learned through those investigations.

3. Rapid prototyping is done to make design ideas concrete so they can be presented to end users and other stakeholders for comment and testing.
4. User testing around the prototype is done with the purpose of collecting preference and usability data from end users.
5. Redesign of ideas and prototypes improves on the prototype based on those data.
6. The process is repeated using iteratively more sophisticated prototypes, increasingly real environments, and an increasingly diverse set of end users and other stakeholders until a satisfactory solution is achieved.

Through this process, the solution is implemented robustly for use in the real world. Human-centered design is informed by and informs approaches to design that come from particular disciplines, and some of the particulars of each of those are also important to good design for learners and learning. These related approaches include user-centered design, user-experience design, and human-systems integration.

USER-CENTERED DESIGN

User-centered design is an approach to designing software to make interactions between the software and those using it fluid and productive.

User-centered design has its foundations in the design of human-computer interfaces. Its focus is on the interactions end users will have with software systems. Nielsen and Molich asserted that there are "five golden rules" when approaching user interface (UI) design:[9]

1. Knowing the end users of the system is critical.
2. Users should be involved in the design process.
3. The user interface must be taken into consideration.
4. Usability is defined, criteria for measuring usability are identified, and measurement data are collected and evaluated to assess those criteria.
5. The design process should iteratively address and fix usability issues.

The design process is an iterative process of research, design, and user testing, with all three focusing on users' wants and needs. All three components of the process might be repeated in each iteration; design and user testing are always repeated.

USER EXPERIENCE DESIGN

User experience design focuses on designing experiences that people want to continue to engage in and return to repeatedly.

User experience (UX) design is rooted in user-centered design but focuses on the experiences people will have while engaging with the implemented design.[10] UX design focuses on end-user satisfaction and those things that affect how fluidly users can engage with the designed system. Good UX design:

- Is iterative
- Includes research, design, and testing
- Involves end users in the design process
- Requires defining what satisfaction and fluidity mean
- Includes criteria and measuring of the extent to which users are satisfied

Game designers use UX design and employ many tricks of the trade for fostering excited engagement.[11] For the gaming industry, end user satisfaction means that users will continue to return to the game and engage with it and will recommend it to others. Fluidity has to do with the ease with which users can carry out the necessary interactions and move on to the next ones. Satisfaction might be measured by collecting data about time devoted to play, frequency of play, and, perhaps, participation in web discussions about the game, and the nature of those discussions. Fluidity might be measured by collecting keystrokes and their timing and looking in web discussions for content associated with fluidity.

To design for learner engagement, learning engineers might take advantage of some of the tricks that game designers use. They might measure satisfaction of learners engaged in a learning experience by collecting data from discussions learners are having with each other, the frequency of their participation in learning activities, their frequency of engagement, and their engagement over time. Particular data to be collected, of course, will depend on the nature of the learning experience and the venue in which learners participate. We discuss more about learning-experience design below. See Chapter 5 to learn about a data collection framework for games applied to learning, and look at Chapter 15 for a brief discussion on some tricks game designers use to keep players engaged that can be applied to learning experiences.

HUMAN-SYSTEMS INTEGRATION

Human-systems integration focuses on people and systems performing together to achieve a set of goals.

Human-systems integration is an approach applied to system development that seeks to optimize total system performance. It's a philosophy and series of processes designed to bring human-centered principles into traditional systems engineering.[12] Human-systems integration is typically applied to large systems that include hardware, software, organizational processes, human personnel, and potentially other components (like facilities) that all operate together. It emphasizes developing systems that effectively and affordably take advantage of the capabilities and limitations of humans.[13] Human-systems integration also focuses on a system's life cycle, from its initial conception, through its development and operation, and even its eventual sunsetting. Core tenets of human-systems integration include the following: [14]

- Focus on human performance throughout the design process
- Optimize the system as a whole, not just as individual components
- Maximize benefits while balancing risks and costs
- Use multidisciplinary design, including both designers and stakeholders

Learning engineers designing highly immersive learning experiences may need to take into account this full set of tenets. See, for example, the Connected Worlds installation at the New York Hall of Science.[15] The learning experience happens in the context of a highly complex full-room embodied interactive simulation. People engaging with the simulation are learning from it; at the same time, every engagement they have with it needs to seem instantaneously responsive. The design of the system included specialized hardware and software designers, learning scientists, learning experience designers, science education experts, and science educators. In addition to the traditional learning components, the team needed to make a wide range of human-system design decisions, including environmental safety, technology maintainability, and development of training for the installation staff on how to use and maintain the system.

[2]

Designing for Variation Across Learners

As Chapter 2 points out, individual learners within a population or cohort differ in a huge variety of ways that are important to consider when supporting their learning. They've lived different experiences resulting in different zones of proximal development. They bring different capabilities and foundational mental models to their learning. They've been exposed to different ways of doing things. They have different interests, different dispositions, and so forth.

The best educational approaches will work for the vast majority of learners in a targeted population. Put simply, a good middle-school math curriculum will catch the interest and support the learning of the vast majority of middle schoolers. A good piece of EdTech designed to teach storytelling will support the vast majority of those for whom it's aimed (whether middle schoolers or second-language learners).

The same learning activities won't work for learners of entirely different developmental levels, interests, or capabilities. Appropriate scope is critical to making a human-centered approach work, as is determining how much of the variation across a population can be accommodated in a design. But even within more targeted populations, there will always be a wide variety of differences to address. This means learning engineers need to investigate (before designing), identifying factors and their variations that will affect learning among the identified population. You certainly have to identify the most common variations, and you'll have to design toward some less common ones as well. Some readers may wonder how to possibly address the huge variations in capabilities and the support needs across a population. This is among the biggest challenges that learning engineering teams face.

Don Norman, a leader in the field of designing human-computer interfaces, also pointed out a subtle challenge in human-centered design regarding population variety.[16] He argued that no single design can address the needs of all users, and that if design teams aren't careful, then human-centered approaches can bias solutions toward the group participating in its creation. Norman further warned that if a design isn't tested with a varied enough set of end users, then this bias will get stronger across iterations. In the years since Norman pointed out this tension, a variety of approaches have been developed that focus on addressing the needs of a large portion of the selected population. These include design thinking, participatory design, and design justice.

DESIGN THINKING

Design thinking emphasizes the need for empathy with the population, such as recognizing their knowledge, capabilities, needs, and wants.

Brown and Wyatt define the **design thinking** process as a combination of inspiration, ideation, and implementation.[17] The inspiration phase starts with framing and scoping the problem and then gathering and synthesizing data. The ideation phase takes those data and uses them to generate ideas for possible solutions. Then, an implementation phase converges on a solution, builds a prototype, tests, and refines the prototype with the focus on delivering the product. The three components of the process are interwoven with one another rather than occurring as individual steps—the whole process and each component are iterative. While the basic human-centered design process (above) was articulated to design physical objects to be used by people, design thinking extends design practice into designing processes, systems of all kinds, and services. Design thinking practitioners focus on designing their products based on what potential users want and need.[18]

Design thinking puts great focus on understanding why people do the things they do and how they interact with each other. A significant component of the inspiration phase includes getting to know or empathizing with the population. Design thinking researchers and practitioners have developed sophisticated methods and practices for building empathy with the population, for example, learning about end users and their interactions in environments. These tools include such techniques as personas, customer journey maps, service blueprints, business model innovation, and rapid prototyping. Some of these are discussed later in this chapter, and while it's beyond our scope to cover all of them in detail, an overview can be found in Chapter 12, Human-Centered Design Tools. More recommendations are also available in the paper "Design Thinking Methods and Tools for Innovation" from the Design, User Experience, and Usability Conference.[19]

PARTICIPATORY DESIGN

Participatory design tells us to include end users, those who know end users well, and other experts on our design teams.

Participatory design,[20] also called co-design,[21] focuses on the design team and on methods for actively engaging the broad range of stakeholders in the design process. Each of the human-centered approaches in this chapter emphasizes the need to include members of the targeted user community or learning population in the design process. Participatory design adds that it isn't enough to simply involve those people in the design process; rather, it's necessary to identify all stakeholders and actively engage representatives from each stakeholder group in the design process.[22] Two common challenges for professional designers are identifying ways of actively engaging stakeholders who aren't educated designers and treating these design team members as integral teammates who bring important expertise.[23]

Most of the approaches discussed earlier assume there's a client who is contracting with a design team to address a challenge. Participatory design begins earlier: professional designers and all stakeholders work together to articulate the challenge and decide which of its aspects to take on, for example, they work together to identify requirements. They then continue working together to develop solutions. Participatory design is conceived as having three basic stages that mostly overlap with the process components of other approaches: initial exploration of work, discovery processes, and prototyping.[24]

- **Initial exploration of work:** All stakeholders meet to share ideas and viewpoints on the situation being investigated and together develop a process for coming to understand the situation. This may include methods such as observations, interviews, walk-throughs and organizational visits, and examinations of artifacts.
- **Discovery processes:** After data are collected, the team clarifies goals and values and agrees on desired outcomes. The goal is to make meaning out of the problem solutions rather than to simply describe them.
- **Prototyping and testing:** Professional designers and stakeholders collaborate to shape project artifacts to fit into the envisioned problem solution.

The whole thing is an iterative process that involves multiple rounds of design and feedback.

DESIGN JUSTICE

Design justice reminds us to make sure we identify ethnic, racial, class, gender, disability, and other variations across our population, that we recognize intersections between these, and that we don't disadvantage particular subgroups more than we disadvantage other subgroups.

Design justice is the newest of these approaches. It seeks to challenge structural inequalities and systems of oppression.[25] Design justice urges us to consider how our designs distribute benefits and burdens and to examine issues of power, penalty, and privilege as we design. This enables designers to be more accountable to those who are intersectionally disadvantaged (for example, at the intersecting experiences of gender, sexual orientation, class, race, ethnicity, disability, and immigration status) and to prioritize the needs of those most affected by our designs. Design justice requires the following:

- In addition to being participatory, our design teams must include designers across identities (for example, women, Black communities), as well as the intersections (for example, based on race, gender, ethnicity, migration status, disability) of those who will be affected by our designs.
- We should make sure to iteratively test our designs with members of those different groups.
- We need to keep track of power relationships as we design (they suggest Patricia Hill Collins' *matrix of domination* to do this) and design to challenge systems of oppression.
- We need to be proactive and systematic in inviting people from disadvantaged groups to use and critique our designs.

As well, design justice tenets remind us that anybody can participate meaningfully in design teams if opportunities for participation are designed appropriately. Design justice is discussed in more detail in Chapter 7, and the KNO example later in this chapter shows participation by community members on design teams.

[3]

Designing for Learners and Learning

Learning solutions can immediately use many of the general techniques already discussed. However, in addition to these, more learning-focused principles and processes should be considered. **Learner-centered design** has its roots in user-centered design but is concerned with *learners* who will *learn* from the implementation of a design rather than on *users* who will *use* a design.[26] Learner-centered design also focuses on the design of learning technologies. Several attributes differentiate computer-aided learners from typical computer users, such as:[27]

1. Learners have low expertise and capabilities in the task domain
2. Learners change in interesting ways during their use of the system
3. Learners will be motivated to engage in learning in very diverse ways
4. Learners are quite diverse in the support they need for learning
5. The most usable computer interactions aren't always the best ways to learn the targeted concepts and skills

Learner-centered design emphasizes tries to build solutions for the diversity of learners, in ways that address the gulf between their knowledge and capabilities and those of an expert, all while keeping learners engaged over time. Learner-centered design teams include subject-matter experts, teachers, designers, and developers and they consider usability and learning outcomes. Since the introduction of learner-centered design, a variety of approaches have added detail to the considerations involved in designing for learners and learning. These include universal design for learning, learning experience design, and design-based research.

UNIVERSAL DESIGN FOR LEARNING

Universal design for learning ensures that learners with disabilities and other variations are considered during the design process.

Universal design for learning began as a framework for designing curriculum materials and learning technologies so that those with disabilities can also interact with them effectively and easily.[28] More recently, it's branched out to focus on all kinds of variations across learners, including social justice and equity issues that go beyond disability. Universal design for learning had two foci: (a) providing flexibility in the ways information is presented and the ways learners are asked to engage, and (b) reducing barriers to learning by providing proper supports. Its goal is to maintain high achievement expectations for all learners regardless of disability status.[29] As required in other human-centered design approaches, it also requires involving end users (in this case, those with targeted disabilities) in the design process.

Ziho Kang is an Associate Professor of Industrial and Systems Engineering at the University of Oklahoma. He and colleagues articulated several guidelines for accomplishing these goals:[30]

- Teachers should appropriately and strategically display information using a variety of representations, for example, analogy, multiple examples, and using a variety of media.
- Learners should be able to choose from a variety of modalities for expressing themselves and demonstrating what they know and are capable of.
- All learners should have a way to engage in every assignment. This means that what's assigned must be doable in some way by all students; there may, for example, be different levels of solving a problem so that all can feel accomplished, nobody will be overly frustrated, and those who can take on more challenges have opportunities to do so.

Recently, proponents of universal design for learning have realized that many of the recommendations they make about designing for those with disabilities also hold when designing for equity across those who bring different knowledge, experiences, and capabilities to the classroom.

LEARNING EXPERIENCE DESIGN

> Learning experience design focuses on designing for adult learners and integrates instructional design, psychology, neuroscience, design thinking, and UX into its methods.

Learning experience design reflects another broad set of approaches that combine elements of adult learning and development, instructional design, psychology, neuroscience, design thinking, and UX design.[31] Learning experience design can be thought of as bringing together UX design and interactive media design principles to design educational experiences.[32] Walcutt and Malone claim it's informed, as well, by industrial knowledge design, experience design, experiential learning, behavioral economics, and human-systems integration.[33]

When adopting a learning experience design approach to design, designers should focus on the ultimate goal of the learning experience (such as improving workplace productivity with up-skilling training versus simply fostering new skills in employees) as well as the larger context around it. Designers should use holistic approaches to user-centered design, borrowed from many files, and design holistic experiences that consider form, function, and aesthetics as well as address senses, emotions, cognition, personal connections and engagement, and social identity. These designs should be robust despite the inevitable errors and biases that each person using the solution will have. And learning experience design encourages designers to think of a learning solution as a collective system, rather than unconnected events, learning activities, or design decisions.[34]

DESIGN-BASED RESEARCH

Design-based research derives from research in the learning sciences and is a methodology for iteratively making designs better while at the same time adding to our body of knowledge learning.

At its most basic, **design-based research** begins with a design that's informed by what's known about how people learn and how to support learning. Designers keep track of each of the design decisions they make and develop a logic model showing how the design's different components are meant to affect and contribute to one another. Rich data descriptions are collected as the design is being carried out, and these allow the designers to compare their predictions to what happens in real-world practice.

Learning outcomes are usually part of the real-world data collection, and these are augmented with important snapshots of what learners are doing and saying. Comparing the designers' expectations to what's actually happening during a learning experience or activity gives insight into what's happening as expected (or not as expected) as well as other surprises. Explanations are derived for any unexpected results, and then refinements are suggested. In cases where explanations can't be derived or where not enough is known to suggest refinements, researchers might be able to identify holes in the theories they're using. They might engage in additional research before moving on and may even, through the data they've collected, be able to suggest new approaches to the professional community. While learning engineers don't necessarily engage in academic research, new scholarly findings on how to better support learning might very well be derivable from a learning engineering effort.

Design-based implementation research is similar to design-based research but focuses on adapting designed learning activities for particular contexts.[35] For example, a curriculum that's been designed for the general middle-school population may need adjustments to work well at a school with a different culture, teachers with different backgrounds, or students with different resources than was assumed by designers. The same iterative process used in design-based research is used to adapt a design for use in special contexts.

Three big ideas that underlie design-based research (and design-based implementation research) are important for learning engineering.

- What happens during a learning experience or set of learning experiences affects what will be learned by the end. Therefore, evaluation of complex designs requires a protocol that lends itself to knowing our intentions and how well the design meets them in practice.
- Design-based research tells us what design process data to keep track of while designing so that issues deep within a component of a complex learning experience can be tracked down for refinement.
- Design-based research provides us with a method, called **conjecture mapping**,[36] for keeping track of refinements and reasons for them over time that then allows guidelines for supporting learning to be derived and refined.

We don't go into detail about conjecture mapping in this chapter (instead refer to Chapter 12, Human-Centered Design Tools). Suffice it to say, it's no small undertaking keeping track of all of the design decisions and why they were made, how design components interact, expected observable outputs of different design components, and how those components together contribute to the results. Tracking all of that *and* the results of using designs in a real-world setting *and* how interpretation of those results inform futures iterations is an even bigger undertaking. Conjecture mapping suggests a framework for doing that. (See also Chapter 4, which includes some advice about using models for keeping track of complex and complicated interactions between parts of designs.)

[4]

User-Centered Design Techniques

User- and learner-centered design approaches contribute several methods that are important to learning engineering, including:

- Personas as a way of keeping track of variations in the population
- Prototyping for quickly getting feedback from a community on ideas
- End user interactions for getting empirical feedback on design decisions

Each of these tools is used in the case studies described a little later in the chapter.

PERSONAS

A **persona** is a description of a subgroup of people who will interact with one's designs or some representative of that subgroup. In other words, a persona is a description of a fictitious user or learner. One persona is created for each of the major subgroups of potential users who will interact with the design being created. When designing for learners and learning, this means creating one to represent each of the major variations across members of the targeted learner population.

The set of personas is used during design to decide which of several options will work better and to guide adaption so that those options work more broadly. Personas are used during critique, to predict how broadly a design will work, and they're used during testing to identify those subpopulations with whom a design should be tested.

Personas are developed using data that are collected before design begins, during the investigative empathy stage. Personas may be the most important resources created for guiding design: The best designs take personas into account during ideation, critiquing and idea refinement, and development of test procedures. The first case study below is from the Age of Learning's *Math Readiness.* That example includes a persona that was developed through interactions with fifty children, two and three years old, and it illustrates how the persona was used to guide ideation and idea refinement.

Included in each persona is a name, photo or sketch, and possible behaviors, goals, interests, and frustrations—all as learned through data collection. The design justice approach emphasizes that personas should be created based on the lived experiences of end users (learners in our case) and other stakeholders and not just on imagining what their capabilities, needs, and frustrations are. Personas should also include other demographic and psychographic information that might affect the ways people will interact with or participate in an implemented design.[37] Development of personas is iterative; they're refined over time as the team's understanding evolves.

PROTOTYPING

Design ideas can be critiqued, tested, refined, and extended only if they are concrete enough so that everyone on the design team, stakeholders, clients, and end users, all have the same understanding of a design in progress. This is done through **prototyping**. A prototype brings design ideas to life, providing the certainty needed to judge the extent to which requirements are addressed.[38] Prototypes might represent a design statically or may be created to simulate actions of and interactions with a proposed product. One of the adages of the design thinking approach is to "prototype early and often." Making a design idea concrete through a prototype allows discovery of design issues early in the process, providing the design team opportunities to get support from stakeholders and clients early in the process so that necessary refinements of vision and scope can be made early in the life cycle. Prototypes range from low-fidelity paper prototypes and wireframes to high-fidelity mock-ups that give a visual representation of the system, to interactive high-fidelity prototypes that look and act like the actual system but with the necessary code or functionality needed to answer questions relevant to the current cycle. Prototyping is done for each iterative cycle, with appropriate end users and stakeholders using each successive prototype to critique or test the design in progress. The value of prototyping is illustrated in the three examples below.

END USER INTERACTIONS

End user interactions should happen early and often in the iterative design process.[39] Early on, to check their assumptions and initial ideas, the design team develops empathy by getting to know the user population and the context of use. Later, the design team interacts with end users to do **end-user testing** of designs in progress. Interactions with end users, whether to understand them or to test designs in progress can be accomplished in a variety of ways, including:[40]

- **User interviews**, or one-on-one interviews with members of a population
- **Surveys and questionnaires** that uncover end users' needs and wants

- **Focus groups** where a facilitator asks end users a set of questions
- **Card sorting** where end users organize topics into meaningful categories
- **Contextual inquiry** where a researcher visits end users in their own environments to learn about their common practices, interests, and so on

[5]

The case studies in this section and the one following it show how two organizations have used the suggestions made by the many methodologies listed. The first section (immediately below) includes the educational game *Math Readiness* and highlights empathy, personas, iterative refinement, and end-user testing.

Age of Learning, Inc.'s *Math Readiness*

Age of Learning, Inc. is a provider of digital learning resources for children ages two through thirteen. One of those learning resources is *My Math Academy*, an adaptive learning game system to help children from pre-kindergarten to second grade (ages four to eight) build a strong foundation in mathematics. At the time of this story, the design team for *My Math Academy* had been working on the set of games for over five years.

Working with research partners, the *My Math Academy* team evaluated its effectiveness in helping children of their targeted population learn math. They found that while *My Math Academy* accelerated math learning in older pre-kindergarteners (four-and-a-half upon entering pre-K) and kindergarteners and increased their engagement, interest, and confidence in learning math,[41] it was not as effective with younger preschoolers (not yet four at the beginning of the school year and the youngest four-year-olds). These children, they found, were missing prerequisite skills and knowledge needed to benefit from interactions with *My Math Academy* games.[42] The company took this as a call for the development of *Math Readiness,* a series of games designed to address mathematics readiness. *Math Readiness* would be used to prepare preschoolers to advance to *My Math Academy.* The target population, they decided, would be two- and three-year-olds.

The *My Math Academy* team, who also were tasked with designing *Math Readiness,* is interdisciplinary; its members have expertise in learning sciences, design research, curriculum development, game design, engineering, art and animation, learning analytics, and efficacy research. The development process followed three phases: exploration, iteration, and validation.[43] They worked collaboratively throughout the phases using Agile development methodologies (see Chapter 11), which calls for nimbly iterating to explore a variety of design concepts, test prototypes, and validate designs. This case study first presents the process of learning about two- and three-year-olds and then the design process for one of the ten games that make up *Math Readiness.* Over the course of getting to know two- and three-year-olds and then designing this game, the team conducted nine interview sessions with over fifty two- and three-year-olds, some for learning about two- and three-year-old children before beginning design and some to test ideas in progress.

EXPLORATION PHASE

What does it mean to be two or three years old? The goal of the exploration phase was to understand the challenge to be solved and the learner population. The team's approach was grounded in the design thinking concept of empathy. They aimed to learn the needs, interests, and capabilities of the children they were designing for: Who are these children? How and why do they behave the way they do? What math readiness skills do they need to learn? How do they learn? Where and when do they learn? How might we engage them in learning? How do we know if and what they are learning? This included consulting the research literature on children of this age, interacting with children of this age to learn more specifics, and developing a persona.

Exploration began by gathering information from the research literature on developmental psychology and design for young children. The team sought to develop a basic understanding of what it means to be two and three and how children of these ages learn and develop. Two books were particularly helpful: *Design for Kids, Digital Products for Playing and Learning* by Debra Levin Gelman[44] and *Designing Games for Children, Developmental, Usability, and Design Considerations for Making Games for Kids* by Carla Fisher.[45] Both books offered specific information about what children can do at different ages. That information, in turn, helped in developing design recommendations that became part of the persona. (See Figure 3.1 for the persona and corresponding design guidelines.)

The team interacted with children during several play-test sessions[46] to gather more specific information about children in the target age group: What did those capabilities the team read in the literature really look like? How do these children's cognitive and motor development impact how they interact with and make sense of digital games? What is their level of engagement with different genres of digital games? How might they respond to the team's ideas? These initial play-test sessions set the foundation for the product being developed.

The team was thinking about designing *Math Readiness* as an open play environment, for example, a clubhouse or playground, where children would explore and visit different areas and play the learning games as they encountered them. To assess the potential of this idea, in one play session, they observed and probed as children interacted with a popular commercial digital game called *Toca Life.*[47] *Toca Life* (https://tocaboca.com) is an open-ended game where children make up stories as they explore designed village-type worlds. As team members observed, they looked for answers to a set of specific behavioral questions: How do children navigate around the village and in the different buildings? What help do they need to learn to navigate? How well do they navigate within buildings? How capable are they of dragging on the screen? How else do they interact with items? What do they enjoy doing?

The team play-tested with five children ages two and three and found that all were very engaged with *Toca Life* and most (four out of five) enjoyed and were able to drag objects and characters around. Some engaged in more advanced role-play mechanics of the game such as cooking, using some game items, and interacting with others. Based on this, they felt comfortable designing a game built around an open play environment. The children's interaction with *Toca Life* also suggested to the team that they would have to design such that the learning games would attract the children and keep their attention, as in the open world of *Toca Life,* the children navigated around the village sometimes in seemingly random ways. They learned also that young children tended to drag with two fingers, which led the team to decide they needed to design the set of games with multi-touch drag.

Based on reading and observations, the team was now ready to develop a persona, that is, a model with enough information in it about a child interacting with a math readiness game that they could use it to predict the way two- and three-year-olds would interact with different functions in the game they were designing. They named their initial persona Lily. Her name and the photo in the persona made her real to the team. The persona includes the amount of exposure to technology Lily has had, her "catchphrase," and details about her family. Knowing that Lily (the typical two- or three-year-old they are designing for) has parents or grandparents available to her suggests the need to consider that Lily might play alone when her parents give her the iPad to keep her occupied and that she might play along with grandma (or other relatives) at other times.

Persona Development: Lily

General

- Lily is two years old
- Speaks English at home
- Doesn't go to school yet

Family

- Parents are married; both work
- Grandparents actively involved in upbringing
- Spends time with parents and at daycare
- No siblings

Catchphrase

- "Mine!"

Tech Exposure

- Mom has an iPhone 11
- Dad has an iPhone 11
- Family has an iPad Air used for fun and to occupy Lily
- Lily's parents are less likely to purchase games that she might get bored of quickly, so she mainly spends time watching videos

Design Guidelines

(1) Lily understands and enjoys making choices but be mindful when asking Lily to choose between two items.

If you ask Lily an either-or question such as, *Lily, would you like cake OR broccoli?* she will likely say (85% of the time!) that she likes the second item (or the item most recently offered) due to recency bias. However, if you ask Lily if she would like cake or broccoli and have her point to which one she wants, she will choose the first or second item roughly the same amount of times.[48]

(2) When using visual communication with Lily, be as literal as possible.

Lily doesn't understand the abstract yet. She understands icons or symbols that are highly representative of the task we are trying to communicate.[49]

Lily cannot read, so pictures and icons are even more important. If we need more than a word or two to describe how something is supposed to work, the interaction is too complicated for her.[50]

(3) Provide moments for surprise and delight throughout the activity.

Lily loves cause and effect. Lily gets a kick out of tapping something and watching or hearing it respond.

She also really likes it when something fun and unexpected happens.[51]

(4) Because Lily's fine motor skills are not yet fully developed, object drop zones and tap zones for Lily should be large.

Lily can drag but is liable to miss her target or experience other difficulties. She is better at tapping.

She tends to use multiple fingers or her whole hand to move objects on the screen or to scroll. When possible, make use of full hand gestures instead of relying on the thumb and index finger alone.[52] Her dragging will improve with practice.

Lily still struggles with small, fine gestures since her fine motor skills are not yet fully developed. She needs big on-screen elements to manipulate. Smaller ones are still difficult for her to interact with.[53]

Lily thinks of "pinching" as picking up a small object or something you do to a friend when you're mad at them, not as a way to shrink things on a screen.[54]

(5) Interactive elements should be as prominent as possible, and non-interactive backgrounds should not be more visually stimulating than interactive elements.

Lily cannot yet distinguish main elements of an interface from the details.[55] If something catches her eye, she will focus on it until she becomes frustrated that it doesn't do anything.

Lily can only see items on screen in two dimensions, not three. Meaning, everything on a screen looks like it's in a single, flat plane to her. If we want to use foreground elements, they should be much clearer and more detailed than anything in the background.[56]

Lily will get overwhelmed when there are too many items competing for her attention. We should pick the smallest possible set of easily identifiable elements (like colors) and use them consistently throughout her experiences.[57]

(6) Allow Lily to get to the interactions as soon as possible.

Lily is impulsive, acting quickly rather than thinking things through. (She's still working on executive function.)[58]

It is critical for Lily to experiment to learn.[59] Experimentation takes many forms: she wants to try stacking blocks in different ways, test boundaries like seeing how far she can be from her parents before being called back, or making funny sounds over and over.

(7) Lily enjoys and learns through repetition.

Lily is willing to repeat practice tasks she finds enjoyable while working toward mastery.[60]

(8) Draw extra attention to any numbers said via voiceover instructions.

We want Lily to think about numbers and hear them as often as possible in everyday language to accelerate her numeracy development.[61]

FIGURE 3.1. Initial persona of a two-year-old, which evolved with more detailed and accurate information as we tested our design ideas. Also included is a summary of how the Lily persona might respond to cues and therefore how to design for her.

Lily's parents might decide what she will play with, while her grandma may give her more choices. These entries in the persona captured variations in the contexts in which children might interact with the game and suggested the need to design parent (or caretaker) materials. Figure 3.1 shows the remainder of the persona too, such as the different ways Lily might respond to cues and therefore how to design for her. It considers that children like Lily are new to the digital world, just learning how to interact with touch screens, and developing fine motor skills, attention span, and listening skills. Another developmental feature of two- and three-year-olds is that they can respond to the same thing in myriad ways; except for that key phrase—*Mine!*—there's a lot of variation in a single child. Thus, creating a single persona with many possibilities was both an accurate way to model an individual child and a way to capture variations across different two- and three-year-olds.[62]

The information in the persona would be used throughout the rest of the development process to answer questions about what Lily would do or how she would react when interacting with suggested game mechanics. It includes a range of behaviors and design suggestions and warnings, covering a large swath of the two- and three-year-old population. When the persona could not provide answers to questions the team had while designing, they knew they needed to find answers through additional observation or testing. As they critiqued and tested their design ideas in later iterations, the initial persona evolved to become more detailed and accurate.

ITERATIVE DESIGN PHASE

The team had generated game ideas during the exploratory phase, and now they began focusing on those ideas: critiquing them, refining them, combining them, and generating more. Because Lily enjoys exploring an open play environment, they decided to organize the learning activities in *Math Readiness* within an environment that Lily can explore. Because Lily enjoys activities where she can make something happen, they decided to design a series of highly interactive games, re-playable music videos, and interactive stories. Because their goal is to prepare Lily to learn pre-K math concepts and skills, these activities would introduce her to counting, tracing numerals, and recognizing and creating patterns. And because it's not possible to predict when Lily will be ready for pre-K math, they decided to include activities that they could use to judge her understanding and allow the game to recommend her readiness to graduate to *My Math Academy.* The rest of this case study focuses on a single game in *Math Readiness* called *Pattern Pathway.* It's designed to help children learn to complete and recognize simple patterns. Because Lily is still developing her motor skills, the team needed to find out more detail about the game mechanics Lily could be expected to manage. They built a prototype and play-tested it with additional two- and three-year-olds. In addition to assessing their motor skills, the team wanted to know more about their enjoyment of dragging game components across the screen; they were imagining a game where children would drag game items to make patterns.

FIRST TESTS OF THE *PATTERN PATHWAY* GAME

Play-testing was to be carried out in three rounds. In the first two, children would be asked to complete AB patterns, which included only two different items that alternated with each other, like ABABAB. In the third round, children would complete an ABC pattern (like ABCABCABC . . .). For the third round, the *hit box,* which is the part of an object that can be used for dragging, was smaller than in the first two rounds. The designers wanted to know how big hit boxes would need to be for successful dragging and dropping. They also included three additional questions:

- How well are these children understanding the game-play mechanics?
- What does it take to get them to understand those mechanics?
- How much do they enjoy the stories that go with each game?

The moderator told each child that they're going to play a game about Shapey who must go over a bridge and that they'll help Shapey. (See Figure 3.2.) Then

FIGURE 3.2. Initial prototype of the *Pattern Pathway* game

FIGURE 3.3. Paper prototype of the *Pattern Pathway* game used in the third test

children listened to Shapey read the pattern aloud ("red, blue, red . . . ") and were asked to choose the next block to help Shapey get across to the other side. They play-tested with six two- to three-year-olds and learned that five out of six were able to drag a block (correctly or incorrectly) to the bridge, indicating that dragging is an interaction that would work for this age group and this concept. They also found that asking the children to help Shapey cross the bridge was simple enough for children to understand and was enjoyable for most. There was one child who had some difficulty dragging the smaller blocks in round three (ABC pattern), which led to the decision to keep the hit box as large as it was for rounds one and two in all of the games.

SECOND TEST OF THE *PATTERN PATHWAY* GAME

At this point, the team decided to use a playground as the open play environment. Children would go to different areas in the playground to play different learning games. In the earlier session with *Pattern Pathway,* they had play-tested with a digital prototype, but at this time in the production process, they didn't have the resources to update the digital build with the new playground theme. Instead, they built a paper prototype of this new game. (See Figure 3.3.)

In this test session, they wanted to check what kinds of instructions and visuals would provide clear guidance so children would know what to do to play the game. (Remember that Lily might not always have an adult with her while playing.) They play-tested with another six children, one at a time with an adult moderator. Three of the children were two-year-olds and three were three-year-olds. They hypothesized that two-year-olds would need more guidance to learn this activity than three-year-olds, and interactions between the adult moderator and each child would allow them to figure out what kinds of audio instructions and online cues would be needed. The moderator asked the two- and three-year-olds to drag step stools to the empty slots; the question was which game instructions resulted in the children recognizing what they should do.

They found that the playground was a fun setting for the children. They were engaged and enjoyed creating their own narratives using the game pieces. However, even though the playground was in the background and not in the foreground, the children were more interested in making Shapey interact with objects on the playground, for example, taking him down the slide or having him play in the sandbox, than completing the pattern as they were asked to do. None of the two-year-olds followed the intentions of the game to complete the pattern. Two of the three-year-olds attended to the pattern, but only one of the three-year-olds replicated it. The team didn't know whether the activity they created was a poor one for these children, if the activity might have had better results if it had been built digitally, if the background called too much attention to itself, or if the time lag (between getting the physical pieces of the game ready and the children actually interacting with the game) was the problem. Using a digital artifact, the children would have been able to interact with the game immediately after turning it on. In a digital game, also, the creators can design what parts are interactable and/or use animation to draw children's attention to the game itself.

THIRD TEST OF THE *PATTERN PATHWAY* GAME

The team developed a digital version of the same game (Figure 3.4) and tested it with another six children. Would the digital version of the game better grab their attention? To invite the attention of the children to the game, the screen was designed with a brighter foreground than background. The playground area in the background was smaller and had less playground equipment in it. And only objects designed for the game itself were interactive. When the children dragged the stepping stools into place, Shapey hopped to the next one. In addition, there was a "helping hand" on the screen that modeled how to drag a stepping stool.

FIGURE 3.4. Digital version of the same game used in the third test

As expected, children's interactions with the game were much more focused on the game itself: dragging the stepping stools to complete the pattern. All of the children attended to the animated objects, and most weren't distracted by the non-interactive elements in the background. The helping hand, however, was not something the children understood. The moderator needed to prompt most of the children to show them that the hand could show how to drag the blocks. A couple of children tried tapping the helping hand. Several children also exhibited "happy tapping," where they rapidly tapped the stool with Shapey on it or the one they needed to drag. One child clicked the slide in the background, and one child tapped the screen with their entire hand. Most children exhibited joy while playing the game, and none tried to exit the game before completion.

The team made modifications to the game, including (a) changing the instructions to make the objective clearer, (b) making game-play mechanics more forgiving and allowing children to drag the stools short distances several times to get them to where they needed to go, and (c) adjusting the art assets, visual drop zone, and animations to help communicate to children where to place the blocks and to help them understand the narrative. A screenshot of the next version of the game is shown in Figure 3.5.

FIGURE 3.5. Final version of the *Pattern Pathway* game

FINAL TESTING

The next round of play-testing was done with another seven children. The team found that with their modifications to enable more flexibility in core game-play mechanics (such as tapping, dragging, swiping), children could easily place blocks in the path. All children successfully interacted with blocks and dragged them to the correct drop zones. All completed the pattern on the pathway, though one needed moderator prompting on the last piece to complete the entire pattern. Children could interact with the first block and make patterns with minimal or no moderator support. The interface was simple enough for the children, and the on-screen visuals were arranged so that children could identify what they could interact with and were not distracted by non-interactive elements in the game. While children were not distracted by the background, one did tap around the screen briefly early on, but once core game play started, he focused on completing the pattern. The children all exhibited joy and excitement while playing the game. Some children giggled after dragging the block to the correct location, and most looked to their parents, apparently proud of having done it successfully.

PREPARING FOR FINAL RELEASE

Once validated, the team moved forward to prepare the game for release. Meanwhile, insights gathered from the design process for *Pattern Pathways* were added to the company's compilation of research-based design guidelines for informing future designs for two- and three-year-olds (Chapter 2). *Pattern Pathways* and nine other *Math Readiness* games are now available for two- and three-year-olds as a precursor to *My Math Academy.* The team moved on to collect interaction data of children playing this and other *Math Readiness* games, and they are analyzing them to inform the next set of improvements.

[6]

The two cases presented below show steps in designing digital interventions for the health sector in Africa. Both demonstrate how participatory design that included members of the targeted community of learners contributed to a good final product. Both also show different ways members of the targeted community of learners can be integrated into design teams and the roles they can play. The first case study is of developing a game on HIV education for a stigmatized population who find it difficult to trust those outside their community. An iterative participatory approach that included a series of meetings created trust and a safe space. The designers listened to members of the stigmatized population, their ideas were appreciated, and they felt safe to openly contribute sensitive concepts that designers then used to make the game engaging and relatable. The second case shows how pictograms on design cards enabled health workers who might not have had the confidence, language, vocabulary, or literacy to articulate their needs or thoughts to the app developers. These cards enabled participation across languages, cultures, and social and power structures.

Leti Arts' *KNO,* for Those at Risk for HIV

This case study describes the design process for an interactive role-playing game that was developed in Ghana to encourage behavior change among a population that was engaging in risky sexual behavior. Key populations—people who inject drugs, men who have sex with men (MSM), transgender persons, sex workers, and prisoners—experience major barriers to accessing HIV prevention, treatment, and other health services. The challenge was to develop tailored and integrated strategies to educate these populations about positive living and accessing HIV prevention, care, and treatment services.

The national prevalence of HIV in adults fifteen to forty-nine years old in Ghana is 1.7 percent. Among key populations, the HIV prevalence is significantly higher. For sex workers, it's 7.0 percent, and for MSM, it's more than twice that at 18 percent.[63] Stigma, discrimination, marginalization, and low levels of HIV knowledge are determinants of key populations' vulnerability to HIV.

An international development project in Ghana was implementing several outreach strategies to overcome these barriers to HIV education and care.[64] A role-playing game was an approach they used to address one key population, MSM. As in role-play, they would have opportunities to make choices in scenarios that replicated what they would normally encounter in real life, experience the outcomes of those choices as game players, and to get to success in the game, come to make decisions that would keep them healthier and get them the services they needed.

The project funded Leti Arts to develop the game. The aim of the role-playing game was to promote safe sex, decrease alcohol consumption, and encourage counseling and testing. It was named *KNO*. With such a generic name, they thought, nobody would find any bias in the name, and nobody for whom it wasn't intended would guess what it was about.

The game provides opportunities for players to take on the role of a character, Kaycey, as he engages in different social scenarios. Users make decisions about behaviors during a night out and consider how to fix mistakes Kaycey makes following a night of overindulgent partying. They're told, "Challenges abound in finding help with his sexual health decisions, but he has no choice but to man up!"

THE PARTICIPATORY DESIGN TEAM: IT TAKES A VILLAGE

Leti Arts is a game design company based in Ghana. They have been building games for both entertainment and education since 2009. The design team included Leti Arts staff, a liaison, and experts from the international development organization that contracted with Leti Arts, representatives of community health organizations, peer educators, government officials, and, most important of all, members of the MSM population the game was targeted for. The HIV counselors, peer educators, members of the targeted group, medical professionals, and others from the different organizations acted as subject-matter experts. The Leti Arts team members managed the project and developed the app.

The Leti Arts team included a project manager, a creative director, and programmers, developers, illustrators, and sound experts. The project manager managed the relationship with the international development project that was funding the game and coordinated the tasks to ensure expectations were met and deliverables were being completed on time. The creative director led the design of the app. Content creators worked with subject-matter experts to design the interactive scenarios, storyboards, and learning experiences; prepare the scripts for narration; and lay out the interactions and flow. The programmers, developers, and UI/UX designers built the front end, back end, and game design. Leti Arts has developed gaming software and stays current with the latest gaming applications. Working together, the members of the participatory design team developed role-play scenarios, characters, user interactions, and alternative experiences of users based on their choices.

THE FIRST CONTENT DEVELOPMENT MEETING

The first workshop was held in the capital of Ghana, Accra. The Leti Arts staff helped others understand the process of game design and the idea of a role-playing game. They guided the team as they identified scenarios for the game. Two ideas emerged for game scenarios that would cover all the different topics.

- **A Safe Night Out.** Kaycey goes out for a night on the town; players interact with the game to make a series of decisions about his behavior. Depending on their choices, they have different experiences and get to make other decisions. In this way, they "experience" the effects of decisions around sex and alcohol use. As they play the game over and over, they get to make better decisions and experience their effects.
- **The Morning After . . .** In this scenario, players role-playing Kaycey consider the effects of the choices he made the night before and act out decision-making about his sexual health, deciding on the best course of action to ensure he stays safe.

After coming up with the two scenarios, the design team continued by creating user interactions and game design flow for each scenario. As they worked, the artist was continuously making sketches based on what he was hearing, sharing his illustrations, and asking for feedback.

Between meetings, Leti Arts staff refined the illustrations and worked on narrations and use of other media, laying out potential routes through the game flow, and the technical details underlying those. Sometimes some of the staff made site visits. One site visit was to restaurants, bars, and other venues members of the MSM community frequent. They sought to learn more about those venues and meet additional members of the MSM community. Another site visit was to health facilities where they interviewed health workers to learn about interactions during counseling sessions. At the next participatory design team meetings, new graphics, versions of the storyline, and insights were shared. Each new design and insight were opportunities to make the app more appealing and worthwhile to the target population.

Over time, the subject-matter experts and Leti Arts staff became more comfortable with one another. As trust and understanding were established within the team, new layers of content emerged, and the complexity of what needed to be developed became more evident.

THE THIRD CONTENT DEVELOPMENT MEETING

In the third content-development session, the members of the MSM population became quite engaged and excited after seeing the artist's illustrations and listening to the storyline. They provided more depth and nuance about the people and interactions within their community, and the game became more real to them. Discussions focused on the names of characters, their backgrounds and professions, the clothes the characters should be wearing, and how they should speak. A suggestion was made that one set of characters in the out-on-the-town scenario should be dressed in Lacoste or Polo shirts and have more introverted personalities, and another set should be dressed in flashier, brighter-colored clothes and be more outspoken and more likely to try (and encourage) new (and riskier) things. As the drawings became more real, researchers also learned more about variations across the end users they were designing for.

It became clear, as well, during this session, that the initial rounds of illustrations did not adequately enough represent the characters and scenes. The lead artist made significant changes to the physiques of the characters after that session, giving them more defined, shaped, muscular bodies than what he had initially imagined. (See Figure 3.6.)

Colors were also discussed and needed to be changed. The initial thematic colors for the app were unappealing to the men from the MSM population. (These are shown in Figure 3.7 on the left.) They wanted the scenes in the night-out scenario to be moodier and more suspenseful and use more contrasting colors, more like the decor in the places they frequented and the clothes they wore. Purple was chosen as the thematic main color, and illustrations were adapted and made consistent throughout

FIGURE 3.6. Changes were made to the initial design of the character after feedback from the targeted population

the app. Figure 3.7 (on the right) shows the opening screen of the night-out scenario, and Figure 3.8 shows the decor of the jazz club.

This session also marked a turning point in support from these design-group participants. They now really wanted Kaycey to succeed in changing his behaviors. They provided additional feedback and insight on the tasks, interactions, and decisions in the game, offering more detailed and real-life advice about the types of decisions people would make in the different scenarios, for example, how men engage with the men in a bar, who they go home with, using condoms, and more.

DESIGNING WITH THE USER IN MIND

The Leti Arts team went through their own journey of understanding the MSM community. In the beginning, this work was based on their preconceived perceptions about the community. As they learned more about the community and began

FIGURE 3.7. Two possible menu screens were considered for when end users open the game. Following design considerations, the initial screen (left) was replaced with a more vibrant screen (right).

to place themselves in the characters, they shifted their perspective and how the case studies evolved. The storyline, characters, and language used for the narratives and visualizations were refined through each iteration.

FIGURE 3.8. Complementary colors were used in the jazz club

The game designers knew that the game needed a constant balance between learning and play to hold players' attention. How could the story be told so that it is engaging and entertaining while not boring and still educational? In the end, the scenarios do not overtly suggest to the MSMs that the app is educating them, but rather, it does so subtly, through narrations, tasks, and decision points. Members of the MSM community offered their expertise as real team members, while Leti Arts experts integrated game mechanics and gamification techniques (points and rewards) to motivate game players and showcase their emerging expertise in engaging ways.

TESTING THE GAME AND ROLLING IT OUT

The game was tested in two locations: in Accra, the capital, and Kumasi, a region north of Accra. It was tested with representatives from two populations: peer educators and potential users. Testing with peer educators resulted in the Leti Arts team refining the night-out story to incorporate a stronger focus on alcohol abuse. Dialogue and decisions were added on how much alcohol to drink and if Kaycey should accept or decline offers from those offering to buy him drinks. Testing with potential users led to additional dialogue refinement.

After incorporating additional feedback from the testing, the game was ready for distribution. To maintain the privacy and security of users, and to make sure they felt safe playing the game, it was never made available to the public. Rather, it was distributed by peer educators. Each peer educator was given an access code to share with the users they are in contact with. New users were invited in by existing users through SMS or email; they were added to a white-list database, created profiles, and were given access to the game. The access screen has never depicted anything that indicates the nature of the game. The data collected included logs tracking distribution and use of the game. The participatory design approach led to a game that is relatable and engaging to members of the key population.

Medic Mobile's Community Health App

How do you encourage participation in the design process when people who need to be members of the design team together speak different languages, come from different cultures, have different perspectives, may lack the confidence to speak, or may be illiterate? Medic Mobile, a nonprofit organization that builds and deploys digital tools to improve health equity worldwide, has developed an approach that brings together relevant people across the health sector, including community members, nurses, and managers who speak different languages, are in hard-to-reach settings, and who don't have internet connectivity. Medic Mobile uses a human-centered participatory design approach to guide use cases, impact workflow design, and build technology road maps. They've also developed a set of cards with drawings as an integral tool in their approach. Participatory design teams use the cards to communicate as they develop use cases, work out expected impact, and lay out workflows and technology road maps as shown in Figure 3.9.[65]

Medic Mobile relies on input from people involved in health care delivery at every stage of design and implementation as they identify opportunities and ideate health care solutions. Most of their projects focus on health care provider workflows, which are complex and remarkably diverse from place to place. Medic Mobile staff can sketch workflows, but sketching takes skills that many participants on their participatory design teams don't have. (See Figure 3.10.)

To assist with the process, their custom-made design cards break down the most common elements in health system workflows. This allows even those who have never articulated workflows before to make sketches of their workflows quickly and easily. Each card has a drawing of a different component of the health care system: community members, health care workers, places, technology, and actions

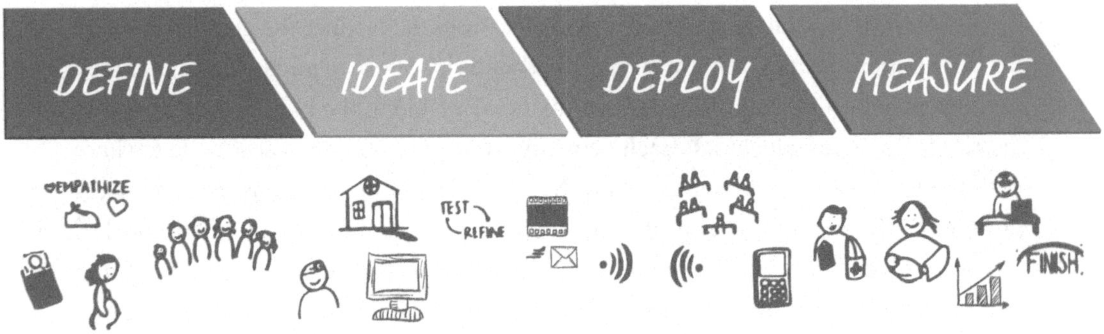

FIGURE 3.9. Medic Mobile's human-centered approach: define, ideate, deploy, measure

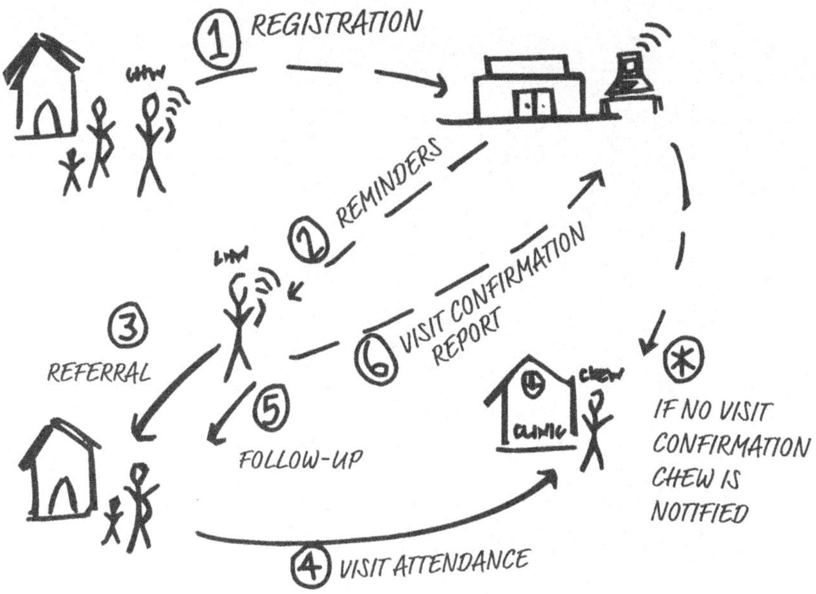

FIGURE 3.10. Sketch of an SMS-enabled antenatal care intervention

In this example mock-up of the workflow or mechanism of action for antenatal care (ANC) intervention, (1) a CHW registers a pregnant woman via SMS; (2) software installed at a hospital automatically creates a schedule of appropriately spaced ANC visits and sends the CHW personalized notifications before each appointment; (3) the CHW revisits the household to refer the woman for ANC; (4) typically the pregnant woman visits the clinic; (5) the CHW follows up a few days later and (6) sends an SMS to confirm that the appointment was attended. If no SMS confirmation is received, the CHW's manager (the CHEW) is automatically notified. Partners often find such workflow sketches more participatory and accessible to input (especially across language, culture, and power barriers) than technical product specifications or detailed written/verbal descriptions alone. New Projects involve many variations of such sketches as designs for technology and service delivery co-evolve.

involved—such as visits to clinics. These cards are a visual way to engage people in role-play to guide the articulation process, help facilitate understanding of the work, and imagine new ways of doing it. For example, the pictures in Figure 3.11 tell stories about the medicine supply chain (part a), how a community health worker gets to the community to visit pregnant women and mothers to check how they are doing (part b), and options for how data are transferred to a ministry of health (part c).

The cards invite everyone from community health workers to scientists and policy makers to be active participants in workshops. Anybody can point to or re-arrange the cards as they speak to explain environments, goals, assets, and pain points. This experience helps to create a feeling that they are all creating something together. This is particularly important when working across language barriers. The design cards take some responsibility from the translators and focus the conversation on the system being laid out on the table. The teams Medic Mobile puts together in

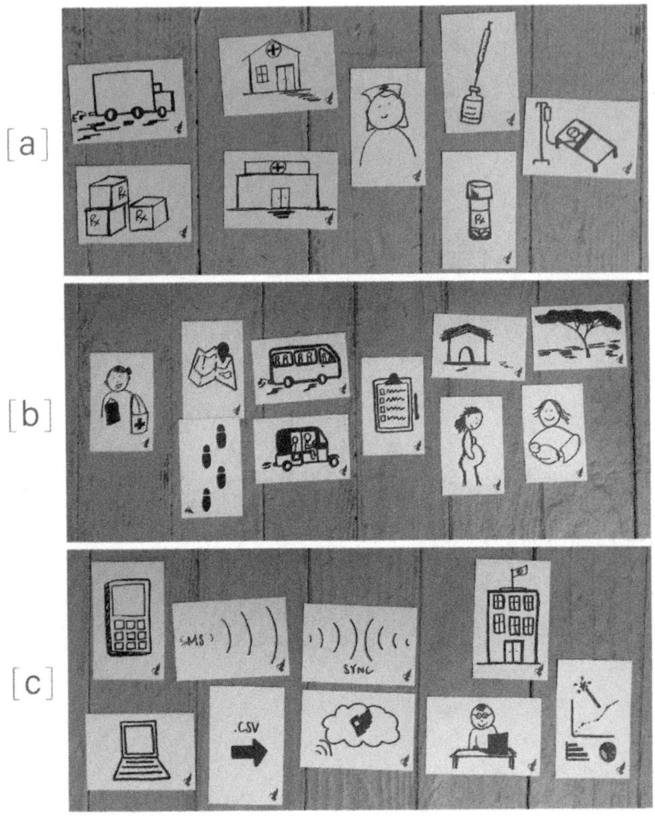

FIGURE 3.11. Medic Mobile's story cards

TOP PANEL: What does the process look like to deliver and track supplies to and at the health facility or hospital for the nurse to administer the medicines?

MIDDLE PANEL: The community health organization is planning a visit to the community to check on pregnant women and new mothers. What transport is available to take her to the location? What information will she collect?

BOTTOM PANEL: What technology is available (feature phone or laptop)? What are the options to transfer data to the ministry of health depending on access to the internet (send to the cloud or collect off-line and sync when internet access is available)? What data do the ministry want? What type of charts and graphs are useful?

designing applications may have people who don't speak the same language or come from different cultures and countries. It could be people in the same country that don't speak the local dialect, Americans or European international development workers involved in projects in rural African communities, or designers from one country in Africa, such as from Kenya, working with target communities in other African countries where the people do not speak Swahili. Design cards give all parties a tool to communicate ideas and explore scenarios in a concrete and tangible form.

Using these cards to make a participatory approach work means that workflows and tools being developed are grounded in the reality of the context and informed by input from health workers on the ground. Designs informed by those who carry out workflows are more likely to be easily integrated into daily work practices. These practices will ultimately lead to creating an improved health delivery system for their communities. ★

- Learning engineering requires human-centered design.
- Human-centered design starts by understanding the challenge from the learners' perspectives and then creates solutions through research-based iterative design.
- Learning engineering's human-centered perspective came from several fields including human-centered design, design thinking, universal design for learning, learning experience design, and design-based research.
- Learners are the central component in the system of learning, and they should be active participants in their own learning.
- Human-centered design is an iterative process that relies on data and data-driven decisions. It doesn't stop with the conception design; it continues as details are added, including implementation details.
- For learning, human-centered design typically involves understanding learner variability (for example developing personas to refer back to during design), making ideas concrete with prototypes, and testing ideas iteratively with representatives of the learner population. The process can include the following:
  - Empathy development via observing or interacting with learners
  - Co-design, or participation of learners in the design process
  - Translation of ideas to rapid prototypes, for example, design cards
  - Testing ideas quickly with learners, for instance, to ensure the learners are meaningfully engaged, for sustainment of motivation and engagement, for feelings of being invited into the process, and for moving learning forward
  - Iterative refinement with simple prototypes, which become more complex and developed with continued user input
  - Iterative refinement during implementation with continued user input
- The mindset of a learning engineering design team should be that the product is the learning experience (or the set of conditions in which learning can be successful) rather than the content or technology.

Learning Engineering is Human-Centered

KEY POINTS

Endnotes

1 Boy, Guy A., and Jennifer McGovern Narkevicius. "Unifying Human Centered Design and Systems Engineering for Human Systems Integration." In *Proceedings of the Fourth International Conference on Complex Systems Design and Management, Paris, December 4–6, 2013,* 151–162. doi:10.1007/978-3-319-02812-5_12

2 IDEO. *The Field Guide to Human-Centered Design: Design Kit.* Palo Alto, CA: IDEO, 2015. www.designkit.org/resources/1

3 Brown, Tim. "Design Thinking." *Harvard Business Review* 86, no. 6 (2008): 1–10. https://hbr.org/2008/06/design-thinking

4 Rose, David H., and Anne Meyer. *A Practical Reader in Universal Design for Learning.* Cambridge, MA: Harvard Education Press, 2006. https://eric.ed.gov/?id=ED515447

5 Walcutt, JJ and Sae Schatz. *Modernizing Learning: Building the Future Learning Ecosystem.* Washginton, DC: Government Publishing Office, 2019. https://adlnet.gov/assets/uploads/Modernizing%20Learning.pdf

6 Anderson, Terry and Julie Shattuck. "Design-Based Research: A Decade of Progress in Education Research?" *Educational Researcher* 41, no. 1 (2012): 16–25. https://doi.org/10.3102/0013189X11428813

7 Dym, Clive L. and Patrick Little. *Engineering Design a Project-based Introduction*, 2nd ed. Hoboken, NJ: Wiley, 2004.

8 IDEO, *The Field Guide to Human-Centered Design.*

9 Nielsen, Jakob and Rolf Molich. "Teaching User Interface Design Based on Usability Engineering." *ACM SIGCHI Bulletin* 21, no. 1 (July 1989): 45–48. https://doi.org/10.1145/67880.67885

10 Dreyfuss, Henry. *Designing for People.* New York: Simon and Schuster, 1955.

Norman, Donald A. *Things That Make Us Smart: Defending Human Attributes in the Age of the Machine.* New York: A William Patrick Book, 1993.

11 Gee, James Paul. "Learning by Design: Good Video Games as Learning Machines." *E-Learning and Digital Media* 2, no. 1 (2005): 5–16. https://doi.org/10.2304/elea.2005.2.1.5

12 Boy and Narkevicius, "Unifying Human Centered Design and Systems Engineering . . . "

13 Boy, Guy André. *Human–Systems Integration: From Virtual to Tangible.* Boca Raton, FL: CRC Press, 2020.

14 Schatz, Sae. "Learning Experience Design." In *Modernizing Learning: Building the Future Learning Ecosystem,* edited by JJ Walcutt and Sae Schatz, 63–106. Washington, DC: Government Publishing Office, 2019. https://adlnet.gov/assets/uploads/Modernizing%20Learning.pdf

15 "Connected Worlds." New York Hall of Science. Accessed December 29, 2001. https://classic.nysci.org/experiencenysci/exhibits/connected-worlds

16 Norman, Donald A. *Emotional Design: Why We Love (or Hate) Everyday Things.* New York: Basic Books, 2005.

17 The phrase "design thinking" grew out of a merger between two design firms, David Kelly Design and ID Two (see in Brown and Wyatt, 2010, page 33). The design processes these firms were using were quite different from standard product design, focusing primarily on designing experiences for consumers in addition to products themselves.

Brown, Tim and Jocelyn Wyatt. "Design Thinking for Social Innovation." *Development Outreach* 12, no. 1 (2010): 29–43. https://doi.org/10.1596/1020-797X_12_1_29

Knemeyer (2015) maintains that user experience and design thinking have shared roots, though the concept of UX precedes design thinking by a decade. Knemeyer even calls them "two sides of the same coin" (page 66).

Knemeyer, Dirk. "Design Thinking and UX: Two Sides of the Same Coin." *Interactions* 22, no. 5 (2015): 66–68. https://doi.org/10.1145/2802679

18 Cao, Jerry, Ben Gremillion, Kamil Ziebak, and Matt Ellis. *UX Design Process Best Practices: Documentation to Move Design Forward.* Mountain View, CA and Gdansk, Poland: UXPin, 2015.

19 Chasanidou, Dimitra, Andrea Alessandro Gasparini, and Eunji Lee. "Design Thinking Methods and Tools for Innovation." In *Proceedings of the Fourth International Conference on Design, User Experience, and Usability: Design Discourse, Los Angeles, August 2–7, 2015,* 12–23. https://doi.org/10.1007/978-3-319-20886-2_2

20 Trischler, Jakob, Simon J. Pervan, Stephen J. Kelly, and Don R. Scott. "The Value of Codesign: The Effect of Customer Involvement in Service Design Teams." *Journal of Service Research* 21, no. 1 (2018): 75–100. https://doi.org/10.1177/1094670517714060

21 Trischler et al., The Value of Codesign.

22 Schuler, Douglas, and Aki Namioka, eds. *Participatory Design: Principles and Practices.* Hillsdale, NJ: Lawrence Erlbaum Associates, 1993.

23 DiSalvo, Betsy, Jason Yip, Elizabeth Bonsignore, and Carl DiSalvo, eds. *Participatory Design for Learning.* New York and London: Routledge, 2017.

24 Spinuzzi, Clay. "The Methodology of Participatory Design." *Technical Communication* 52, no. 2 (2005): 163–174.

25 Costanza-Chock, Sasha. *Design Justice: Community-Led Practices to Build the Worlds We Need.* Cambridge, MA: MIT Press, 2020.

26 Quintana, Chris, Jim Eng, Andrew Carra, Hsin-Kai Wu, and Elliot Soloway. "Symphony: A Case Study in Extending Learner-Centered Design Through Process Space Analysis." In *Proceedings of the SIGCHI conference on Human Factors in Computing Systems, Pittsburgh, PA, May 15–20, 1999,* 473–480. https://doi.org/10.1145/302979.303136

Soloway, Elliot, Mark Guzdial, and Kenneth E. Hay. "Learner-Centered Design: The Challenge for HCI in the 21st century." *Interactions* 1, no. 2 (1994): 36–48.

Soloway, Elliot, Shari L. Jackson, Jonathan Klein, Chris Quintana, James Reed, Jeff Spitulnik, Steven J. Stratford, Scott Studer, Jim Eng, and Nancy Scala. "Learning Theory in Practice: Case Studies of Learner-Centered Design." In *Proceedings of the SIGCHI Conference on Human Factors in Computing Systems, Vancouver, April 1999,* 189–196. https://doi.org/10.1145/238386.238476

27 Soloway, Guzdial, and Hay, "Learner-Centered Design."

28 Rose and Meyer, *A Practical Reader in Universal Design for Learning.*

29 Patzer, Yasmin and Niels Pinkwart. "Inclusive E-Learning: Towards an Integrated System Design." *Studies in Health Technology and Informatics* 242 (2017), 878–885. https://pubmed.ncbi.nlm.nih.gov/28873900

30 Kang, Ziho, Mattlyn R. Dragoo, Lauren Yeagle, Randa L. Shehab, Han Yuan, Lei Ding, and Stephen G. West. "Adaptive Learning Pedagogy of Universal Design for Learning (UDL) for Multimodal Training." *Journal of Aviation/Aerospace Education and Research* 27, no. 1 (2018): 23–48. https://doi.org/10.15394/jaaer.2018.1752

31 Hudson, Jane. "Putting Learning Experience Design into Workplace Learning." *Training and Development* 44, no. 5 (2017): 7.

32 Benedek, András. "MindTheGapp™ Between Standards and Practice of Mobile Learning Experience Design." *International Journal on Advances in Education Research* 2, no. 1 (2015): 14–36.

33 Walcutt, JJ and Naomi Malone. "Lifelong Learning." In *Modernizing Learning: Building the Future Learning Ecosystem,* edited by JJ Walcutt and Sae Schatz, 61–82. Washington, DC: Government Publishing Office, 2019. https://adlnet.gov/assets/uploads/Modernizing%20Learning.pdf

34 Schatz, "Learning Experience Design."

35 Fishman, Barry, William Penuel, Anna-Ruth Allen, Britte Cheng, and Nora Sabelli. "Design-Based Implementation Research: An Emerging Model for Transforming the Relationship of Research and Practice." *Teachers College Record* 115, no. 14 (2013): 136–156. https://eric.ed.gov/?id=EJ1018453

36 Sandoval, William. "Conjecture Mapping: An Approach to Systematic Educational Design Research." *Journal of the Learning Sciences* 23, no. 1 (2014): 18–36. https://doi.org/10.1080/10508406.2013.778204

37 Moule, Jodie. *Killer UX Design: Create User Experiences to Wow Your Visitors.* Victoria, Australia: SitePoint, 2012.

38 Moule, *Killer UX Design.*

39 Roscoe, Rod D., Russell J. Branaghan, Nancy J. Cooke, and Scotty D. Craig. "Human Systems Engineering and Educational Technology." In *End-User Considerations in Educational Technology Design*, edited by Rod D. Roscoe, Scotty D. Craig, and Ian Douglas, 1–34. Hershey, PA: IGI Global, 2018.

40 Cao, Gremillion, Ziebak, and Ellis. *UX Design Process Best Practices.*

41 Thai, Khanh-Phuong, Hee Jin Bang, and Linlin Li. "Accelerating Early Math Learning with Research-Based Personalized Learning Games: A Cluster Randomized Controlled Trial." *Journal of Research on Educational Effectiveness* (2021): 1–24. https://doi.org/10.1080/19345747.2021.1969710

42 Betts, Anastasia, Khanh-Phuong Thai, Daniel Jacobs, and Linlin Li. "Math Readiness: Early Identification of Preschool Children Least Ready to Benefit from Formal Math Instruction in School." In *Proceedings of the International Academic Forum International Conference on Education, Hawaii, January 2020.* https://doi.org/10.22492/issn.2189-1036.2020.40

43 Roughly equivalent to investigation, ideation, and testing in the learning design process diagram presented in Chapter 1.

44 Gelman, Debra Levin. *Design for Kids: Digital Products for Playing and Learning.* New York: Rosenfeld Media, 2014.

45 Fisher, Carla. *Designing Games for Children: Developmental, Usability, and Design Considerations for Making Games for Kids.* Burlington, MA: Focal Point, 2015.

46 A play-test session is a session in which play is used to explore or test a set of ideas.

47 Toca Boca. *Toca Life: World.* Toca Boca. IoS/Android/Kindle Fire. 2020. https://tocaboca.com

48 Sumner, Emily, Erika DeAngelis, Mara Hyatt, Noah Goodman, and Celeste Kidd. "Cake or Broccoli? Recency Biases Children's Verbal Responses." *PLOS ONE* 14, no. 6 (2019): 1–9. https://doi.org/10.1371/journal.pone.0217207

49 Gelman, *Design for Kids.*

50 Gelman, *Design for Kids.*

51 Tech.eu. "Toca Boca - Emil Ovemar (20th May 2014)." Video, 4:52. August 10, 2015. https://youtu.be/ONPG7n5AQXQ

cf. Gelman, *Design for Kids.*

52 Gelman, *Design for Kids.*

53 Gelman, *Design for Kids.*

54 Gelman, *Design for Kids.*

55 Gelman, *Design for Kids.*

56 Gelman, *Design for Kids.*

57 Gelman, *Design for Kids.*

58 Fisher, *Designing Games for Children.*

59 Fisher, *Designing Games for Children.*

60 Fisher, *Designing Games for Children.*

61 Magargee, Suzanne D. and Judith E. Beauford. "Do Explicit Number Names Accelerate Pre-Kindergarteners' Numeracy and Place Value Acquisition?" *Educational Studies in Mathematics* 92, no. 2 (2016): 179–192. https://doi.org/10.1007/s10649-016-9682-y

62 While the literature on personas suggests developing several personas, each focusing on a different subset of the user population, this single persona included what was needed to design toward variations across this population in development, use of technology, and interaction with caregivers.

63 World Health Organization. "Ghana: HIV Country Profile 2019." Accessed December 29, 2021. Interactive Demographic and Socioeconomic Data. https://cfs.hivci.org/country-factsheet.html

64 FHI 360. *Hidden No More: Innovative Approaches for Reaching Key Populations for HIV Care and Treatment in Ghana.* Durham, NC: FHI 360. www.fhi360.org/sites/default/files/media/documents/resource-linkages-ghana-approaches-2016.pdf

65 Holeman, Isaac, and Dianna Kane. "Human-Centered Design for Global Health Equity." *Information Technology for Development* 26, no. 3 (2020): 477–505. https://doi.org/10.1080/02681102.2019.1667289

METHOD

CHAPTER 4

Learning Engineering is Engineering

by Avron Barr, Brandt Dargue, Jim Goodell, and Brandt Redd

Learning engineering is a process and practice that applies the learning sciences using human-centered **engineering** design methodologies and data-informed decision-making to support learners and their development.

Without Margaret Hutchinson Rousseau and her team of engineers and scientists, large-scale production of penicillin wouldn't have been possible during World War II. Many more lives would have been lost, and it might have impacted the outcome of the war—and the world as we know it today.

Margaret was a Massachusetts Institute of Technology (MIT) trained chemical engineer. This chapter features stories from people trained as engineers and who applied its general principles to learning engineering. Bror Saxberg was trained as an electrical engineer (at MIT) and medical doctor (at Harvard University) and later became a learning engineer. Piotr Mitros was trained as an electrical engineer and later became a learning engineer. He also developed the MITx platform, which is now Open edX.

Avron Barr, a co-author of this chapter, is a software engineer, expert in artificial intelligence, and a learning engineer. Co-author, Brandt Redd comes from a family of engineers and has applied his software engineering background and deep knowledge of the learning sciences to the field of learning engineering.

We will explore in this chapter some common principles that apply to any kind of engineering—mechanical engineering, civil engineering, chemical engineering, software engineering, and learning engineering.

[1]

Bror Saxberg knows a lot about the science of learning and the practice of learning engineering. His medical doctorate from Harvard Medical School and doctorate of philosophy in electrical engineering and computer science from MIT give him a unique background and credibility. After proving to be an expert learner, he took on the personal mission to help others learn at scale. Before his doctorates at MIT and Harvard, he was a Rhodes scholar, earning a master's degree in mathematics at Oxford University. But his career isn't limited to academic achievements. He has brought his expertise into real-world situations, promoted learning engineering practices, and impacted hundreds of thousands of students.

Bror's stature and light complexion reflect his Nordic heritage. His father Borje "Bud" Saxberg emigrated to the US from Finland on a scholarship from Oregon State University. Bud Saxberg joined the faculty of University of Washington in 1957 after marrying his wife Margaret, a Norwegian student, and after the birth of Bror.[1] Bror's father and mother encouraged him to gain a deeper understanding of mathematics. As a result, Bror now says "deep exposure to mathematics gave me an enormous toolkit to engage and understand the principles and problem-solving of engineering."[2] Additionally, his father's career as a teacher helped inspire his interest in teaching and learning.

After doing research in cognitive science related to human and machine vision at MIT's Artificial Intelligence Laboratory, Bror learned about putting people, ideas, technology, and finances together into successful organizations while at management consulting firm McKinsey and Company. Later, he applied his knowledge as Chief Academic Officer at K12, Inc., a company that provides online curricula to virtual charter schools, home-school parents, and schools that want to supplement course offerings, and then as Chief Learning Officer at Kaplan University[3] (now Purdue University Global, an accredited online college serving 28,000 students with 175 degree-programs). He was also general manager for the multimedia division of DK Publishing.

More recently, as vice president of learning science at the Chan Zuckerberg Initiative, his career moved from cognitive scientist to learning engineer, to one who advances the practice of learning engineering at scale, prompting him to remark:

> I rely on scientific research about learning and minds, but I use it to solve real problems. I am, essentially, a learning engineer.[4]

Bror is articulate, precise, and energetic when discussing learning engineering. His face lights up when talking about how learning works and about discoveries that lead to better learning.

He acknowledges that while learning engineering builds on the science of learning, it's not limited to blindly applying existing scientific discoveries. As with any engineering task, we should ask, *What's the science behind this? How do we use that science to make robust learning environments?* And beyond that, we should look to new experimentation, the collection and analysis of data to understand weaknesses in the current approach in context and for specific learners, and to test the effectiveness of alternative solutions. Engineering also involves making trade-offs and navigating real-world constraints to achieve practical outcomes. For example, "'how do we measure learning progress over short and long time frames?' Education [and training] cannot be defined by a few numbers; still, we shouldn't shy away from objective information to improve the student experience."[5] We'll examine more of Bror's story in Chapter 6.

[2]

In March 2012 MIT launched the MITx platform, the predecessor to edX, the **massive open online course (MOOC)** platform created by Harvard and MIT that now hosts over 3,000 university-level courses offered by 150 schools, nonprofit organizations, and corporations. These courses are taken by about thirty-three million students worldwide. Some courses are offered at no charge. edX runs on the free edX open source software platform. The global nonprofit, edX is transforming traditional education, removing the barriers of cost, location, and access. The story of the Open edX platform is a good illustration of engineering mindsets and methods applied to a learning solution.

Piotr Mitros began building MITx in mid-November 2011, and the first course on it was launched to MIT students less than three months later, in early February 2012. By the beginning of March, the course was available to the world. The coders had a rapid development cycle, in part because Piotr had been working on the concepts behind MITx (and Open edX) for many years.

In 2007, as a graduate student at MIT, he worked on a project with Obafemi Awolowo University (OAU), based in Nigeria. It had thirty-thousand students. The electrical engineering department had seven-hundred students, and about a dozen instructors, of whom three were full faculty.

Even though the faculty were hard working and highly qualified, the teacher–student ratios severely limited the traditional education model. Piotr applied an engineering mindset to the problem. He came up with models that blended technology, peer learning, and human instruction. He wasn't able to implement these at OAU, but they became the basis of the MITx project and eventually the Open edX platform.

In 2007, Piotr discussed this with Rafael Reif, the current president of MIT who was the school's provost then. "At the time, I was a graduate student, with very little savings, and no credibility." It would take a few more years before a project would be funded. The time wasn't wasted, however. Piotr became an early employee at a medical imaging startup. There he developed the analog electronics for a new medical instrument that can remotely image the surface of the heart, shaving hours off of a particular type of atrial surgery and dramatically increasing its accuracy. It's been used on thousands of patients, saving many lives.

When he built the MITx platform, Piotr had a lot of practical experience teaching and training as an engineer but admits he wasn't an experienced learning scientist or learning engineer. "Fortunately, I had support from people who were such experts." The learning gains achieved on the MITx platform would have been impossible without the contributions of others. Piotr spoke to as many experts as he could and integrated the most promising concepts into a coherent system. Many of these concepts came from his thesis advisor, Jerry Sussman (a student of Seymour Papert's and a renowned computer science educator), David Prichard (a top physics education researcher with a deep understanding of the science of how people learn), David's graduate students (especially Daniel Seaton), and Chris Terman (one of the highest-regarded lecturers at MIT). In addition, as he had helped Sebastian Thrun launch the original AI course that led to his founding of Udacity, Piotr stood on his shoulders and on those Sebastian learned from, including Sal Khan and Peter Norvig.

LEARNING ENGINEERING IS OFTEN A TEAM SPORT IN WHICH THE LEAD DEVELOPERS DEPEND ON OTHER EXPERTS

* SEE CHAPTER 10, TOOLS FOR TEAMING

Critically, this group helped him sort truth from fiction—what we know works from what we don't yet know—which is a key process for any learning engineer and one that he wasn't yet qualified to engage in, as it's a skill that takes years of careful work to develop.

Engineers need focus to solve complex technical problems like, in the case of learning engineering, *How can we optimize student learning, engagement, and growth?* A team approach recognizes the value of others who focus on project management, human resources, implementation, and other factors of success, allowing learning engineers to focus on engineering.

By integrating expert input and prior work, Piotr's engineering goal for the design of Open edX was to build an engaging, pedagogically effective platform as quickly as possible.

Cost is central to engineering. The design process was to take what was known about how people learn and come up with simple ways to implement those techniques in a learning platform where content could be authored at reasonable cost. He estimates that the cost of content and platform development for the original Open edX platform and course were roughly a half-million dollars. Jerry Sussman and Piotr worked more than full time. Chris Terman worked half-time. Anant Agarwal probably ramped up to about quarter-time over the course of the project. In addition, teaching assistants, consultants, and others helped.

Piotr and the team worked to understand the challenge by sorting through concepts by **return on investment**, with a large amount of thought on how to implement effective techniques with low investment into either platform or course development. The set of techniques he converged on for the original platform were:

- Moving from passive to active and then to constructive learning
- Complex multi-concept problems
- Continuous formative assessment
- Remediations for knowledge gaps and misconceptions
- Immediate feedback
- Mastery learning
- Self-paced learning

This design focused on a limited number of proven learning approaches, known to be effective for the kinds of courses originally intended for the platform. Note how this approach contrasts with traditional scientific research that tends to push into new areas, either researching new interventions or going into further depth around one intervention. In contrast, good learning engineering uses a broad array of robust, established techniques based on previous research with well-replicated results. Engineers also may use data differently than research scientists. For some scientific studies, outlier data are filtered out as "noise" so that generalized findings may be discovered. Engineers are more concerned with outlier data, the specific conditions in which a system tends to fail.

The scaling of cost is important to learning engineering as well. For example, consider how these costs scale:

- $1 in per-student cost,
- assuming an average of 1,000 students per course,
- equals $1,000 cost per course.

- $1,000 in per-course delivery cost,
- assuming 1,000 courses on a platform,
- equals $1,000,000 for the total run-time platform cost.

- But $1,000 in platform development or maintenance costs,
- assuming just 1 platform,
- is still only $1,000 per platform.

At scale the per-course delivery costs add up, so finding ways to reduce those incremental costs was a big part of the engineering challenge. For the Open edX platform, with millions of students, thousands of courses, and one platform a lot of attention was paid to making course creation both economical and effective, and only some attention was paid to the platform development costs.

In many cases, Piotr took techniques from intelligent tutoring systems or adaptive systems and modified them to minimize course authoring costs while retaining the same cognitive processes and benefits. For example, Piotr used a combination of techniques that allow students to both navigate and contribute to remediations. His approach leveraged the MOOC context to crowdsource content tagging, relying on learners' intelligence and a good user interface design instead of machine intelligence that might take more time and resources to build.

For the original iterations of the platform, course authoring expertise was not a constraint; as a platform designed for MIT professors, there was an assumption that the people engineering courses would be able to program and use sophisticated technologies. Learning engineering, like other engineering fields, often requires expertise in specialized tools. Mechanical engineers use computer-aided design; software engineers use integrated development environments. In this case, the system was engineered to make course authoring efficient for expert users, rather than make it easy for anyone to author content. It was possible for the original MITx platform to be deployed quickly based on the assumption that these professionals would be able to invest their time into learning how to properly construct courses using existing software engineering tools. It was assumed that course authors could already use professional tools like version control systems, Python, data visualizations, and that they could effectively apply the learning sciences. Or, if they couldn't already, it was assumed that they'd learn to do so.

As pointed out in Chapter 1, understanding the challenge includes understanding the context of a learning engineering team. If this project wasn't contextually situated at MIT, the challenge might have been constrained by the need for more usable course authoring tools. In fact, the edX platform now includes edX Studio, a tool for developing edX courses without requiring software development expertise. Even so, learning engineering is a team sport and not all members of the team need expertise in all of the tools. For example, Anant Agarwal captured videos at home, which he handed off to editors, who in turn handed them off to a student to integrate into the course. Learning engineering often depends on the skills of a multidisciplinary team.

[3]

Engineering is the application of creativity and science to solve problems, and learning engineering is the application of the learning sciences to creatively solve problems for learners and learning. Different engineering domains differ in the problems to be solved and the science to be applied in solving those problems. Mechanical and chemical engineering apply sciences such as physics, material science, and chemistry, whereas learning engineering applies, for example, cognitive, sociocultural, behavioral, and motivational sciences.

Each engineering domain is unique. There are, however, some overarching principles that apply to any kind of engineering. Whether it's software, civil, or learning engineering, the application of engineering includes:[6]

- Addressing specific problems
- End users who are intended to benefit from the solution
- Testability
- Maintainability
- Integrity
- Well-defined external integration
- Ethics
- Management

In general, an engineer should:[7]

- Understand the absolutes, context, and "the possible" of ethical practice
- Be able to communicate with a purpose targeted to a group or population
- Be aware of the constraints of public, private and academic practice

- Be able to apply fundamental science to system applications
- Be able to execute at all levels of design: problem definition, estimation, figure of merit, rules of thumb, and sanity checks
- Be able to execute total system design for sustainability
- Be aware of contextual design variables: performance, constraints, variation, and process capability
- Practice through team projects: problem definition, information acquisition, data analysis, trade-off analysis, and optimization

In other words, an engineer must systematically account for all implications of the design and the final product built to that design. An engineer must think of how the solution will be used and how it will be built—not just what materials are used in the architecture but also the processes used in construction. How will it be supported and maintained? How could it be misused? To help consider and account for both sets of bullets above, the engineering process is systematic and methodical with periodic reviews. Knowledge of human nature, trend analysis, and imagination also help. This is just as important for learning engineering. In the story above, Piotr Mitros' team had to consider how the learning system design supported instructors, teaching assistants, authors, school administrators, information technology administrators, and managers—as well as learners. They had to ensure the design was applicable for all scales of use, and they had to consider constraints such as privacy laws at all levels of use. They had to evaluate risks of data breaches and even cheating. Some of that is done through careful, systematic reviews, and some requires experimentation and studies.

One way that engineers manage the complexity of all the unknowns is by creating and using **models**.[8] Models may be used as a simpler representation of the complex system or to simulate very complex systems in a way that would be difficult or costly in the real world. Civil engineers use models of population growth and other demographics to ensure solutions are "right sized" for the life of their use. Civil engineers, for example, use models of material strength to ensure safety over time, even as the population who uses a bridge or road grows. They use models of weather as well as models of how materials decay and erode to ensure that their solutions last. Some of these models aren't precise; rather, they're estimates that usually have a safe margin of error that must be understood by the engineer. Some, like models of the strength of materials, are as simple as trigonometry tables or even the multiplication tables we used when learning math. For many of these models, the engineer must be able to extrapolate to a finer level represented in the table.

Engineering models, such as computational fluid dynamic models are very precise, high-fidelity models. They're used in the aerospace industry to perform tests and validations on new designs, for example, for wing shapes. These models can retain the complexities of, and even add more complexities that are difficult or impossible to test in the real world. To bring it back to learning engineering, models of learners can be used to test learning systems or concepts. Piotr Mitros' team also used models of learning such as moving from passive to active and then to constructive learning.

Models are used to describe aspects of a system and mathematical relationships for understanding and analyzing the system. Different models of the same system may be developed to understand the system from different perspectives. For example, there could be one model of the edX platform representing learner interactions, another modeling software architecture, another modeling the content used in a course, and another modeling the data used within the system. (See Chapter 6 for some interesting stories about how data are used to build models that help optimize learning, predict learning outcomes, and improve learning engineering products.)

Engineers have a mindset; they think about problems to be solved as a part of a system. **Systems thinking** offers a wide perspective that includes seeing overall structures, patterns, and cycles in systems, rather than seeing only the separate and specific events in a system.[9] In learning engineering this includes considering the context in which learning takes place, for example, how the learning environment impacts a person's ability to learn. It also includes the learner as a part in the system. For example, how does the system adapt learning experiences for learners with widely varying backgrounds and needs? What affordances allow learners to direct that adaptation? How is a learner's ability to learn affected by that adaptation?

Systems of various components add complexity to the overall design. Engineers manage complexity by thinking of systems as a set of interoperable components or **modules**. Modularizing the system allows engineers to divide up the challenge into less complex subsystems. Modules of a system have design **constraints** and **tolerances** appropriate for the role they play within the overall system. **Interfaces** handle the interactions among modules for the system to work as intended. The system functions when (a) it includes modules to do all of the required functions, (b) the modules interoperate with properly functioning interfaces, and (c) each module performs within tolerances (that is, within the permissible limit or limits of variation).

Engineers are also concerned with the environment in which the system will operate. When designing a system, an engineer may specify the typical **operating conditions** under which a component of the system is expected to operate and the tolerance or acceptable range in which the component or system is expected to function. For example, electronics engineers designing early smartphones might have recognized that typical LCD screen components didn't function when the temperature was below freezing or above 90° F / 32° C. If the phone was expected to work in colder temperatures then the engineers needed to design a way to keep the screen from freezing, for example by adding insulation to keep it warmer. If the phone was expected to work in warmer temperatures, like in hot climates, then the engineers needed to incorporate a cooling module as well as a sensor and an interface to control when the cooling module turns on or off.

In **trade-off analysis** an engineering team makes decisions that balance cost, utility, and other factors. An interesting example is energy production using solar cells. The more solar energy (sunlight) goes in, the more usable energy you get out. So solar cells are most efficient when pointed directly at the sun. You can add more solar energy going in through mirrors and lenses, like magnifying glasses, focusing the sun directly on the cells. However, heat destroys the cells; they must be kept cool for longevity. An engineer of the system must balance everything using trade-off analyses. For instance, air conditioning might cool the cells, but how much energy does that use?

Learning engineers also leverage system thinking, trade-off analysis, and modular design. They're also concerned with constraints, tolerances, and operating conditions. If the components of a learning solution are designed for one environment, and that operating environment changes, the system may need to be re-engineered to tolerate a different environment. For example, the traditional classroom model of instruction wasn't designed to operate in a global pandemic. The previous system had components to address student engagement that failed when the operating conditions changed. Even as schools reopened with remote learning and hybrid options, student participation levels plummeted. The system components that previously supported student participation—physical space, cultural norms, and in public K-12 education, truancy laws and bussing—just failed to function during the pandemic. While the system has always failed to effectively engage some students, even in districts that were able to ensure devices and connectivity for all students found that 20 percent or more of students were not showing up. Just like the engineers of the phone with the temperature-sensitive LCD screen, the most innovative colleges, school districts, and independent schools designed new modules to supplement or replace the parts of their systems that failed under the new operating conditions. These learning engineers also developed new sensors and instrumentation to monitor student engagement within the new remote learning environment.

[4]

Great teachers, instructional designers, and learning scientists know how important feedback is to learners as part of the learning process. In Chapter 1, we examined learning engineering as a process that involves data-informed feedback loops to iteratively improve solutions for learning. In this chapter on engineering, we can't talk about feedback loops without getting into **engineering control theory**. Conveniently, this theory can be adapted to education and training reasonably well as soon as you get over some vocabulary hurdles.

Figure 4.1 shows a basic control system. One example might be a cruise control for your car. In that case, the reference is the speed you want to go, for example, 65 miles per hour. The controller translates that reference to an input value, the throttle position. Then the system (including the engine, transmission, drive train, tires, and so on) produces an output, the actual speed of the car.

In control theory, this is an **open-loop control system**, meaning that it has no feedback. To get a predictable output the controller must have a very good mathematical model of the system and the system itself must be very precise. Open-loop systems are used when the acceptable margin of error is large, for example, for a cooling fan.

A car with an open-loop cruise control would slow down as it climbed hills and speed up when it descended. For more precise control, real cruise controls use a feedback loop. A sensor detects the output value (the speed of the car) and returns it to the controller. The controller takes the difference between the feedback and the reference values and adjusts the input (throttle) accordingly. This is called a **closed-loop control system**.

Mathematically, taking the difference is subtraction so we call this negative feedback. In contrast, positive feedback sends systems wildly out of control because it amplifies any error. A familiar example is pointing a microphone at a speaker. The terrific squeal that you hear is a positive feedback loop.

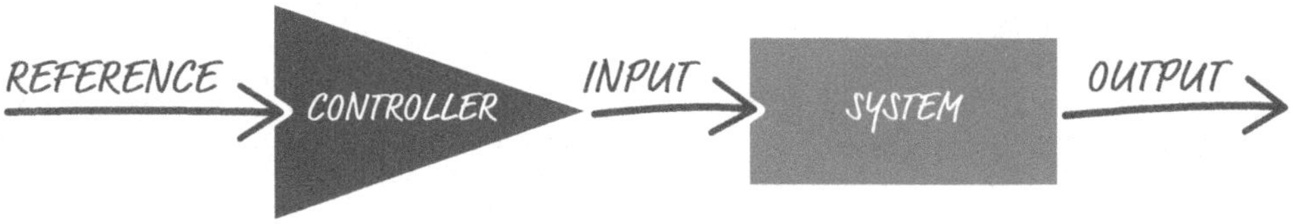

FIGURE 4.1. An open-loop control system

So, when talking about control systems, closed loop is better than open loop, and negative feedback is good while positive feedback is bad. The precise engineering terminology is the opposite of what we might use in casual conversation. Let's now apply this to education.

A Personalized Learning System

If we take the closed-control loop diagram in Figure 4.2 and make a few word substitutions, we get a personalized learning system as shown in Figure 4.3. The learner is a part of a system that can benefit from feedback. Skills and other capabilities are an output that can be measured through assessment (sensor), and the controller in the system informs decisions to vary instruction, including instruction in the form of formative feedback to the learner.

For a moment, let's ignore the feedback loop. In an open-loop learning system, a set of learning objectives (such as those established through academic standards, competency definitions, or skills descriptors) are translated into instruction in the form of textbooks, lectures, and exercises. These activities are delivered to learners resulting in skills. Conventional schooling is much like this. To handle a class of a dozen or more students, all students engage in the same activities. But remember that open-loop systems require a very precise system and a large acceptable margin of error. Students come to us with different personalities, talents, preferences, and backgrounds. The result is a wide margin of error as illustrated by the spectrum of grades assigned at the end of a course.

Good teachers and good curriculum do better than this. They find ways to provide feedback as often as possible and frequently adapt their teaching to the needs of

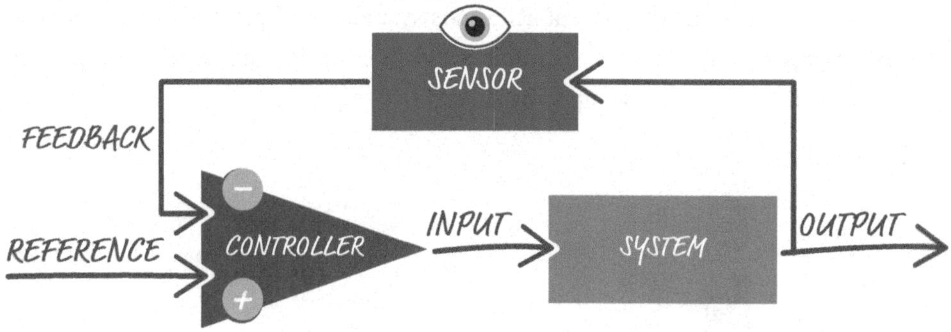

FIGURE 4.2. A closed-loop control system

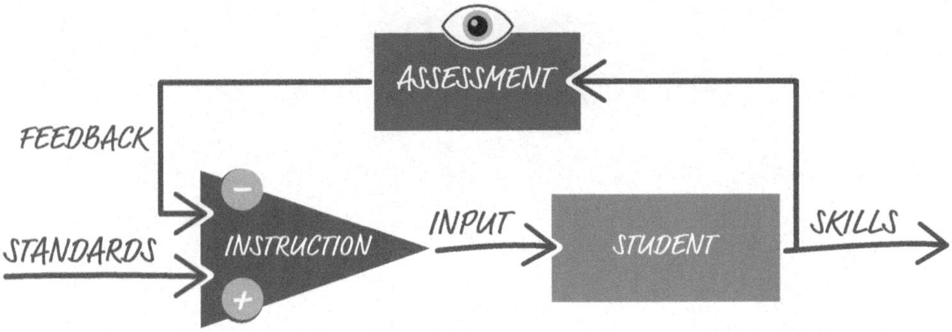

FIGURE 4.3. Control theory for learning, a personalized learning system

the class or individual students. Good students can also use feedback to adapt their learning to match the instructional methods being used. Both kinds of adaptation require feedback from quizzes, assessments, measurements, and observations. To do this well, the feedback should be compared with the standards for what's intended to be learned and instruction adjusted, including instructional feedback, to the individual learner.

Multiple Feedback Loops

Remember that a system is an assembly of multiple subsystems. Those systems work independently but also contribute something to the overall system. Additionally, it's important to think of a system as being very dynamic. Each subsystem may have its own feedback control loops as well as the system itself. Similarly, effective learning has multiple, nested, feedback loops. An inner loop is feedback that a learner receives immediately while doing a learning activity. An outer loop is feedback that a learner gets between learning activities, such as new assignments or suggestions for what to do next. Additional loops can guide the learner on the best paths toward long-term learning goals connected with personal and career goals. Figure 4.4 shows learner feedback loops aligned to the levels defined by the Advanced Distributed Learning (ADL) Initiative's Total Learning Architecture[10] and as considered in the IEEE's Conceptual Model for Adaptive Instructional Systems.

We can visualize the innermost feedback loops in a process model as shown in Figure 4.5. In the inner loop, the learner receives feedback while doing an activity. The outer loop uses data from the activity and other data to inform macro-level feedback—guidance on the selection of the next activity.

Now let's consider three more insights we can gain from control theory: the

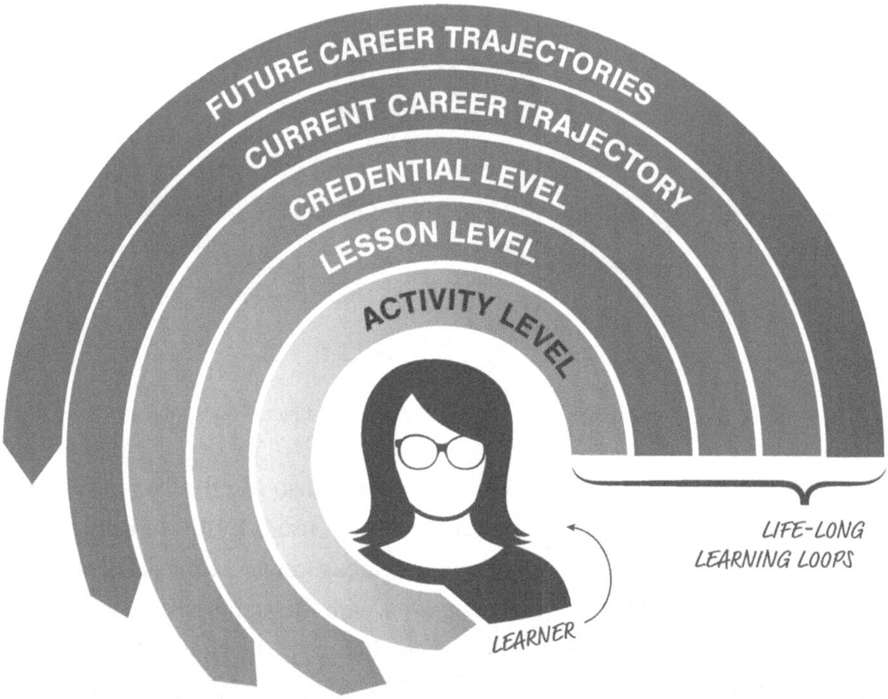

FIGURE 4.4. Learner-centered adaptive instructional systems may provide multiple learner feedback loops

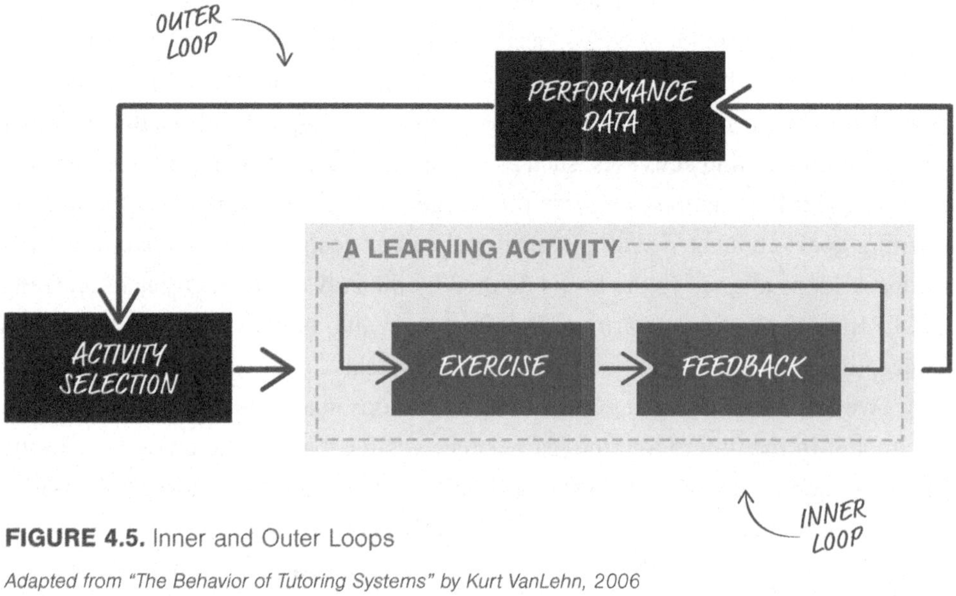

FIGURE 4.5. Inner and Outer Loops

Adapted from "The Behavior of Tutoring Systems" by Kurt VanLehn, 2006

role of a transfer function, speed and frequency of feedback, and sensitivity to what is being measured.

Transfer Functions

A **transfer function** is a mathematical description of the relationship between the input and the output of a system. Let's use the automobile example. The input is the position of the gas pedal (more correctly called the accelerator pedal, as we'll see in a moment). The output is the speed of the car. Pressing the pedal to a certain position doesn't directly make the car go a corresponding speed. Rather, pressing the pedal causes the car to accelerate at a rate proportional to the pedal position. If you keep the pedal pressed to the floor, the car will continue to accelerate to higher speeds until it reaches the limits of its construction. (For calculus fans, this means that the transfer function of a car's drivetrain involves an integral.)

The transfer function is important because it's incorporated into the design of the controller. When an engineer designs a controller, they use the transfer function to anticipate what will be the result of a particular input. Typically, they take the inverse of the function to determine what input is required to achieve the desired output. Getting back to our example of a car cruise control, some versions have an option to maintain a consistent distance behind the car in front, adjusting the speed to match that car. The operator can choose which transfer function is used, consistent speed, or consistent distance. For those drivers that prefer saving fuel over driving at a consistent speed, there could be a transfer function based on fuel consumption.

The educational and training equivalent of a transfer function is a learning theory—a description of how a learning activity will result in new knowledge. Learning theories help us select activities that will effectively help a student learn a particular skill.

A personalized learning system will inevitably express one or more learning theories in the selection of activities. It's important to align the theory to the population of learners (or learner), domain, and context. There are personal differences in the way each person learns. In engineering terms, this means that each learner has their own personal transfer function. And that transfer function may change over time. (See Chapters 2, 3, 9, 12, and 15 on the learning sciences, human-centered engineering design, tools for human-centered design, and learner motivation for useful learning theories for your learning engineering toolbox.) We can think of people in a school as being parts of a system; feedback can go to different parts of the system (for example, instructors, learners, tutors, or tutoring software). The different transfer functions direct the feedback to different parts of the system. An adaptive system might even decide which transfer function to use or where to direct the feedback, such as to different controllers, to get optimal results. In learning, an adaptive system would direct different feedback to online instruction, to an instructor, an advisor or counselor, and to the learner.

Speed of Feedback

For feedback to be most effective, it must be frequent, fast, and rich. Feedback must come often so that course corrections are made frequently. It must be fast, ideally immediate; otherwise it's too late to affect the learning process. And it should be rich. "Incorrect" is not nearly so meaningful as, "You misplaced the negative sign in step 3."

Frequent, fast, and rich feedback depends on frequent, fast, and rich assessments. In conventional schooling, assessment is expensive. It costs a lot of teacher time to compose, administer, and score assessments. This is an excellent opportunity to apply technology. Computer supports can minimize the effort required to compose, administer, and score assessments. And computers can tabulate the results into effective teacher and student dashboards. The result is a more personalized and effective learning experience. Or, as an engineer might say, more predictable output with a smaller margin of error.

The time from the moment an output is measured to a resulting change in the input is called a **propagation delay**. In educational terms, this is the time from when a learner's capability (such as knowledge or skill) is assessed until the moment their activity is affected by the feedback from that assessment. In a traditional math class the student does homework one day, submits it the next day, and receives graded homework back the next day after that. Thus, the propagation delay is two days (or two class periods). Fast feedback means a shorter propagation delay. With more immediate feedback, learners have the chance to refine their understanding and capabilities more quickly. Measurements that require human grading will naturally be slower. Many online learning systems offer near instantaneous feedback.

Frequency of Feedback

Frequency of feedback is a measure of how often the output (such as knowledge or skill, in our case) is measured and feedback generated. In a traditional classroom, mathematics feedback is daily (or once per class period). Some traditionally taught courses may only have two or three graded activities in the entire course. However, this may be a pessimistic way to measure frequency. For example, if students can check their answers in the back of the book, then feedback is both faster and more frequent. A more ideal condition gives feedback after each attempted answer, but this is only better if it's the right kind of feedback. Research suggests that timeliness and quality of feedback both matter.[11] Of course, this guideline must be applied judiciously; it's often worth giving a learner time to make it through to the end of something instead of interrupting.

Richness of Feedback

A third component of educational feedback is richness. In mathematics, this might be the difference between being told that an answer is wrong versus being informed about exactly what mistake was made. In a writing course, it might be the difference between a simple score versus detailed feedback about how the student might improve their essay. For job performance, rich feedback would give an employee insight into how to improve performance and how to recognize an error in the future and distinguish between a job well done and subpar performance.

Students can influence all three feedback factors. For example, college English students who seek help at a writing lab will get faster, more frequent, and richer feedback than students who don't make use of the resource.

Control theory tells us that faster and more frequent feedback compensates for inaccurate measurements and poorer transfer functions. In education language, this means that if we can make feedback faster and more frequent then we can compensate for a less-than-perfect learning theory and suboptimal assessments. Of course, it would be nice to have everything—fast, frequent, and rich feedback as well as good quality assessments and a solid learning theory. But it's useful to know that some of these factors can compensate for others. Additionally, we also know from the learning sciences that too much feedback to the learner can be unproductive for learning. We know, for example that too much new information produces cognitive load, and we know that in learning there's a level of desirable difficulty.

Physical and electronic systems are designed using **filters** and **dampers** to prevent over-correcting. For example, if the feedback to the controller in a car's cruise control system were too precise it would continuously apply the brake and then the gas, the brake and then the gas. In signal processing, a filter is a device or process that removes some unwanted components or features from a signal. A damper may be used to reduce the amplitude of mechanical vibrations in a physical system, such as a soft pedal on a piano or the shock absorbers on a car.

One-on-one tutors have a lot of raw data in various formats and fidelity levels while observing a learner working on a problem. They watch carefully as the student makes mistakes. Great tutors will not immediately correct a learner but give them a chance to discover their own errors and self-correct. The tutor is, in effect, acting as a filter or damper and a controller.

Sensitivity to What's Being Measured

Feedback loops are a very effective tool—so effective that if the wrong thing is being measured or the wrong feedback is offered then the wrong skill will be optimized. A recent manifestation of this are complaints in United States K-12 education about "teaching to the test." The concern is that because summative tests are used to evaluate schools then the only skills that will be taught are those that are on the test. This concern is valid. Multiple studies have shown that a focus on conceptual understanding results in better test performance than test-focused instruction.[12]

The problem with determining the right feedback is also manifest in the combination of skills that a particular problem might require. For example, a mathematics story problem might require reading, visualization, and problem-solving skills in addition to the ability to solve the resulting mathematical equation. To offer effective feedback to a learner's wrong answer, the system (whether human or automated) must be able to detect which of these skills wasn't applied properly. One way to determine the root cause of the wrong answer is to examine the answers given for similar questions. If the root cause still can't be deduced with enough certainty to provide good instructional feedback, some adaptive instructional systems may select other questions to test the possible root causes. In many cases, the analysis requires interacting with the student to discover the steps they followed to answer the question.

It's tempting isolate skills and only assess one at a time. There are two reasons why this won't work. First, most learning goals involve applying multiple skills together. Second, the demand for some skills simply can't be eliminated. For example, nearly every assessment requires reading and following directions. Similarly, most real-life situations require the application of multiple skills learned to varying degrees of competence.

APPLYING FEEDBACK LOOPS

To summarize, engineering offers us the following insights about using feedback in education and training:

- Select and use appropriate models, understanding the limitations of each. Choose your learning theory deliberately and measure its effectiveness. Iteratively adjust the model based on data.
- Use multiple levels of control loops with various feedback mechanisms. Adapt not only to what the student has and has not mastered but to the individual learning patterns and affinities of each student. Provide quizzes and other knowledge checks as well as tests.
- Fast and frequent feedback can compensate for lower quality in other areas of the system. This can hide problems. You may think you have a good learning theory when, in fact, fast feedback is making the difference; however, it's also an opportunity to make deliberate trade-offs.
- Ensure the control loops use the proper outputs as feedback. Be sure you are measuring what you think you are measuring. And remember that every assessment measures multiple skills.
- Feedback loops based on data also inform the iterative learning engineering process. (See Chapters 5 and 6 on data instrumentation and analysis for a deeper discussion on this.)

[5]

The first course on the edX platform was a course on circuit design. In place of lectures, the Open edX platform had learning sequences, which interleaved short videos, text, exercise, and interactives.

Engineering relies on **prototypes** before fully developing solutions. Often this starts with **paper prototypes** that sketch out **wireframes** of an idea and then to rough models before implementing a **minimum viable product** (MVP) that can be tested with a small set of users. The MITx platform was designed as such a prototype. Piotr was surprised when the first prototype worked well. The course team received strong positive feedback from a pilot group of on-campus students, and a month later, strong positive feedback from online students. (Indeed, 98.6 percent of alumni rated the course as good as or better than an in-person experience.) Obviously, there was a sample bias and experimenter bias to the early results, but they were sufficient to raise $60 million funding for the edX project.

In the prototype platform, courses were designed based on constructive learning—closely related to but not to be confused with constructivist learning theory, which is the idea that people actively construct or make their own knowledge.[13] In contrast, constructive learning uses flexible technology that allows learners to connect new information to their prior knowledge in the modality that's most effective for them. A presentation might walk students through a derivation, but ideally, students themselves would do the work through interwoven exercises.

In practice, the constructive feedback approach was too time-intensive with regard to professional development for course instructors. Anant Agarwal, who created course videos, also ran one of the larger research groups at MIT's Computer Science and Artificial Intelligence Laboratory and was director of the laboratory. He had around ten hours per week to record videos and the original approach was a change from his teaching style. These **constraints** called for a different approach.

ENGINEERING ALWAYS INVOLVES CONSTRAINTS. Every problem to be solved has limits that must be considered when designing and developing the solution. These constraints may include limited resources, time, or technology to develop the solution. Other limits can be based on the learner populations to be served and contextual factors in the environments where the solution will be implemented. Engineering design also must consider ***engineering tolerance***–the permissible limit or limits of variation of any component in the system. Each module or component of a system should only allow variations that don't significantly affect the functioning of the overall system in a negative way, within the intended implementation conditions.[14]

Based on the constraints, most of the learning sequences in the edX circuit design course came to be designed as simple understanding-check exercises interwoven with lecture-style presentations, albeit with a screencast of a slideshow deck annotated with a digital stylus. This change led to active learning—still ahead of traditional university courses—but not as much of a constructive learning approach.

For the homework assignments in the course, Piotr did a survey of past problem sets for the MIT version of the course. He found that the vast majority of problems could be adapted into either numeric responses, circuit schematics, or equation responses. He built technology to support equations and numeric responses, while Chris Terman built a circuit schematic editor and simulators. Note that he did not implement multiple choice questions, since those did not allow for the model of mastery learning designed for the course, where students could make as many attempts as they needed to answer open-ended questions.

Jerry Sussman put an incredible amount of time into creating the problems themselves, which were complex, multi-concept analysis and design problems. Of note, many problems had multiple solutions. For example, given a very basic problem like picking a pair of resistors for a resistive divider that attenuates a voltage threefold, all that matters is the ratio of the resistors. As a result, many problems could be graded by short Python scripts. (While these set a high bar for expertise to the engineering of the course content, a five-line script doesn't add significant time to content creation for experienced programmers. This further highlights learning engineering as a rigorous, skilled discipline and team sport.)

The platform was designed to support iterative improvement of courses based on data. Every action in the course was collected, archived, and preserved, including context in an engineered (and since well-documented) format. The system supported A/B testing of learning activities, randomly assigning alternative experiences, and collecting data to determine which worked best. It had a pluggable architecture for components (XModules, later renamed XBlocks) which allowed for creation of a variety of learning experiences. As of this writing, the open-source community has authored hundreds of XBlocks that plug into the Open edX platform.

[6]

Design patterns are repeatable solutions to commonly occurring engineering problems. A civil engineer is familiar with common bridge architectures and which types work best in certain contexts. In software engineering, design patterns establish best practices and promote shared understanding that improves the quality, consistency, and maintainability of code. Software engineers use named design patterns so that everyone on the team can work together and employ consistent coding approaches based on those known patterns. Learning engineering teams can also use design patterns; for example, the learning sciences concepts in Chapter 9 lend themselves to design pattern templates. Here's an example design pattern for a deliberate practice technique (with constructive feedback) applicable to tutoring or coach contexts.

Example Design Pattern: Deliberate Practice

Deliberate practice with feedback is a pattern of learning often employed with a human or software-based tutor or coach. It supports learning and development after the learner has gained initial conceptual understanding of the problem space. It can be paired with other learning modalities such as worked examples and as part of a cognitive apprenticeship process. This design pattern helps learners retain knowledge, apply knowledge, and build expertise.

Applicable Contexts: Artificial, online, simulated, and real-world environments

Inputs: Data about learner needs and prior learning

Instrumentation: During the learning experience, data are observed and collected about the conditions that require a learner response as well as each learner response

Design Considerations: How will observed behaviors and learner performance be used to adapt the problem and/or problem space (performance challenge) based on learner variability and progress? Which implied learning events or behaviors are most relevant, such as demonstration of mastery, motivational factors, or trying to game the system?

Pattern:

1. Ideally, begin with a baseline prediction about the learner's competence* and prior learning; use this to assign a problem or performance task at an appropriate level of difficulty. If this information is unavailable then fill the baseline model through other means, such as by collecting data via a pre-test.
2. Use historical data, algorithms, or human (expert) insights to predict the probability that the learner will demonstrate competence on the problem or task at any given time based their prior learning, performance, or forgetting curves.
3. Use a pedagogical or andragogical model about learner development for the desired skill mastery, for example, sequencing from novice to expert in a

* *Intelligent tutoring systems may use knowledge inference analytics, such as knowledge tracing, to establish predictions about learner competence. (See Chapter 18 for a discussion.) A reusable competency definition and measurement criteria may be predefined for the skill or task. (See Chapter 8.)*

domain, controlling the level of difficulty for a task or problem, addressing common misconceptions, or controlling cognitive load. Iteratively improve this model using data collected from learners who attempt the problems or tasks.

4. Assign or present problems or performance tasks at a level of **desirable difficulty** and with adaptations (like hints) appropriate for the learner's variability.
5. The learner responds to a problem or part of performance task.
6. Observe the learner's responses and indicators of, for example, affective states (like boredom or confusion), engagement, or system abuse (gaming).
7. Give **unrequested** or **requested feedback** as needed. Sometimes the feedback is informed by a learner's mistake or misconception demonstrated in the previous attempt. Sometimes feedback is requested, such as in the form of a hint. In all cases, feedback is informative, motivational (considering the learners emotional state and response), timely, elaborate, effective, and strategic.
8. Learner reattempts the problem task until completed successfully or the answer/task is demonstrated by the tutor.
9. Assign additional problems or performance tasks with adjustments based on new data from the prior attempt. (That is, repeat the process from step 4.)
10. Continue this process until the learner has demonstrated mastery of the required competencies.

[7]

The need to apply engineering principles to the development of learning experiences and learning conditions has never been greater. Part of meeting that need is the emergence of the learning engineer as a distinct profession. Traditional models of developing and delivering instruction are increasingly breaking down under changing conditions in the world, such as shifts in the economy and employers' need for new kinds of talent. Schools, institutions, and training organizations are already under enormous pressure to adapt. A global pandemic and innovations in information technology have changed how everyone works and learns.

What will it mean to be a citizen and contributor in a future world that's changing at an accelerating rate? How can systems of learning be developed to equip people for this constant change? Even academic systems that were considered state of the art for previous generations failed to meet the needs of many. How can the science of learning be applied at scale so that all people have opportunities to reach great learning outcomes, opportunities that thus far have been afforded only to some? Just like it took engineering to scale the production of penicillin during World War II, and it took engineering to produce and distribute the COVID-19 vaccines, it will take engineering to develop and scale the systems of learning that are needed by future populations of humanity. ★

A professional engineer is **competent** by virtue of his/her fundamental education and training to apply the scientific method and outlook to the analysis and solution of engineering problems.

. . . His/her education will have been such as to make him/her **capable** of closely and continuously following progress in his/her branch of engineering science by consulting newly published works on a worldwide basis, assimilating such information and applying it independently.

. . . His/her education and training will have been such that he/she will have acquired a **broad and general appreciation** of the engineering sciences as well as **thorough insight** into the special features of his/her own branch.

– Conference of Engineering Societies of Western Europe and the United States of America, 1961[15]

- Science aims to discover truths about the world. Engineering aims to create scalable solutions to problems that work within a range of conditions. Engineering is a systematic problem-solving process.
- Constraints (like cost or time) and trade-offs are central to engineering.
- Learning engineering requires engineering mindsets, including a systems perspective, ability to envision the future, and a scientific approach.
- Systems are designed using models of various degrees of fidelity.
- Scalability of complex systems is achieved in part by breaking them into modules, with interfaces between those modules. Interoperability is improved by using standard interfaces.
- Parts of a system have design constraints and tolerances.
- In an open-loop system, the controller uses what it knows about the conditions to set the input. In a learning context, instructional designers use what they know about learners (like age and demographics) and the learning content (like media type and depth of knowledge) as inputs.
- In a closed-loop system, the controller compares feedback from the output to adjust the input. Similarly, in learning engineering, the outputs (how well students are learning) must be compared to the desired output.
- Negative feedback means measuring the difference between the output and the reference (goal) and adapting accordingly.
- Faster, more frequent, and rich feedback is generally better, especially for dynamic systems, and can even compensate for less-than-ideal conditions in other parts of the system.
- Use filters and dampers to prevent over-correcting.
- Engineered systems (and human learning) work best with multiple feedback loops. Each subsystem may have their own feedback control loops as well as the system itself.
- The science of learning is not being applied at scale. Therefore, we see the need for a new profession to produce scaled solutions.

Learning Engineering is Engineering

KEY POINTS

Endnotes

1 Gardner, Nancy. "Bud Saxberg's Half-Century: Business Prof Celebrates 50 Years at the UW—and Counting." UW News. University of Washington, April 5, 2007. www.washington.edu/news/2007/04/05/bud-saxbergs-half-century-business-prof-celebrates-50-years-at-the-uw-and-counting

2 University of Washington. "Bror Saxberg." Alumni Profiles. UW Electrical Engineering. Accessed September 29, 2020. https://vannevar.ece.uw.edu/people/alumni/profiles/bror_saxberg.html

3 Shaughnessy, Michael F. and Bror Saxberg. "Interview with Bror Saxberg." *Educational Technology 54*, no. 5 (2014): 50–53. www.jstor.org/stable/44430307

4 University of Washington, "Bror Saxberg."

5 University of Washington, "Bror Saxberg."

6 Twelves, Tim. "Engineering Principles." Last modified July 22, 2013. http://wiki.c2.com/?EngineeringPrinciples

7 Kimerling, Lionel C. "3.003 Principles of Engineering Practice." MIT OpenCourseWare, Slideshow. Spring 2010. https://ocw.mit.edu/courses/materials-science-and-engineering/3-003-principles-of-engineering-practice-spring-2010/lecture-notes/MIT3_003S10_lec01.pdf

8 "Model." In *Guide to the Systems Engineering Body of Knowledge (SEBoK)*. Version 2.5. Hoboken, NJ: Trustees of the Stevens Institute of Technology. Accessed October 15, 2021. www.sebokwiki.org/wiki/Model_(glossary)

9 McNamara, Carter. "What Is Systems Thinking?" In *Field Guide to Consulting and Organizational Development: A Collaborative and Systems Approach to Performance, Change and Learning*, 405. Minneapolis, MN: Authenticity Consulting, 2006.

10 Smith, Brent, Jerry Gordon, Trey Hayden, and Andrew Johnson. *2019 Total Learning Architecture Report.* Washington, DC: ADL Initiative, 2020. www.adlnet.gov/assets/uploads/2019%20Total%20Learning%20Architecture%20Report.pdf

11 Wees, David. "The Role of Immediacy of Feedback in Student Learning." *The Reflective Educator,* March 31, 2010. https://davidwees.com/content/role-immediacy-feedback-student-learning

12 *Learning about Teaching: Initial Findings from the Measures of Effective Teaching Project. Policy Brief. Met Project.* Washington, DC: Bill & Melinda Gates Foundation, 2010. https://files.eric.ed.gov/fulltext/ED528388.pdf

"Improving Math Performance: What Do You Think Is the Single Most Important Factor in Dramatically Improving Students' Math Performance in Your School?" No Child Left Behind: Blue Ribbon Schools. US Department of Education. www2.ed.gov/programs/nclbbrs/math.pdf

Jerald, Craig. "Teach to the Test? Just Say No." *Reading Rockets,* November 7, 2013. www.readingrockets.org/article/teach-test-just-say-no

Newmann, Fred M., Anthony S. Bryk, and Jenny K. Nagaoka. *Authentic Intellectual Work and Standardized Tests: Conflict or Coexistence? Improving Chicago's Schools*, 10. Chicago, IL: Chicago Consortium on School Research, 2001. https://consortium.uchicago.edu/sites/default/files/2018-10/p0a02.pdf

Newmann, Byrk, and Nagaoka, "Authentic Intellectual Work and Standardized Tests," 29.

13 McLeod, Saul. "Constructivism as a Theory for Teaching and Learning." *Simply Psychology,* July 19, 2019. www.simplypsychology.org/constructivism.html

14 Phillips, Steven D., Bruce Borchardt, and G. Caskey. *Measurement Uncertainty Considerations for Coordinate Measuring Machines.* Gaithersburg, MD: National Institute of Standards and Technology, US Department of Commerce, 1993. https://nvlpubs.nist.gov/nistpubs/Legacy/IR/nistir5170.pdf

15 Closing quotation sourced from Christensen, Steen Hyldgaard, Christelle Didier, Andrew Jamison, Martin Meganck, Carl Mitcham, and Byron Newberry, eds. *Engineering Identities, Epistemologies and Values: Engineering Education and Practice in Context, Volume 2.* Dordrecht: Springer, 2015, 170.

MEASURE

CHAPTER 5

Learning Engineering Uses Data (Part 1): Instrumentation

by Erin Czerwinski, Jim Goodell, Steve Ritter, Robert Sottilare, Khanh-Phuong Thai, and Daniel Jacobs

Learning engineering is a process and practice that applies the learning sciences using human-centered engineering design methodologies and **data-informed decision-making** to support learners and their development.

Data-informed decision-making is an essential and integral part of learning engineering. Without it, you may be doing learning design, but you are not doing learning engineering. Data-informed decision-making has two parts, instrumentation and analytics.

- **Instrumentation** is the part of the learning engineering process responsible for designing, developing, and implementing the data collection used within the learning solution to inform iterative improvements to the learning solution.
- **Analytics** is the part of learning engineering responsible for analysis and use of data within the learning solution to inform iterative improvements to the learning solution.

Instrumentation uses sensors to capture data along with software and hardware to process and store data for analysis.

- **Sensors** are human-computer or environment-computer interfaces that capture data.

- **Data pipelines** are the software and hardware infrastructure for capturing, processing, and storing data.

The learning engineering process is different from one person or team designing a course and later having other researchers collect data as part of an efficacy study. Learning engineering addresses design of data instrumentation while designing the solution. The process assumes the data will be used to inform at least one iteration of the design.

The learning engineering process includes understanding what data to collect, designing, and developing instrumentation, and using data to inform iterative design and development. As we discuss in Chapter 4, engineering involves trade-offs. It is not always practical or possible to collect data that might be valuable, and collecting more data is not necessarily better.

In addition to informing iterative design and development, some systems also use instrumented data to inform feedback directly to learners, instructors, and other stakeholders, including:

- Feedback to learners and instructors during a learning experience
- Feedback between experiences to help determine what to do next
- Feedback that guides the learner on pathways toward longer-term goals

In some cases, new instrumentation hardware or software doesn't need to be developed. For example, online learning platforms may have built-in software to capture learner responses (taps, clicks, or keystrokes) and log that data with context metadata to a file or database. The learning engineering team developing a new activity or lesson can use that built-in capability. You may be surprised to learn how much about a learner's experience and cognitive state can be derived from taps, clicks, or keystrokes without any special hardware. For example, a learner's level of boredom, confusion, frustration, and concentration may be detectable with just data from a keyboard and mouse or touch screen.

However, a learning engineering team should not assume that current data collection is sufficient to answer new questions. "Data must be developed using a sound theoretical framing about what it is that we are trying to measure, rather than trying to align existing clickstream and telemetry data with constructs after-the-fact," according to the Society for Learning Analytics Research (SoLAR).[1]

Other times, the problem to be solved by the learning engineering team requires development of new sensors, new properties, or new data pipelines to capture, store, tag, and process the data. Even if the instrumentation exists, the learning

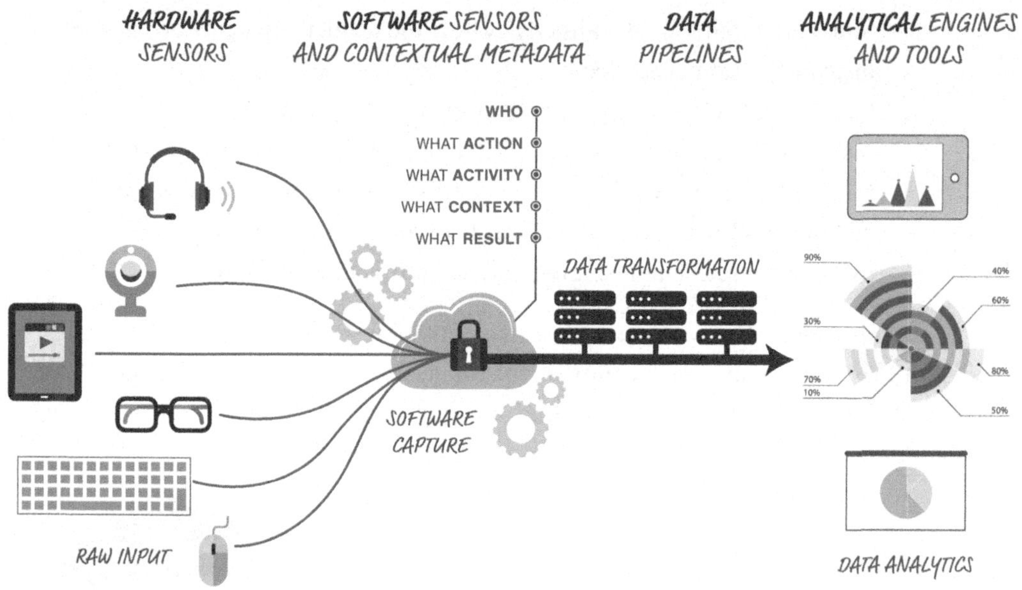

FIGURE 5.1. Hardware and software sensors capture learner actions. Those data are captured, processed, and stored through data pipelines for use within various analytical engines and tools.

engineering team must understand what subset of data is relevant to the current challenge and what conclusions can be drawn from it.

Chapter 1 explained that data are important in all parts of the learning engineering process. Curating and defining the kinds of data to be instrumented is part of understanding the challenge. Instrumentation design and development happen in the creation phase. The instrumentation is put into use during the implementation phase to collect data, and instrumented data are used within the investigation phase to discover opportunities for improvement (new challenges).

In the challenge and creation phases, a learning engineering team might consider data requirements as modular challenges leading to the development of instrumentation. Considerations include the following:

1. **Question:** What's the question we want answered? Who cares? Why?
2. **Method:** How can we answer it using data? What analysis techniques?
3. **Metrics:** What do we need to calculate from the data to answer?
4. **Data:** What specifically defined data elements are needed for the metrics? What algorithm will be used?

5. **Sources:** What systems already collect the needed elements or what new instrumentation is needed?
6. **Quality:** Check assumptions about the existing sources and instrumentation, for example, with data profiling tools. Was it intended for a different purpose? Does the quality hold up for the new purpose and metrics? Are there other aspects of quality that will impact use of existing sources and instrumentation for this new purpose?

In this chapter, we will examine instrumentation stories from the US military, an innovative university, and a company that makes software for children ages three to ten. We also will examine open source and standards-based platforms for instrumentation of online, game-based, and experiential learning data.

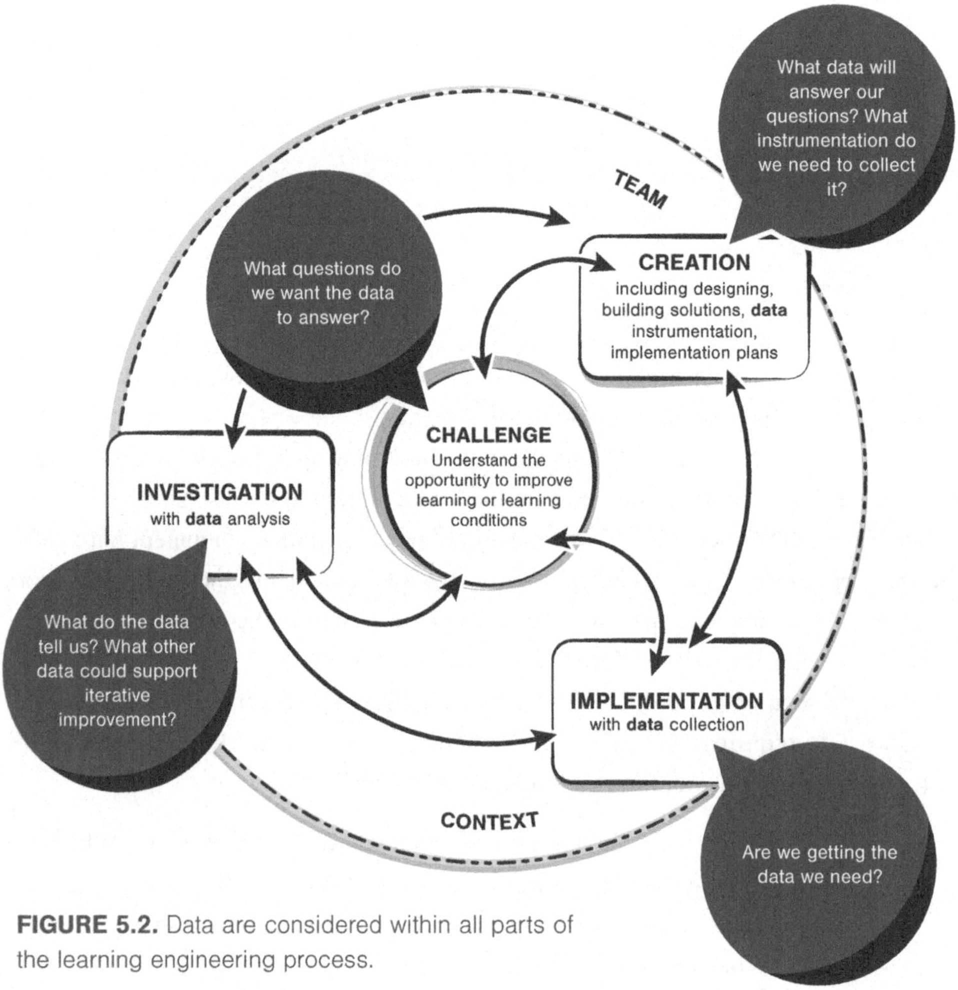

FIGURE 5.2. Data are considered within all parts of the learning engineering process.

[1]

Flight simulators at Boeing, language learning apps like Duolingo, learner positioning systems like Gooru, and software for middle school mathematics like ASSISTments and MATHia are all adaptive instructional systems. These systems capture data about learner experiences and responses and use those data to adapt the learning experiences. They collect the data using sensors.

In the case of military training, sensors can be things like heart rate monitors. For example, well-trained snipers must learn to control their heart rate and shoot in between heart beats.[2] An adaptive instructional system for a sniper might monitor their heart rate, physical orientation of the weapon, and the accuracy of their shot.

Training for soldiers, athletes, and astronauts uses many other kinds of physiological sensors, such as galvanic skin response sensors to measure sweat (an indication of stress), eye tracking (to monitor what the trainee is paying attention to), and respiratory sensors. Just because your task must be measured doesn't mean your sensor is up to the job. Sensors have limits. One such limit is that sensors can be obtrusive. Obtrusive sensors might be attached to the body of the learner or very close to it. On the other hand, unobtrusive sensing means that learners usually are not aware of the sensor or its function during use. Over time, body-worn sensors that might be obtrusive at first can become unobtrusive if they aren't causing discomfort.

When designing sensor suites to collect data about individual learners or teams, context matters. It is generally OK to be a bit obtrusive when you are exploring the efficacy of sensor data as a basis for some inference or prediction of learner states (for example, emotions, stress or other learner states that influence learning) as long as it doesn't interfere with the performance of the task being learned. If you need to implement your solution in an operational environment, make sure that the sensor hardware doesn't interfere with their job.

Bob Sottilare is familiar with the use of sensors. His work supports the largest training organization in the world: the US military. At the US Army Research Laboratory, he developed automated authoring, instructional management, and analysis tools and intelligent tutoring systems (ITSs) and standards for adaptive instructional systems. He is the father of the Generalized Intelligent Framework for Tutoring (GIFT), an award-winning open source, artificial intelligence–based adaptive instructional architecture (see www.gifttutoring.org).

One of Bob Sottilare's undergraduate students, while interning for Sottilare, wanted to investigate the efficacy of measuring heart rate unobtrusively. A few

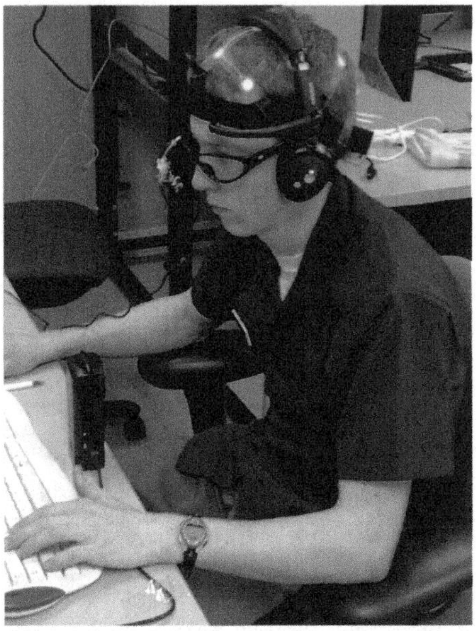

FIGURE 5.3. A West Point cadet testing two low-cost EEG sensors that measure electrical activity of the brain and a low-cost eye tracker

Credit: Robert Sottilare

years before that, Bob had been at an affective computing conference at the University of Memphis and he ran into Rosalind Picard, who ran the MIT affective computing laboratory. (*Affective* here means relating to moods, feelings, and attitudes.) One of her grad students had developed a method to use webcams to measure heart rate. The webcams collected data through red-green-blue channels. It turns out that if the green and blue channels were eliminated and the camera was pointed just above a person's eyes, the intensity of the red channel could be sensed, and a person's heartbeat could be visualized. At first, this seemed like a much less obtrusive alternative for measuring heart rate. However, sensors have limits. In this case, distance was a major limitation. As the user moved away from the camera, the number of pixels focused on the sweet spot of heavy blood flow between and above the eyes lessened and so did the accuracy of the heart rate monitor.

Bob's intern wanted to see if he could duplicate the informal results explored by Rosalind Picard. Bob and his student set up an experiment in the lab to see if they could accurately measure heart rate with this method. Like the original experiment, they found that distance had a huge effect on accuracy, but there were other factors that they didn't think about beforehand. Low ambient light also affected accuracy. They noticed that the experimental trials early in the day showed more accuracy. They had the lights turned down in the lab, but the lab faced east, and the morning sun meant more ambient light in the morning and less later in the day. Even when a sensor is designed to measure a specific factor, such as heart rate, other conditions can influence the results. This was especially true in this case. These sensors not only suffered in accuracy due to the environment, but also failed to be unobtrusive (which was their intended use) because the camera needed to be close to the person's forehead.

Another time, Bob was working with others to conduct another experiment.

They were collecting galvanic skin response data using Bluetooth. They had run several trials, which were ruined by dropout (no data available) because the Bluetooth communication failed. They also ended up with intermittent and low-quality data. Sensors have limits. One such limit is that some sensors are not suited to a task, even if it may seem so at first. Testing sensors to make sure they give desired data before implementing those sensors is important. Additionally, one sensor may not be able to give the desired data. Sometimes it takes a mix of sensors to capture all the data you need to predict a set of states.

Even if the sensor is suitable for the task, the technology to collect the data from the sensor may be a limiting factor. For example, an enormous amount of interesting data could be captured from simultaneous video streams from millions of users of an app, but the data pipeline required to capture all that data might be prohibitive. Most solutions require less data to answer the questions related to the learning engineering challenge. Trade-offs are required.

Sensors and their data pipelines have limits and require trade-offs.

Another limiting factor is that sensor data can be perishable, just like that donut you ate this morning. Fresh donuts and fresh data as you need them are always best. For example, for some military training it may be important to know the person's level of anxiety and how well they are coping with a stressful situation. If you have a really accurate model of the learner's anxiety based on physiological sensor data, then it is only good while the individual learner's physiology is not influenced by some external factor, like caffeine intake. Since people eat or drink all kinds of things that change their heart rate, blood pressure, brain function, and other factors. It is highly likely that trying to use yesterday's data today will result in significant errors. In the case of a sniper, starting to drink coffee could completely change what their biological data look like.

DATA ARE PERISHABLE. A model of the learner's current state based on sensor data becomes less accurate with every new experience or external influence.

The US Army also has developed sensors that capture other kinds of data such as the radio communication between members of a squad. A team works best when communication is efficient. These sensors can encode the communication to determine how well the team is following communications protocols. Those data support constructive feedback during after action reviews to help the squad improve its performance. "The After Action Review (AAR) was developed by the United States Army in the 1970s to help its soldiers learn from both their mistakes and achievements."[3] The encoding might include what command was given, what response was given, the time between command and response, and the contextual conditions that prompted the exchange.

This encoding of raw sensor data resembles the encoding of raw log data collected by learning apps like Duolingo. The raw data capture that you tapped on the screen, and the encoded data add meaning, such as which word you tapped, what prompt you were given, when the question was displayed, how long it took you to respond, and other information about the prompt that helps Duolingo predict if you will get the answer right the next time you are asked to translate the same word.

[2]

Data standards help streamline the development of instrumentation and ensure that data collected are comparable. One suite of standards now being maintained by the IEEE Standards Association is called Experience Application Programming Interface (xAPI) as described in Figure 5.4. Others like IMS Global's Caliper™ and frameworks that have served as de facto standards like the ADAGE Framework are described later in this chapter.

You may be thinking, "I'm not an experienced software engineer. Isn't instrumentation using standards like xAPI only for full-time geeks?" Not according to Anthony Altieri, founder of Omnes Solutions. In a 2017 *Learning Solutions* article, he showed how instructional designers can send an xAPI statement from a web page to a Learning Record Store (LRS) with just four steps and just four lines of JavaScript code.[4]

1. Define a variable that holds the URL address of the LRS and the username and password to authenticate
2. Tell the browser to use that variable for the LRS
3. Define the xAPI statement
4. Send the statement

It may be easier if all you are doing is editing some values in a template web page. Chapter 13, Data Instrumentation Tools, includes a simple example.

EXPERIENCE API (xAPI) AND THE LEARNING RECORD STORE (LRS)

xAPI is an open set of standards used in training and education applications for instrumentation. API stands for **application programming interface**—a way for two programs, systems, or apps to communicate.

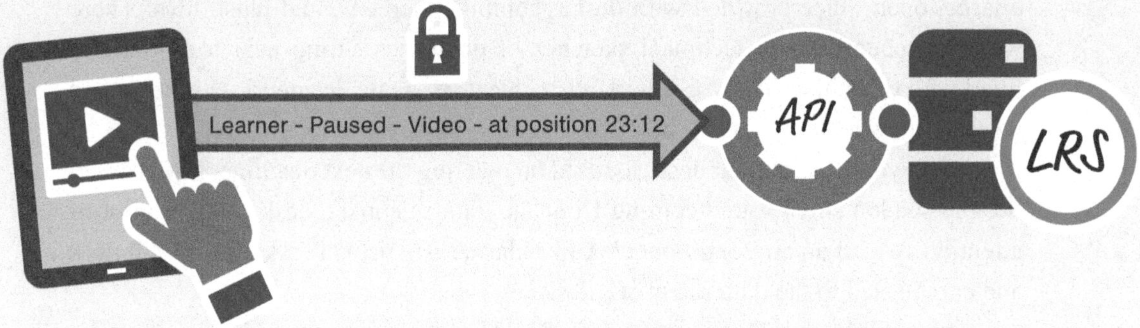

xAPI is used in both distributed learning and traditional contexts, such as courses delivered via learning management systems. First developed by the US military's Advanced Distributed Learning Initiative, xAPI is now part of a suite of international standards maintained by the IEEE Standards Association.

xAPI data are structured as statements with these parts: an **actor** (for example, learner), a **verb** (for example, tapped/clicked), an **object** (for example, a button), with a timestamp, and other relevant info. Consider the following examples:

ACTOR	VERB	OBJECT	RESULT	CONTEXT	TIMESTAMP
"a learner"	"paused"	"this video"		"position 23:56"	"2022-06-09T11:20..."
"a learner"	"answered"	"this question"	"3"	Question URL	"2022-06-09T11:22..."
"system"	"scored"	"this question"	"correct"	Question URL	"2022-06-09T11:22..."

The standard support **Profiles** for different kinds of learning interactions, for example, watching a video, answering a test question, or reading an e-book.

xAPI includes **independent LRSs**. Data from multiple platforms or activities may be collected into a common LRS rather than being locked in the data store of a learning management system.

FIGURE 5.4. xAPI high-level summary. Open source resources are available through IEEE SA Open. xAPI Open Source Repository: https://gitlab.com/ieee-sa/xapi
See also https://standards.ieee.org/initiatives/opensource/index.html

[3]

In 2015, a data scientist was working in his office in Glendale, California. It was a large, open office crowded with desks, computer screens, and plush toys. There were whiteboards with technical sketches of databases sitting next to bookcases filled with titles like *BIG 3rd Grade Math.* Educators, game designers, engineers and researchers were hard at work building an educational game for children.

Everyone was at their desk, focused on meeting the next deadline. It was quiet. So, the sudden shrill sound coming from the data scientist's desk brought a lot of attention. Was it an air conditioner? A fire alarm? An airplane taking off? All eyes and ears turned to the data scientist's desk.

"My apologies, it's my computer's fan. The data are just too big."

That may have been the moment when **big data** had arrived at Age of Learning, and on the new project they were working on, which would come to be called *My Math Academy.*

It was around 2015. Big data (and loud fans) had earlier arrived at mobile gaming companies like Zynga or Supercell. These mobile app developers already had developed a strong skill set in tracking how users were using apps, using data to segment users into different groups, and to predict their behavior.

Video games were changing as well. Games weren't just Mario and Zelda anymore. The things that people had learned about the motivational aspects of games were being applied in educational products since the 1980s, but the educational games industry had its ups and downs. But gamification was seeing a comeback through mobile apps. Gaming was once again coming to education in a big way.

And educational technology was changing. Coursera, and several other providers had launched recently, doing massively online courses. ABCMouse had become a hit success for educating young children. Education was moving beyond the textbook, beyond the print-sheet, and beyond the static website. Educational technology was embracing video and embracing interactivity.

Age of Learning (the company that makes ABCMouse), was looking to do something new, and to use big data and video game design in an entirely new way. The three ingredients of education, video games, and big data were thrown into an oven and baked for several years, and a new product, called *My Math Academy,* would emerge.

Lessons in Data Instrumentation

My Math Academy is a program designed to teach, practice, and assess basic math skills for children between ages three and ten. It is composed of many small games, each designed to teach, practice, or assess a particular skill. As they were building it, the Age of Learning team knew that they wanted to do careful data instrumentation. It was a key part of bringing big data, game design, and education together.

This was because they knew about the potential value of having a large data set. Researchers like Zoran Popović[5] and Ryan Baker had been successful in capturing meaningful insights about children's learning by analyzing data about how they played video games and interacted with adaptive learning systems. (Read more about Ryan Baker in Chapter 6.)

There wasn't really a big data set for children of this age with educational data. There could be new insights about how people learn—for example, how often do children confuse the number 3 with the similar looking number 8? Or how easy is it to count if you can't recognize numbers yet? They hoped they could apply the insights they would gain to building a product where kids could not only enjoy their experience but could also learn effectively and efficiently.

Their first goal was to build a good, comprehensive data set for analysis. They learned a lot of lessons along the way. They didn't know exactly what they would be looking for, so they opted to log with a lot of detail.

Comprehensive logs were a challenge and a source of great debate. Some team members wanted to log only what they thought they would need and would have a clear use for. Others wanted to log every single event that happened, without any plan for how to interpret the data.

They settled on a plan, based on the ADAGE framework—an open API for data collection in educational games. (See the inset on the next page for more details.) With ADAGE they would log down to a click level, and they would carefully track all meaningful events in the game. They made sure to label things carefully, so a human could read through the logs. They also tracked context, so an analyst could easily figure out what else was going on, without doing a heroic parsing effort. In the end, they got a little more data than they needed.

The game designers' and data team's dialogue went something like this:

Game designers: Today we are going to ship a new game. Please help us instrument the data.

Data team: Of course!

Game designers:	Should we tell you what we want to know in advance, so you can prepare accordingly?
Data team:	No no, we will simply track everything. There is no need to worry about it now!

ADAGE FRAMEWORK. The Assessment Data Aggregator for Gaming Environments (or ADAGE) framework is a set of data collection and analysis tools on a shared, open source platform that uses big data techniques to transform clickstream data from game and design systems into formative feedback for usability testing and evidence of learning.[6] The framework was designed to test whether click-stream data could provide reliable evidence of learning. ADAGE was used as a framework for video games in education research to demonstrate evidence of player learning. One goal of the framework and related research was to attend to the ways in which game play can provide a powerful new form of assessment. ADAGE consists of two main layers: (1) the semantic template that determines which click-stream data events could be indicators of learning; (2) the learning telemetry that captures data for analysis.[7] The framework was used with and in popular game platforms and open source code repositories still exist. (See https://github.com/wids-eria/adage.)

The data team settled on a strategy to track all the clicks within the games. They tracked to know if a child was clicking an important button or not. They tracked timestamps. They also tracked context, so they knew exactly what educational game the child was playing when the button was clicked.

Things started well enough. A few days after they shipped, the game designers asked how many questions each student was getting right or wrong. They had the data. The logs had been appropriate, and it wasn't hard to load the data into R (a data analytics tool set) to report the results.

However, things soon turned. The next question was, "How long does it take to answer a question?" The answer was not in the logged data (because the students didn't need to click when a question started). They couldn't do the analysis without first reshipping the gaming and adding instrumentation.

The data team learned a lesson: trying to track everything would track too much and not enough. The more questions you know in advance, the easier it is to track the right stuff. So, the data and design team began working together to try to figure out in advance what questions they might need from the data. And sometimes, no matter how hard they tried, they just wouldn't know until after they shipped.

LESSON: Instrumentation can be an iterative process.

The team knew that analyzing poorly annotated logs was difficult, so they chose to make the logs easy to interpret. The game designers wanted to know how many games were passed successfully. They were trying to get a sense of if the games were too easy or too hard.

Game designers: Can you tell us which games are easy and which are hard?

Data analyst: Sure, the data are all ready to go.

And so, the data analyst loaded the data into his computer. And he found all the instances where the students had SUCCEEDED. And he added those all up and did a very nice report.

Data analyst: Here is your report! I have counted all the SUCCEEDS.

Game designers: But where are the FAILS? Surely students SUCCEED and FAIL, right?

Data analyst: No, they SUCCEED and CANCEL.

The game designers were a little confused. "That does not sound right," they said. The analyst went back to his data. There were two columns. One was called OUTCOME, and the other called SCORE. OUTCOME had two values, SUCCEED and CANCEL. SCORE had two values, PASS and FAIL (and sometimes it was empty too).

Data analyst: They should have called it COMPLETE and CANCEL, instead of SUCCEED and CANCEL, and then I never would have made that mistake.

LESSON: Language really matters, and it's worth taking time to come up with good data labels.

The team knew that inconsistent logs were hard to work with, so they chose to have clear rules for how to log data, and to have software that made those rules easy to check and enforce. This was one of the hardest parts. Because the team was designing the game in an iterative way, they weren't sure about all possible future features. They had to be careful with the naming conventions. This is a subtle art.

Game designers:	We have invented a new game. It is beautiful and immersive and educational. We should add data logs to it so we can answer important questions and iterate on the design.
Data team:	No problem. We'll study this game more carefully and figure out the best way to instrument the logging.
Game designers:	It does resemble a multiple-choice question on an exam. You could log it in a similar way!

And so, the game designers left and the analysts played the game.

Data analyst:	Before we discuss the instrumentation, let us order a pizza.

The pizza was ordered.

Data analyst:	It should arrive in thirty minutes. Now onto the business at hand: I've played the game. The audio says, "pick the number 3," and it shows the student the numbers, 3, 4 and 5. The student must tap on the number 3. What shall we call the number 3?
Second analyst:	It is the correct answer!
Another analyst:	No, it is the target choice.
Another analyst:	No, it is the correct choice.
First data analyst:	No, it is the target answer.
Second analyst:	Or the chosen answer.

And then the pizza arrived.

Second analyst:	It's been an hour and we have not named this simple thing? This is taking much too long!
Veteran data analyst:	No, it's taking about the right amount of time. I remember when SUCCEED was confused with PASS. It's worth spending the time up front to get the language right. Let's make a decision, tell the developers, and keep our new word and our common understanding of it long into the future.

This is an example where an existing standard or profile could have saved a lot of time and provided labels that would be valuable across platforms within and beyond the specific learning engineering team needs, not just across learning activities. And when a standard profile doesn't exist it may be helpful to develop one with others and publish it openly.

In 2021 the ADL Initiative launched an xAPI Profile Server supporting the open authoring, management, and publishing of xAPI profiles.[8] xAPI profiles provide a template for assembling sets of xAPI statements. These profiles model the vocabulary, patterns, sequences, and concepts of learning activities within a domain. Each xAPI profile is designed for a specific interaction type (for example, video) or subject matter (for example, diagnostic medicine). While any given learning activity could involve thousands of different data points about a learner's performance, an xAPI profile constrains what data are collected and in what formats. This helps learning engineering teams to know what to collect, and it supports interoperability—so that different systems use similar data collection schemas for related learning experiences.

LESSON: Take time when choosing data labels, definitions and vocabulary. Use standards when available; if standards don't exist, help create new standards or reusable profiles.

The team knew that bad data are difficult to analyze, so they chose to invest heavily in manual and automated quality assurance. They knew there were a lot of people and layers involved in data instrumentation—from in the game, to in the server, to the database, to the analyst. They made sure each layer had its own documentation. Some months passed.

Game designers:	Can you tell us if people are learning more, now that they have played the game for several months?
Data analyst:	Surely we have the data for this! We can do it.
Veteran analyst:	*(Now, a bit more "veteran.")* I don't quite remember what is a SUCCEED and what is a PASS.
Data analyst:	I don't really remember either, it's been many months since we thought about this. Let's read through the code I wrote several months ago and try to figure it out.

They read through the code, and eventually figured it out.

Veteran analyst: This same problem has come up twice. Let's take the time to write a data dictionary. It will define all the columns in our tables, with all these little things that we figured out.

Data analyst: That's great, it will also be much easier to share the data as new people join the project.

So, they created a data dictionary, where they documented each column, and the data inside. They used it many times in the future. There were a few good references they looked at for how to create good data dictionaries, including ceds.ed.gov. They also had the help of good software references, like metacat and metabase.

LESSON: Maintain a data dictionary for your data definitions, aligned to standard definitions when available.

The team knew that products change over time, as do technologies. They accepted that the data flow from an educational game, like water, flows down a stream. You can put some rocks here and there, but you can't really control where it goes. And once the flow starts, you can't really go back and change it, you just have to adapt. Using the data to change the app, and to help students learn, is the best part. After the game had shipped, the educators and data scientists and game designers all gathered.

Game designers: We built an educational game for three- to five-year-olds. We have seen them play it. They love it, and they seem to be learning.

Educators: Excellent! By the way, three- to five-year-olds, you say? A three-year-old is very different than a four-year-old. That's 30% of a life!

Game designers: Good point! Maybe we can look at each game and see the pass rate based on the user's age. If it's very high or very low, then maybe something isn't right.

And so, the data scientists took a look. Initially, they thought there wasn't much of a difference between a three-year-old, a four-year-old, and a five-year-old. It's the kind of thing that any teacher of children that age would say was obvious, but you might not know that if you were a mere game designer or programmer. When they looked at the data, it was clear that users of a certain age would stay with the game longer than other users. Four-year-olds would stay the longest, but younger or older kids would drop off.

They took a look at each game within the system and noticed that each game had a particular age where the pass rate was around 75%. But it would be higher or lower as you got further from the target age.

Data analyst: There does seem to be a correlation between cancellations, pass rates, and age. Each game seems to have an optimal age.

Game designers: Aha! Why don't we show students their initial games based on their age? Maybe people will have a better first experience and will stick around longer.

Educators: Good idea!

And so, it was done, and they saw that students stuck around longer!

LESSON: Data from good instrumentation gives visibility into opportunities for improvement.

[4]

Whether you or your team is using simple instrumentation, like data logged when a learner submits a web form, or something more sophisticated, it always involves some kind of sensor which may include a hardware interface (like a touch screen) and software instrumentation. These sensor data then travel on a data pipeline and are stored somewhere.

Standards such as IMS Global's Caliper, described in Figure 5.5, provide an interoperable pipeline for collecting data captured from an online activity, such as an activity launched from a learning management system using the Learning Tools Interoperability (LTI) standard. IMS members include commercial learning management platform vendors that also provide analysis and data visualization software features.

IMS Global is a US-based 501(c)6 businesses association that facilitates standards development led by member-based work groups. IMS Global has testing

IMS GLOBAL CALIPER

Commercial learning management systems may use IMS Global's Caliper standard for instrumentation. It's similar to xAPI in purpose and messaging format but has a governed vocabulary and is engineered with a focus on capture and transport of analytics data tightly coupled with existing IMS teaching and learning standards. Unlike xAPI, Caliper doesn't specify a separate LRS as part of the standard. In place of an LRS, IMS provides the Comprehensive Learner Record Standard, a collection of discrete achievement assertions (academic, co-curricular, and skills-based achievements) that can be issued to the learner. The Caliper standard is built to complement existing IMS Global open standards and is well suited for use by organizations that use those other IMS standards such as Common Cartridge, LTI, OneRoster and QTI.

Caliper includes a Sensor API for transmitting basic learning events in a simple and standardized format. Also, like xAPI, Caliper includes defined profiles that model learning or supporting activities. As of April 2021, the IMS Global website listed the following standard profiles which it also certifies for technical compliance:

Annotation Profile
Assessment Profile
Assignable Profile
Basic Profile
Feedback Profile
Forum Profile
Grading Profile
Library Profile
Media Profile
Reading Profile
Resource Mgmt Profile
Search Profile
Session Profile
Survey Profile
Tool Launch Profile
Tool Use Profile

At the IMS Quarterly meeting, on August 15, 2016, IMS members and xAPI developers determined that Caliper and xAPI are not equivalent, they have different origins, and there may be cases where one or the other is preferred, as well as cases that support both or a translation of data from both. While both xAPI (Actor/Verb/Object) and Caliper (Actor/Action/Activity) use a data model based upon a triple statement structure, there are differences in the detailed structure and usage of the Object and Activity definitions. However, it should be possible for each specification to make use of the other's Verb/Action. The most significant differences noted in analysis are in the transport layers for the specifications.

FIGURE 5.5. Caliper is the IMS Global Learning Consortium's set of standards for learning metrics. See www.imsglobal.org/activity/caliper and www.imsglobal.org/initial-xapicaliper-comparison

programs that enable products to be certified compliant with specific standards and features of the standards. IMS conformance certification for Caliper Analytics is available for Contributing and Affiliate-level members.

IMS Global offers its member organizations a certification service for testing applications that emit Caliper messages over HTTP. Each Metric Profile defined in the Caliper Analytics specification serves as a separate unit of certification. Edtech suppliers may certify their products for one, some, or all relevant Metric Profiles.[9] For example, vendors that offer assessment products might certify a product as having a compliant sensor API for the Caliper Assessment Profile designed to track attempts, completion times, and item skips and responses as learners take assessments and engage with individual assessment items. A learning management system vendor would certify its platform as being compliant to receive those assessment event messages from compliant sensor API.

Chapter 13 has process tools for deciding what data to collect and for designing instrumentation for the collection of those data. The chapter also includes references to open-source software resources for instrumenting learning experiences. ★

- Instrumentation includes “sensors” to collect data at the source and a “pipeline” to move, process, and store those data.
  - Sensors are hardware and software human-computer or environment-computer interfaces, like a touch screen on a phone and the software that handles the taps.
  - Sensors have limits.
  - Sensors may already exist or need to be developed.
  - Sensors may be obtrusive.
  - Sensor data may be perishable.
  - Raw data from sensors can collect events like taps and clicks but other things can be derived from those observations, such as a learner’s level of boredom or frustration.
- The learning engineering process starts with the challenge. Knowing in advance what questions you want to answer with the data should guide what data to collect and review.
- Iteration is needed throughout data collection, review, and analysis.
- Domain-specific frameworks help establish repeatable approaches and practices.
- Data standards provide an opportunity for interoperability and faster development of data pipelines. Experience API (xAPI) with its Learning Record Store (LRS) and Profile Server provide an infrastructure for instrumentation supported by IEEE. Caliper from IMS Global provides a standard for instrumentation that’s tightly integrated with other standards such as LTI, which is popular for launching activities from within a learning management system.
- Maintain a data dictionary and use standard data definitions.
- Engineering involves trade-offs.

Learning Engineering Uses Data (Part 1): Instrumentation

KEY POINTS

Endnotes

1 Kitto, Kirsty, John Whitmer, Aaron Silvers, and Michael Webb. *Creating data for learning analytics ecosystems.* Beaumont, Alberta: Society for Learning Analytics Research (SoLAR), 2020. www.solaresearch.org/wp-content/uploads/2020/09/SoLAR_Position-Paper_2020_09.pdf

2 "Fight Science: Ultimate Soldiers: A Well-Trained Sniper Uses Mind Over Matter to Control His Own Physiology." Video, 4:45. National Geographic. January 25, 2010. https://youtu.be/yX2bVJm94b0

3 Henshaw, Todd. "After Action Review (AAR) Process: Nano Tools for Leaders." Wharton@ Work. Wharton Executive Education. April 2012. https://executiveeducation.wharton.upenn.edu/thought-leadership/wharton-at-work/2012/04/after-action-reviews

4 Altieri, Anthony. "Getting Started with xAPI: Four Lines of Code." *Learning Solutions Magazine.* May 17, 2017. https://learningsolutionsmag.com/articles/2322/getting-started-with-xapi-four-lines-of-code

5 "Zoran Popović." University of Washington, Paul G. Allen School of Computer Science & Engineering. https://homes.cs.washington.edu/~zoran

6 "Wids-eria/ADAGE: Assessment Data Aggregator for Gaming Environments." GitHub. Games + Learning + Society / Learning Games Network / Wisconsin Institute for Discovery UW Madison. Last modified September 23, 2015. https://github.com/wids-eria/ADAGE

7 Halverson, Richard, and V. Elizabeth Owen. "Game-Based Assessment: An Integrated Model for Capturing Evidence of Learning in Play." *International Journal of Learning Technology 9,* no. 2 (2014): 111–138. https://doi.org/10.1504/IJLT.2014.064489

8 "xAPI Profile Server to Launch in 2021." ADL Initiative, US Department of Defense. December 2, 2020. https://adlnet.gov/news/2020/12/02/xAPI-Profile-Server-to-Launch-in-2021

9 "Caliper Analytics." IMS Global Learning Consortium. Updated August 2021. www.imsglobal.org/activity/caliper

ANALYZE

CHAPTER 6

Learning Engineering Uses Data (Part 2): Analytics

by Michelle Barrett, Erin Czerwinski, Jim Goodell, Daniel Jacobs, Steve Ritter, Robert Sottilare, and Khanh-Phuong Thai

Learning engineering is a process and practice that applies the learning sciences using human-centered engineering design methodologies and **data-informed decision-making** to support learners and their development.

This chapter is a high-level introduction to data analysis for decision-making within the learning engineering process. It addresses the use of data for feedback to the learner and people supporting learners, and it addresses the use of data to inform iterative improvements to engineered solutions. It gives some high-level guidance to non-statisticians as to how to think about data.

Learning engineers use data to measure the effect of conditions on learning within a rapid cycle for improvement. This involves understanding the data from the instrumented learning (including the context around learning experiences) and how to determine whether the quality of the measure is sufficient for the decision at hand. **Analytics**—the systematic computational analysis of data—is central to the investigation phase of the learning engineering process introduced in Chapter 1.

Data-informed design decisions are needed because human intuitions about what helps people learn are often wrong. Looking at data from simple trials can keep the work focused on the most important design features and avoid costly diversions. For example, when Ken Koedinger's team at Carnegie Mellon University was developing a cognitive tutor (an intelligent tutoring system) for Geometry, they wondered if they should build in a diagramming tool. In a lot of problems presented to students, the system showed a diagram, and Koedinger was wondering, "maybe that's an important part of figuring out how to solve a geometry problem—to be able to draw the diagram." But before they invested in developing diagramming software, they did a study: "In some we gave the diagram, in some we didn't, in some we didn't give it but prompted them to draw it [on paper]," he said. "There was almost no difference at all, and we did that before we built the diagramming tool fortunately. And we decided not to build it because it wasn't the root cause of difficulty."

[1]

Would you think that you could do better on a test by studying less with cheaper instructional materials? That's exactly what one learning engineering team found.

At Kaplan Inc., Bror Saxberg was chief learning officer, overseeing the research and development of innovative learning strategies and consistent academic standards for Kaplan University courses and Kaplan products. Like Ken Koedinger at Carnegie Mellon University, Bror and his team recognized that if there were questions that the current science didn't answer, his team would need to do their own experiments. Although they looked to outside research to inform interventions and course design, they recognized that they lacked evidence about what worked for their specific student population and delivery model. So they created a research pipeline to test the impact of interventions on student learning and implement the best approaches at scale. "The Pipeline was conceived of in 2013 by Bror Saxberg and David Niemi, Vice President of Measurement and Evaluation for Kaplan, Inc., along with colleagues who saw a need for Kaplan University to accumulate credible evidence about what worked to measurably improve learning and outcomes for adult, online students."[1] Some of the research had surprising results.

Within Kaplan is the Kaplan Test Preparation group. This group is one of the leaders in preparing students for the Law School Admission Test (LSAT). Saxberg explains that about 25 percent of this test includes "challenging logical reasoning problems with complex question stems and distractors."[2] The Kaplan Test Preparation group knew that these problems weren't only a significant portion of the test but also very difficult to master. Their idea, which seemed like an obvious one, was to use video to prepare students for these test items. The video they produced included embedded practice questions for students to answer and typically took more than an hour for students to complete. A workbook also was provided as a part of the video test preparation.

It seemed a solution to the problem was found, but there was also an alternative.

A Kaplan Test Preparation learning engineer considered that the logical reasoning portion of the test was very complex and was likely to "overload the working memory of most learners."[3] (See Chapter 2 for an explanation of cognitive load theory.) This engineer believed that a video was not the best way for students to get a grasp on these logic problems. Instead, he proposed students study **worked examples**, which are examples of the logical reasoning problems found on the test worked out and supplemented with expert commentary.[4]

The worked examples were designed to limit split attention by aligning each statement in the question to its explanation, allowing students to focus on one thing at a time. It offered expert thinking for each part of the question and reduced the explanation to the minimum required to understand the logic.

At this point, two methods had been developed for helping students prepare for the logical reasoning part of the test. To find out which method was more effective, Kaplan conducted a study. There were four different conditions students were put in before taking a twelve-question post-test (see Figure 6.1). One group of students prepared using the videos and workbook for an average preparation time of about ninety minutes. Another group studied eight worked examples for an average time of about nine minutes. Another group studied fifteen worked examples for an average time of about fifteen minutes, and the control group didn't prepare at all for the post-test. An example of the worked examples is shown in Figure 6.2.

EXPERIMENTAL CONDITION	AVERAGE TIME SPENT
Test only (Control)	0 minutes (no test preparation)
Videos and workbook	90 minutes
15 worked examples	15 minutes
8 worked examples	9 minutes

FIGURE 6.1. Experimental conditions in the Kaplan LSAT study

The study found that the two worked example conditions "worked statistically significantly better at helping learners master" the logical reasoning problems. Additionally, it was found that the video and workbook students didn't do much better than the students who didn't prepare at all for the test. Perhaps most surprising of all was that the group that did the best was the eight-question worked examples group—the students who only studied for about nine minutes. That group did better than even the group that took more time to study more worked examples.[5] Figure 6.3 shows the study results.

WORKED EXAMPLE

QUESTION	EXPERT THINKING
Linguist: Most people can tell whether a sequence of words in their own dialect is grammatical. Yet few people who can do so can specify the relevant grammatical rules. Which one of the following best illustrates the principle underlying the linguist's statements?	The underlying principle here is: People can apply sophisticated rules without being able to specify those rules.
(A) Some people can write cogent and accurate narrative descriptions of events. But these people are not necessarily also capable of composing emotionally moving and satisfying poems.	Nothing here is about rules or applying rules.
(B) Engineers who apply the principles of physics to design buildings and bridges must know a great deal more than do the physicists who discover these principles.	Making a distinction about people that can apply rules and different people who discover the rules.
(C) Some people can tell whether any given piece of music is a waltz. But the majority of these people cannot state the defining characteristics of a waltz.	Correct. This is saying some people can apply the rules (defining characteristics) for identifying a waltz without knowing specifically what those rules are.
(D) Those travelers who most enjoy their journeys are not always those most capable of vividly describing the details of those journeys.	The second part of this sounds a bit like the second part of the linguist's underlying principle (describing details) but it is not describing *rules*. And the first part is not about *applying* any rules, it is just about enjoying something.
(E) Quite a few people know the rules of chess, but only a small number of them can play chess very well.	This one is almost the opposite of the linguist's principle, people who know the rules but can't apply them.

FIGURE 6.2. An example for LSAT reasoning like the ones tested by the Kaplan team. The question is on the left, and expert reasoning is on the right.

Adapted from Khan Academy, www.khanacademy.org/test-prep/lsat/lsat-lessons

The takeaway from this example isn't that worked examples are the solution to every learning problem or that studying less is better for learning. The takeaway is that the best solution in this case was one that took into consideration that students were working with complex problems that would overload working memory. The team developed a theory based on recent research about worked examples, designed

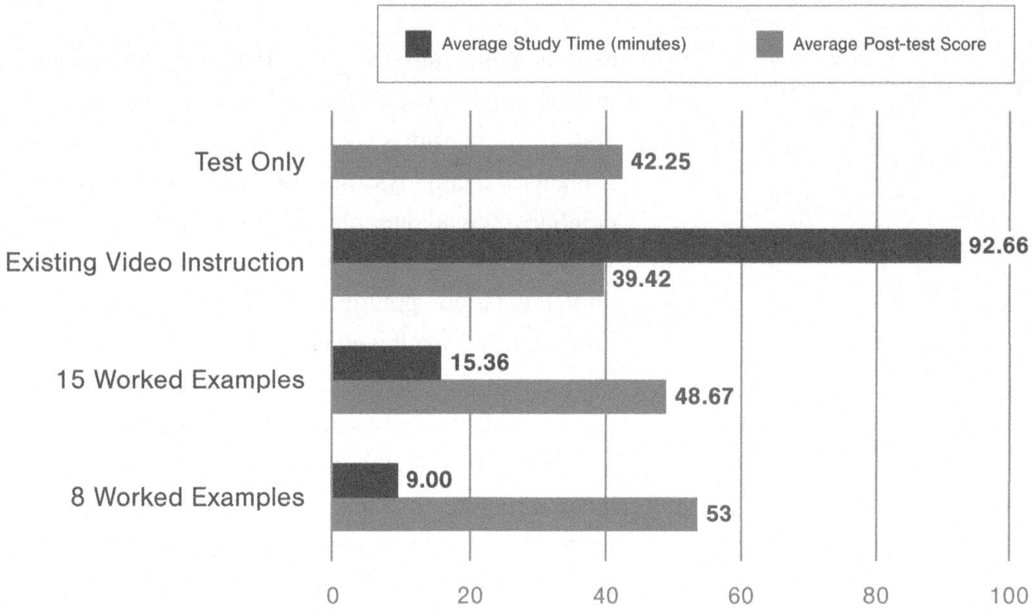

FIGURE 6.3. Kaplan study results: fewer worked examples outperformed longer videos

an alternative preparation method, tested it in context, and let the data decide the best option. The solution in this case likely can't be applied to other cases; learning engineering research isn't about discovering generalizable learning science findings. Learning engineering research deals with highly contextualized cases within specific courses or products for specific learner populations. This research then can be applied to these specific cases to improve learning outcomes.

[2]

Data Analysis is a Team Sport: Making Sense of Data

The challenge for learning engineering is to improve learning or learning conditions. Data analysis and analytics help us to answer whether our creation effectively improved learning or learning conditions. The findings also typically pique curiosity, generating additional questions for exploration.

Edmentum is a company that provides research-based curriculum, assessments for learning, and educational services for K-12 educators and learners. The roots of the company trace back to the early 1960s and the University of Illinois at Urbana-Champaign under the name PLATO. The company created what many

> PSYCHOMETRICS IS THE SCIENCE OF MEASURING MENTAL CAPACITIES AND PROCESSES

experts would agree was the first computer-assisted instructional system designed for widespread use.[6] Today, Edmentum serves millions of teachers and students and employs an active learning engineering practice to evaluate the contributions of product features, instructional curriculum and content, and implementation practices to learning outcomes. Edmentum's learning engineering processes include roles across the organization, such as learning engineers, psychometricians, learning designers, content and assessment developers, implementation consultants, user interface and user experience (UI/UX) designers, data scientists, software engineers, and product managers.

Roles in any particular learning engineering team or at any other organization may be defined differently even if the same titles are used. Edmentum's learning designers are experts in pedagogy, instructional design, and the specific content being taught. Edmentum's research data engineers manage the data pipeline and conduct ETL (extract, transform, load) processes that make raw data usable for research purposes. This role includes capturing feedback data and supporting experiments; they also have the technical expertise to help with instrumentation and sensors. Finally, Edmentum's learning engineers bring expertise in experimental design and learning sciences, particularly within the context of online and adaptive instructional systems. They also have strong technical data skills. In some ways, their roles are akin to UX researchers—but with a focus on what learners are doing in a system to achieve learning outcomes (which Edmentum's psychometricians help measure). These learning engineers test hypotheses with data analyses and plan follow-up experiments to test additional hypotheses where needed. When it comes time to examine data analyses and decide on next steps, each of these roles has an important contribution to make.

Why so many different areas of expertise? While organizations may not use the same titles or organizational structure as Edmentum, interpreting analytic results requires consideration of a large variety of facets. Let's look at a simple example from Edmentum's archives.

SCENARIO

Here's the situation: The results from a formative assessment delivered immediately following online instruction are yielding a poor pass rate. In other words, students who are asked to demonstrate knowledge on a topic—on which they have just received instruction—aren't able to do so according to the measure provided to them. What's more, the pass rate is no better than the scores on the pre-test. This is a basic descriptive analysis, simply calculating the percent of students who pass the formative assessment. Yet the interpretation of those results benefits from different perspectives with far more effective resulting actions. For this simple example, a few roles are critical to the discussion:

Learning engineer: What are the potential causes of this result? Who should be consulted and what additional analyses should we pursue? What actions should we take as a result of this finding?

Learning designer: Is there evidence that the instruction could lead to confusion or doesn't address a common misconception? Is the skill being taught chunked properly? Are there elements of instruction that may be distracting or unintentionally increase cognitive load? Are there other pedagogical approaches for this instruction that may be more successful?

Content and assessment developers: Is the instructional content and the assessment content aligned so that the construct taught is the construct measured? Are there errors in the instructional or assessment content? Are the pre-test and post-test measuring the same construct?

Psychometrician: Is the passing score set properly to distinguish between students who have mastered the content versus students who haven't? Is there evidence any of the assessment content has multiple correct responses, a highly attractive distractor that may indicate a mis-key, a scoring issue that isn't correctly assigning credit to a correct response? Is there evidence of construct-irrelevant variance, for example, linguistic complexity incommensurate with a learner's profile, accommodations not being assigned for students who require them? Is there evidence students are speeding through the assessment, answering at random, or are otherwise disengaged? Are the pre-test and the post-test at the same level of difficulty?

Implementation consultant: Is there evidence teachers may be implementing the system in an unintended way, for example having the students take the assessment prior to instruction? Is this context, setting, or group of students unusual?

Software engineer: Is there an error in our calculation of a pass? In our attribution of formative assessment items to the skill?

UI/UX designer: Is there evidence of construct-irrelevant variance, for example, the submit button located in an unusual place? Do we need to include additional ways for students to engage in the instructional or assessment content, for example, universal design for learning.

As you can see, a very simple analysis can result in alternative hypotheses and possible investigations. If the focus of interpretation is too narrow, it is highly possible that an impactful revision is missed. In the scenario above, Edmentum took multiple actions, including internal process revisions to better target and align instructional and assessment content based on evidence-centered design principles, a UI update, and correction of mis-keyed assessment items. In addition, regular monitoring processes were established to allow for ongoing and continuous improvement.

As the analyses become more sophisticated, moving from descriptive to predictive and prescriptive analytics, it may become challenging for all participants to understand and interpret the analyses performed. However, the importance of bringing together a team for this interpretation isn't diminished and may even be more critical as the methods themselves (for example, deep learning) can yield less immediate transparency. Therefore, those engaging in generating the analytics should invest in simple and clear communication of methods and results such that all relevant roles can join the party.

[3]

Learning Analytics

For some kinds of learning, one-on-one tutoring works a lot better than group instruction. In 1984, Benjamin Bloom and his students found that learners tutored using a certain approach performed so much better that a student likely to get a 'D' based on classroom instruction might get an 'A' if tutored.

Great human tutors and teachers are "mind readers," able to infer in real time what a student is feeling (frustrated, board, engaged) based on close observation of posture and facial expressions. And by close observation, and through deep understanding of how people learn the topic at hand, they can infer what the learner might be thinking when faced with a problem. They can infer misconceptions or missed steps in the process by closely observing actions, reactions, and answers given.

The approach that Benjamin Bloom found was so successful with tutoring is called **mastery learning**. With mastery learning, the student must master the current learning objective before moving on to the next one. Bloom's dilemma was that the model of one-on-one human tutoring with mastery learning was too costly to implement at scale. Learning analytics may help solve that problem.

One thing that makes a difference in one-on-one tutoring versus group instruction is the amount of data available to the human tutor. A tutor can more closely observe one learner at a time. The classroom teacher must take in information about many students simultaneously. The better that a tutor can "read the mind" of students, the better feedback they can provide to guide the learner toward mastery.

Ryan Baker, a professor at the University of Pennsylvania, studies how data from online interactions can better be used to improve learning. Most of his research is with intelligent tutoring systems, but any learning experience will do if properly instrumented.

Ryan is the founder of the field of education data mining and a superstar in the field of learning analytics. His advice is to "have a data analyst [on your team] who knows something about education." He said the current data analysis tools make it easy to make a lot of mistakes and not understanding the context also leads to wrong conclusions.

Baker and his colleagues have figured out ways of using the kinds of data collected by tutoring systems like Duolingo and Khan Academy's practice exercises to gain real-time insights similar to those that human tutors have. This is possible without actually watching the learner. It can be done in some cases just using data from students' interactions with a touch screen or keyboard.

There's value in human tutoring that can't be replaced by a machine, but by using data from instrumented learning experiences, tutoring systems combined with human teachers/tutors are moving closer to the kinds of results that Benjamin Bloom observed with one-on-one human tutors. Data instrumentation and analytics can collect the data and provide feedback to learners directly or augment a teacher's ability to notice when a student needs a certain kind of feedback.

Real-time analytics used from instrumented classrooms (for example, using video) can be used to signal to an instructor when a student is bored or frustrated. It augments the human capability of the instructor to process data on many students in the classroom.

Over a decade ago, Ryan (among others) discovered ways of using transaction logs to detect when students were gaming the system in online intelligent

BIG DATA LEARNING ANALYTICS

Big data are extremely large data sets that may be analyzed computationally to reveal patterns, trends, and associations, especially relating to human behavior and interactions.* Data from instrumented learning experiences have created unprecedented opportunities for analytics to find patterns, predict outcomes, and gain insights for optimizing learning. For example, a set of techniques called **knowledge tracing** is used to model each learner's mastery of concepts or skills based on data collected from engagement with a sequence of learning activities. Knowledge tracing data can help provide learners with personalized feedback and can help learning engineers discover imperfections in learning experiences and opportunities for improvement.

When looking for patterns in big data, the raw data may have millions of transactions from thousands of learners and many variables. This may be too big to process efficiently. Big data analytics uses big data reduction methods to find patterns or features in the data most relevant to the previously identified challenge. For example, **dimensional reduction** reduces the number of variables by eliminating irrelevant properties or combining attributes into fewer variables. For example, analysis that involves location data with both city and zip code could reduce the size of the data set by eliminating one or both if the analysis is not concerned with location. In other cases, variables highly correlated can be combined, data with missing values eliminated, or features are extracted from a source data set into a derived data set for further analysis.

Machine learning is an application of artificial intelligence that provides systems the ability to automatically learn using algorithms and statistical models to analyze and draw inferences from patterns in data. In machine learning, data-driven predictions or decisions are based on a **training data set** used to develop the model, then a **validation data set** is used to tune the model and know when the model has had the right amount of training, finally a **test data set** is used to evaluate the final model.

For big problems that cannot be easily solved by one team, artificial intelligence engineers issue a global challenge called a shared task. The development of Natural Language Processing—the technology used by Alexa, Siri, and Cortana—advanced much more rapidly than it would have otherwise because of shared tasks. It is often about getting the right data into the hands of the people who can, and are interested in, solving a problem.

In learning engineering, the research team at Duolingo used a shared task to find out which learning algorithms could best predict what mistakes each learner will make in the future.† Anonymized lesson histories from millions of Duolingo learners made the research possible. In another shared task, participants started with English prompts and generated sets of plausible translations in five other languages. For evaluation, Duolingo provided sentences with handcrafted, field-tested sets of possible translations, weighted and ranked according to actual learner response frequency. These machine learning shared tasks helped advance the field overall while solving a specific challenge in Duolingo's learning engineering process of iterative improvement.

---

* "big data, n.1." OED Online. Oxford University Press, December 2020. Web. Retrieved Jan. 2021.

† https://venturebeat.com/2020/08/18/how-duolingo-uses-ai-in-every-part-of-its-app. Retrieved Jan. 2021.

DIG INTO BIG DATA AND LEARNING ANALYTICS AT RYAN'S FREE MOOC: BIG DATA IN EDUCATION

tutors, such as when they were doing practice problems. Just like students might ask a human tutor for help when they get stuck on a problem, they could ask the tutor for a hint. Within each problem, the tutor has a set of available hints that increasingly get closer to revealing the answer. Sometimes rather than putting in the effort to practice, students gamed the system by asking for hint after hint until the answer was given. Ryan and his colleagues used analysis of transaction log data to determine when asking for a hint is productive for learning and when it's counterproductive. Further research has examined what kinds of feedback helps bring about productive learner behaviors, and Ryan has also investigated interventions to help nudge learners away from gaming and other unproductive behaviors toward more productive learning behaviors.

In 2006, Ryan learned a hard lesson, that quantitative analysis doesn't tell the whole story. The intervention was a puppy character, Scooter the Tutor, displayed on the screen. "If kids use the software properly then Scooter would look happy, and he danced around. If they misused the software Scooter, looked sadder and sadder. Eventually if students had failed to learn and continued to game the system, Scooter would give them supplementary exercises that were different in kind but covered the same stuff they bypassed."

The idea was that it would reduce the incentive to game because there'd be a direct penalty for gaming. "So, we deployed it, and lo and behold it worked! The data showed that students gamed the system about half as much. And when students didn't game the system, they learned significantly more. Rather than falling further behind, which is what we'd seen in previous studies, they actually caught up to the students who hadn't gamed."

This looked like a big victory. Ryan documented the positive findings from his experiments in his doctoral dissertation and in journal articles.[7] But the data didn't tell the full story. For a solution to scale, people need to use it. In this case, it turned out, teachers and students didn't like Scooter. And that was a surprise. "The school system that we'd been working with didn't want to use it because the teachers didn't like it. And so we dug a little deeper. We actually asked, 'how did you like it,' 'how did it affect your learning,' 'what did you think about it?'"

By surveying students and teachers, the additional qualitative data revealed unfortunate truths about the scalability of the solution.

- "Students who never gamed, who only saw the happy dancing dog, said they liked it; they said it helped their learning, despite the fact that it didn't."
- Students who gamed the system, who the data showed benefited by the intervention, said they didn't like Scooter and that Scooter hurt their learning. "Now do I think they actually thought it hurt their learning? No. I think they didn't like it, but they were willing to tell us (and they probably told their teacher) that they thought it hurt their learning."

This speaks to the importance of human-centered design (as discussed in Chapter 3). The other thing Ryan and his team learned was that Scooter promoted bad behavior. "Scooter got really angry and caught fire. It wasn't meant to look like catching fire. It was meant to look like anger lines, but it looked like catching fire. And some of the middle school boys came up with this game that they played where they tried to see who could get Scooter to catch fire first."

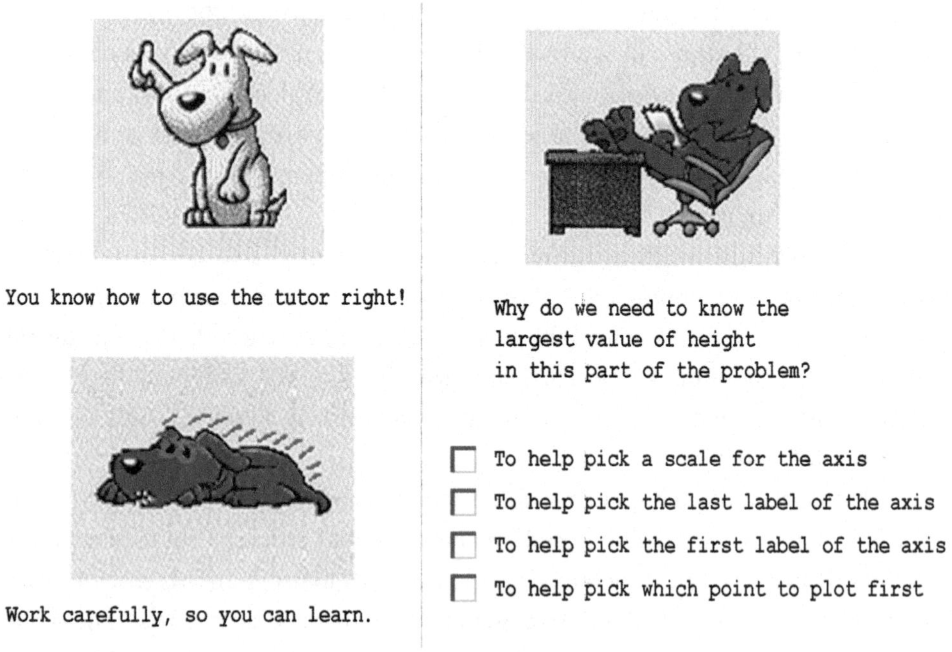

FIGURE 6.4. Scooter the Tutor—looking happy when the student hasn't been gaming harmfully (top-left), giving a supplementary exercise to a gaming student (right), and looking angry (unintentionally looking on fire) when the student is believed to have been gaming the system (bottom-left)

This is an example of data from an experiment showing that an intervention can be effective in the context of a small-scale experiment, but it can fail to scale due to contextual factors outside of the cognitive science. "It failed because we didn't consider the other dimensions of our solution and its adoption," Ryan told us.

There's an interesting postscript to this story, however, that emphasizes the importance of context. A key concept in the learning engineering process described in Chapters 1 and 2 is that learners are contextually situated. Part of that context is the culture of the school, organization, or community. After Ryan's initial development of Scooter the Tutor, researchers in other countries used translated versions of Scooter to run studies themselves. "In some countries, they liked Scooter and found him helpful. In some countries, the students never really got any interventions because everyone would go off and talk about the answer before they would even type it into Scooter. It was really fascinating—the diversity of ways that students in different countries respond to the same agent. That's another really interesting learning engineering challenge; we can't just assume that we build something once, in one context, and forever that's how it's going to be."

Data standards make it easier to create, share, and integrate data. They provide data integrity, accuracy, and consistency, clarify ambiguous meanings, minimize redundant data, and the means to document intended use and rules. To share, exchange, and understand data, we must standardize the format as well as the meaning.[8] See Chapter 14, Software and Technology Standards as Tools.

[3]

As a cognitive scientist at Carnegie Learning, Martina Pavelko was used to thinking deeply about the particular ways that students learn to solve math problems. The compendium of strategies, misconceptions, skills and feedback used to guide students through this process is part of the cognitive model that drives instruction in the MATHia intelligent tutoring system.

But now Martina was asked to look at this process from a different perspective. Carnegie Learning was going to try to simplify the process of creating these cognitive models in order to make them more accessible to new cognitive scientists, and to enable cognitive scientists focused on topics other than mathematics to create new content. Martina needed to introspect into her own process—and those of other cognitive scientists—to accomplish this task.

Martina had also earned a masters' degree in applied learning science, and she'd previously worked as a chemistry teacher. She brought the precision of a chemist to the task, and her academic preparation and years of teaching gave her the instinct to know what would work with students and be acceptable in the classroom.

Authoring tools used to create instructional content make assumptions about roles and responsibilities in the authoring process, and one particular challenge was deciding where to draw the line between writing the cognitive model (the general AI system that can guide students through solving math problems) and writing the content (the specific math problems that students will need to solve). Consider a particular word problem that a student could be asked to solve. Mathematical thinking and content are related; the story expressed in a word problem might lead to different misconceptions or strategic approaches than another, but writing a word problem requires a very different skill set than writing a cognitive model. A good word problem is written clearly and at an appropriate level for students, expresses a story that is interesting to students, and requires students to apply the appropriate mathematics.

A cognitive model is a descriptive or computational representation of human thinking about a given concept, skill, or domain for the purposes of comprehension and prediction. A cognitive model of learning, is an account of how humans gain accurate and complete knowledge.[9]

Martina quickly recognized that a key set of decisions for the new tool revolved around the relationship between cognitive model authoring and content authoring. In discussion with other cognitive scientists and engineers, she was asked what seemed to be a simple question: How many word problems do you need?

Martina's immediate answer was that standard practice was to write 200 problems for each topic. No student would ever do all 200, but this database of problems seemed to be enough to cover the different skills that students would need to learn within the domain of mathematics as well as to provide enough variety in the problem set that students sitting next to each other would not get the same problem.

Following standard practice was not a satisfying answer, and initial discussions with others focused on questions that reflected a mathematical approach to the problem: what's the probability that two students sitting together will be working on the same problem? How many problems per skill do we need and how does this question change for skills that tend to co-occur? MATHia's algorithm for picking problems for individual students is complex; it considers the student's past history, strengths, weaknesses and other factors, and characterizing the problem mathematically seemed difficult. Since they were focused on authoring tools for creating new content, it did not initially occur to them that existing data might help them understand this problem. Instead of focusing on new content, they decided to first understand better how their existing content was being used. Were there mathematics topics that needed fewer than 200 problems? Were there ones that needed more? More importantly, what factors influenced not only the number of problems needed but the variety?

Carnegie Learning hosts a biweekly **data jam**, a meeting where representatives of different departments—including Cognitive Science, Research, Engineering, Product Management and Marketing—get together to talk about difficult issues related to understanding or collecting data. At Carnegie Learning, data analytics is a team sport. Martina, along with Hao Li, a learning engineer in the research department, took the problem to the data jam. The meeting led to a different perspective on the problem. Instead of thinking about how many problems a topic needed, they started talking about problem use. The right number of problems (and the right distribution of problem types) should, ideally, lead to a situation where every problem is used equally often. Problems that address difficult skills, where students might need to complete ten problems to reach mastery need to be more frequent than problems that address easier skills, where students might need only three or four to reach mastery. By examining existing content, they discovered many cases where the problem bank was less than optimal. In several cases, there were some problems that were rarely used while others were used for almost every student.

Instead of focusing on new content, they decided to first understand better how their existing content was being used.

This project started with a focus on authoring tools for new content and did not initially focus on analytics on existing data, but the emphasis on data changed the project and the authoring process substantially. They moved toward a system where, instead of trying to author the complete problem bank up front, they author a minimal set of problems based on their assumptions about skill difficulty and other factors. When the system is delivered, they monitor the distribution of problem presentations to determine whether there are gaps in the problem bank that need to be filled.

[4]

In Chapter 4 we examined techniques used across fields of engineering. One of those techniques is building models. In creating tutoring systems, data are used to model things about the learner cognitive states such as the ability to recall some knowledge or do some skill. Models are also used to predict a learner's affective state or behaviors under given conditions. And models are used to predict how well a given learning activity will bring about a given learning outcome for a group of learners or an individual.

A big part of learning analytics applied to intelligent tutoring systems has to do with creating, testing, and tuning predictive or descriptive models. Remember when Bror Saxberg and the team at Kaplan found that studying eight worked examples was more effective than studying fifteen worked examples? They also found that fifteen worked examples were better than, for example, *zero* worked examples.

What if we want to predict the optimum number of worked examples? Figure 6.5 shows the three data points from which we can build a simple predictive model. With just three data points and reported margins of error in the data from the original study we will not be able to get an accurate prediction, but we can use those three points to illustrate the concept of predictive modeling.

WORKED EXAMPLES	POST-TEST SCORE
0	42.25
8	53
15	48.67

FIGURE 6.5. Data points from the Kaplan study

One way we can build a predictive model is to fit a curve onto the three points we have. The following analysis illustrates the concept of fitting known data points to a curve (a parabola). Remember the quadratic formula $y = ax^2 + bx + c$? We have three points that we can plug into three equations, and each equation has three unknown variables: *a, b,* and *c.* The quadratic function tool at mathepower.com can help us develop this model for the number of worked examples. And, interestingly, it also gives a worked example showing how to calculate the parabola formula from

You are looking for a quadratic function with points at:

- $x = 0, y = 42.25$
- $x = 8, y = 53$
- $x = 15, y = 48.67$

Mathepower found the following function:

$f(x) = -0.131\,x^2 + 2.39\,x + 42.25$

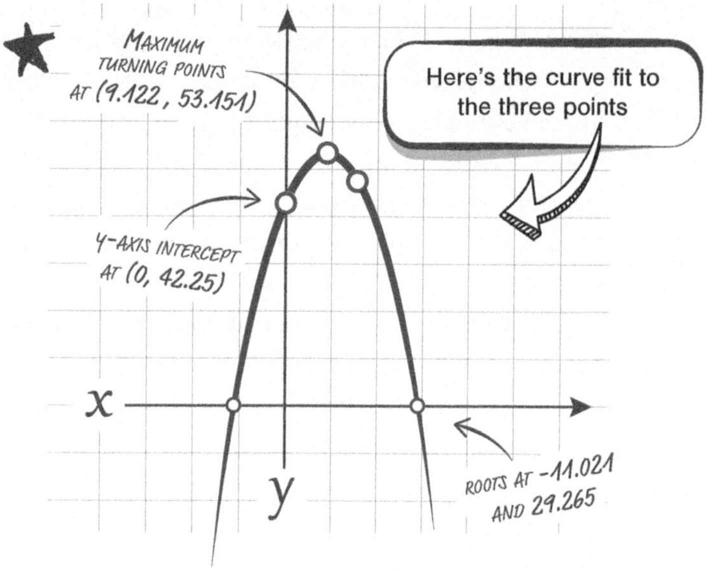

Here's a worked example showing how Mathepower calculated the function for the curve

$$f(x) = ax^2 + bx + 1c$$

THESE INPUTS	GIVE THESE EQUATIONS	AND SIMPLIFY TO THIS SET
Point (0, 42.25) is $f(0) = 42.25$	$0a+0b+1c = 42.25$	$c = 42.25$
Point (8, 53) is $f(8) = 53$	$1a \cdot 8^2 + 1b \cdot 8 + 1c = 53$	$64a + 8b + c = 53$
Point (15, 48.67) is $f(15) = 48.67$	$1a \cdot 15^2 + 1b \cdot 15 + 1c = 48.67$	$225a + 15b + c = 48.67$

THIS IS A SYSTEM OF 3 EQUATIONS WITH 3 VARIABLES, SO USING THEM TOGETHER, WE CAN SOLVE FOR A, B, AND C

225 divided by 64 = 3.516, so LINE-3 was multiplied by -3.516 times LINE-2 to cancel out the a variable in LINE-3

$c = 42.25$	LINE-1
$64a + 8b + c = 53$	LINE-2
$-13.125b + -2.516c = -137.658$	LINE-3

To isolate the a variable, LINE-2 was divided by 64

$c = 42.25$	LINE-1
$a + 0.125b + 0.016c = 0.828$	LINE-2
$-13.125b + -2.516c = -137.658$	LINE-3

To isolate the b variable, LINE-3 was divided by -13.125

$c = 42.25$	LINE-1
$a + 0.125b + 0.016c = 0.828$	LINE-2
$b + -0.192c = 10.488$	LINE-3

SUBSTITUTING THE KNOWN VARIABLES ACROSS EQUATIONS GETS: $a = 0.131$ $b = 2.39$ $c = 42.25$

INSERTING THOSE VALUES SHOWS THAT THE FUNCTION EQUALS: $f(x) = -0.131x^2 + 2.39x + 42.25$

FIGURE 6.6. Data points from Kaplan study plugged into the quadratic function tool at mathepower.com the three points! * Figure 6.6 shows the mathepower.com outcome.

The solved function serves as a model predicting that the optimum number of worked examples is about nine (9.122 to be more precise). We can see an estimate of that by looking at the peak of the graph. We can also predict the scores of students that study more or less worked examples by plugging the number into the formula or looking at the graph. What might someone score if they studied five worked examples? What about twenty?

But this is just a model, and models are not perfect. Testing the model with additional real data from learners' interactions is an important next step. With new insights from testing, we can iteratively refine the model. It would be expensive to test every possible option but data from testing even one or two additional conditions could give additional insights into the accuracy of the model.

We can also add parameters to the model to make it more precise and then test again, such as the time spent studying each worked example. We can A/B test various worked example features. With test data we can find outliers, such as learners who don't do as well with nine worked examples. And from that, we can iteratively test alternative activity designs or other conditions that might work better for those learners.

With machine learning, a kind of artificial intelligence, a predictive model may be trained using existing data that reflect the kind of variables. Chapter 18, Data Analysis Tools describes other kinds of predictive and descriptive models used in learning analytics and education data mining and techniques used to test those models.

[5]

Carnegie Mellon University has a large computer science and engineering cohort of students. Incoming freshmen have such variability in their math backgrounds that some struggle to hit the ground running in their first year as they attempt to catch up to their peers in the mathematics courses. This presented a challenge that learning engineering techniques could help address.

The Eberly Center for Teaching Excellence and Educational Innovation is a

---

* *Note: In this specific case the data points had margins of error showing levels of uncertainty about the measurement. Fitting a curve to uncertain points leads to uncertain predictions, but to illustrate a simple predictive model based on fitting to a curve we'll assume we have error-free data points.*

centralized campus office that helps faculty use learning science research, collect data, and "...design and implement meaningful educational experiences." In addition to the services offered by the Eberly Center, CMU has packaged its educational technologies into a toolkit that supports the spectrum from learning design through analysis and iterative improvement. This ecosystem of tools is called the OpenSimon Toolkit.

Using the OpenSimon Toolkit, Marsha Lovett, Director of the Eberly Center, worked with her learning engineering, data science, and computer science colleagues to solve the freshman math challenge. Specifically, they designed a set of self-paced modules targeting the prerequisite skills that incoming students lacked so that all students started with the same baseline competency. The system was also instrumented to provide data to faculty about the areas where new students might still be weak.

Marsha and her team built three modules and packaged them into a course called Discrete Math Primer. They used the **Open Learning Initiative** platform within OpenSimon; it's a kind of online textbook-replacement courseware. Each of the Discrete Math Primer modules targeted a primary math skill: logic, sets, or functions. Each module included practice and assessment questions that provided data about students' number of attempts, correctness, and need for hints. Pre- and post-tests measured learning gains in a summative fashion.

One way to model learning is using a **learning curve** that shows the rate of a person's (or group of people's) progress at learning a new skill over time. Learning curves show what we can't necessarily see with just the raw data. Using

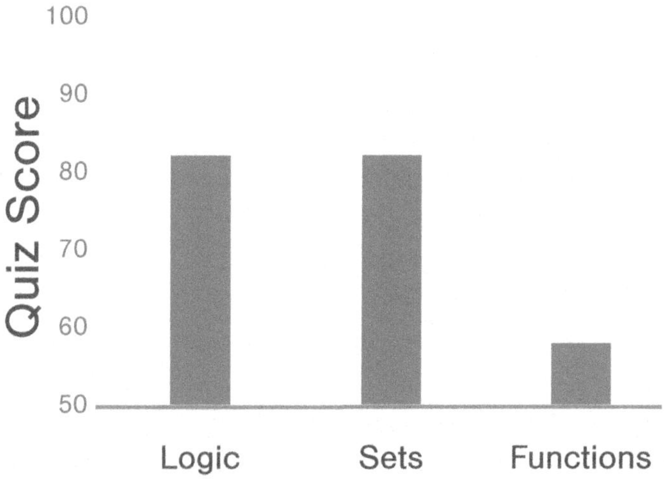

FIGURE 6.7.
2016 post-test data from CMU's Discrete Math Primer

LearnSphere[10] as a data repository and analysis infrastructure, and **DataShop**[11] analysis tools for generating learning curves, CMU could chart the learning or lack thereof taking place. These analyses also provided key information about which skills students needed more practice with as well as where there were holes in the analytics being collected.

The course was first offered to students in the summer of 2016. In the first delivery of the course, they found that students were generally improving, according to post-test data at the conclusion of the modules—except in functions. (See Figure 6.7.) However, using **learning curve analysis** on each individual skill, the data appeared to be more nuanced than this. The learning curves in Figure 6.7 provide a visualization of the data for two of the skills: logic and functions. The number of opportunities to practice a skill is shown along the x-axis, and the error rate is on the y-axis. With each attempt at practicing the same skill, the number of errors a student will generate should decrease.

Ideally, learning curves should generally look like the dotted line shown in the functions module graph on the right in Figure 6.8. It starts high and goes down in a smooth line. For the logic module learning curve (on the left of Figure 6.8), learning doesn't seem to be occurring—students aren't improving with this skill over time. And although the learning curve for the functions module looks better, it has some strange anomalies where the error rate goes back up, such as right before the fifth and fifteenth attempts. These anomalies show where learning isn't taking place as expected, but they don't tell us the causes of the anomalies. Finding the cause of the anomalies requires more investigation. It could be that learning can be improved by providing more practice opportunities for a given skill, more scaffolding in the course in the form of more or better instruction, or by breaking down the skills further to provide more practice opportunities in finer-grained skills. These are just a few of the next steps that were taken on this Discrete Math Primer.

With a few new refinements for the course identified, Marsha and her team went to work. They added more practice and feedback on targeted skills and improved the summative assessments. The improved course was delivered, and more data were collected and analyzed in the summer of 2017. This analysis and subsequent improvement provided even better results.

CMU departments were pleased. The changes to the course, targeting individual skills for improvement interventions, led to a significant increase in the students' understanding of functions.

But there was still room for iterative improvement. Data from subsequent courses showed that students were still struggling with transfer of the concepts to

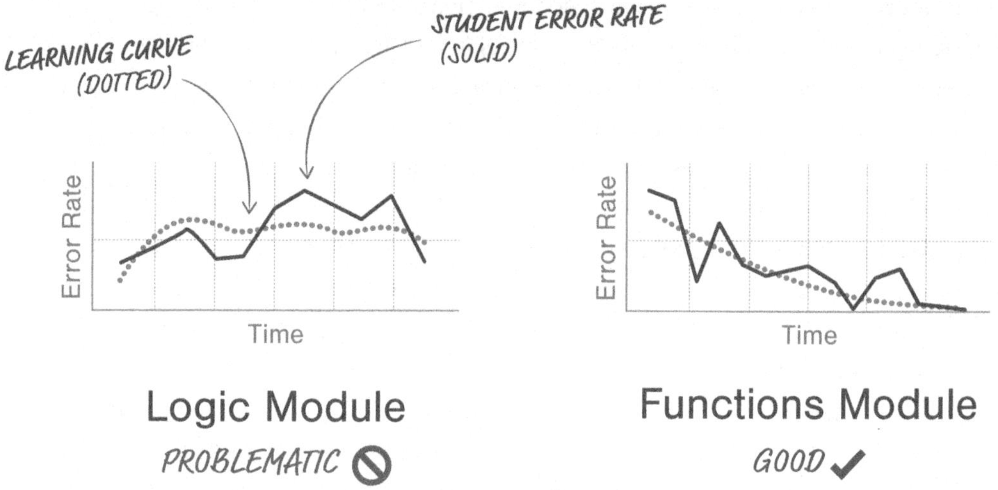

FIGURE 6.8. 2016 learning curve analyses from CMU's Discrete Math Primer. The right side shows that learning is taking place (as error rates fall over time), while the left side indicates an issue with the learning or assessment experience.

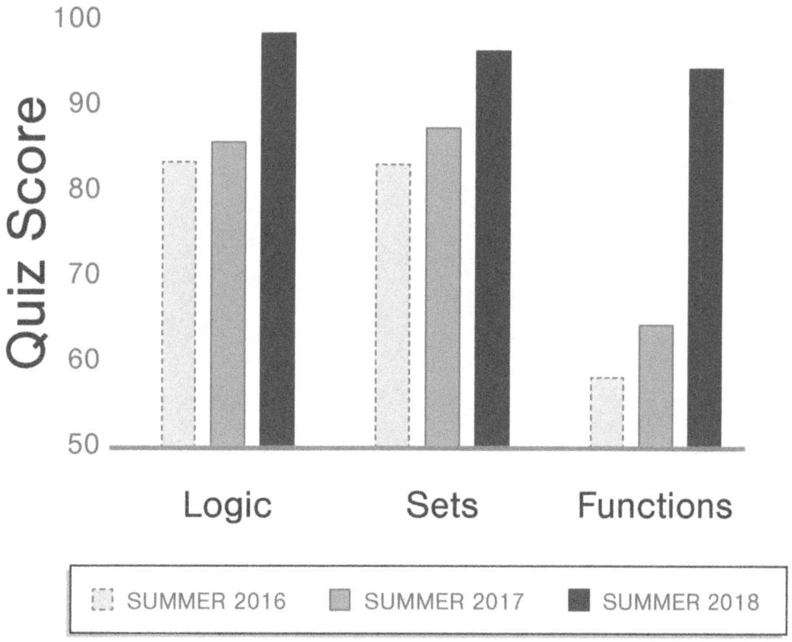

FIGURE 6.9. 2016–2018 post-test data from CMU's Discrete Math Primer

open-ended problems. Since open-ended questions are difficult to auto-grade in an online course, the next improvement step was to add cognitive tutor authoring tools to the course. These tools provides an interface for developing complex problems with multiple steps. By integrating them into the course, Marsha and her team were instrumenting it for finer-grained data collection during each step in a problem. For the students, cognitive tutors provide practice in individual skills, with feedback given with each step in a problem. The results of this iteratively improved course resulted in even more significant learning gains for the students, evidenced by the following year's post-test data. See Figure 6.9 for a comparison of the 2016, 2017, and 2018 course outcomes.

CMU's Discrete Math Primer is still in use today and is used by more faculty each semester. The success of this iterative problem solving also has resulted in the math faculty requesting more modules for their majors. Learning engineering processes have given the students a way to come up to speed with their peers, and the faculty a tool for supporting struggling students. ★

- Analytics, the systematic computational analysis of data, is central to the investigation phase of the learning engineering process.
- Data analysis is needed because human intuition is often wrong.
- Findings from the learning sciences can inform theories that can be tested by analyzing data from experiments.
- Research within learning engineering focuses on identifying highly contextualized findings about learning within specific products or conditions for specific learner populations.
- Learning engineering—and data analysis for learning engineering—is a team sport often requiring psychometricians, learning designers, content and assessment developers, implementation consultants, UI/UX designers, data scientists, software engineers, and product managers.
- Big data are extremely large data sets that may be analyzed computationally to reveal patterns, trends, and associations, especially relating to human behavior and interactions.
- Quantitative data doesn't always tell the whole story.
- Learning is contextually situated and so are the results of any experimental data.
- Data can be used to question existing practices and assumptions.
- In learning engineering, data are sometimes used to model things about the learner, to predict a learner's state or behavior under given conditions, and to predict how well a given learning activity will bring about a given learning outcome.
- Learning curve analysis shows a learner's progress at learning a new skill over time. One form of learning curve analysis measures error rates on assessment problems; as a person masters a skill their errors should go down.

Learning Engineering Uses Data (Part 2): Analytics

KEY POINTS

Endnotes

1 Brown, Jessie and Martin Kurzweil. "Engineering Learning at Kaplan University." *Ithaka S+R.* Last modified October 6, 2016. https://doi.org/10.18665/sr.284711

2 Saxberg, Bror. "Executing the Change to Learning Engineering at Scale." In Chris Dede, John Richards, Bror Saxberg (eds.). *Learning Engineering for Online Education: Theoretical Contexts and Design-Based Examples,* 1st ed. New York: Routledge, 2018, 166–193. https://doi.org/10.4324/9781351186193

3 Saxberg, "Executing the Change to Learning Engineering at Scale."

4 Saxberg, "Executing the Change to Learning Engineering at Scale."

5 Rudman, Larry, John Sweller, and David Niemi. "Using Cognitive Load Theory to Improve Logical Reasoning for the LSAT." In *Proceedings of 2013 Annual Meeting of the American Educational Research Association, San Francisco, CA, April 29, 2013*

6 Jones, Steve. "The Friendly Orange Glow: The Untold Story of the PLATO System and the Dawn of Cyberculture." *New Media & Society* 20, no. 11 (2018): 405–408. https://doi.org/10.1177/1461444818784306

7 Baker, Ryan S. "Designing intelligent tutors that adapt to when students game the system." PhD diss. Carnegie Mellon University, 2005. http://reports-archive.adm.cs.cmu.edu/anon/hcii/CMU-HCII-05-104.pdf

Baker, Ryan S., Albert T. Corbett, Kenneth R. Koedinger, Shelley Evenson, Ido Roll, Angela Z. Wagner, Meghan Naim, Jay Raspat, Daniel J. Baker, and Joseph E. Beck. "Adapting to When Students Game an Intelligent Tutoring System." In *Proceedings of the International Conference on Intelligent Tutoring Systems, Jhongli, Taiwan, June 26–30, 2006.* Berlin, Heidelberg: Springer. https://u1lib.org/book/774357/133d6d

8 Data Management. "Data Standards." US Geological Survey. Last modified May 3, 2021. www.usgs.gov/products/data-and-tools/data-management/data-standards

9 Lane, H. Chad. "Cognitive Models of Learning." In *Encyclopedia of the Sciences of Learning,* edited by Norbert M. Seel. Boston: Springer, 2012. https://doi.org/10.1007/978-1-4419-1428-6_241

10 "A Community Data Infrastructure to Support Learning Improvement Online." LearnSphere. Carnegie Mellon University, 2018. http://learnsphere.org

11 "DataShop @CMU: A Data Analysis Service for the Learning Science Community." Carnegie Mellon University. Last modified October 31, 2021. https://pslcdatashop.web.cmu.edu

12 Closing quotation sourced from Hey, Tony, Stewart Tansley, and Kristin Tolle, eds. "Jim Gray on eScience: A Transformed Scientific Method." In *The Fourth Paradigm: Data-Intensive Scientific Discovery.* Redmond, VA: Microsoft Research, 2009, xix.

People now do not actually look through telescopes. Instead, they are "looking" through large-scale, complex instruments that relay data to data centers, and only then do they look at the information on their computers.

– Jim Gray[12]

VALUES

CHAPTER 7

Learning Engineering is Ethical

by Jordan Richard Schoenherr*

An act has no ethical quality whatever unless it be chosen out of several all equally possible. – *William James*

What is Ethical in Learning Engineering?

Education and training are replete with questions of values and ethics.[1] For example, questions arise during instructional design and delivery about who should teach a course, what material will be covered, how that material will be presented, and how a learner's knowledge will be assessed. The answer to each of these will have value implications within, and outside of, the learning context. Additionally, a number of ethical issues define the learning context, including accessibility, copyright and intellectual property rights, learner privacy, and diversity.[2]

The value-laden nature of instructional design and learning engineering mustn't be overlooked.[3] In parallel, there has been growing recognition that the values of learners need to be incorporated into the process of design.[4] In other words, not only are the products of learning engineering value-laden, so too are its processes. Design decisions and other learning engineering activities should be informed by frameworks that consider values and ethics—from the perspective of learners, educators, and communities.

This chapter considers how to address ethical learning engineering in a principled, systematic manner. It offers an ethical sense-making approach and a practical framework for ethical sense-making in learning engineering.

* *The author would like to thank Jodi Lis for her insightful feedback throughout the writing process for this chapter.*

[1]

Ethics in the Learning Engineering Process

Using the learning engineering process described in Chapter 1, ethical considerations can be identified at each stage.

The challenge stage involves understanding the **ethical affordances** (or ethical features) of the problem space. This includes understanding the learner population, the technologies available to instructional designers and learning engineers, and the sociocultural context where learning will occur. At this stage, value-based design frameworks can be used to identify the general questions that should be asked during the design process and the appropriate means to assess the ethical affordances of a design. As well, learners themselves should be engaged to understand what values are important to them and how these values might be considered in framing the challenge.

In an iterative creation stage, learning engineers and instructional designers will begin to identify vulnerabilities in the design that result from bringing together early models and mock-ups, piloting assessment instruments and educational interventions. At this stage, a preliminary assessment of performance can help us determine whether specific design characteristics or features discriminate against some populations of learners. This assessment focuses on discrimination with respect to successful participation in designed activities, successful learning, and engagement and motivation responses with the learning activities and content (for example, level of challenge, connections to interest). Learning engineers must then consider how, or whether, to address these issues and be prepared to justify their decisions.

Adoption introduces other social and ethical concerns. Implementation may be carried out in unintended ways, leading to unintended unethical consequences. As well, during the implementation phase, the learning engineering team must consider information ethics, especially issues concerning privacy, consent, and user autonomy. These considerations must be incorporated into implementation design. This requires an understanding of a community, their relationships, and values. For instance, the requirements of privacy are not only determined by legislation but also by sociocultural traditions.

The investigation stage provides an opportunity to investigate possible improvements to the current solution and to potentially correct weaknesses in areas of value sensitivity. This is also a phase in which data are analyzed. Careful consideration should be given to avoid bias in interpretation of those data, in protecting learner privacy, and in interpreting the data through a lens of ethical sense-making.

Outside of the process model outlined in Chapter 1, we must also consider a parallel set of concerns for the technology ecosystem. As learning engineering technologies (for example, learning management systems, adaptive instructional systems) and approaches (for example, human-centered design, anti-discrimination design) become widely adopted, there will be competition and cooperation by individuals and organizations. Here, ethical questions will also play a key role. We must consider how technologies can be standardized as well as their transparency, their accessibility, and their interoperability. As technologies evolve, we must ensure that learners can access and understand their data and the methods used to create them by developing standards that reflect the best practices of learning engineering communities.

[2]

Ethics: From Principles to Practice

In both Eastern (for example, Confucius) and Western (for example, Aristotle) philosophical traditions, the discipline of ethics has been considered a competency. Virtues reflect qualities or traits that must be cultivated over time. Like any competency, ethical sense-making requires knowledge to identify the features of a situation that are *ethically* relevant. These features, or ethical affordances, don't necessarily exist objectively within the world. Rather, much like technical affordances, ethical affordances require an understanding of how an individual interacts with their environment. Even if a learning engineer considers the ethical affordances associated with the intended function of a product, unintended uses might introduce new ethical issues.

ETHICAL PRINCIPLES, NORMS, AND CONVENTIONS

Given their roles and responsibilities, prescriptive norms apply to learning engineers. Typically, these norms are defined in laws, codes of conduct, or guidelines. These norms can be defined for a specific knowledge domain, such as health professions education, or for a kind of product developed by learning engineers, such as adaptive instructional systems (AIS) or autonomous systems, more generally.[5]

As the multiplicity of principles suggests, although learning engineers might simply believe that the design process ends once a product, instrument, or process has been completed, they must also consider how their innovations are adopted by specific communities.

PROFESSIONAL CODES OF CONDUCT

Education, training, and engineering professions have available codes that consider social and ethical issues associated with instruction.

Education. Professional associations at all levels of education have adopted codes of ethics. For instance, the Association for Educational Communications and Technology's (AECT) *Code of Professional Ethics* presents a set of values that express a commitment toward learners, society, and their profession.[6] In terms of learners, ethical practice requires promoting independence in the pursuit of learners' goals, participation in educational programs, and protecting the rights (especially privacy), health, and safety of learners. In addition to these positive norms, the AECT code also emphasizes nonmaleficence in terms prohibiting actions related to stalking, bullying, harassment, defamation, and retaliation. Emphasis is also placed on the consideration of varying points of view, which suggests a recognition of the need to avoid personal biases. On a broader scale, the AECT also notes that instructional designers and educators need to differentiate between individual and organizational views, accurate representation and communication of educational issues to the public, and promotion of diversity. Similar principles have also been articulated by the National Education Association[7] and the International Society for Performance Improvement.[8]

Training and Talent Development. Paralleling approaches in academia, the learning and development (L&D) industry has also recognized the need to develop its own principles. For instance, the Association for Talent Development has developed a code of conduct that describes expected behaviors and practice that should occur in the context of professional training and development. Like other codes, it considers the personal, professional, and social obligations of talent developers. The order of the eleven values described in the code indicates priority, with "the rights and dignities" of the individual followed by the development of "human potential." The code also addresses issues related to privacy, copyright law, confidentiality, and professional integrity. The Talent Management Institute provides a more comprehensive list of twenty-eight values that prioritize "knowledge and compliance of the law," conduct with stakeholders, and upholding professional integrity followed by broad ethical issues, such as avoiding biases and prejudice, reporting misconduct, and assigning credit.[9] However, many of these values appear to overlap (for example, loyalty, prudence, care for clients, fair dealing with clients, and no misrepresentation). Many other codes of conduct and guidelines are also available that reflect extensions of organizational and business ethics.[10]

Engineering. Engineering fields also have professional codes that relate to general and specific affordances. For instance, the IEEE has identified nine ethical principles, including the safety and health of the public, avoidance of conflicts of interest, as well as treating individuals fairly while avoiding harassment. Given the breadth of the society's membership, technical affordances are only considered at a very general level. For instance, the fifth principle states that members should "seek, accept, and offer honest criticism of technical work, to acknowledge and correct errors, to be honest and realistic in stating claims or estimates based on available data, and to credit properly the contributions of others." Despite its generality, this principle and others place a high value on technical competencies.

In addition to its code of ethics, the IEEE has recently identified general principles to ensure ethically aligned design.[11] These principles are directed toward developing trustworthy autonomous and intelligent systems that support human values. They include human rights, well-being, data agency, effectiveness, transparency, accountability, awareness of misuse, and competence of designers. For instance, data agency requires that individuals have control over their identity and can securely share their data. Transparency requires that the processes used when processing data are discoverable; whereas awareness of misuse requires that preventative steps be taken to minimize risk and misuse of data.

Another notable set of principles has been developed by the Association for Computing Machinery (ACM). The ACM has identified three broad sets of ethical principles pertaining to general, professional, and leadership responsibilities. Both the structure and the content of the ACM code are notable. For instance, by specifying three levels of responsibility (as an individual, group member, and leader), the code addresses the specific demands of different roles. The ACM also adds several principles. For example, the principle of nonmaleficence (avoid harm) and beneficence (help) are fairly standard, but they also recognize that ethical issues can arise when modifying, retiring, and replacing systems.

Psychology. In that learning engineering is fundamentally about cognitive and social psychological processes, learning engineers should also consider principles developed in psychology. To address ethical concerns, the American Psychological Association (APA) has developed norms to encompass activities such as research, practice, and teaching. The APA has identified five equal principles that should "guide and inspire" the activities of psychologists.[12] As Figure 7.1 demonstrates, each of these has applicability to learning engineering. For instance, learning engineers shouldn't only consider design features in terms of the learning environment, learning algorithms, and the provision of feedback; they should also consider how these learning systems are implemented and the associated ethical implications. This is something we will return to below. Similar sets of norms have been adopted by other organizations (for example, the National Commission for Health Education Credentialing, 2020).[13]

NATIONAL AND REGIONAL STANDARDS AND GUIDELINES

In addition to organizational and professional codes of conduct, learning engineers must also be aware of national and international standards. Although a complete review of these is outside the scope of this chapter, a few notable frameworks are considered.

Ethical AI. At a general level, UNESCO has developed recommendations for the ethics of artificial intelligence noting that "living in digitalizing societies requires new educational practices, the need for ethical reflection, critical thinking, responsible design practices, and new skills, given the implications for the labor market and employability." [14] They identify four core values:

1. Respecting, protecting, and promoting human dignity, human rights, and fundamental freedoms
2. Recognizing and promoting environment and ecosystem flourishing
3. Ensuring diversity and inclusiveness
4. Living in harmony and peace

These values inform ten principles of systems design, including human oversight and determination, transparency and explainability, awareness and literacy, and multi-stakeholder and adaptive governance and collaboration.

Ethical use of personal information. Perhaps the most noteworthy standards for legal and ethical use of data are provided in the General Data Protection Regulation (GDPR), a regulation in European Union law on data protection and privacy in the EU and the European Economic Area. While it's law in the EU, it's also being used

PRINCIPLE	APA DESCRIPTION	LEARNING ENGINEERING EXAMPLES
Beneficence and Nonmaleficence	"Psychologists strive to benefit those with whom they work and take care to do no harm."	Learning engineers should develop learning and assessment methods and products that help learners and organizations. They shouldn't develop methods that are associated with the dissemination of disinformation or misinformation or misrepresent the state of knowledge in a domain. Learner data should be used only for the intended purpose, and learners must be aware of this purpose, providing valid consent.
Fidelity and Responsibility	"Psychologists establish relationships of trust with those with whom they work."	Learning engineers should ensure that they have the trust of their employers and their users. They should understand the obligations that they have to these parties and declare conflicts whenever possible. They should seek to minimize real, apparent, or potential conflicts of interests and respect intellectual property.
Integrity	"Psychologists seek to promote accuracy, honesty, and truthfulness in the science, teaching, and practice of psychology."	Learning engineers must engage in a process of knowledge translation to facilitate stakeholder understanding of learning engineering.
Justice	"Psychologists recognize that fairness and justice entitle all persons to access to and benefit from the contributions of psychology and to equal quality in the processes, procedures, and services being conducted by psychologists."	Learning engineers should develop products, processes, and services that are equally accessible to all, that recognize differences in social norms and culture, and that steward diversity of approaches and perspectives. Learning engineers should avoid working with any individual or organization associated with fraud, corruption, or human rights violations, for example, working with organizations that use slave labor. Learning engineers should respect democratic institutions that promote procedural fairness and social justice.
Respect for People's Rights and Dignity	"Psychologists respect the dignity and worth of all people, and the rights of individuals to privacy, confidentiality, and self-determination."	Learning engineering must promote the autonomy of the learner. Learners must understand the assessment context, be provided with tools that allow them to challenge it, and foster well-being. Learning engineering must ensure that learner data remain confidential, anonymous, and be protected. Learners should be informed of how their data are used, provided with applicable retention standards, and options for data erasure.

FIGURE 7.1. Excerpts from the APA principles and their applicability to learning engineers

as a guideline for ethical treatment of personal data in other countries. In the United States, the state of California adopted the California Consumer Privacy Act that has similar provisions to GDPR.

A significant issue raised in this framework is the so-called "right to be forgotten." The guideline states that "[a] data subject should have the right to have personal data concerning him or her rectified and a 'right to be forgotten' . . . "[15] Similar requirements have been echoed in learning engineering, in terms of standards for integrated/comprehensive learner records.

Governmental and nongovernmental organizations have also suggested ethical design principles. For instance, the United Kingdom developed *Government Design Principles* that include considering users' needs, using available data to inform design, consistency (rather than uniformity), ensuring broad accessibility of design, and understanding the context of use.[16] Similar approaches have been adopted elsewhere too. For instance, the community-driven *Principles for Digital Development* defines broadly applicable tenets including closing knowledge gaps in communities and presenting data in an easily accessible format as well as diverse, responsible, and rigorous data collection and use practices.[17] Finally, perhaps the most innovative example is the *Guiding Principles of the Internet of Education.* The group who developed the principles frames their approach as an "ongoing conversation across a global community of practice."[18] The ten principles are:

1. One open internet of education
2. Distributed governance
3. Effective collaboration
4. Open standards
5. Open participation
6. Proportional influence
7. Diversity, equity, and inclusion
8. Data dignity
9. Agency and access control
10. Life-long learning

These principles create a framework that aligns with many learning engineering ethical ideals, such as open standards and participation, proportional influence (number and diversity of learners), the promotion of life-long learning, and decentralized control to support sharing between stakeholders.

[3]

Ethical Sense-Making for Learning Engineering

An ethical sense-making approach to learning engineering can be defined by principles that incorporate actionable strategies.

- **Design requires ethical sense-making.** Designing ethical systems and conditions for learning requires we acknowledge that the environments we work in are often ambiguous. Even when we're familiar with their features, we must question our assumptions. As designers, we must consider both the affordances that liberate users and the anti-affordances that constrain their actions. We must also consider whether specific groups of learners will experience more rewards or costs than others. Ethical sense-making should be promoted through design, empowering users to think clearly and critically.
- **Design affects communities.** Engineering designs are human artifacts. They're both tools and symbols. Learning engineering teams must consider the impact of their designs on communities. Community engagement is essential. Understanding how a community sees itself, how they see others, and the community's needs, as well as their deep sociocultural and linguistic traditions, takes time, respect, humility, and deference.
- **Learning engineering affects individuals.** Designs affect individual users, who are each a unique combination of traits, strategies, and personal histories. Designs must promote learners' understanding of the systems and processes they're using. Designers must ensure that users can critically challenge both technical and ethical affordances of a design by promoting autonomy.
- **Learning engineers are community leaders.** Depending on the needs of a community, the role of a learning engineering team will vary. Regardless, designers must acknowledge that they are responsible for their design—its use, disuse, and misuse. They must be accountable to their stakeholders.
- **Learning engineers will experience conflicts of commitments.** Participants in the learning engineering process are embedded in multiple communities. As professionals, we have commitments to our professions. As employees, we have commitments to our organizations. As educators, we have commitments to our students. As persons, we have commitments to our community. Conflicts of interest are inevitable. They must be declared and mitigated. Team members must be conflict competent.

- **Learning engineers are advocates.** Wherever possible, designs and algorithms within a learning engineering solution should be transparent. Both the affordances and anti-affordances of a design should be made clear to users. Transparency always will be relative to the competency of the individual and the community. Designers must be advocates and leaders for social and ethical issues. They must engage in knowledge translation between communities.

FRAMEWORK FOR APPLYING ETHICAL SENSE-MAKING IN THE LEARNING ENGINEERING PROCESS

An approach for ethical sense-making in learning engineering is shown in Figure 7.2. First, the APA's principles are adopted as a starting point because they address the kinds of situations learning engineers will encounter in most experimental and applied settings. Next, these principles are applied to the stages of the learning engineering process. The corresponding matrix requires that teams consider how each ethical principle is presented at each stage by asking a series of corresponding questions. (See Chapter 17 for the detailed application of this approach.)

Principle	Challenge	Creation	Implementation	Investigation
Beneficence and Nonmaleficence				
Fidelity and Responsibility				
Integrity				
Justice				
Respect for People				

FIGURE 7.2. Sense-making Ethical Evaluation Matrix (SEEM) for Learning Engineering

[4]

Ethical Examples from Health Care Education

When people think about the health care professions, white lab coats, stethoscopes, prostrate patients, and a caricature of the Hippocratic Oath (*do no harm*)[19] likely come to mind. Beyond these stereotypes, the health care professions are defined by specific professional competencies and guided by numerous legal and professional standards. For instance, the Canadian Medical Association Code of Ethics defines a set of virtues (compassion, honesty, humility, integrity, and prudence) that should inform decision-making inclusive of patients' values and experiences. Health care professions are expected to use this code to inform every area of practice, including medical education.

Health care and health care education often involve uniquely challenging situations that illustrate **boundary conditions**[20] for ethical sense-making (see Figure 7.3). For example, medical training sometimes requires the use of donated human remains.[21] Here, values and ethics range from codes of conduct (see the left side of Figure 7.4) to more symbolic gestures of respect. For instance, the University of Ottawa has erected monuments to donors (refer to the right side of Figure 7.4), holds an annual commemorative service for families of donors,[22] and publicly acknowledges these contributions with medals of recognition. Although symbolic, "loved ones, who sometimes feel their altruistic gifts go unnoticed, cherish this concrete form of appreciation."[23]

Educators in the health care professions might be aware of ethical issues in ways that may not be immediately clear to other teachers and trainers. Even so, they can still miss some ethical considerations. On occasion, I sometimes collaborate with health educators. Two case studies from that experience illustrate examples of ethical blind spots in education related to learner participation in studies and the recognition of the contributions of others.

LEARNER PARTICIPATION IN STUDIES

In health professions education, activities are often first designed as a means to develop a competency (a hypothetical set of knowledge and skills) in learners. Educators might decide to conduct educational studies as a secondary objective. However, I've found that they didn't always perceive the ethical affordances of the situation

ETHICAL BOUNDARY CONDITIONS

The term **boundary condition** is used in the social sciences as well as in the physical sciences, mathematics, and engineering. Boundary conditions specify situations in which relations between variables change depending on the values of other variables. Boundary condition in ethics reflects the extremes of object or entity. Defining boundaries in the case of categories of objects (rather than physical entities) can be extremely problematic. For instance, when determining a boundary, we might attempt to differentiate between ethical and unethical behavior by identifying a set of criteria, such as what causes more good than harm or what contains more features associated with good or bad behavior.

In practice, "good" and "bad" behaviors overlap such that in one set of circumstances an action might be correct, while in another, the same behaviors might be incorrect—like stealing to support one's family versus stealing to advance one's position. In practice, this creates a region of uncertainty that can result in ambiguity and misclassification, as shown in Figure 7.1. Depending on the individual and circumstances, this region can be larger or smaller.

FIGURE 7.3.A. Simplified general model of ethical decision-making

In mathematics and engineering, the boundary conditions are a set of conditions that must be satisfied to solve a boundary value problem. A solution to a boundary value problem is a solution that also satisfies the boundary conditions. Figure 7.2 illustrates a boundary value problem.

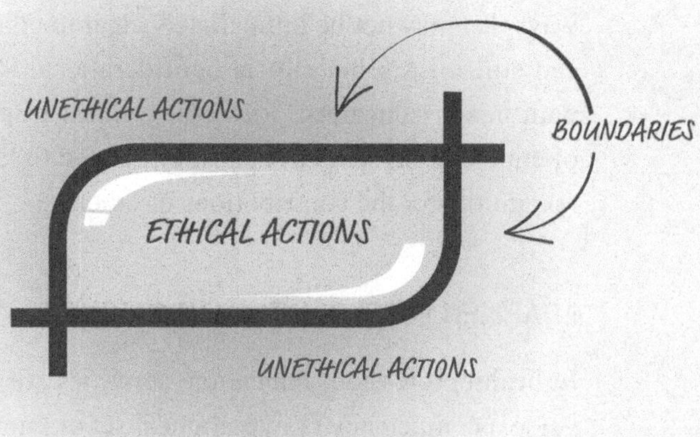

FIGURE 7.3.B. Illustration of a boundary value problem for ethical actions

in the same way that I did. For instance, in a few cases, I had to ask colleagues to request an ethics review for their educational studies.

For these educators, if education research didn't include patients, research ethics approval often consisted of a short review and a waiver. My concerns also stemmed from my background. In contrast to many of my medical colleagues, I focused on obtaining informed consent and recognizing that the learner might feel pressured to participate in a study or simply fail to withdraw from a study because they were already enrolled in the course.

Thus, while informed consent was a principle that both my colleagues and I shared, I found that those educators didn't understand its application in this context. Much like the notion of behavioral traces, they viewed learners' data as byproducts of the educational activity. Consequently, they considered the ethical implications with a different disciplinary lens. In addressing these concerns, my colleagues became aware of the ethical implications. Thus, whether working in a multidisciplinary team or with diverse groups of stakeholders, identifying issues related to values and ethics can be quite revealing.

Code of Conduct in the Anatomy Laboratory

...2. Fulfill the expectations of the donors and honor their wishes by studying the bodies with purpose and respect. Treat the donated bodies and prosections as you would wish your own body, or that of a member of your family, to be treated.

3. All donated bodies and prosections should be handled with respect. Neither the donated bodies nor any parts thereof are to be positioned or displayed in inappropriate, comical or obscene manners.

...6. NO unauthorized photographs from mobile devices or digital camera are ever to be taken...

FIGURE 7.4. Excerpts from McGill anatomy laboratory code of conduct (left). Monument commemorating individuals who donated their remains (right). Inscription: "In memory of those who have generously given their body for the advancement of science and medical education."

Credit: Faculty of Medicine, University of Ottawa

RECOGNIZING THE CONTRIBUTIONS OF OTHERS

Ethics in instructional design and learning engineering requires recognizing the contributions of all stakeholders. In medical simulation centers, many tasks use existing training systems. (See Figure 7.5, left.) Training sessions that use these materials tend to focus on the development of team decision-making and communication skills. Instructional designers in health professions education often assumed that the use of these technologies was sufficient to promote the acquisition of complex skills. However, many novel training tasks were created to address more foundational skills. In many cases, elegant training solutions were developed by technicians that worked at the simulation center at the request of clinicians. Many of these training tasks were exceptionally novel, using a variety of materials and techniques, for example, multi-layer synthetic tissue models with shampoo packets to model abscesses. (See Figure 7.5, right.) In many cases, technicians described the design and developmental process in a manner that suggested their autonomy, with little to no input from the clinicians. However, other than interpersonal expressions of thanks, technicians were often not formally acknowledged as contributors in instructional design in publications or presentations.

During a formal presentation about the ethics of contribution in research, I observed these value conflicts directly. I used the lack of acknowledgment as a talking point to illustrate how junior team members, students, and technicians are

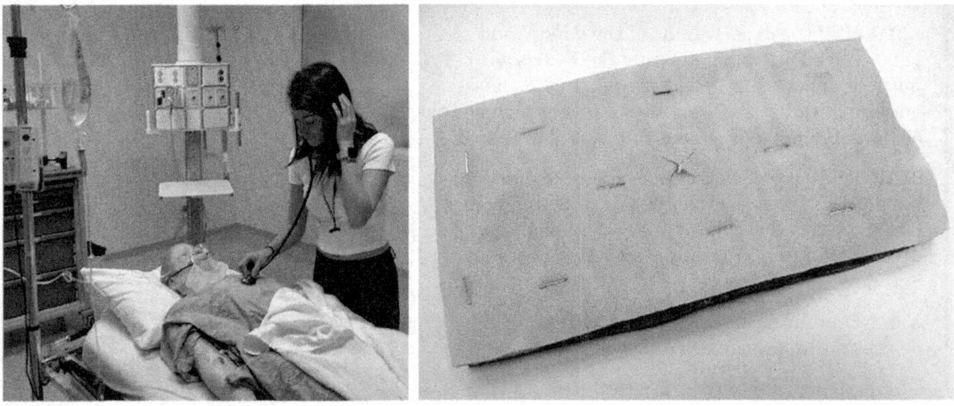

FIGURE 7.5. Research assistant demonstrating the simulation environment with a mannequin located in a full-scale model of an emergency room (left). Sample of a used synthetic tissue abscess model (right). The model consists of synthetic skin (rubber), foam, shampoo packets, and duct tape and staples to secure the layers. Learners probe the sample to find the location of the abscess, make an incision, palpate, and clean the synthetic wound.

Credit: Jordan Richard Schoenherr

often overlooked. A clinician sitting in the audience quickly put up their hand and confidently asked in a rhetorical manner "Why would *we* put their [technicians'] name on a paper? We pay them." In the case of this clinician, thanks and remuneration were appropriate forms of recognition for the contributions of technicians whereas authorship was reserved for others. Following the discussion, I was tentatively approached by other clinicians. They thanked me for raising and discussing concerns about the need to recognize team members even though it was a taboo topic. Similar concerns can also arise in student-educator projects wherein differing expectations can lead to inappropriate recognition.[24]

[5]

Ethical Sense-Making

The existence of a plurality of ethical frameworks, guidelines, and codes highlights the fact that ethics requires more than mere compliance with a set, or sets, of principles. Learning engineers must interpret these principles, resolve conflicts between different (often incommensurable) values, identify ethically relevant features of a situation, and consider how relational structures can impact learning and decision-making. They must engage in an ethical sense-making process and be conscious of the ethical dimensions of instructional design.[25]

There's a great temptation to address ethical concerns *after* we've designed a course or instructional technology. Research suggests that we often rationalize our ethical intuitions.[26] Ethical sense-making requires considering moral reasoning abilities, the effects of stress and divided attention of moral judgments, and situational factors that determine what values are made accessible by features of the environment.[27] A few general features of ethical sense-making should be considered when engaging in learning engineering in that they affect the judgments of learners, instructional designers, and academic administrators:

- **Moral development is thought to progress through three broad stages: children are driven by punishment and reward, teens and young adults by adherence to social conventions or those of society, whereas adults can use ethical principles.** Ethical principles can reflect a focus on utility, deontological principles, or care. These are the kinds of principles embodied in professional standards and guidelines. However, not everyone successfully progresses through these stages.[28]

- **Failures of attention and time limitations can lead us to neglect values and ethics.**[29] For instance, researchers suggest that when individuals are completing a task and don't believe their performance is being monitored, they're more likely to attempt to deceive evaluators. However, reminders of codes of conduct immediately before a task can increase academic integrity.[30] Sharing is also promoted when individuals believe they're being monitored[31] whereas the experience of anonymity can increase in antisocial behaviors.[32]
- **Similar norms and conventions are evidenced across cultures.** Cross-cultural values fall into two distinct clusters based on individual-focused (care and fairness / proportionality) and group-focused moral motivations (authority, loyalty, and sanctity / purity).[33] Contextual factors and group influence can determine which norms are relevant at any given time.[34] However, individuals often tend to devalue members of other groups when considering ethical responses.
- **Psychological studies have also demonstrated that even if we apply certain norms to our group, we do not necessarily apply them to others.** Learners and educators use social categories and identities to understand the learning environment.[35] The mere mention of sex or race before a task can lower a learner's performance. This is further supported by studies of academic impostor syndrome that demonstrate some learners don't feel they deserve their achievements.[36]
- **Engaging in effortful reasoning doesn't guarantee moral behavior.** Reasoning can be associated with *less* ethical behavior.[37] These findings suggest that individuals often *rationalize* choices based on their affective responses.
- **Empathy is an important factor in determining moral judgments.**[38] Factors that promote empathy tend to increase helping behavior. In contrast, when individuals are directed toward thinking about abstract values (for example, monetary incentives), they tend to request and give less assistance. For instance, research suggests that framing a task as a business game[39] reduces collaboration relative to when a task is framed as a community game.[40]

Learning engineering teams must take these factors into consideration. Factors that decrease ethical behavior, such as anonymity, divided attention, ambiguous ethical standards, and rationalization, can present challenges for both learners and learning engineers. In that many of these biases might be implicit for learners and educators, they require specific consideration during the design process.[41] By adopting an ethical sense-making approach to design, we can take these factors into consideration.

[6]

Ethical Examples from Everyday Education

I was once approached by a student who wanted to discuss concerns they had about the lecture content. In the lecture, I presented a brief (anonymized) story of an acquaintance of mine who struggled with a particular mental health issue to illustrate the diversity and complexity of human behavior and the ubiquity of such concerns. When they spoke to me, the student stated that they felt the discussion misrepresented the mental health issue, making reference to inappropriate, normative standards. Moreover, they felt that the discussion of psychological disorders was inappropriate in academia because it might cause students psychological distress. These kinds of discussions are growing in number as the roles of learners and educators are being negotiated. They illustrate the need to understand the value of ethical sense-making in the daily business of academia.

At the core of ethical sense-making is the need to understand context. Simply identifying a conflict in values isn't sufficient for resolving the issue. In this case, further discussion provided considerable insight into the source of the student's concerns. First, the student indicated that they had personal, ongoing experience dealing with mental health issues. They acknowledged that these particular issues were emotionally charged. Second, they had in fact misattributed something stated in the textbook to my lectures, a general psychological phenomenon referred to as failure of source monitoring. After I listened to and acknowledged the student's perspective, the student thanked me for hearing what they had to say, noting that not all lecturers had done so in their experience. The student acknowledged their reaction and that they understood my intent. I also reinforced that students should feel comfortable raising their concerns, additionally noting that these topics were within the scope of the course and should be addressed in academia.

In this case, the simple act of gathering more information to understand someone else's perspective, to empathize with the student, promoted interpersonal respect and allowed for the discussion of sensitive issues. By listening, educators not only support dialogue, but they can also gain an understanding of how learners approach the material and adapt their courses. This incident also illustrates that educators can't be complacent in terms of how material is presented to students. They must address aspects of the textbook or other learning resources and clearly distinguish between personal and academic perspectives of both learners and educators. Beyond these issues, instructors also must ensure that they take into consideration potential differences in cultural norms for interactions between students and instructors. What might be perceived as disrespectful behavior (for example, question course content, curt emails) might not be perceived as such by the student.

[7]

Ethics in Assessment and Design

Learning engineering requires a framework that addresses both the underlying technical and value-laden dimensions of design. This framework must be applicable to traditional approaches to pedagogy and assessment as well as more advanced learning technologies that reflect adaptive or intelligent learning systems.

ETHICAL ASSESSMENTS

Samuel Messick developed a general value framework for use in assessment.[42] (See Figure 7.6.) He acknowledged that the development of training and assessment instruments has always been informed by values. In contrast to earlier frameworks, Messick assumed that construct validity was the principal means to evaluate the utility of instructional design and assessment. The foundation of assessment reflects an instrument's construct validity in terms of the amount and kind of evidence as well as whether it reflects a representative sample of the information and processes associated with the competency of interest.

Concurrently, we must also consider whether an assessment instrument is suited for its purpose. For instance, a five hundred–item assessment might have considerable construct validity supporting its use but might not feasibly be implemented within an organizational context due to the time required for its completion. Messick also stressed the need to understand the broad value implications of an assessment instrument. For instance, high or low scores could result in promotion or termination within an organization or in a student passing or failing a course. These reflect value judgments about whether an employee or student is good or bad. Finally, Messick suggests that we go further to consider the social consequences of our assessment. For instance, a test can be used to classify and label someone with a learning disability that could result in changes in their social status.

	Test Interpretation	Test Use
Evidential Basis	Construct Validity	Construct Validity + Relevance / Utility
Consequential Basis	Construct Validity + Value Implications	Construct Validity + Relevance / Utility + Value Implications + Social Consequences

FIGURE 7.6. Facets of Construct Validity

Adapted from Messick (1995)

VALUE-BASED DESIGN

Complementing value-based approaches to psychometrics are valued-based approaches to design. Here, we consider four broad approaches that attempt to integrate user-centered design frameworks: value sensitive design, reflective design, design justice, and anti-discrimination design.

Value Sensitive Design. Friedman and colleagues define **value sensitive design** as "a theoretically grounded approach to the design of technology that accounts for human values in a principled and comprehensive manner throughout the design process."[43] Values must be included throughout the iteration of the design process (outlined in Chapter 1), which incorporates conceptual, empirical, and technical aspects of the process. According to value sensitive design, the three kinds of investigations can be defined as:

- **Conceptual**: Specifying the fundamental values that are relevant to design, thereby providing a common point of comparison for all members of a design team
- **Empirical**: Using qualitative and quantitative methods adopted from the social sciences to examine how technology works within the implementation context
- **Technical:** Examining the extent to which specific technologies support or interfere with the realization of human values (retroactive analysis) or design technologies to support values that have been identified within the conceptual design phase

The value sensitive design approach incorporates many elements of ethical sense-making in that it considers the ethical affordances of a system. These aspects of design have become increasingly important given that the exploitation of users' patterns of behavior has become increasingly apparent.[44] Although the practical outcomes of adopting a value sensitive design approach might align with ethical sense-making, designers should make more deliberate attempts to identify how social and cognitive processes are impacted by specific design decisions.

Reflective Design. An alternative approach, referred to as **reflective design**, stresses "analysis of the ways in which technologies reflect and perpetuate unconscious cultural assumptions, with design, building, and evaluation of new computing devices that reflect alternative possibilities."[45] This approach consists of six principles and design strategies shown in Figure 7.7.

PRINCIPLES	STRATEGIES
Reflection is required to critically identify what values are embedded within a design, what values are comparatively neglected, and what methods can be used to address marginalized values	Ensure that users can take responsibility for and control the meaning-making process when engaged with socio-technical systems
Reflection should be used by designers to understand their assumptions and role within the design process	Engage users in the design process to develop a digital scaffolding that facilitates their comprehension of new concepts and new system features
Designers should facilitate users' understanding of their relationship with technologies	Use feedback collected from or about users as input into the system or to help guide the evaluation of a system
Skepticism should be promoted, enabling users to critically consider how technology affects their choices and behavior	Users' feedback should be collected and used through the design process, rather than at the end
Acknowledge that reflection and action are not mutually exclusive	Systems should be used in an analogous manner to experiments
Mutual engagement of designers and users in the development and use of technologies can facilitate reflection	Consider a variety of metaphors adopted from different disciplines to understand the design space

FIGURE 7.7. Principles and strategies for reflective design

Adapted from Sengers et al. (2005)

In its critical approach to design, the reflective design process embodies a number of features of ethical sense-making. Rather than adopting a designer-centered approach wherein a designer "[stands] aloof, benignly passing down opportunities for reflection," reflective design suggests that technologies should be designed to engage designers and their users in a continuous process of meaning-making. Thus, the basic features of ethical sense-making can be used in the process of reflective design to direct designers to vulnerabilities they face in engaging users in effortful reflection on their relationships with technology.

Design Justice. Perhaps the most critical approaches to design are the **design justice** principles (also discussed in Chapter 3). Described as a living document, the principles are directed toward reformulating and restructuring the design process, including the role of the designer and other stakeholders.[46] Designers are referred to as facilitators rather than experts and assume that the lived experience of all stakeholders makes them experts. A central feature of the theory that informs design justice is that design can reinforce existing biases. For instance, when learners are forced to choose a response on a multiple-choice question, a design necessarily limits the correct response, failing to consider why learners selected an alternative response. In many cases, learners might simply be wrong. However, the response alternatives selected by an instructional designer might reflect cultural biases. Within clinical psychology, the pathologizing of homosexuality in early versions of the *Diagnostic and Statistical Manual* presents such an example.[47] If learners are presented this information in a course and a corresponding question on a test, they would be required to respond in a manner that runs counter to their beliefs.

Instead, much like reflective design, design justice assumes that the goal of design should be to empower, sustain, and heal communities. Consequently, communities should be seen as the leaders and controllers of a collaborative design process that attempts to use existing approaches that are well-adapted to the community and to offer new, nonexploitative design solutions. These principles represent an important framework. However, like all frameworks that have a number of values, conflicts can arise.

Anti-discrimination Design. The final framework that we will consider here is referred to as **anti-discrimination design**. Like design justice, it takes as its focus discriminatory practices that might be embedded within the design. It additionally provides a useful typology of three classes of design features:

- **Non-Affordances and Poor Affordances:** Non-affordances reflect a failure to include affordances that are apparent to the user. Rather than reflecting a design failure, they reflect an absence of specific features. In contrast, poor affordances are perceived by the user but lack a clear identification of what the features do, for example, bad design.

- **Discriminatory Non-Affordances and Poor Affordances:** Non-affordances and poor affordances that result in a disadvantage (or advantage) given to a specific set of users. These issues arise when examining design from the users' perspective. For instance, if auditory cues are used as an affordance, the design will disadvantage individuals with hearing impairment.
- **Disaffordances and Dysaffordances:** These issues arise when examining design from the users' perspective. Disaffordances fail to recognize relevant user identity groups. Dysaffordances additionally require unaccommodated users to misrepresent themselves. For example, learners using an online learning application might be forced to select a specific disability, gender, or racial category due to an absence of other options.[48]

Crucially, the anti-discrimination design framework also emphasizes the importance of stewardship associated with the role of designer or engineer. For instance, D. E. Wittkower notes that:

> . . . even if a developer team somehow were absolutely diverse, absolutely self-aware, and absolutely politicized, such a strategy for anti-discriminatory design wrongly implies that the socially privileged designer has neither ability nor responsibility to engage in anti-discriminatory design. In other words, a developer working on her own should not excuse herself from the responsibility to attempt to think through diverse user experiences.[49]

VALUE-BASED DESIGN AND ETHICAL SENSE-MAKING

At their core, value sensitive design, reflective design, design justice, and anti-discrimination design share features with an ethical sense-making approach. Namely, designers must consider the mental models of the members of the communities learning engineering will impact. Rather than limiting themselves to the technical features that they, and users, perceive within a system, they must consider the ethically relevant features of a system. This requires understanding what learners and their community perceive as a value. Designers often will find themselves in ethically ambiguous or ambivalent situations. For instance, designers will potentially be faced with value conflicts, for example, communities might not wish to accept certain members, they might wish to promote values that are at odds with those of the designer, or human rights. Most troubling, designers might be faced with the decision of compromising on certain values to assist with a community. By adopting an approach based on ethical sense-making, instructional designers and learning engineers can reflect on how they have included values within design as well as how their design choices can create affordance and anti-affordance. ★

Although learning engineers might simply believe that the design process ends once a product, instrument, or process has been completed, they must also consider how their innovations are adopted by specific communities.

- Ethical decision-making occurs at every learning engineering stage.
- Learning engineers must consider values and ethics while selecting the content, pedagogical approaches, assessment strategies, and content delivery methods as well as throughout the learning engineering process, such as during design or experimentation. Many situations might seem ethically ambiguous or neutral in the absence of reflection.
- Learning engineers must consider how the learning context can impact learning performance and perception. They must consider learner community values as well as the physical and social environments of the implementation context.
- Professionals who engage in learning engineering are guided by professional codes of conduct as well as national and international guidelines that contain high-level ethical principles.
- Learners and educators are continuously engaged in ethical sense-making, which is sensitive to factors including stress, divided attention, the social environment, and task framing. These can increase or decrease pro-social behavior and adherence to social norms.
- Boundary conditions are used to specify situations in which relations between variables change depending on the values of other variables. Ethical boundary conditions establish gray areas where the same action may be ethical or unethical depending on contextual variables.
- Ethical affordances are contextually relevant design features that comply with established ethical principles and respect the values of stakeholder communities. Anti-affordances are contextually relevant design features that fail to comply with established ethical principles or fail to respect the values of stakeholder communities.
- Including values and ethics in design requires an understanding of the ethical affordances of a system. This requires operationalizing how learners interact with a system. Stakeholders should be engaged through all stages of development, implementation, and technology diffusion to ensure their concerns have been taken into account.

Learning Engineering is Ethical

KEY POINTS

Endnotes

1 Here, values is used to refer to non-ethical values (for example, preferences, social norms and conventions) whereas ethics is used to refer to individual morality and values defined in formal ethical systems.

2 Moore, Stephanie L. and James B. Ellsworth. "Ethics of Educational Technology." In *Handbook of Research on Educational Communications and Technology,* 113–127. New York: Springer, 2014. https://doi.org/10.1007/978-1-4614-3185-5_10

3 Mabry, Christie Knittel and Tony O'Driscoll. "Lessons from Adult Education: Identifying and Exploring Emerging Ethical Issues in Technologically Enhanced Performance." *Performance Improvement Quarterly* 16, no. 4, (2003): 78–93. https://doi.org/10.1111/j.1937-8327.2003.tb00296.x

4 Bødker, Susanne. *Through the Interface: A Human Activity Approach to User Interface Design.* Boca Raton, FL: CRC Press, 1990

5 Schoenherr, Jordan Richard. "Designing Ethical Agency for Adaptive Instructional Systems: The FATE of Learning and Assessment." *Adaptive Instructional Systems: Design and Evaluation, HCII 2021, Lecture Notes in Computer Science*, vol. 12792, edited by Robert A. Sottilare and J. Schwarz, 265–283. Cham: Springer, 2021. https://doi.org/10.1007/978-3-030-77857-6_18

6 "AECT Code of Professional Ethics 2018." Association for Educational Communications and Technology, 2018. www.aect.org/docs/AECT_Code_of_Ethic-Current.pdf

7 "Code of Ethics for Educators." National Education Association, September 14, 2020. www.nea.org/resource-library/code-ethics-educators

8 "Code of Ethics." International Society for Performance Improvement, 2002. https://ispi.org/general/custom.asp?page=CodeofEthics

9 "The Code of Ethics." Talent Management Institute, 2021. www.tmi.org/about-talent-management-institute/tmi-code-of-ethics

10 Jones, Campbell, René Ten Bos, and Martin Parker. *For Business Ethics,* 1st ed. New York, London: Routledge, 2005. https://doi.org/10.4324/9780203458457

11 "Ethically Aligned Design: A Vision for Prioritizing Human Well-being with Autonomous and Intelligent Systems—Version II Request for Input." IEEE Global Initiative on Ethics of Autonomous and Intelligent Systems, 2018. https://standards.ieee.org/content/dam/ieee-standards/standards/web/documents/other/ead_v2.pdf

12 Schoenherr, Jordan. "Moral Economies and Codes of Conduct: The Social Organization of Canadian Experimental Psychology." *Scientia Canadensis: Canadian Journal of the History of Science, Technology and Medicine* 41, no. 1 (2019): 31–54. https://doi.org/10.7202/1065958ar

13 "Code of Ethics for the Health Education Profession." Coalition for National Health Education Organizations (CNHEO), 2020. http://cnheo.org/code-of-ethics.html

14 Ad Hoc Expert Group for the Preparation of a Draft Text of a Recommendation the Ethics of Artificial Intelligence. "Outcome Document: First Draft of the Recommendation on the Ethics of Artificial Intelligence." Paris: United Nations Educational Scientific and Cultural Organization (UNESCO), 2020. https://unesdoc.unesco.org/ark:/48223/pf0000373434

15 Council of the European Union. *Proposal for a Regulation of the European Parliament and of the Council on the Protection of Individuals with Regard to the Processing of Personal Data and on the Free Movement of Such Data (General Data Protection Regulation).* Brussels: Council of the European Union, 2015. See especially page 68. https://data.consilium.europa.eu/doc/document/ST-9565-2015-INIT/en/pdf

16 Central Digital and Data Office. "Guidance: Government Design Principles." United Kingdom Government. Last modified September 10, 2019. www.gov.uk/guidance/government-design-principles

17 "Principles for Digital Development." Accessed December 29, 2021. https://digitalprinciples.org

18 "The IoE Guiding Principles." Internet of Education. Accessed December 29, 2021. www.internetofeducation.org/#Guiding-Principles

19 Formally, this is referred to as the Principle of Nonmaleficence.

20 Busse, Christian, Andrew P. Kach, and Stephan M. Wagner. "Boundary Conditions: What They Are, How to Explore Them, Why We Need Them, and When to Consider Them." *Organizational Research Methods* 20, no. 4 (2017): 574–609. https://doi.org/10.1177/1094428116641191

21 Champney, Thomas H. "A Proposal for a Policy on the Ethical Care and Use of Cadavers and Their Tissues." *Anatomical Sciences Education* 4, no. 1 (2011): 49–52. https://doi.org/10.1002/ase.199

Jones, D. Gareth and Mike R. King. "Maintaining the Anonymity of Cadavers in Medical Education: Historic Relic or Educational and Ethical Necessity?" *Anatomical Sciences Education* 10, no. 1 (2017): 87–97. https://doi.org/10.1002/ase.1618

22 "Body Bequeathal Program." Department of Innovation in Medical Education, University of Ottawa. Last modified December 22, 2021. https://med.uottawa.ca/department-innovation/division-clinical-and-functional-anatomy/body-bequeathal-program/memorial-service

23 "Medal of Recognition." The Ottawa Hospital. Last modified December 30, 2016. www.ottawahospital.on.ca/en/clinical-services/deptpgrmcs/programs/organ-and-tissue-donation-program/donor-awareness/medal-of-recognition

24 Schoenherr, Jordan Richard. "Social-Cognitive Barriers to Ethical Authorship." *Frontiers in Psychology* 6 (2015): 877. http://dx.doi.org/10.3389/fpsyg.2015.00877

25 Osguthorpe, Russell T., Richard D. Osguthorpe, W. James Jacob, and Randy Davies. "The Moral Dimensions of Instructional Design." *Educational Technology* 43, no. 2 (2003): 19–23. www.jstor.org/stable/44428816

26 Haidt, Jonathan, and Jesse Graham. "When Morality Opposes Justice: Conservatives Have Moral Intuitions that Liberals may not Recognize." *Social Justice Research* 20 (2007): 98–116. https://doi.org/10.1007/s11211-007-0034-z

27 Schoenherr, Jordan Richard. "Ethical Sensemaking and Autonomous and Intelligent Systems: Identifying the Ethical Affordances of A/IS." *Frontlines in AI Ethics*, edited by Andrew Hampton and Jeanine DeFalco. London: Routledge, forthcoming.

28 Kohlberg, Lawrence. *Moral Development.* McGraw-Hill, 1973.

29 Darley, John M., and C. Daniel Batson. "'From Jerusalem to Jericho': A Study of Situational and Dispositional Variables in Helping Behavior." *Journal of Personality and Social Psychology* 27, no. 1 (1973): 100–108. https://doi.org/10.1037/h0034449

30 Mazar, Nina, On Amir, and Dan Ariely. "The Dishonesty of Honest People: A Theory of Self-Concept Maintenance." *Journal of Marketing Research* 45, no. 6 (2008): 633–644. https://doi.org/10.1509/jmkr.45.6.633

31 Shariff, Azim F. and Ara Norenzayan. "God is Watching You: Priming God Concepts Increases Prosocial Behavior in an Anonymous Economic Game." *Psychological Science* 18, no. 9 (2007): 803–809. https://doi.org/10.1111/j.1467-9280.2007.01983.x

32 Diener, Edward, Scott C. Fraser, Arthur L. Beaman, and Roger T. Kelem. "Effects of Deindividuation Variables on Stealing Among Halloween Trick-or-Treaters." *Journal of Personality and Social Psychology* 33, no. 2 (1976): 178. https://doi.org/10.1037/0022-3514.33.2.178

33 Haidt, Jonathan and Jesse Graham. "When Morality Opposes Justice: Conservatives Have Moral Intuitions that Liberals May Not Recognize." *Social Justice Research* 20, no. 1 (2007): 98–116. https://doi.org/10.1007/s11211-007-0034-z

34 Lapsley, Daniel K. and Darcia Narvaez. "A Social–Cognitive Approach to the Moral Personality." In *Moral Development, Self, and Identity*, edited by Daniel K. Lapsley and Darcia Narvaez, 189–212. Mahwah, NJ: Lawrence Erlbaum Associates Publishers, 2004.

35 Cikara, Mina, Rachel A. Farnsworth, Lasana T. Harris, and Susan T. Fiske. "On the Wrong Side of the Trolley Track: Neural Correlates of Relative Social Valuation." *Social Cognitive and Affective Neuroscience* 5, no. 4 (2010): 404–413. https://doi.org/10.1093/scan/nsq011

36 Osborne, Jason W. "Testing Stereotype Threat: Does Anxiety Explain Race and Sex Differences in Achievement?" *Contemporary Educational Psychology* 26, no. 3 (2001): 291–310. https://doi.org/10.1006/ceps.2000.1052

Spencer, Steven J., Claude M. Steele, and Diane M. Quinn. "Stereotype Threat and Women's Math Performance." *Journal of Experimental Social Psychology* 35, no. 1 (1999): 4–28. https://doi.org/10.1006/jesp.1998.1373

Steele, Claude M. and Joshua Aronson. "Stereotype Threat and the Intellectual Test Performance of African Americans." *Journal of Personality and Social Psychology* 69, no. 5 (1995): 797–811. https://doi.org/10.1037/0022-3514.69.5.797

37 Mulder, Laetitia B. and Eric van Dijk. "Moral Rationalization Contributes More Strongly to Escalation of Unethical Behavior Among Low Moral Identifiers than Among High Moral Identifiers." *Frontiers in Psychology* 10 (2020): 2912. https://doi.org/10.3389/fpsyg.2019.02912

Fiske, Alan Page and Tage Shakti Rai. *Virtuous Violence: Hurting and Killing to Create, Sustain, End, and Honor Social Relationships.* Cambridge: Cambridge University Press, 2014.

38 Hoffman, Martin L. *Empathy and Moral Development: Implications for Caring and Justice.* Cambridge: Cambridge University Press, 2001.

39 Vohs, Kathleen D. "Money Priming Can Change People's Thoughts, Feelings, Motivations, and Behaviors: An Update on 10 Years of Experiments." *Journal of Experimental Psychology: General* 144, no. 4 (2015): e86. https://doi.org/10.1037/xge0000091

40 Liberman, Varda, Steven M. Samuels, and Lee Ross. "The Name of the Game: Predictive Power of Reputations Versus Situational Labels in Determining Prisoner's Dilemma Game Moves." *Personality and Social Psychology Bulletin* 30, no. 9 (2004): 1175–1185. https://doi.org/10.1177/0146167204264004

41 Wittkower, Dylan E. "Principles of Anti-Discriminatory Design." In *Proceedings of the 2016 IEEE International Symposium on Ethics in Engineering, Science and Technology (ETHICS), Vancouver, May 13–14, 2016*, 1–7. https://doi.org/10.1109/ETHICS.2016.7560055

42 Messick, Samuel. "Validity of Psychological Assessment: Validation of Inferences from Persons' Responses and Performances as Scientific Inquiry into Score Meaning." *American Psychologist* 50, no. 9 (1995): 741–749. https://doi.org/10.1037/0003-066X.50.9.741

43 Friedman, Batya, Peter H. Kahn, Alan Borning, and Alina Huldtgren. "Value Sensitive Design and Information Systems." In *Early Engagement and New Technologies: Opening Up the Laboratory*, edited by Neelke Doorn, Daan Schuurbiers, Ibo van de Poel, and Michael E. Gorman, 69–101. Dordrecht: Springer, 2013. https://doi.org/10.1007/978-94-007-7844-3_4

44 Bösch, Christoph, Benjamin Erb, Frank Kargl, Henning Kopp, and Stefan Pfattheicher. "Tales from the Dark Side: Privacy Dark Strategies and Privacy Dark Patterns." Proceedings on Privacy Enhancing Technologies, no. 4 (2016): 237–254. https://doi.org/10.1515/popets-2016-0038

Gray, Colin M., Yubo Kou, Bryan Battles, Joseph Hoggatt, and Austin L. Toombs. "The Dark (Patterns) Side of UX Design." In *Proceedings of the 2018 CHI Conference on Human Factors in Computing Systems*, 1–14. New York: Association for Computing Machinery, 2018. https://doi.org/10.1145/3173574.3174108

45 Sengers, Phoebe, Kirsten Boehner, Shay David, and Joseph Kaye. "Reflective Design." In *Proceedings of the 4th Decennial Conference on Critical Computing: Between Sense and Sensibility*, 49–58. New York: Association for Computing Machinery, 2005. https://doi.org/10.1145/1094562.1094569

46 Costanza-Chock, Sasha. "Design Justice: Towards an Intersectional Feminist Framework for Design Theory and Practice." In *Proceedings of the Design Research Society, Limerick, Ireland, June 25–28, 2018.* https://ssrn.com/abstract=3189696

47 Zucker, Kenneth J., and Robert L. Spitzer. "Was the Gender Identity Disorder of Childhood Diagnosis Introduced into DSM-III as a Backdoor Maneuver to Replace Homosexuality? A Historical Note." *Journal of Sex and Marital Therapy* 31, no. 1 (2005): 31–42. https://doi.org/10.1080/00926230590475251

48 Wittkower, DE. "Disaffordances and Dysaffordances in Code." In *Selected Papers of #AoIR2017: The 18th Annual Conference of the Association of Internet Researchers, Tartu, Estonia, October 18–21, 2017.* https://journals.uic.edu/ojs/index.php/spir/article/view/10174

49 Wittkower, "Disaffordances and Dysaffordances in Code."

TOOLS

SHORT PRACTICAL CHAPTERS
WITH EASY-REFERENCE CHECKLISTS, GUIDES, + TEMPLATES

STRATEGY

CHAPTER 8

Tools for Understanding the Challenge

by Erin Czerwinski and Jim Goodell

Learning engineering is a repeatable process that starts with a challenge. This chapter introduces practical tools for understanding those learning engineering challenges to be solved by a learning engineering team.

The challenges learning engineers address are focused on helping every targeted learner be successful in reaching learning goals. This might include creating things that help learners make progress toward a goal (for example, refer to the section in Chapter 2 on addressing learners' zones of proximal development and scaffolding) or things that help targeted learners overcome barriers as illustrated in Figure 8.1.

Learning engineering teams are often asked to examine learning conditions to determine what factors could be adjusted to improve learning for one or more targeted populations of learners. This chapter provides tools to help elaborate on

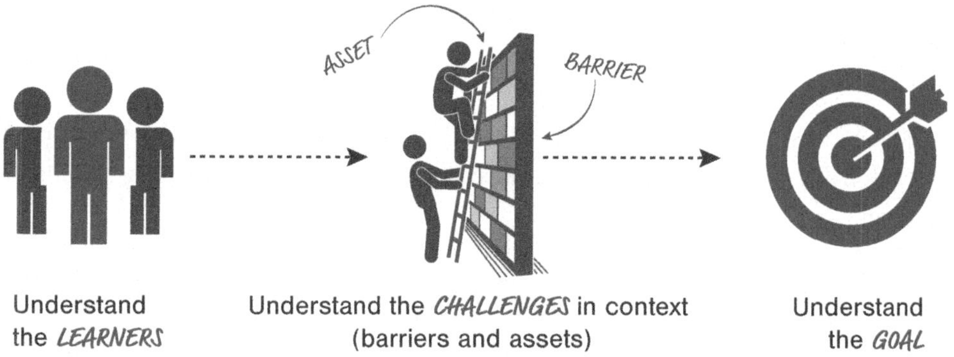

FIGURE 8.1. Learning engineering challenges can be thought of as barriers that must be overcome—and assets to use to assist—on the way to a goal

what needs to be learned, the conditions that might need to be addressed, and the complexities of that learning. The four tools include task analysis, the five whys technique, cause and effect analysis, and failure mode and effects analysis.

Supporting learning so that every targeted learner can be successful requires knowing quite a bit about who the learners are; what they already know, are capable of, and have experienced; what resources they bring to their learning; what their interests and goals are and what will keep them engaged; the context in which the learning is to happen and the resources and constraints associated with those contexts; the capabilities, practices, preferences, and content knowledge of those helping the learners to learn (such as teachers, family, and peers); what tends to be difficult about learning the new skills; and more. Consequentially, to fully understand the learning engineering challenge, consider using the kinds of tools discussed in this chapter in conjunction with tools from other chapters, including:

- Chapter 9, Tools from the Learning Sciences
- Chapter 12, Human-Centered Design Tools
- Chapter 15, Tools for Learner Motivation
- Chapter 16, Implementation Tools (to understand conditions and constraints)
- Chapter 18, Data Analysis Tools

> Analysis is the study we do in order to figure out what to do.
> – *Allison Rossett and Kendra Sheldon*[1]

Task Analysis

> Task analysis is used when a targeted skill isn't already precisely defined. This approach is frequently used to unpack the component skills and knowledge needed to accomplish a task.

Various task analysis methods attempt to unpack the declarative, procedural, and strategic knowledge a person must have to perform a task in a given context (defined by a set of conditions and available tools). **Behavioral task analysis** identifies the observable or directly measurable behaviors. **Cognitive task analysis** is used for tasks that require high-level reasoning, such as decision-making, problem solving, or judgments. Task analyses should also uncover necessary mindsets, attitudes, or habits of mind / practice. Training expert Donald Clark identifies the following kinds of information captured during a task analysis: [2]

- **Conditions:** Tools or equipment needed and the task environment
- **Performance Measure:** How well must it be performed?
- **Frequency:** How often is the task performed, for example, hourly or daily?
- **Difficulty:** Use a standard scale, such as from one to five
- **Importance:** How important is this compared to performers' other tasks?
- **Steps:** Knowledge and logical steps for performing the task

Uncovered information might also include:

- **Dependent Attitudes:** What habits of practice or thinking are helpful?
- **Transferable Skills:** What skills used in other contexts can be applied?

Task analyses should identify various methods a person might use to successfully perform the task using different sets of tools in different contexts (in this way predicting a set of learner differences and different ways a learner might carry out the task). Learners come with deficiencies in what they know; they also come with funds of knowledge—things they already know and are capable of. A single, rigid solution path or a deficiency-based learning experience can be unmotivating for learners who have other ways of knowing and/or doing. Performance task analysis includes identifying the variety of ways the task can be carried out, the variety of ways each part of the task can be carried out, and the different prior knowledge and skills learners might engage to learn the task. The most effective learning experiences offer learners opportunities to learn and demonstrate a skill using multiple approaches. They are developed with an understanding of learners' funds of knowledge as well as what they haven't yet attained.

HOW TO USE

The analysis process involves interviewing and/or observing a variety of people who do the task competently and/or analyzing documentation of the tasks being performed. In an academic context, the list of tasks may be defined by academic standards. In a training context, the process of task analysis starts by analyzing the job or role. Let's say we already know the task, for example, training employees to estimate the cost of a new carpet installation for an irregularly shaped room. We'll need to unpack the task into its steps. Then, for each step, we inquire about what a person must:

- Know prior to doing the step
- Perceive during, for example, the set of rectangles making up the room
- Attend to during, for example, the customer, care with customer property
- Do during the step

While interviewing or observing someone doing the task, ask them to tell you:

- What they're thinking at each step
- What they're observing
- When they make a decision, what assumptions they make
- How they know their decisions are right and the work product is correct

A template like the one below can be useful. Also see Chapters 6 and 18 for information on learning curve analysis; effective task analyses should specify tasks in enough granularity to support future learning curve analyses. Learning engineering best practices call for competency definitions with data-justified specificity, meaning we want to be able to prove that the competency is at the atomic level with data.

PERFORMANCE TASK ANALYSIS TOOL TEMPLATE

Task: ______________________________

Task Step	Know	Perceive	Attend To	Do

FIGURE 8.2. Performance Task Analysis template

Five Whys Technique

Based on some understanding of current conditions, use this tool to identify why the learning is less than optimal. Then use the root cause that is identified as the next challenge to be solved by the learning engineering team.

The **five whys technique** was developed by Sakichi Toyoda, the founder of Toyota, in the 1930s. Toyota executives would go and see what was happening on the shop floor (rather than just think about solving a problem from the boardroom), and then they'd use analysis techniques to examine the issues they identified. The five whys is a root-cause analysis technique,* and it works well with other human-centered design approaches. Learning engineers might use the five whys to figure out why learners are failing at a given task or are challenged by a particular topic.[3]

HOW TO USE

In its simplest form, use this procedure: (1) Identify a problem, (2) ask *why?*, and (3) based on that answer ask *why?* again. (Repeat up to five times—or more—as needed.) Sometimes the root cause is discovered in fewer or more than five steps. It's helpful to unpack as much as possible. Don't stop at the symptoms of problems.

Example: The vehicle will not start.

1. *Why?* The battery is dead.
2. *Why?* The alternator isn't functioning.
3. *Why?* The alternator belt has broken.
4. *Why?* The alternator belt was beyond its useful life and not replaced.
5. *Why?* The vehicle wasn't maintained to the suggested service schedule.

Note that sometimes depending on where you are in the learning engineering process, you may have access to data or research that can inform the answers to your root cause questions. This is exemplified in the next example where a root cause was discovered with analysis of data and interviewing some learners to better understand why they were having difficulties.

Example: Students are failing multiplication word problems on a standardized test.

1. *Why?* Students are missing about half of the problems on the tests even though they performed better on in-class multiplication word problems.
2. *Why?* Based on the data, students are missing the same sets of problems.
3. *Why?* Examining the troublesome problems reveals that they all prompt students to "find the product" of two or more numbers.

---

* *Caution: Not all problems have a single root cause. For more complex problems the method must be repeated asking a different sequence of questions each time. In those cases, use this method with the "fishbone diagrams" tool discussed later in this chapter.*

4. *Why?* Talking to the students reveals that they don't know what the word "product" means in mathematics. (Note, during this step, it's important to go talk with learners, just as the Toyota executives visited the shop floor to understand what was going on. A simple template like the one that follows may be used to assist with this.)
5. *Why?* The teacher succeeded in ensuring that students in the class were proficient in multiplication as an operation but failed to expose them to the terminology used in the standardized assessment. In-class practice problems before the test didn't use the word "product."

THE FIVE WHYS TOOL TEMPLATE

Condition: ____

Why?	
Why?	
Why?	
Why?	
Why?	

FIGURE 8.3. Five Whys template

Cause and Effect (Fishbone) Analysis

This technique helps explore all possible causes of a problem. Use it to investigate the root causes of more complex or multifaceted challenges.

The five whys technique is designed to help identify a single condition or root cause that, if changed, could result in an improvement or desired outcome. In contrast, cause and effect analysis, developed by Kaoru Ishikawa in the 1960s, is better suited for those situations where the multitude of root causes that might be preventing an ideal outcome. This technique is also called **fishbone analysis*** because a completed diagram can look like the skeleton of a fish. The technique is fully defined in the 1990 book, *Introduction to Quality Control.*[4]

HOW TO USE[5]

1. Start by asking why an ideal outcome isn't being reached.
2. Instead of just one, consider multiple reasons.
3. Record each answer as a branch in the diagram.
4. For each branch ask *why?,* and record the answer as a subsequent branch until the various root causes are found.

Note, in the following example, interacting with the learners is essential to getting at reasons for difficulties. You may need to use another tool, such as the five whys, to get at the root causes of each of the identified difficulties.

Example: Some of our learners don't automatically know that ¼ is greater than ⅛. "Why don't learners know the relative value of fractions?" Answering the question may require some investigation, such as asking learners or doing follow-up assessments. Let's say we asked learners, "Why do you think ¼ is less than ⅛?" and they provided these responses:

> "No one taught me about numbers with a line between them." (From this we might theorize the learner wasn't exposed to the idea of fractions or didn't retain the concept from a prior learning experience.)
>
> "Because 8 is greater than 4." (From this we can infer that their mental model for quantity is imperfect and must be expanded.)
>
> "Oh, I was wrong, I was looking at the numbers on the bottom and forgot it was a fraction." (In this case, we might infer that the learner has been exposed to fractions but hasn't yet sufficiently retained that knowledge or developed skills to consistently apply it.)

Starting with these three initial branches might result in a fishbone diagram as shown in Figure 8.4.A, and based on this, we might identify different kinds of solutions as shown in Figure 8.4.B.

---

* *Also known as Cause and Effect, Ishikawa, Herringbone, and Fishikawa Diagrams.*

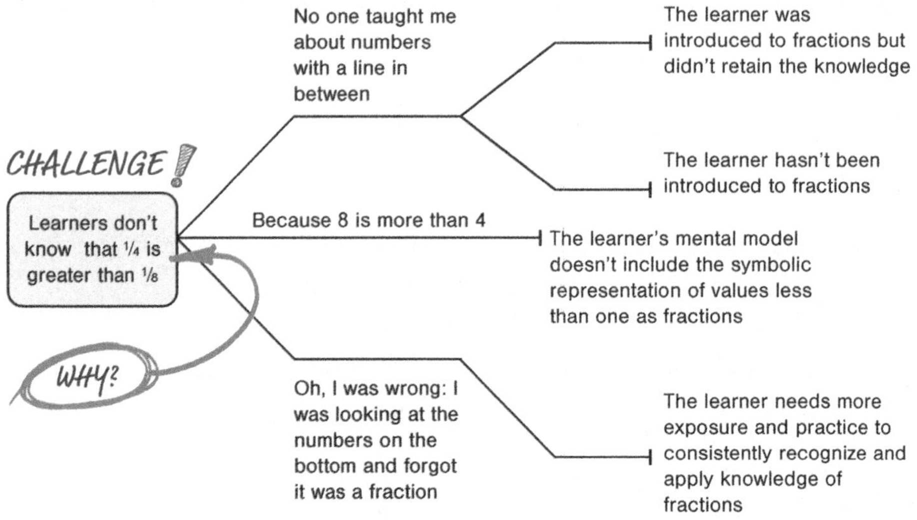

FIGURE 8.4.A. Example fishbone diagram (step 1)

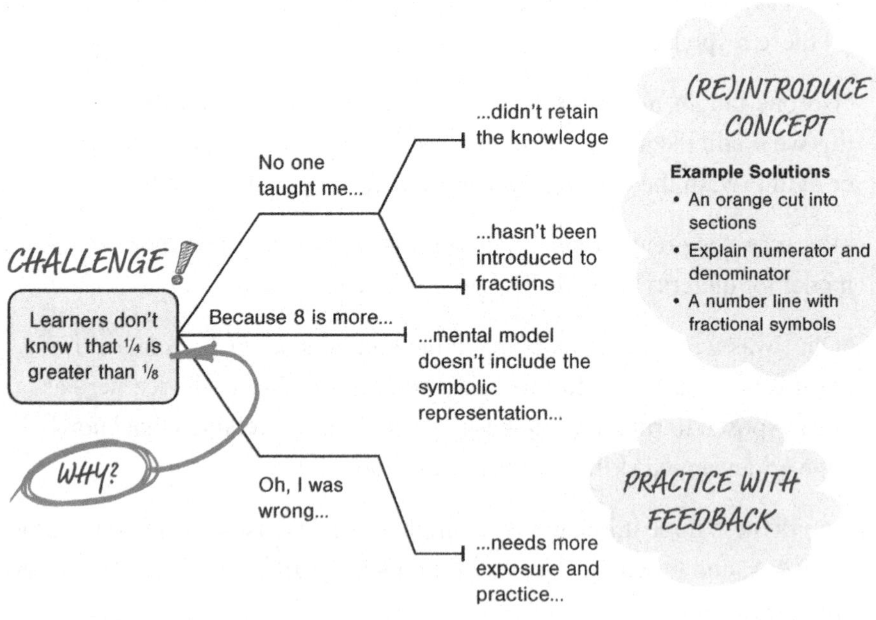

FIGURE 8.4.B. Example fishbone diagram (step 2)

ALTERNATIVE FORM

The fishbone analysis template in Figure 8.5 is adapted from a model by the Carnegie Foundation for the Advancement of Teaching. It takes a slightly different approach, for example, creating main category branches from the problem statement. Use it when you want to organize potential causes by category, for example, separating learner motivational or behavioral causes from learner cognition causes.

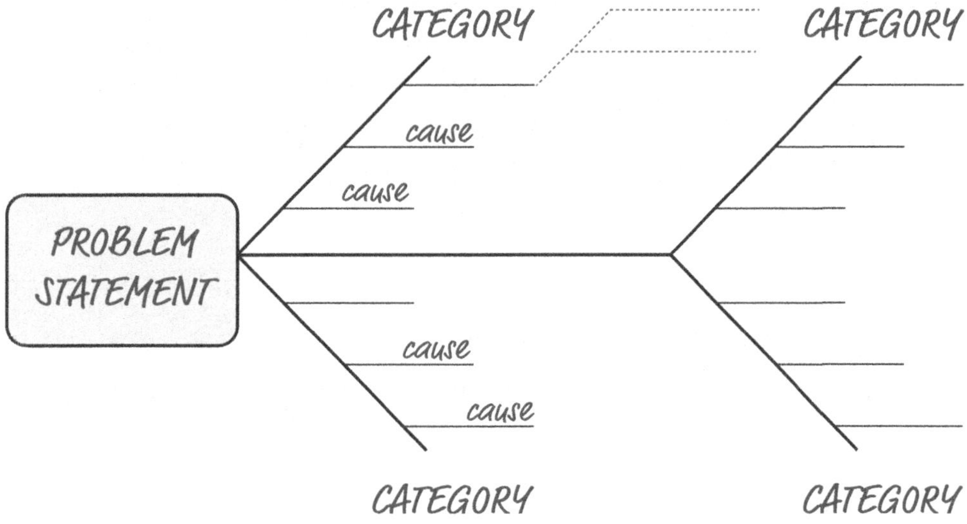

FIGURE 8.5. Alternative fishbone diagram template

Failure Mode and Effects Analysis

Use this technique to prioritize what challenge (or challenges) to address. This technique helps you look at all of the things that possibly could go wrong; it's most useful at the beginning of the create stage to uncover and address potential problems that would be more expensive to correct later. (Caution: Don't let this process cause "analysis paralysis" that slows down Agile design and development.)

This technique (originally known as *failure mode, effects, and criticality analysis*) was first published in 1949 by the US Department of Defense. The technique grew out of systems engineering and quality control. It builds on tools like cause and effect analysis to try to predict failures before they happen. **Failure mode and effects analysis** is also effective in improving the design of business processes and systems. When using it, start by looking in detail at the proposed solution and then identify where that solution might fail.[6]

HOW TO USE[7]

(One example process; there are variations.)

1. Review the learning objectives, domain pedagogies, and what's known about the learner population, learning environment, and other contexts.
2. Brainstorm potential failure modes.
3. List potential effects of each failure.
4. Assign severity rankings. (That is, rate the severity of each effect.)
5. Assign occurrence rankings.
6. Assign detection rankings. (How likely is it the failure will be detected?)
7. Calculate a risk priority number (severity × occurrence × detection).
8. Develop the action plan (design and development requirements) to address the highest priorities.

An example of failure mode and effect analysis comes from the Prince of Songkla University, Thailand, which used it to understand a challenge in their Industrial Engineering bachelor's degree program.[8] The program includes placing students in industrial settings for on-the-job training, but industry partners complained that students were being placed in jobs they weren't yet capable of performing. University faculty used this analysis to uncover issues in the complex situation, which spanned diverse stakeholders, factors, and education/industrial contexts. They examined all potential failure points and then evaluated each using five-point rubrics:

1. **Severity:** Likelihood of the customer noticing the failure or the level of worst results, particularly in terms of safety and system functionality (5 = Student can't do the job to 1 = Student comfortable with the job)
2. **Occurrence:** Likelihood of a specific failure (5 = Very high probability of its occurrence to 1 = Very low probability of its occurrence)
3. **Detection:** Degree of existing control plan or verification program that can pinpoint potential failures before they occur (5 = Can't predict and no detection of failure to 1 = Can predict and detect)

Next, they created a risk priority number, which is an index based on the multiplication of *severity* by *occurrence* by *detection* metrics. An example of (part of) what this analysis might have looked like is below:

Failure Mode	Severity	Occurrence	Detection	Risk Priority
Students lack key admin info about jobs	4	4	4	64
Students lack essential skills	4	3	4	48
Industry partners not accurately defining jobs	4	2	3	24
. . .	. . .	. . .	. . .	. . .

FIGURE 8.6. Partial example of how a failure mode and effects analysis might be scored. The numeric scores in this figure are fictional for the purposes of illustration.

After identifying all of the potential failure modes, the faculty then ranked the top five most serious issues. Then the team used the five whys technique, presented earlier in this chapter, to uncover root cause. They found that four of the five high-priority issues could have been prevented with better communications between the department and the industrial partners. Only one of the top-five issues pointed to the need to better prepare student before on-the-job training. Once they had that clarity, they were able to identify actions to prevent each issue from reoccurring in the future. ★

Endnotes

1 Rossett, Allison, and Kendra Sheldon. *Beyond the Podium: Delivering Training and Performance to a Digital World.* 1st ed. San Fancisco: Jossey-Bass / Pfeiffer, 2001.

2 Clark, Donald. "Task Analysis in Instructional Design." *Instructional System Design: The ADDIE Model: A Handbook for Learning Designers.* Last modified September 21, 2015. http://knowledgejump.com/hrd/isd/tasks.html

Clark, Donald. "Task Analysis Tools." Knowledge Jump. Last modified October 18, 2011. http://knowledgejump.com/hrd/needsalt.html

3 Mind Tools Team. "5 Whys: Getting to the Root of a Problem Quickly." Mind Tools. Last modified December 12, 2021. www.mindtools.com/pages/article/newTMC_5W.htm

4 Ishikawa, Kaoru. *Introduction to Quality Control.* Japan: Taylor & Francis, 1990.

5 See also: Mind Tools Team. "Cause and Effect Analysis: Identifying the Likely Causes of Problems." Mind Tools. www.mindtools.com/pages/article/newTMC_03.htm

6 Mind Tools Team. "Failure Mode and Effects Analysis (FMEA): Spotting Problems Before a Solution Is Implemented." Mind Tools. Last modified December 12, 2021. www.mindtools.com/pages/article/newTMC_82.htm

7 Venuk, Cecelia Marie. "Failure Modes and Effects Analysis (FMEA)." *Presentation at the Albuquerque Quality Network Conference, Albuquerque, NM, February 23, 2012.* www.osti.gov/servlets/purl/1097206

"10 Steps to do a Process FMEA." FMEA Training from QualityTrainingPortal. Accessed December 12, 2021. https://fmea-training.com/10-steps-process-failure-mode-and-effects-analysis

Kane, Robert and Rosalie Kane. "Guidance for Performing Failure Mode and Effects Analysis with Performance Improvement Projects." The Centers for Medicare and Medicaid Services, United States Department of Health and Human Services. Last modified February 18, 2014. www.cms.gov/Medicare/Provider-Enrollment-and-Certification/QAPI/downloads/GuidanceForFMEA.pdf

8 Sinthavalai, Runchana and Napisporn Memongkol. "A Case of FMEA Implementation in the Educational Sector and Integration with CRM and QFD Concepts." Paper presented at *IEEE International Engineering Management Conference, Estoril, Portugal, June, 28–30, 2008.* New York: IEEE. https://ieeexplore.ieee.org/abstract/document/4618036

CHAPTER 9

Tools from the Learning Sciences

by Jim Goodell, Janet Kolodner, and Aaron Kessler

This chapter builds on the foundations outlined in Chapter 2. It summarizes concepts from the learning sciences, and it provides some scaffolding to help organize your thinking around their application.

Before using these tools, you should have already examined the challenge (see Chapter 8) and used a modular design approach to isolate specific opportunities or problems to be addressed. First use the following checklist to consider the applicable category or categories that apply to your challenge.

Learning Sciences Concept Categories—Check all that apply:

- ❑ Create or improve the conditions for learning
- ❑ Help learners understand new ideas
- ❑ Help learners retain knowledge
- ❑ Help learners apply knowledge
- ❑ Help learners build expertise
- ❑ Motivate learners
- ❑ Measure learning and optimize feedback

Next use the checklist that follows to identify concepts that apply. Then during iterative design, development, and instrumentation; refer back to these checklists and consider how your solution incorporates the relevant concepts. Use a worksheet to track which concepts were implemented. Following the checklist on the next page, the remainder of this chapter includes definitions of the learning sciences concepts for reference. It also incorporates an example design pattern, to show how you might integrate the learning sciences concepts into your learning designs.

CATEGORY	SAMPLE CONCEPTS TO CONSIDER
Create or improve the conditions for learning	❑ **Agency:** What people think about their own learning matters ❑ **Cognitive Capabilities:** Improve learners' capacity to learn ❑ **Hierarchy of Needs:** Foster physiological / emotional well-being ❑ **Personalization:** Use learner models to inform tailored interventions ❑ **Variability:** Learning is different for everyone
Help learners understand new ideas	❑ **Concrete to Abstract:** Start with concrete examples and then expand ❑ **Feedback:** Effective feedback is specific, timely, actionable . . . ❑ **Metacognition:** Help grow or scaffold metacognitive thinking ❑ **Novice vs. Expert:** Help novice learners see and build connections ❑ **Productive Failure:** Safe failure (and feedback) can aid learning ❑ **Scaffolding:** Give support to make the task just challenging enough ❑ **Spaced Learning:** Mitigate forgetting by studying over time
Help learners retain knowledge	❑ **Active Learning:** Foster learning through doing ❑ **Cognitive Load:** Avoid working memory overload ❑ **Connections:** Emphasize cognitive connections and transferability ❑ **Personal Connection:** Use authentic, personally meaningful tasks ❑ **Zone of Proximal Development:** Find the "just right" challenge level
Help learners apply knowledge	❑ **Challenge:** Set the right level of desirable difficulty ❑ **Prior Experience:** Remember, there's no learning from scratch ❑ **Reinforce:** Use it or lose it ❑ **Transfer:** Help learners apply knowledge to new contexts ❑ **Unlearning:** Help learners let go of biases and misconceptions
Help learners build expertise	❑ **Communities:** Foster real-world applications through social learning ❑ **Memory:** Help build long-term (vs. working) memory ❑ **Mentorship:** Model ideas and skills ❑ **Novice vs. Expert:** Help novice learners see and build connections
Motivate learners	❑ **Core Drives:** Tap into learners' core drives to foster motivation ❑ **Engagement:** Motivation is learner-centric ❑ **Hierarchy of Needs:** Foster physiological / emotional well-being ❑ **Motivation Types:** Consider intrinsic vs. extrinsic motivators ❑ **Relevance:** Use authentic, personally meaningful tasks
Measure learning and optimize feedback	❑ **Feedback:** Effective feedback is specific, timely, actionable . . . ❑ **Metacognition:** Help grow or scaffold metacognitive thinking ❑ **Novice vs. Expert:** Help novice learners see and build connections ❑ **Productive Failure:** Safe failure (and feedback) can aid learning ❑ **Scaffolding:** Give support to make the task just challenging enough

ACTIVE LEARNING: Foster learning through doing

Learners are more likely to engage enthusiastically and to be able to integrate what they're learning with their prior knowledge when asked to achieve a goal that is meaningful to them, work on a project, or solve a problem. After learning their new understanding or capability is more likely to be well integrated with what they already know. However, such project-based learning only works well when scaffolded so that learners understand the objectives, ask good questions, carry out robust investigations to answer those questions, reflect on their experiences, and take advantage of failures.

AGENCY: What people think about their own learning matters

Helping learners understand that many aspects of successful learning, such as strategy and effort, are under their control fosters agency. Relatedly, when learners see failure as an opportunity to find out what they still need to learn—rather than an indicator of self-worth or fixed intelligence—they're more likely to persevere. A growth mindset is encouraged with process-focused feedback and an environment that treats mistakes as opportunities to reflect and learn.

CHALLENGE: Set the right level of desirable difficulty

When learners work at the edge of their mastery (while maintaining high expectations for performance) it pushes them past their current abilities. Like in athletics, while practice isn't always fun and drills can be difficult, a deliberate training process leads to improvement. The right level of challenge with the right level of support (scaffolding) promotes effective learning while offsetting the motivational and cognitive costs of floundering and frustration.

COGNITIVE CAPABILITIES: Improve learners' capacity to learn

Learning is dependent on general cognitive capacities such as attention, executive function, working memory, and processing skills. When necessary, interventions should be applied to develop or strengthen these cognitive capabilities.

COGNITIVE LOAD: Avoid working memory overload

Cognitive load is the effort used in working memory. Working memory (sometimes referred to as short-term memory) is where new learning starts, but it has limited capacity and requires greater mental effort. In some cases, a heavy cognitive load can impede learning. Cognitive load theory suggests that learning experiences should be designed so that they don't overload working memory.

COMMUNITIES: Foster real-world applications through social learning

Learning communities (grounded in communities of practice) allow students to socially situate, construct, and organize knowledge compatible with experts in the domain. Encourage social learning through communities to help learners bridge the gap between academic understanding and real-world application.

CONCRETE TO ABSTRACT: Start with concrete examples and then expand

Learning starts with concrete information and gradually moves to more abstract understanding. Learners often need to start with imperfect but concrete conceptual models, anchored in a single context, and then over time replace those with more accurate and abstract understanding that can be applied to more than one problem or context.

CONNECTIONS: Emphasize cognitive connections and transferability

Does the learning experience or environment help learners make connections to prior learning? Does it help learners connect across knowledge domains, for example, to transfer something learned in school to a real-life task? Help make the connections among different concepts, or among theoretical ideas and real-world applications, obvious. Help learners practice using new knowledge or skills in different contexts or problem variations.

CORE DRIVES: Tap into learners' core drives to foster motivation

People are motivated by different things at different times. Core drives include curiosity, meaningfulness, accomplishment, empowerment, ownership, social influence, scarcity, unpredictability, and avoidance. Good learning experiences and environments tap into these drives so that learners are motivated to engage deeply, remain engaged over time, and re-engage after becoming disengaged.

See also Chapter 15, Tools for Learner Motivation, for specific strategies based on the science of motivation.

ENGAGEMENT: Motivation is learner-centric

Learning isn't something done to students by a teacher. It's a process in the learner's brain of adding and changing existing knowledge. Learning only happens if learners actively participate in the process. Learners are more likely to persevere if they believe their talents can be developed through hard work, good strategies, and input from others.

FEEDBACK: Effective feedback is specific, timely, actionable . . .

Descriptive feedback gives learners information about the quality of their ideas and performance that they can use to adjust. Deliver effective feedback, which is specific, understandable, timely, non-threatening, and actionable.

HIERARCHY OF NEEDS: Foster physiological / emotional well-being

Before higher levels of motivation can be attained, a person's basic survival needs (for example, not starving and feeling safe) and psychological needs (for example, belonging and esteem) must be met, more or less. Learners with good nutrition, sleep, and exercise will have better cognitive skills. Aerobic exercise can improve brain plasticity. Sleep is critical for solidifying learning. Nutrition is important for brain health. Similarly, learners who feel they're a part of a positive, supportive learning community will be better able to focus on learning. To the extent possible, set these conditions to enable learning.

MEMORY: Help build long-term (vs. working) memory

The difference between a novice and an expert brain has a lot to do with how each uses the two kinds of memory. Working (short-term) memory is slower, error prone, more deliberate, has limited capacity and limited retention, requires greater mental effort, and is the place where new learning starts. In contrast, long-term memory has long retention, is efficient, operates automatically (without effort), and when trained error-free. Experts use long-term memory to do complex tasks effortlessly. Help novices grow their long-term memory by exposing them to many varied patterns of a concept and by helping them grow, connect, and enhance their mental models.

MENTORSHIP: Model ideas and skills

Mentor learners by modeling of ideas and skills while engaging in real world activities. This allows novice learners to begin developing expertise. Instructional tactics such as demonstration and talk-aloud can help.

METACOGNITION: Help grow or scaffold metacognitive thinking

Metacognition is thinking about one's own thinking and learning. A metacognitive learner knows when they're on the right track and when they're having difficulties. Metacognitive strategies include self-explanation, asking for help, starting over, and persevering. A good way of helping learners develop metacognition is to prompt them to reflect on or articulate what they're learning—metacognitive scaffolding. Did I already know that? How would I explain that to someone else? Does it conflict with what I thought I knew or could do? How well do I know this? On what parts of this do I need help or more practice? For measurement and feedback, consider assessing learners' metacognitive skills. Also, develop assessments that prompt learners to express their thought processes (rather than just giving a final answer). See the design pattern below for an example of how to help learners build their metacognitive skills through prompting.

MOTIVATION TYPES: Consider intrinsic vs. extrinsic motivators

Intrinsic motivators (internal goals) tend to be more powerful than extrinsic rewards. Use strategies, such as those outlined in Chapter 15, to foster intrinsic motivation.

NOVICE vs. EXPERT: Help novice learners see and build connections

Compared to novices, experts not only have more content knowledge, they've also organized that knowledge for deeper understanding, rapid retrieval, and contextual application. Experts can see patterns and understand under which conditions and contexts to apply knowledge. Experts can also select and retrieve important aspects of their knowledge without effort. It may be necessary to help learners restructure their knowledge so that it's organized more like the knowledge of experts. That takes intentional practice with feedback. Explicitly help learners see and practice building connections between concepts at each level of learning. Also, when it comes to measurement and feedback, consider measuring efficiency of application and transferability (not just retrieval of discrete facts and highly contextualized skills) as learners move from novice to experts.

PERSONALIZATION: Use learner models to inform tailored interventions

In one-on-one tutoring, tutors construct mental models of what a learner knows and can do based on observations and interactions. In intelligent tutoring systems, learner models are dynamically built from data about a learner and their interactions. In both cases these models are useful for diagnosis, feedback, coaching, and the prescription of learning activities. Tailoring such interventions to learners' unique cognition, metacognition, and motivational factors can greatly improve learning outcomes.

See also Chapter 13, Data Instrumentation Tools, for more insights on collection of data used to optimize feedback.

PRIOR EXPERIENCE: Remember, there's no learning from scratch

Learning is an active process in which a learner constructs meaning by mapping new information onto prior knowledge. As we experience life our brains try to fit new information into what we already know about the world. Learning works best when we have the background knowledge to make sense of the new information. Learning doesn't work if the prerequisite knowledge on which to anchor the new knowledge is missing. Help learners by understanding their prior experiences and then connecting new knowledge or skills to them.

PRODUCTIVE FAILURE: Safe failure (and feedback) can aid learning

Failure provides an opportunity to learn. When a learner tries out some thinking or a new skill and it doesn't work as well as they expected, the opportunity presents itself to figure out why and correct or improve their capabilities. Use a wrong answer during learning-embedded assessments as an opportunity to provide feedback, or provide feedback on project-based activities that help learner reflect on why they failed and how to correct those issues, gaps, or misconceptions in the future.

REINFORCE: Use it or lose it

A newly learned skill or knowledge component is generally forgotten over time if not reinforced with practice and applied. Use techniques like spaced learning, or create tasks that require learners to build upon and practice their new knowledge and skills, so that they're reinforced over time.

In Chapter 4, Learning Engineering is Engineering, we introduced design patterns–repeatable solutions to commonly occurring engineering problems. The following design pattern is an example of an instructional strategy that addresses the learning sciences concept of metacognition.

Example Design Pattern: Metacognitive Prompting *

Explicit verbal, text, or visual reminders prompt learners to engage in specific cognitive processes, such as remembering previous instructions. Metacognitive prompting involves asking questions and giving reminders that encourage metacognitive thinking such as planning, monitoring, and evaluating one's thinking processes.

How It Works: Metacognitive prompts are designed to enhance metacognitive skills, including self-awareness, self-monitoring, self-regulation, reflective judgment (evaluating the accuracy of knowledge), integrative thinking (integrating separate pieces of information or seemingly opposing perspectives), and emotional intelligence (the ability to understand one's own and others' emotions). These skills act as a "multiplier" to all other cognitive competencies. Metacognitive strategies help learners to independently make sense of situations, transfer their knowledge to new contexts, and evaluate themselves. These skills also help learners better plan, practice, evaluate their own learning then adjust their behavior to best meet their goals.

Applicable Contexts: All

Inputs: None required

Instrumentation: None required

Design Considerations: Is the learner already familiar with the concept of "metacognition," or at least, the value of metacognitive skills like self-awareness and self-regulation? Will you incorporate the prompts before, during, and/or after a learning activity? Will you use metacognitive prompts as a self-directed, teacher-led, or group activity?

* *Schatz et al. (2012). Making Good Instructors Great: US Marine Corps Small Unit Decision Making Instructional and Assessment Techniques Handbook, pp. 84–85.*

Pattern:

1. Explain the concept of metacognition and its benefits. Use direct instruction to help learners initially understand the distinction between "thinking" (that is, cognition) and "thinking about thinking" (that is, metacognition). Explain core metacognitive skills and how these skills "multiply" learning and cognitive performance.
2. Before, during, and/or after an activity that introduces new concepts, help learners activate metacognitive thinking through questions or prompting. First, determine which phases to add the prompts into.
    - **Preparation (Pre):** Metacognitive prompts during the preparation phase generally involve planning, such as encouraging learners to set goals, organize their thoughts, anticipate, or predict.
    - **Execution (During):** Prompts during execution often involve monitoring, such as summarizing or elaborating on new concepts, self-assessing comprehension, or using mental strategies (like mnemonic devices).
    - **Reflection (Post):** Metacognitive prompts during the reflective phase generally involve evaluating, such as self-assessing performance, reflecting on feedback, or considering ways to apply the recent lesson.
3. Next, determine which metacognitive skills are most appropriate to activate and how to prompt them. These can be delivered asynchronously (such as via automated scripts in an e-learning course), by a teacher (such as through tutoring or mentorship), or drawn out through peer-learning activities.

    Here are some examples:

    - **Frame:** Ask how individual parts fit into an overall task
    - **Attend:** Cue learners to the critical pieces of information
    - **Self-Regulate:** Ask learners what "mental tricks" they use
    - **Extend:** Ask about similar concepts that relate to the lesson
    - **Reflect:** Ask learners to describe (paraphrase) what they just learned
    - **Experiment:** Make learners "stretch" to solve new problems
4. Prompt learners. If possible engage in a dialogue to encourage reflection.
5. In a group setting, consider leading a group discussion. Allot time for the discussion and encourage learners to describe the metacognitive strategies that they personally found useful.

RELEVANCE: Use authentic, personally meaningful tasks

Learners are more likely to become intrinsically motivated and engaged over long periods of time if what they're asked to do is personally meaningful and authentic, if they imagine they're capable, if they know when and who in the world carries out such tasks, if they have the available resources that someone in the real world engaging in that task would have, and if associated activities and assessments fit into the flow of what they're trying to achieve. Learners often need help to know how a new learning experience is meaningful to them and encouragement that they're capable of learning the associated knowledge and skills.

SCAFFOLDING: Give support to make the task just challenging enough

Scaffolding provides the structure and support learners need to construct their own learning with tasks more complex than they could handle without that support. Scaffolding includes hints, prompts, conceptual frameworks (for example, advance organizers), process support, focus support, and strategic guidance. Its goal is to provide just enough support to make tasks achievable without losing useful complexity or context. Scaffolding may be added and removed based on each learner's current needs. For measurement and feedback, build in the opportunity for learners to get hints and worked examples during formative assessments. If possible, use data to adjust the level of difficulty for an assessment task, removing and adding scaffolding for a desired level of difficulty.

SPACED LEARNING: Mitigate forgetting by studying over time

Studying the same amount of content over time (rather than cramming all at once) can dramatically improve learning, long-term recall and flexible use of that content. Increasing the time between repetitions over time is most effective.

TRANSFER: Help learners apply knowledge to new contexts

Transfer refers to ability to apply existing knowledge and skills to new contexts. Transfer is difficult. It requires recognition that you know something, understanding of how to apply it in a new context or form, and the disposition to do so. Often, learners can use existing knowledge when prompted before they can independently recognize that their knowledge is relevant. Being able to transfer learning requires practice in a variety of circumstances. Create varied conditions and coach learners on what knowledge or skills might be useful for different contexts. The better someone can reuse their knowledge, the more robust their learning becomes.

UNLEARNING: Help learners let go of biases and misconceptions

Sometimes a learner has mistaken, imperfect, or incomplete mental models that must be replaced with corrected or improved ones. Developers of learning experiences should not only know the subject matter but also common points of learner confusion and how to address them. Use formative assessments and other opportunities to identified learners' gaps, biases, and misconceptions, and then help them unlearn those unhelpful ideas or skills.

VARIABILITY: Learning is different for everyone

Existing knowledge is the foundation on which new learning is anchored. New learning is also dependent on cognitive capacities such as attention, executive function, working memory, and processing skills.* All of these personal characteristics are variable. In addition, different cultural influences and experiences impact development from the beginning of life. To be most effective, it's important to consider learners' variability and, to the extent possible, tailor learning experiences to work with and build upon those individual or group differences.

ZONE OF PROXIMAL DEVELOPMENT: Find the "just right" challenge level

Tasks that are outside of a learner's current independent ability—but that are achievable with help (scaffolding)—are within a learner's Zone of Proximal Development. Every learner's zone is different, and a learner's zone is different at different points in time. Learning activities should be adaptive or adaptable to consider the probable zones and to provide the relevant scaffolding required for success. Good scaffolding helps learners succeed past what they can do by themselves and helps them grow their capabilities over time. ★

---

* *Note: There is no evidence that people have particular fixed learning styles (for example, visual versus auditory). Learners' preferred mode of learning may vary over time, by context, and by learning objective. Adaptive and adaptable learning experiences offer multiple modes and levels that consider differences in the learners to be served.*

TEAM

CHAPTER 10

Tools for Teaming

by Dina Kurzweil and Erin S. Barry*

Learning engineering requires a team. This chapter defines teams and learning engineering teams. It examines stages of team development, practices for team formation, and shared competencies of a learning engineering team. Finally, this chapter provides insights about effective team communication and common barriers faced by teams with strategies for overcoming team dysfunctions.

What's a team?

> A team is a small number of people . . . who are committed to a common purpose, performance goals, and approach for which they hold themselves mutually accountable.[1]

For teams to be effective, the common purpose or goal needs to be clear so that team members can work interdependently to achieve the common outcome.

Additionally, team members should have a shared commitment and responsibility to complete the common purpose or goal. It's important for all members of the team to understand each member's role and expectations and have mutual respect for what each person brings to the table. On some teams, the leader sets the vision, selects the members of the team, and sets out the procedures to follow, while the team members execute accordingly. In contrast, other teams allow all team members to contribute to decision-making about vision, selection of team members, and procedures in addition to the execution of tasks. To have effective

---

* *The opinions or assertions contained herein are the private ones of the authors and are not to be construed as official or reflecting the views of the Department of Defense, the Uniformed Services University of the Health Sciences, or any other agency of the US government. The authors have no financial disclosures.*

team performance, cohesiveness, morals, and ultimately outcomes, the team should clearly understand who's involved in each step, and they should have the flexibility to change these dynamics based on evolving contexts and situations. Finally, teams should periodically have meaningful discussions about the overall goals as well as roles of each team member. This helps to maintain a positive and safe environment where team members feel comfortable speaking up.[2]

Why have a team?

Why should we work in a team? Everyone has unique experiences, perspectives, opinions, gifts, communication and leadership styles, strengths, and weaknesses that, when brought together, strengthen potential solutions and can solve problems that couldn't otherwise be solved alone. When dealing with larger or complex problems, the power of a team can far exceed any one person's ability. It's extremely rare for someone to independently have all of the capabilities needed to take on learning engineering challenges including expertise in engineering processes, learning sciences, software engineering, data science, instructional design, artificial intelligence and machine learning, pedagogy and andragogy, user experience design, and product testing as well as mastery of regulatory policies and technical standards.

What's a learning engineering team?

Learning engineering teams bring together specialists who can help transform learning environments, expand best practices, implement learner-centered design, and enable data-driven decisions. These specialists have a combination of knowledge and experience as well as the ability to filter their individual knowledge through the lenses of their combined experience. In other words, the value of effective teams doesn't only come from each member's own abilities; it also comes from their abilities to work together.

Learning Engineering Team Composition

Different learning engineering challenges require different mixes of talent, but they typically require contributions from the following domains:

- ❑ Assessment, measurement, and evaluation
- ❑ Data science

- ❑ Education and training professions
- ❑ Instructional design
- ❑ Learning environment engineering
- ❑ Learning experience design
- ❑ Learning sciences
- ❑ Project management
- ❑ Software engineering
- ❑ Subject-matter expertise

Team Organization

While organizations may be managed operationally around functional teams, learning engineering teams may require cross-disciplinary effort drawn from different departments. For example, dynamic or interworking teams may be needed to complete particular tasks. Carnegie Learning's bi-weekly "data jams" described in Chapter 6 are an example of this. Below are some different types of teams that can be found within organizations:

- **Dynamic or task force teams:** These teams are brought together to quickly address a task or problem and are dissolved once it's been completed or solved.
- **Functional teams:** Functional teams are more enduring. Their members belong to the same functional area and respond to a single leader, who's responsible for the team and its outcomes. This type of team doesn't dissolve once a project is complete; instead they move on to a new project together.
- **Interworking teams:** These teams are made up of members from different areas of activity, and their members usually have the same hierarchical level. This type of team usually comes together to focus on a task or problem with a multidisciplinary view, and the team dissolves once the project is completed.
- **Matrixed teams:** Matrixed team members usually belong to different functional areas and respond to different managers or leaders, but an organization assembles them into a temporary team to implement a specific project. After its completion, the team dissolves. Typically, members of matrixed teams perform other tasks related to their home department, but as far as the project is concerned, they answer to the project leader.

Team Formation

Every learning engineering challenge is different, and the work required in each stage of the learning engineering process also varies. The mix of talents needed, the roles assigned to team members, the contributions required for each role, and the overall work will vary by challenge and stage. For example, the implementation phase requires a different team composition than creation phase. Similarly, implementation of a global learning platform like Duolingo requires a different team than implementation of a single course delivered to a few students or the design of donkey carts in West Africa to get children to school. Even when the reporting structures and titles for people in an organization are relatively static, the composition of teams and assigned roles should be aligned with the challenge, context, and work required for the given stage of a project. It may be helpful to think of team formation (or re-formation) as a step between each phase of the learning engineering process. Between stages of the learning engineering process ask:

- What problem is the team being formed to solve?
- What team competencies are required to address the problem's context?
- What are the organizational contexts in which the team must operate?
- How will the organizational contexts dictate the work to be done and the processes that need to be followed?

	PHASES			
WHAT AREAS OF EXPERTISE ARE NEEDED?	Challenge	Creation	Implementation	Investigation
Assessment, measurement, and evaluation				
Data science				
Education and training professions				
Instructional design				
Learning environment engineering				
Learning experience design				
Learning sciences				
Project management				
Software engineering				
Subject-matter expertise				

FIGURE 10.1. Worksheet for team roles by learning engineering process phase

TEAM VARIATION WITHIN THE LEARNING ENGINEERING PROCESS

The learning engineering process, defined in Chapter 1, is iterative. (It's not a linear process!) Steps may be revisited multiple times before moving on, and steps may be revisited again throughout the process. Similarly, learning engineering team development takes on many forms, is iterative, and can be repeated at any stage. The team member roles and overall composition may need to evolve over time. Teams may need to integrate new people based on requirements and expertise at each stage of the process. The following describes eight team functions. Figure 10.2 shows these functions mapped to the learning engineering process from Chapter 1.

1. **Developing:** During the challenge phase, the team develops a firm grounding in the problem or challenge. These are often complex and will likely require decisions about what's to be done.
2. **Coalescing:** Also during the challenge phase, the team works together to understand the context of the problem and problem space. They should have at least one advocate who has a firm grounding in the context of the learners (and other stakeholders). That advocate (or advocates) must be able to explain the situation to the rest of the team.
3. **Assigning:** The talents needed from each team member and their alignment to a particular aspect of the problem will depend on the specific problem to be addressed. Make sure to reassess and reassign members between stages of the learning engineering process either by adjusting the team composition, each person's expected contributions, or by handing off the project or tasks to a separate team.
4. **Planning:** During the creation phase, the team plans how it will address the challenge using multiple rounds of iterative development. They also curate internal products to guide the work, such as standards, experimentation protocols, and style guides. This stage should also include plans for who will provide peer review and who will provide final sign-offs.
5. **Developing:** Also during the creation phase, the appropriate team members will iteratively develop products and instrumentation to address the challenge, testing each iteration with end users. Subgroups or individuals may focus on developing parts of the overall solution, including instrumentation and implementation plans.
6. **Implementing:** During the implementation phase, the team must be

prepared to support the implementation of the product and to document any issues that arise. This may mean adjustment of implementation plans as well as tactical and personnel challenges.

7. **Analyzing:** During the investigation phase, the team examines the solution's ability to fully and ideally solve the problem. This is a critical review point. Upon completion of an analysis the team might discover, for example, that it needs more data, additional or different testing, or to make new design decisions. In other words, following the analysis phase, it's likely that the learning engineering team will need to revisit one of the prior stages (or repeat the analyzing phase with variations).
8. **Iterating:** Team members working on each stage of the process must look for opportunities to improve the solution in future iterations. Each member is responsible for contributing to continuous improvements—examining what's working in the current iteration as well as what might be a challenge or opportunity for the next.

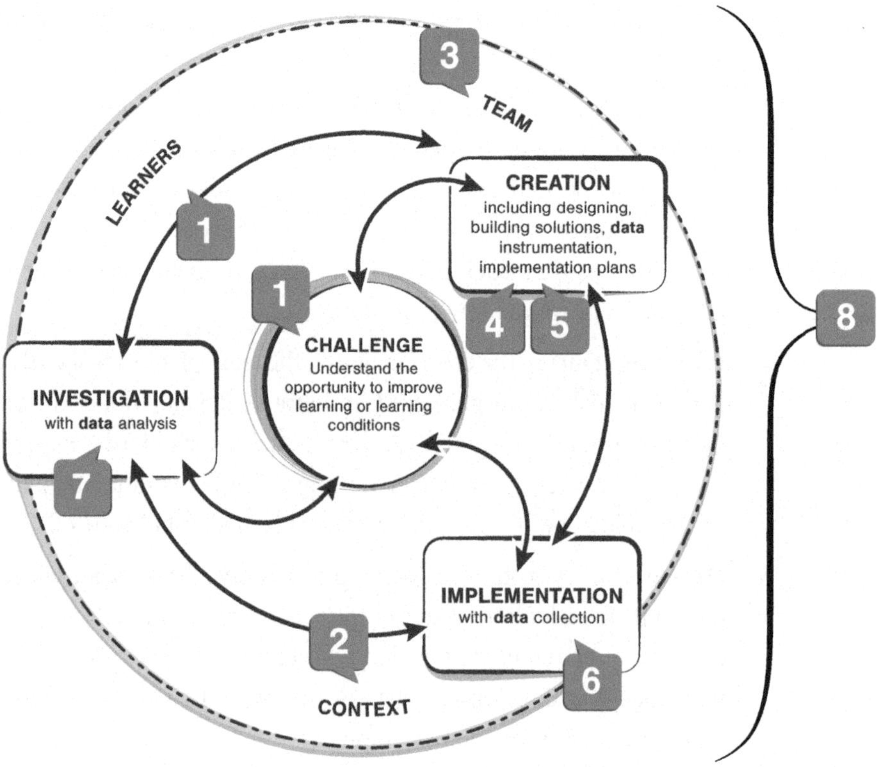

FIGURE 10.2. Suggested phases during which to apply the outlined team processes

TEAM DYNAMICS

Bruce Tuckman, an early psychology researcher focused on team dynamics, developed a four-phase model of the team development process that provides a framework on the nature of team dynamics and their evolution. The four stages are:

1. **Forming:** In this stage, individuals are trying to get to know each other and the organization and have not formed a commitment to the team. Project leaders provide direction and outline expectations. Leaders can also facilitate a discussion about the results to help the group understand each other, their differences, operating and communication styles.
2. **Storming:** In this typically rocky stage, team members may challenge the leader and each other. The leader coaches members on how to manage conflict and focus on goals. The leaders also facilitate related training.
3. **Norming:** After individuals have worked through conflicts, the team begins to develop. People begin to appreciate differences and work together. The leader begins to be more of a facilitator, offering encouragement and guidance.
4. **Performing:** At this stage, the team is fully functional, members are able to manage their relationships, and work toward shared goals. Team members feel accepted and communicate openly with the leader. The leader focuses on delegating responsibilities and must identify when the team is moving into a different stage.

TEAM LEADERSHIP

The choice of who leads a team should account for context. Some teams are small, such as an instructional designer teaming with an instructor. Larger teams who are collectively designing learning experiences, platforms, or other complex solutions may need a project manager who coordinates across the various other specialists and sets the direction for the work. Similarly, as teams go through different stages of development, different styles of leadership should be considered for optimal team performance. During the earlier stages of team development, the leader may need to be more involved and directive. When teams get to the norming and performing stages, shared leadership becomes more realistic as everyone understands each other's roles and can step in with their needed expertise.

TEAM CHECKLIST

Teams formed to address any part of a learning engineering process can leverage general team building principles to move from storming to norming and performing. Use the checklist below as a guide to move through team formation processes:

- ❑ **Develop ground rules**
  It's important to develop ground rules, such as how to deal with accelerated or delayed project timelines, how concerns will be handled, who to talk to about what and when, and how to promote the work of others and the team.

- ❑ **Have clearly defined roles**
  Each member must understand their own role as well as the roles of others. This will help members to know what they're doing, how they can help each other when needed, and how to avoid stepping on others' toes.

- ❑ **Create a vision and goals**
  The team must have a clear way ahead that's known by all members. The vision doesn't prescribe details of every step on the path forward.

- ❑ **Provide clear communication**
  Communication at all organizational levels must be clear for all to understand.

- ❑ **Build trust and cooperation**
  Once the team is formed, its members must have mutual trust and be willing to cooperate with one another. Without those, failure is inevitable.

- ❑ **Value ideas**
  Team members must value each other's ideas and contributions. If team members don't feel valued, they won't feel like part of the team, leading to lower performance and satisfaction.

- ❑ **Acknowledge unstated feelings**
  Leaders must acknowledge and use social awareness to account for others' behaviors and emotions. If a team member isn't pleased with a certain path and it's noticed by the leader, it's useful to acknowledge that not everyone may agree with the path forward and allow for all thoughts to be heard.

- ❑ **Allow sharing (and often)**
  All members of the team need to share ideas and thoughts around the project. Being heard allows individuals to feel like a part of the team.

Communication

Communication is an important aspect for teams to be effective and successful. Communication includes providing a clear message (sending), and importantly, it also includes making sure that the message sent is understood by the person receiving the message (receiving). Communication is both verbal (using words) and nonverbal (sounds, facial expressions, body language, and paralanguage). When communication is clear, open, and honest, there's increased trust on the team and decreased conflict.

COMPETENCIES OF TEAM MEMBERS

Learning engineering teams will be more successful if they have some knowledge of concepts and vocabulary used in the domains of the other professional specialties on the team. For example, if a software engineer on the team knows something about terms used by learning scientists, and if the instructional designer knows about some of the ways that learning analytics can provide insights. This shared vocabulary will help all team members work more effectively together. It's also important that a member or some members of the team can communicate well with stakeholders, clients, and leaders of the organization they're supporting.

COMMUNICATION STYLES

It's important for us to understand our own communication styles as well as those of others. There are many tools available to look at communication styles; one tool, called DISC, is illustrated in Figure 10.3. It helps you identify your preferred style of communication (dominance, influence, steadiness, correctness) and information about the other styles. It's a great tool to use with teams to provide awareness on each person's communication style to help you modify your behaviors. Adapting to others' communication styles can help ensure that the message sent is the message received. One of many DISC assessment tools is available online at: www.extendeddisc.org/what-is-disc.

Team Functioning and Dysfunctioning

Some common characteristics seem to be strong indicators of a team that isn't functioning at its peak or that needs intervention. What makes good teams and what

DOMINANCE	*INFLUENCING*	*STABILIZING*	*CAUTIOUS*
Forceful	Expressive	Restrained	Compliant
Strong-minded	Emotional	Satisfied	Careful
Pioneering	Influential	Easy mark	Correct
Domineering	Attractive	Willing	Precise
Determined	Stimulating	Even-tempered	Fussy
Demanding	Captivating	Patient	Timid
Self-reliant	Companionable	Kind	Open-minded
Persistent	Playful	Self-controlled	Agreeable
High-spirited	Talkative	Good-natured	Soft-spoken
Impatient	Convincing	Contented	Resigned
Aggressive	Good mixer	Gentle	Respectful
Nervy	Poised	Accommodating	Conventional
Argumentative	Confident	Relaxed	Cooperative
Restless	Inspiring	Considerate	Well-disciplined
Courageous	Optimistic	Sympathetic	Diplomatic
Positive	Eager	Lenient	Exacting
Adventurous	Enthusiastic	Loyal	Adaptable
Will power	Entertaining	Good listener	Humble
Competitive	Life-of-the-party	Obedient	Tolerant
Vigorous	Persuasive	Neighborly	Cautious
Outspoken	Eloquent	Reserved	Strict
Dogged	Animated	Obliging	Devout
Assertive	Gregarious	Nonchalant	Docile
Bold	Outgoing	Moderate	Perfectionist

FIGURE 10.3. Communication styles based upon the DISC model

Table CC-BY the Chute Institute, 2013

makes bad teams? See the tool in Figure 10.4 for qualities of dysfunctional teams as well as ways to work towards fixing these qualities to improve team performance.

For teams to be effective, there are many elements that need to be considered in order for all members of the team to work effectively. Team members who embrace and encourage both leader and follower roles are beneficial for team collaboration. For effective team performance, cohesiveness, morals, leadership, planning documentation, and communication plans should be clearly understood. Identify who's involved in each step, and have flexibility for changing context and situations. The characteristics and competencies of the team should be formally recognized. Finally, teams should have meaningful discussions of the overall goals and roles of each team member to maintain a positive and a safe environment for all members to speak up and share thoughts and ideas at any time.[3]

TEAM DYSFUNCTION AND IMPROVEMENT STRATEGIES

DYSFUNCTIONS	WHAT TO DO TO BE EFFECTIVE
Lack of trust Avoidance of accountability Lack of cohesion	• Be genuine and show vulnerability • Understand your role and team members' roles • Hold each other accountable • Use open, honest communication • Provide constructive feedback
Unaddressed or unresolved conflicts	• Frame conflict as positive • Address the conflict in a timely manner • Use open, honest communication • Maintain mutual respect • Listen—not just to respond but to hear other perspectives • Work toward resolution so that all parties feel like they're heard and valued and reach agreement with next steps
Inequality among team members	• Clearly describe roles and responsibility for each member • Clearly communicate roles/responsibilities to the team • Value all team members • Find ways to show that each member is part of the team • Find ways to train members to meet their needs on the team • Help team members reach individual goals for themselves • Consider the context of the situation, as it may determine who can/is able to do certain tasks

<table>
<tr><th>DYSFUNCTIONS</th><th>WHAT TO DO TO BE EFFECTIVE</th></tr>
<tr><td>Ineffective communication and communication breakdowns</td><td>• Communicate, communicate, communicate!
• Use clear, open communication
• Make sure that the message sent is the message received
• Listen to understand, not to respond</td></tr>
<tr><td>Lack of commitment</td><td rowspan="2">• Determine deadlines and who's involved in meeting them
• Commit to decisions with confidence
• Focus on team / collective results</td></tr>
<tr><td>Inattention to results</td></tr>
<tr><td>Not adaptable</td><td rowspan="2">• Use techniques from team dynamics and above in this table
• Help members to adapt to changing contexts
• Allow members to support each other</td></tr>
<tr><td>Unsupportive team environments / negative atmosphere / culture</td></tr>
<tr><td>Weak leadership</td><td>• Identify leadership's motivation
• Identify triggers for weak decision-making
• Follow the chain of command if necessary</td></tr>
<tr><td>Poor decision-making</td><td>• Consider context for poor decisions
• Add more time to the decision-making process
• Look to others for more ideas
• Develop multiple paths for decisions and track outcomes</td></tr>
<tr><td>Diversity not valued</td><td>• Educate your team
• Commit to diversity of thought
• Attack head on, biases, styles, etc. that limit diversity
• Acknowledge that silence doesn't mean there's no problem
• Discuss body language and language in general
• Consider the effects of power on diversity of thoughts, ideas, creativity, and outcomes</td></tr>
<tr><td>Lack of goal and objectives for the team</td><td>• Develop a goal for the team and clearly communicate it
• Allow input from others (those above, below, and peers) to make sure the goal is measurable and achievable, while also meeting the mission of the organization</td></tr>
<tr><td>Poorly defined roles and responsibilities</td><td>• Have clearly defined roles for each member of the team (think short job descriptions for each person)
• Communicate these role descriptions with the entire team</td></tr>
</table>

FIGURE 10.4 Team dysfunction and resolution cheat sheet

★

Endnotes

1 Katzenbach, John R., and Dennis K. Smith. "The Discipline of Teams." *Harvard Business Review, March–April* (1993), https://hbr.org/1993/03/the-discipline-of-teams-2

2 Barry, Erin S., Karlen S. Bader-Larsen, Holly S. Meyer, Steven J. Durning, and Lara Varpio. "Leadership and Followership in Military Interprofessional Health Care Teams." *Military Medicine 186,* no. Supplement_3 (2021): 7–15.

3 Barry et al., *Military Medicine,* 7–15.

Hackman, J. Richard. *Leading Teams: Setting the Stage for Great Performances.* Harvard Business Press, 2002.

WORK PROCESSES

CHAPTER 11

Lean-Agile Development Tools

by Michelle Barrett and Jim Goodell

This chapter introduces Agile development approaches commonly used in software development and explains how these tools can be used with the learning engineering process.

Managing work across functions, time, and budget is difficult, and each management strategy has pros and cons. We present a variety of management approaches well suited to learning engineering.

Agile Development

Agile is a set of methods and methodologies that help a team to think more effectively, work more efficiently, and make better decisions. Agile is also a mindset, which opens up the planning, design, and process improvement to the team. Everyone shares the same information, and everyone on the team has a say in how the practices are applied.

Agile was originally coined in February 2001 by a group of software engineers who were tired of seeing software development projects fail. Frustrated by delivering software customers didn't like after years of development, they envisioned a better and more collaborative way of working that would engage customers early and often to mitigate the risk that what was being built was not what was wanted, thereby accommodating change.

To change a way of working deeply ingrained in many organizations is no small feat. So those engineers, self-described as "organizational anarchists," developed the Agile Manifesto.[1]

We are uncovering better ways of developing
software by doing it and helping others do it.
Through this work we have come to value:

Individuals and interactions over processes and tools
Working software over comprehensive documentation
Customer collaboration over contract negotiation
Responding to change over following a plan

That is, while there is value in the items on
the right, we value the items on the left more.

Along with the Manifesto, several principles were developed, the first of which is satisfying the customer through early and **continuous delivery** of software. Since the introduction of the Agile Manifesto, professionals other than software engineers have noticed that applying Agile practices to their work has similarly improved their ability to respond to change to better meet customer needs. We'll return to outline some of the practices that have been successfully used in a learning engineering context. But first, a quick detour through Lean.

Lean Development

Lean has roots in manufacturing, specifically, automotive manufacturing. Eiji Toyoda, nephew to the founder of Toyota, experimented with methods to make the Toyota manufacturing lines deliver productivity, quality, and variety. What he developed was an approach that became the Toyota Production System. Based on a study of this system, Lean principles were first described in *The Machine that Changed the World: The Story of Lean Production—Toyota's Secret Weapon in the Global Car Wars That Is Now Revolutionizing World Industry.*[2]

Lean principles are all about removing delay and waste, which is defined as any action or step in a process that doesn't add value to the customer. Waste can include defects, overproduction, waiting, transportation, inventory, motion, and extra processing. To eliminate waste, a relentless focus on **continuous improvement** is employed. Problems are seen as learning opportunities and teams are tasked with making improvements in response to those opportunities.

You'll see Lean in many contexts now, including manufacturing, entrepreneurship, analytics, organizational design and process, and—you got it—Agile. Lean-Agile combines the principles of Lean (continuous improvement) with the principles of Agile (continuous delivery).

The principles of Lean (continuous improvement) are a good fit with the iterative learning engineering process shown in Chapter 1, and the Agile principles align well with learning engineering as human-centered design, explained in Chapter 3.

Lean-Agile in Learning Engineering

Burr Settles is one of the early employees of Duolingo, as the tenth engineer and the twentieth overall employee. What's more, Duolingo is his first and only corporate job to date. And to top it off, Duolingo is a relatively young company, with its first beta product out for testing November 30, 2011. By this time, companies had been experimenting with Agile for over ten years, and Lean was twenty years old. So when asked about project management at Duolingo, specifically experiences with methods that preceded Agile, Burr said, "Oh, they never really tried that." Duolingo was operating Agile from the start. "In the beginning, if it couldn't be done in two weeks, we didn't do it."

What does it mean to operate Agile? What's important to understand about Lean-Agile is that it represents a collection of principles meant to enable teams to deliver maximum value to customers. Methods and practices aligned with those principles are widely used today.

Scrum

Have you ever watched a rugby game? It's beautiful to watch a self-organizing team of fifteen individuals move the ball down the field to the goal, orchestrating together and in the moment to respond to changing conditions. It's from this game that Agile Scrum found its name.

Scrum is a framework that values honesty, openness, transparency, empowerment, and collaboration. In order to facilitate those values, Scrum includes specific roles, activities, artifacts, and their specified rules. Because it creates a language for roles and activities, it can feel daunting to a newcomer, even cult-like. In addition, because of its structured roles and activities, for teams new to Scrum, the approach can feel dogmatic and sometimes even contrary to the Agile principles themselves. But if you keep in mind a self-organized team working together to move a ball down the field, many of the activities begin to make sense. Everyone on the Scrum team owns the success of the project.

FIGURE 11.1. A rugby scrum *Credit: Alain Vermeulen*

ROLES

Product Owner: This role is responsible for maintaining a product backlog, which is simply a list of work to be done, in priority order. The work is described from the perspective of the user to whom the work will bring incremental value and focuses on what must be done rather than how to do it. These are called user stories. Each item in the list is ordered by priority by the product owner. The product owner is responsible for understanding the most important needs of the user and company and representing that to the team.

Scrum Master: This role is a servant leader for the team. They help remove impediments and foster an environment for high-performing team dynamics, continuous flow, and relentless improvement.

Development Team: The team members decide how to complete the work described on each item of the backlog and complete the work. A team is expected to represent the skill sets needed to drive the work to completion and deliver the incremental value. The team members decide who completes which tasks; this isn't assigned by the Scrum master or product owner.

ACTIVITIES

Stand-up: A short daily meeting in which each team member describes work they completed the day before, work they plan on completing the current day, and any blockers or impediments they may have to completing the work.

Sprint: A regular increment in time (two weeks is typical, but other increments also are used) during which the team completes work they committed to complete during planning.

Sprint Planning: A meeting that occurs at the start of the sprint during which the team examines capacity and pulls in work from the backlog and commits to its completion by the end of the sprint.

Sprint Review: A meeting that occurs at the end of the sprint during which the team presents all work completed during the sprint. This includes a demonstration of the functional value delivered.

Grooming: A meeting held by the product owner during which the acceptance criteria (for example, what does it mean for the work to be complete and satisfactory to the user) for items in the backlog are discussed with the team and the team asks questions, gets clarifications, and estimates a size for the backlog item.

Retrospective: Perhaps the most important meeting of them all, the retrospective occurs at the end of the sprint. Everyone on the team reflects on what went well, what didn't go well, and what they will collectively change in the next sprint to improve.

> The . . . "relay race" approach to product development . . . may conflict with the goals of maximum speed and flexibility. Instead, a holistic or "rugby" approach—where a team tries to go the distance as a unit, passing the ball back and forth—may better serve today's competitive requirements.
>
> – *Takeuchi and Nonaka, 1986*[3]

Kanban

Kanban is a Lean method used to support teams as they work to continuously improve their processes. In its simplest form, Kanban helps the team analyze the process they are using to deliver value for incremental change. To do this, teams visualize the work as it is flowing through the team's process so that problems in workflow are more easily identified and can be remedied by the team.

The primary tool of Kanban is a kanban board. A very simple kanban board might look like the figure below. On each sticky note is a work item to be completed, similar to the user story used in Scrum.

All teams will have a fixed capacity for work in progress (the middle column). At some point, they simply can't take in any more work without introducing waste such as additional wait time or poor quality with rework loops. Therefore, teams may choose to impose work-in-progress limits to specified columns in the kanban board, representing the maximum allowable items allowed in a column at any point in time. Under these conditions, items may only be pulled into the column for work if the team is not at the work-in-progress limit.

Scaled Agile

In larger companies or institutions, the coordination of multiple Agile teams can be daunting. Agile teams are designed to be driven by the team members, thereby challenging many long-held governance, budgeting, and release planning processes,

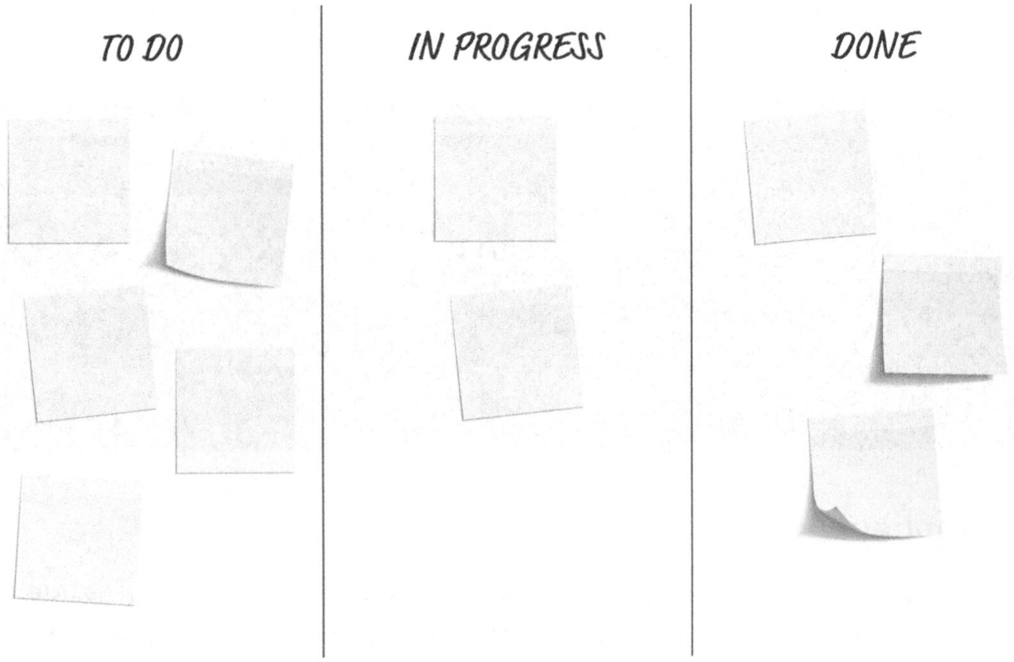

FIGURE 11.2. An example kanban board

along with top-down decision-making. However, research indicates that Lean management and continuous delivery processes positively drive job satisfaction and software delivery performance, both of which positively drive organizational performance. Therefore, methods for collaboration among Agile teams are needed to harness the power of Agile while addressing dependencies, milestones, suppliers, and so on. One well-known method is SAFe (Scaled Agile Framework) Agile. This framework provides for planning across Agile teams in program increments, which typically represent several sprints of work. The website www.scaledagileframework.com is a great reference for learning engineering teams navigating the terminology and methods of Lean, Agile, and SAFe.

Application of Agile Tools and Processes to Learning Engineering

You now may recognize the learning engineering process as one focused on continuous improvement to provide maximum value to learners and those supporting them. You may also recognize elements of Scrum and/or Kanban that can help facilitate team collaboration and delivery of value by your team. It's possible that members of your learning engineering team are also members of other teams using Scrum or Kanban, or that technical work your learning engineering team needs done must flow through the Scrum processes. If your learning engineering team is operating within the context of a medium-to-large organization, you could find that you are expected to participate in SAFe activities for collaboration with other teams.

Let's think about the Learning Engineering process introduced in Chapter 1, and how a team might choose to use Agile to navigate this process. First, the process starts with a problem to be solved in a given context. Let's start with a very simple example of Kanban application to the learning engineering process. Let's say we have a problem to be solved in a given context, and we represent the work in the following user story. We create a user story for each of the problems the team will work on. (See Figure 11.3, and also refer to Chapter 12, Human-Centered Design Tools, for more information on user stories.)

FIGURE 11.3. Simple user story outline

AS A (TRAINER, EDUCATOR, LEARNER, OTHER)
WHO IS (CONTEXT),
I WANT (A GOAL)
SO THAT (PROBLEM TO BE SOLVED).

ACCEPTANCE CRITERIA
1. MUST...
2. MUST...

Kanban Tools for Learning Engineering

A learning engineering kanban board might look something like Figure 11.4. You will see that the columns in the kanban board mirror the major steps in the learning engineering process. In this example board, at this moment, there are three user stories in the backlog, one user story in each of the challenge and creation stages, four user stories in implementation, one story in investigation, two stories in review, and one that has been completed. Thus, this team is actively working on a total of nine learning engineering problems simultaneously. Each story that is done represents results or findings that will serve to inform the problem to be solved—the ultimate value of the learning engineering process. Therefore, this method also supports the measurement of value the team provides over time.

As work is completed, stories are moved across the board. If the team has work-in-progress limits, then work can only be pulled into a subsequent step if there is capacity to do so, never exceeding a work-in-progress limit. As this board is used, steps in the process where the work slows down or builds up will become visible to the team, indicating the team might want to consider a process improvement they think will improve the flow.

Regular retrospectives provide the avenue for sharing ideas about process improvement, even for teams using the simple Kanban approach. Feedback from every team member should be gathered. A simple and common format is presented below.

If a learning engineering team implements nothing else from the Lean-Agile methods, the combination of Kanban with retrospective is the one to implement.

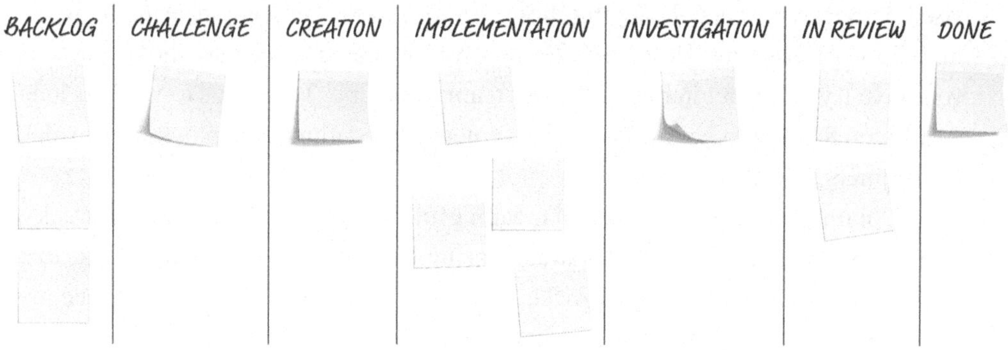

FIGURE 11.4. A learning engineering kanban board might look like this

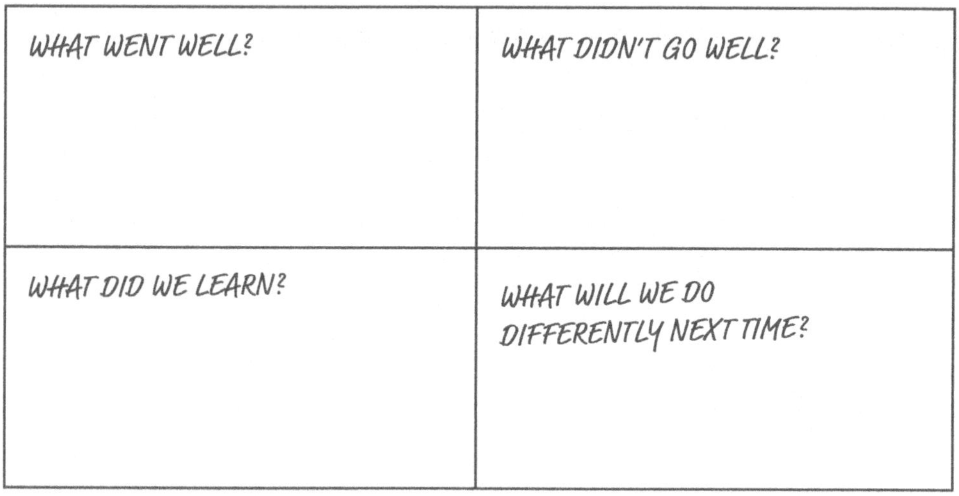

FIGURE 11.5. Regular retrospectives encourage continuous improvement

Visualizing the work to be done, understanding work-in-progress limits, and conducting reviews of the board for process improvement will result in considerable benefit to the team.

Getting Started with Lean-Agile

Adopting new practices like Lean-Agile can feel overwhelming at first. In this chapter, we briefly introduced concepts, roles, and activities typically seen in organizations that use Lean-Agile methods. We have provided samples of tools that can be used for applying Kanban or Scrum methods to a learning engineering effort based on our experience deploying these methods to learning engineering teams in multiple organizations. However, the best way to understand how these methods work is to try them and iterate with your team over time. This tends to work as long as the team focuses on continuous improvement and continuous deployment of value to customers and stakeholders.

Duolingo no longer expects all meaningful work to be complete in two weeks. As the company grew beyond a software startup, they also matured to recognize that Scrum is not a one-size-fits-all approach. For example, Burr and his team have recently been working on a project to add a knowledge state modeling service underneath Duolingo's flagship product. This is obviously a large learning engineering effort, one with many stakeholders. The overall effort is expected to span more than a two-week sprint for development and requires a healthy runway of research preceding the start of development. The cadence of Scrum is not appropriate for the early research stage but is appropriate for the development stage, and Burr and his teams have the freedom to use the methods that fit the stage and state of the project. But Burr never lost sight of the ultimate goal—to deliver value to his customers. In fact, when the research started in September, he made an oath to stop shaving until there was a live feature in the platform using the knowledge state service. And the teams delivered.

He ended up shaving on March 31, several months ahead of expectation. ★

Endnotes

1 Cunningham, Ward. "Manifesto for Agile Software Development." *Agile Manifesto Website,* 2001. https://agilemanifesto.org

2 Womack, James P., Daniel T. Jones, and Daniel Roos. *The Machine that Changed the World: The Story of Lean Production—Toyota's Secret Weapon in the Global Car Wars that is Now Revolutionizing World Industry.* Simon and Schuster, 2007.

3 Takeuchi, Hirotaka and Ikujiro Nonaka. "The New New Product Development Game." *Harvard Business Review 64,* no. 1 (1986): 137–146. (See page 137.)

CHAPTER 12

Human-Centered Design Tools

by Sae Schatz, Khanh-Phuong Thai, Scotty D. Craig, Jordan Richard Schoenherr, Jodi Lis, and Janet Kolodner

This chapter catalogs some human-centered design tools that build on the concepts and processes introduced in Chapter 3, Learning Engineering is Human-Centered.

The goal of human-centered design is to understand the interactions among people and the other elements of a system and then apply theory, principles, and data to support human well-being and overall system performance. The "system" we're talking about is the collective assembly of all the stakeholder groups, system subcomponents, and interactions among them. In a school context, this could include everything from its management climate, classroom layout, and teaching methods to the EdTech user interface, subject matter being covered, and students' personal characteristics. Figure 12.1 shows a concept of the multilayered system in which learners and learning experiences are embedded. Each of these different layers plays a role in the ultimate success or failure of learning engineering solutions.[1]

To design the most effective learning experiences, we need to use human-centered design techniques that take into account our whole system—from the context of use and learner characteristics down to their mouse clicks and data elements. And we need to plan for human variability, limitations, and imperfections. As discussed in Chapter 3, disciplines such as user-centered design,[2] user-experience design,[3] design thinking,[4] human-systems integration,[5] design justice,[6] and participatory design[7] provide useful tools for this. There are also unique applications of these techniques for learning contexts, and they go by names such as learner-centered design,[8] learning-experience design,[9] universal design for learning,[10] and design-based research.[11] (Check out the endnotes for links to additional resources for these

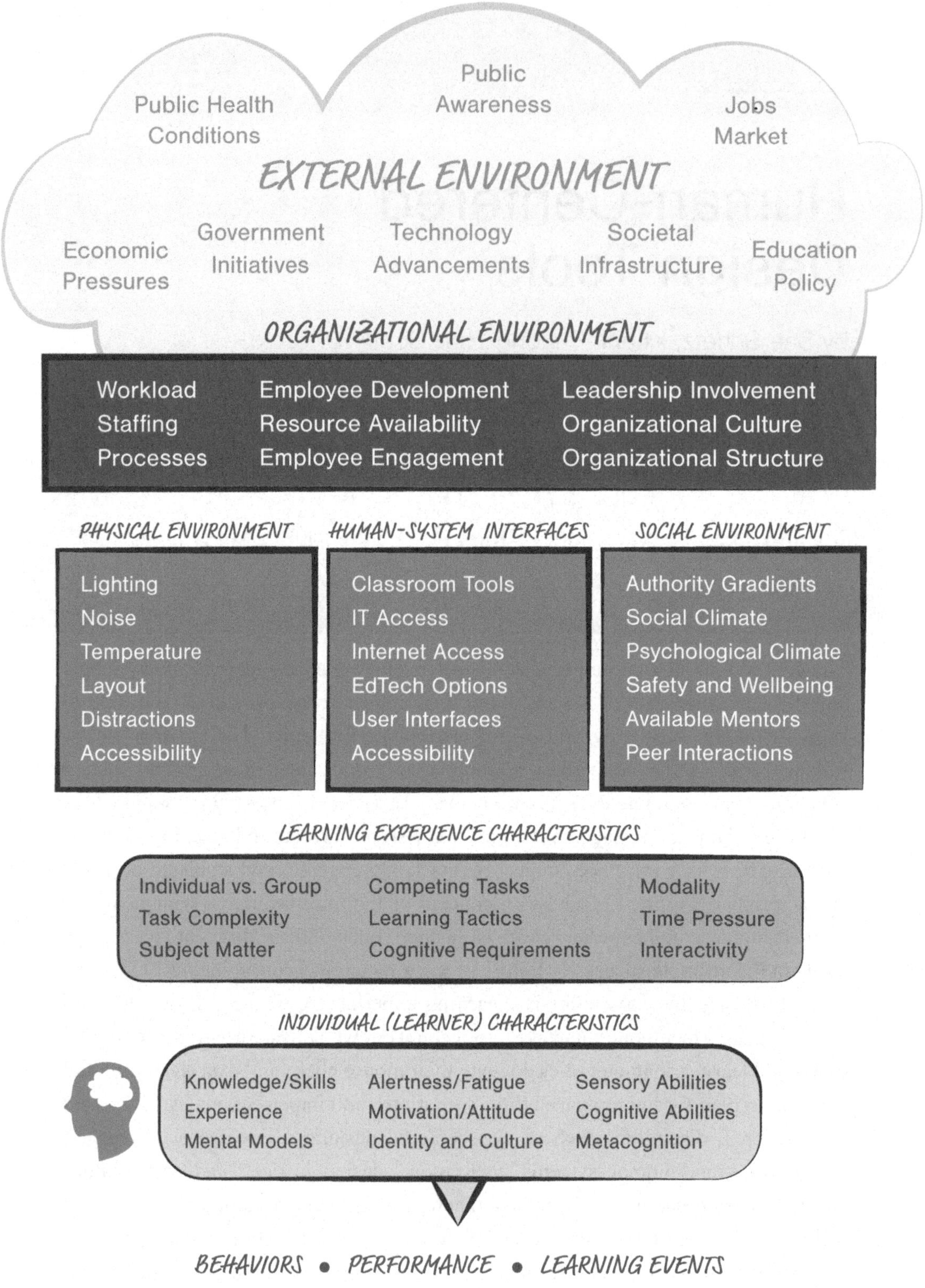

FIGURE 12.1. Examples of interacting subcomponents in a system

disciplines.) The remainder of this chapter includes an introductory set of human-centered tools that are generally applicable to most learning engineering solutions.

Stakeholder Analyses

Stakeholders are the humans—people or groups—affected by, or in some way involved with, a system. They may include learners, teachers, educational staff, managers, system administrators, learning engineering collaborators, and many others. Also, different stakeholders may interact with a system at different times. For example, curriculum developers may be active stakeholders early in a system's life cycle but then only periodically after the final product is released. So, who are your stakeholders, and how will they interact with your learning experience?

- ❑ Identify who your stakeholders are for all life-cycle phases
- ❑ Identify how they'll use, affect, or be affected by your system
- ❑ Elicit and document stakeholders' expectations
- ❑ Understand the context of how and when they'll interact with your system

A common way to categorize stakeholders is with a stakeholder analysis diagram. These come in various forms, but often look like Figure 12.2. To create a

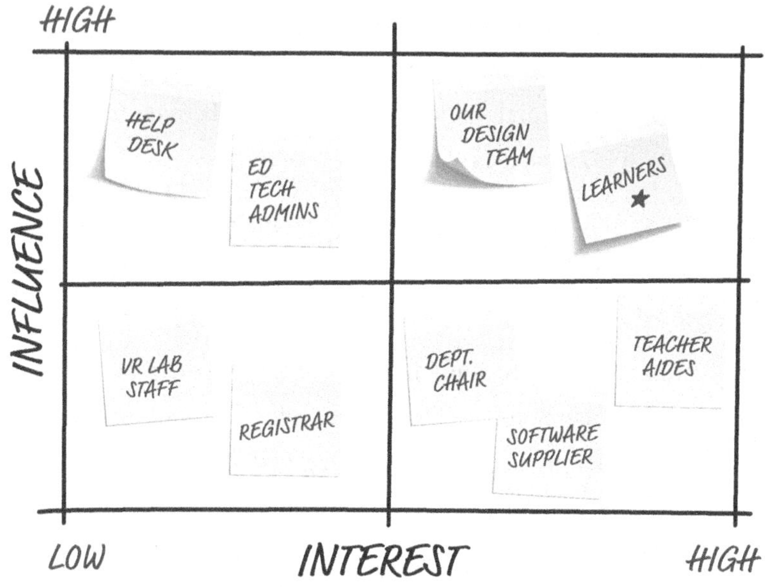

FIGURE 12.2. Identify and map all of your stakeholders

stakeholder analysis, start by brainstorming about the possible stakeholders and then organize them into groups, such as based on their level of interest (or involvement) in the project as well as their ability to influence its success.

STAKEHOLDER NEEDS ASSESSMENT AND ANALYSIS

Once you've identified your stakeholders, the next step is to think about their attributes and needs—making sure all are understood, identifying any conflicts, and prioritizing them as necessary. It's important to complete these assessments early, so that critical system requirements are well understood before starting development. Following a stakeholder needs assessment, you'll also want to complete a corresponding needs analysis. The difference is that a needs *assessment* simply identifies your stakeholders' needs while the *analysis* helps you get to the root cause of why those needs exist. (See Chapter 8 for root-cause analysis tools.)

There are many ways to effectively perform stakeholder needs assessments and analyses. Pick the tools most appropriate for your situation. **Qualitative methods** focus on exploring personal observations, thoughts, or experiences. Some of these research approaches include:

- ❑ Stakeholder elicitation, such as interviews or focus groups
- ❑ Open-ended reactions or attitudinal surveys
- ❑ Behavioral or cognitive task analyses
- ❑ Field observation, ethnography, and participatory analyses
- ❑ Design-based research (although this can also be quantitative)[12]
- ❑ Reviews of published case studies

Quantitative methods use more objective approaches, typically involving statistics or computational methods of some kind. Some of these approaches include:

- ❑ Trend analyses
- ❑ Quantitative analyses of published studies, like meta-analyses
- ❑ Likert-style questionnaires with close-ended answer options
- ❑ Computational methods, like modeling and simulation
- ❑ Experimental and quasi-experimental studies

Note, whenever you're conducting research with stakeholders—even just simple interviews—make sure to consider research ethics. Refer to the ethical frameworks in Chapter 7 and the tools for making ethical decisions in Chapter 17.

IDENTIFY LEARNER VARIATIONS

It's important to understand the range of diversity within a population rather than just designing to its middle or so-called "average." Learning engineers need to uncover typical variations as well as **edge cases** among both dominant and non-dominant subgroups, particularly from the learner population. This allows for the creation of designs that accommodate and can be adapted broadly. In addition to using the research methods described above, consider some basic questions about each learner subgroup, such as from the checklist below:

- ❑ Who are my learners, and what will they learn?
- ❑ What are my learners' different interests related to what they'll learn?
- ❑ Why would these learners want to learn the targeted skills and content?
- ❑ Given that, how might they become engaged in learning?
- ❑ What prior knowledge and experiences do they bring with them?
- ❑ What range of abilities do different learners possess?
- ❑ When and where will they learn?
- ❑ How do they engage in this environment?
- ❑ How do they see themselves in this environment? How do they identify?
- ❑ How might we design learning activities that connect to varying identities?
- ❑ How might we ensure learners' equitable access and empowerment?

Participatory Design Techniques

As discussed in Chapter 3, participatory design techniques invite stakeholders into the design process directly, not only to gain empathetic understanding of their needs but to guide iterative development of the solution intended to meet those needs. In other words, participatory design involves interacting with members of the targeted learning populations and other stakeholders that support them within the design process itself. For example, you may collaborate with instructors to understand their teaching experiences, practical constraints, and knowledge about their learners during the create stage of the learning engineering process. There are many different ways to integrate stakeholders into the design process, and regardless of the approaches selected, the goal is to actively engage representatives from each stakeholder group in the process.

Stakeholders can play many valuable roles. However, since most people lack a background in human-centered design, you'll likely need to use participatory design methods to help coax stakeholders into explicitly articulating their tacit knowledge—or, as the saying goes, to help them make the invisible visible. There are numerous useful collaborative methods, including the three outlined here: design cards, card sorting, and affinity diagrams. In addition to the following tools, the tools for understanding the challenge in Chapter 8 can be used with participatory design.

DESIGN CARDS

Design cards are cards that each depict a single concept via text or imagery. Design cards can be used in various ways to guide collaborative idea generation and critique, prompt the team to consider the wider spectrum of key issues, or help participants sequence or prioritize concepts, such as for modeling of workflows or processes. And the value of design cards doesn't end with the initial design phase. For instance, they can be used as cues to help stakeholders critique aspects of a design in support of development iterations. Using a set of learning sciences concept cards might help end users respond to various questions about the prototype design, such as "How well did we do in addressing this aspect of learning?"

A set of cards typically covers a comprehensive topic, but beyond that, there's much variation. A set may reference more generalizable concepts (such as instructional tactics) using text, or it might include personalized images created for a specific context. For example, in Chapter 3, Medic Mobile used custom-made cards to describe elements of a health system. Each card included a single, sketched concept, such as community members, health care workers, places, technology, and activities. By using the cards during participatory design workshops, stakeholders were better able to conceptualize the wider system, engage in detailed discussions about the health care workflow, and share stories from their own experiences.

You can make your own design cards based on the principles in this book or your unique learning engineering context, or you can search online for pre-made cards suitable for your design challenge. For instance, Transcend, a nonprofit that works with K-12 schools, has developed a set of cards that helps educators identify the most relevant concepts from the learning sciences for a particular educational experience.[13] Similarly, InGlobal Learning Design offers a set of design mindset cards with thought-provoking and playful prompts that teams can use to help stimulate collaboration and generate better ideas.[14] Famed design firm IDEO also offers cards for co-designing schools, such as its equitable learning practices cards.[15] (In addition to its cards, IDEO launched a nonprofit business for educators that offers a number of open-access tools. See www.designkit.org for details.)

CARD SORTING

Card sorting is one specific use of cards. Simply put, in a card sorting activity, stakeholders categorize the cards into conceptual piles. This technique is popular for user interface and user experience (UI/UX) design, because it demonstrates how end users mentally "lump and split" concepts. UI designers might use that information to create menus for an app or a website's navigation. Card sorting can also be used for other kinds of classification or prioritization activities—anything where grouping is important. When performing a card sort, simply create the cards and then either define the groupings (closed sort) or let the end users create their own (open sort).

AFFINITY DIAGRAMS

Similar to card sorting, affinity diagrams ask stakeholders to sort concepts into logical groupings. Unlike typical card sorts, though, affinity diagrams begin with a blank set of sticky notes, and they're designed for groups of stakeholders to complete collaboratively. Affinity diagrams are useful in situations where a team needs to sort through a large number of concepts—particularly when some of those concepts might still be unknown to the larger group. Consider using this technique to rapidly uncover concepts and their relationships—for instance, if the team is approaching a brand-new design project or has an incomplete picture of a complex context.

To complete an affinity diagram, follow these steps:[16]

- ❑ Ask participants to silently jot down concepts, one per sticky note
- ❑ Post the ideas for everyone to see, like on a real or digital white board
- ❑ Collectively sort the notes into conceptual categories
- ❑ Promote an existing card or create a new header card for each group
- ❑ Create superheaders if two or more groups have a strong relationship
- ❑ Redraw the concepts and categories as a finished document

Figure 12.3 shows a simplified example of what an affinity diagram might look like if stakeholders were asked to identify and then sort data science knowledge and skills into a set of learning objectives.

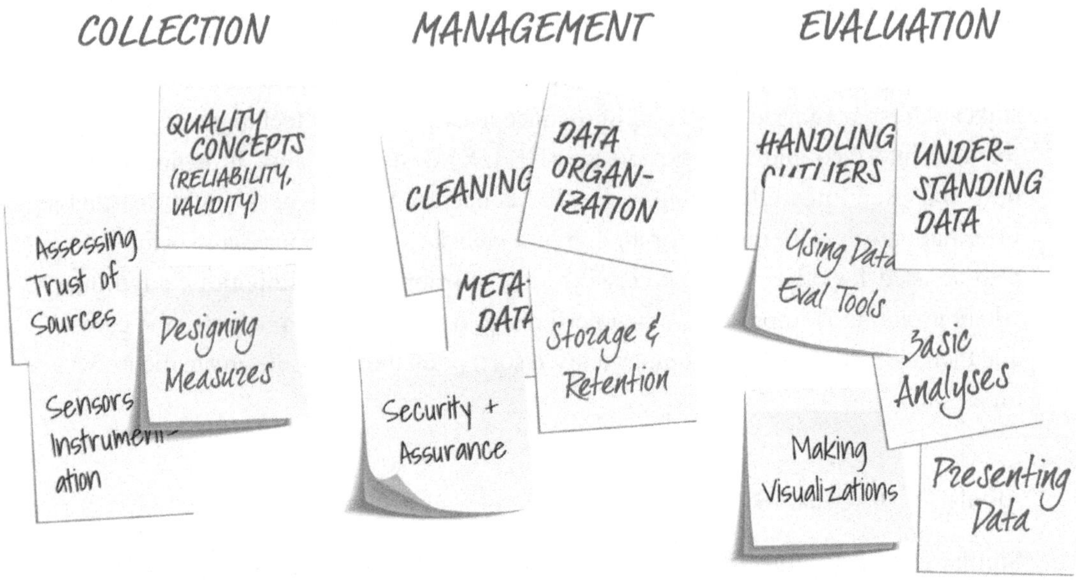

FIGURE 12.3. Example of an affinity diagram with potential data science topics

Personas

As described in Chapter 3, personas are representations of key stakeholders. Typically, a project will require several (say, three to twelve) personas to represent different stakeholder groups or meaningful variations within a single group.

> [A persona is] not a description of a real, single user or an average user. The persona represents patterns of users' behavior, goals, and motives, compiled in a fictional description of a single individual. It also contains made-up personal details, in order to make the persona more "tangible and alive" for the development team.[17]

Personas should be based on qualitative and quantitative demographic data; use what's been learned about the learner population (or populations as well as other stakeholders) to guide your generation of real-world persona variations.[18] It's important that your sets of personas cover the major variations across those who will engage with the implementation of your design. Ideally, personas should help surface variations in each relevant group, including different goals, backgrounds, cultures, and cognitive and physical abilities consistent with the general demographics. As you work on your personas consider the following:

- ❑ Name
- ❑ Personality and traits
- ❑ Culture and background
- ❑ Social context (such as peers, mentors, and family)
- ❑ Abilities and disabilities
- ❑ Prior knowledge and experiences
- ❑ Goals
- ❑ Motivations (likes)
- ❑ Frustrations (dislikes)
- ❑ Environment and other learning context factors
- ❑ Access to relevant tools or technologies

Scenarios, User Stories, and Use Cases

Narrative is a powerful tool in human-centered design. For example, learning engineers can write **scenarios** about the personas they develop. These help highlight a persona's motivations, context, and other characteristics and tell the story about how a representative learner can be expected to navigate the learning experience being designed. Here's a brief example:

> *Daniel sat at his family's shared computer and logged into his school's learning management system. His sister played nearby, watching cartoons on the television, and Daniel had to work hard to pay attention . . .*

User stories have some similarities to scenarios, but the practice of writing user stories grew out of software development and Agile management. (See Chapter 11 for more information on Agile.) User stories are meant to be short (only one or two sentences), informal, and easy to read, and they should describe how a person interacts with the intended system. A development project may have dozens or hundreds of these small user stories. The idea is that each should describe one meaningful feature of the in-development solution, and the product team should be able to accomplish the development of a user-story feature in one sprint. Bigger features that can't fit into a single user story are called epics, and related user stories might be combined under a collective epic.

There are several user story templates; the most common one is below:

As a ___(STAKEHOLDER)___ **I want to** ___(TASK)___ **so that** ___(DESIRED RESULT)___

An example user story made in this template might be:

> *As a teacher, I want to know which students didn't complete their assignments by the deadline so that I can check in with them.*

Finally, **use cases** are more like recipes. Use cases are written descriptions of how different stakeholders are expected to engage with a system. A set of use cases should show the variety of ways stakeholders might interact with a system, their different reactions, and the various outputs that might ensue. Each use case typically includes the following:[19]

- ❑ **Actor:** Who's interacting with the system (which stakeholder or group)?
- ❑ **System:** What product or experience is the actor interacting with?
- ❑ **Goals:** What does the actor want to accomplish?
- ❑ **Preconditions:** What must be true before this use case would take place?
- ❑ **Triggers:** What event caused the use case to begin?
- ❑ **Basic Flow (Success):** How does an actor complete the path successfully?
- ❑ **Alternative Flows:** What different or unsuccessful paths exist?

A brief (simplified) example is shown in Figure 12.4.

USE CASE	Access Assignment In-Box
ACTOR	Teacher
SYSTEM	Learning Management System (LMS)
GOALS	Identify students who have (or have not) submitted their assignments
PRECONDITIONS	Assignment was released (opened) to students in the LMS
TRIGGERS	Actor with admin privileges opens an active assignment
BASIC FLOW	After releasing an assignment in the LMS, the teacher opens the assignment in-box to see the class's submission statuses. If the assignment deadline has passed, then the teacher collects the names of the late students and may follow up with them through the LMS, email, or text messaging.

FIGURE 12.4. Simplified use case example

Human-Centered Requirements Definition

In general, the tools and analyses discussed so far in this chapter inform the *design* of a learning engineering solution, but at some point, design activities need to mature into tangible *development* work. Defining system requirements supports that process. **Requirements** are succinct, formal descriptions of what a system must accomplish, how well it needs to function, and applicable constraints or limitations.

A successful project is likely to have dozens, if not hundreds, of requirements to inform its components' functionality and performance expectations. But not all requirements are the same. As you consider your goals and constraints, look for requirements that fit each of these categories (and note the examples of each listed after the requirement category in parentheses):

- ❑ **Functional requirements:** What a component does ("plays movie")
- ❑ **Nonfunctional requirements:** Qualities of a system ("usability")
- ❑ **Project drivers:** Reasons or goals for the project ("reduce attrition")
- ❑ **Project constraints:** Restrictions on the process ("must be under $1M")
- ❑ **Project issues:** Project management conditions ("iterative design")

Writing effective requirements—especially human-centric ones—is a critical part of systems development. In fact, research shows that many failed projects are caused, at least in part, by a failure to sufficiently consider human-centered requirements. For example, one large-scale study on technology-based development in the United States found that only 34 percent of projects were successful, 15 percent completely failed, and 51 percent were only partially successful. Projects most frequently failed because of "(1) an inadequate understanding of the intended users and the context of use, and (2) vague usability requirements, such as 'the system must be intuitive to use.'"[20] To avoid these traps, it's important to know a lot about who will interact with your system, where and how they'll interact with it, and what they really care about—and then to translate those design factors into effective system requirements that articulate the corresponding concrete functions and qualities. Also, make sure to consider concepts unique to a *learning* experience. For example, which of the learning science concepts from Chapter 9 apply? What kinds of learner variability does your system need to support? Which tools for learner motivation (from Chapter 15) should be included? And from Chapter 13, what data elements need to be collected, and what instrumentation is necessary to support those requirements?

There are plenty of existing requirements templates and spreadsheets available online. Some templates are very simple, like sticky notes on a kanban board as shown in Figure 11.2; other projects require more details or formal management processes. Find an approach that fits your needs or customize the example shown in Figure 12.5, which is adapted from the Volere Requirements Template.[21]

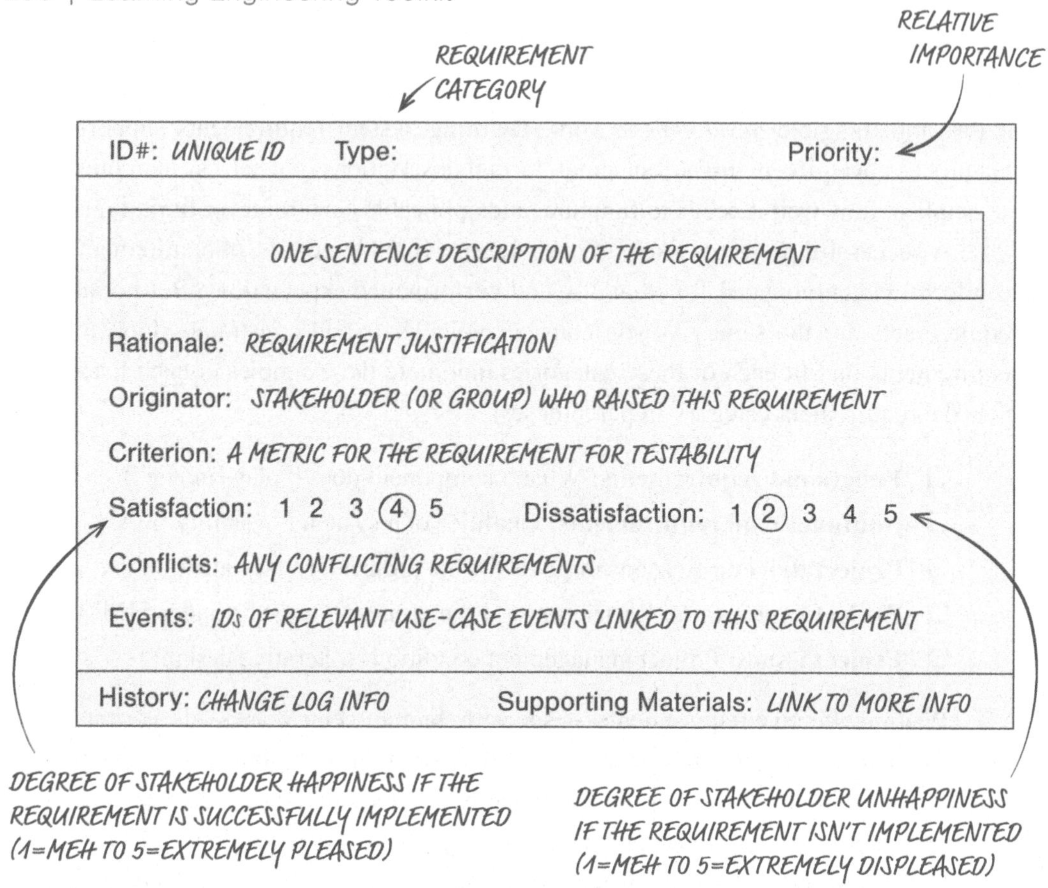

FIGURE 12.5. Example of a requirement template

LOGIC MODELS AND CONJECTURE MAPPING

A significant challenge in iteratively designing learning experiences is keeping track of the reasons for decisions made along the way—for instance, design choices made based on theoretical principles, forced by necessary trade-offs (such as from constraints or competing priorities), or revised in response to new information uncovered through iterative testing. Two specialized techniques, logic models and conjecture maps, can help you keep track of decision-making over time.

A **logic model** is a representation of the design team's expectations about the connections between a system, its policy inputs (resources, strategies, activities), and its desired outcomes.

> In the most basic terms, logic models provide a kind of map for a program or initiative, helping clarify a program or policy's destination, the pathways toward the destination, and markers along the way. . . . [A] logic model helps clarify both what the program, initiative, or policy

is and what it is not. This kind of clarification is helpful in building an evaluation design that can capture the program's or policy's influence and impact.[22]

Figure 12.6 shows a simplified logic model structure. In practice, you'd fill in such a table with summaries derived from more detailed supporting tables, and you'd fill out each of those through a collaborative design activity. Logic models are useful throughout a learning engineering project—from initial planning through iterative testing, implementation, and evaluation. They're best developed early (for instance, to clarify goals, make underlying beliefs explicit, identify logical assumptions and gaps, and build consensus) and then revisited periodically (for instance, to help clarify when and how to conduct evaluations or to refine components based on testing results).

The US Department of Education's Institute of Education Sciences has published an open-access toolkit for building logic models for learning-oriented projects. Its toolkit includes templates, examples, and even suggested agendas for participatory design workshops.[23]

Problem Statement:					
Resources (Inputs)	**Strategies and Activities**	**Outputs**	**Short-term Outcomes**	**Long-term Outcomes**	**Impacts**
What resources are or could reasonably be available?	What will the activities, events, and such be?	What are the initial products of these activities?	What changes are expected in the short term?	What changes do you want to occur after the initial outcomes?	What are the anticipated changes over the long haul?
Assumptions:					

FIGURE 12.6. Sample components of an education-themed logic model[24]

Similar to logic models, conjecture maps help articulate the logical relationships between initial beliefs and desired outcomes, but in contrast to logic models, **conjecture maps** tend to be more detailed and focused. Conjecture mapping is used to document the relevant features of a learning experience (such as the

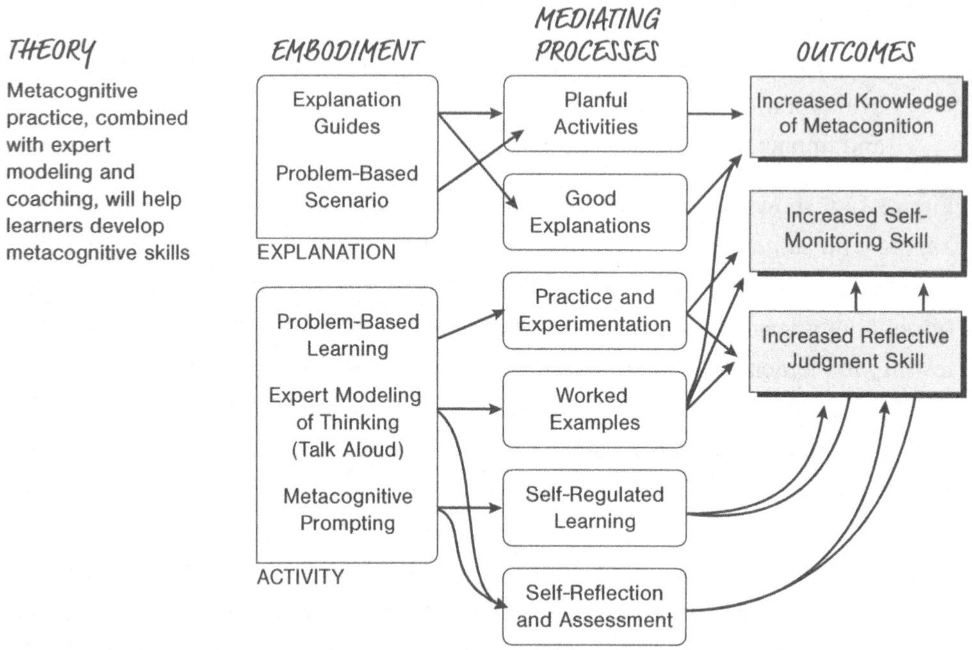

FIGURE 12.7. Example conjecture map

FIGURE 12.8. Example theory of change activity (step 3)

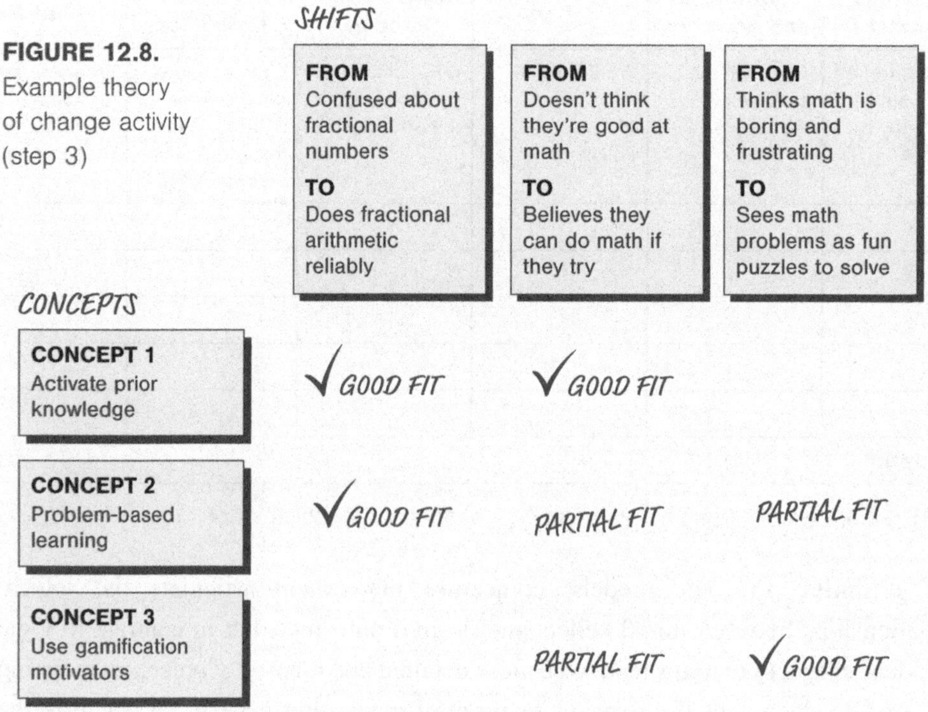

materials, technologies, and environment) and explain how they're predicted to work together to produce the desired outcomes.[25] The idea is to draw an explicit line from a conjecture (or set of conjectures) derived from theories about how people learn, to how the conjecture(s) will be embodied within a particular learning experience (such as through specific instructional interventions or technologies), to the mediating processes (in other words, how the embodied interventions are expected to effect change), and finally to the desired outcomes. (See Figure 12.7.) Conjecture maps can be used in conjunction with logic models or other requirements engineering processes, but they're also useful standalone tools, particularly when it comes to testing, diagnosing, and refining the pedagogical (or andragogical or heutagogical) components of a learning engineering solution.

If you're not sure which conjectures or mediating processes to include, then it may be useful to complete a theory of change activity. A "**theory of change**" is a description of why and how change—such as achieving learning outcomes or fostering learner motivation—is desirable and achievable in a particular context. The open-access IDEO Design Kit includes an activity template and worksheet,[26] and it describes the activity process in five steps:

1. Write out each shift (like learning or motivation) you're trying to create
2. Identify possible concepts or activities that may achieve those outcomes
3. Create a matrix of goals by concepts; mark those most likely to succeed
4. Narrow down your set of priorities
5. Document your final decisions

Figure 12.8 shows an example snapshot of step three in the process. Refer to the IDEO Design Kit for additional details.

Prototyping

A prototype is a draft version of a design that allows for demonstration of its concepts.[27] Prototypes can range from low-fidelity paper drawings to high-fidelity interactive models that showcase features on a subset of content. Early in the design process, it's useful to create quick and inexpensive prototypes like hand-drawn sketches.[28] Use these to refine ideas, communicate with the rest of the learning engineering team, and get feedback from stakeholders. As design and development work progresses, the prototypes need to become gradually more realistic. Mid-fidelity prototypes might include **wireframes** (user interface sketches done by hand or with a digital design application,[29] such as shown in Figure 12.9) and **storyboards** (sketches of the flow of an experience over time). High-fidelity prototypes are typically functional—albeit pared down or incomplete. For example, an advanced software prototype might include a fully functional computer-based application with realistic user interactions that cover one learning module within a curriculum.[30] The IDEO Design Kit offers worksheets and advice on how to prototype and iteratively evaluate your prototypes. It recommends you "find fast and scrappy ways to do your testing. This stage of the design process could take anything from a few days to a few weeks, depending on what you're testing and how many rounds of prototyping you want to do."[31]

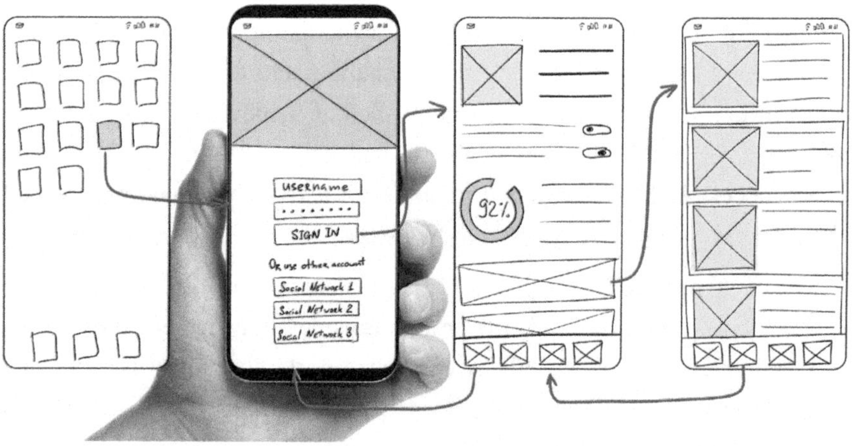

FIGURE 12.9. Early prototypes can be quick, hand-drawn sketches

End-User Test and Evaluation

Each part of a learning engineering design can (and, resources permitting, should) be tested, but testing doesn't need to be difficult or complex. Consider this advice from famed usability expert Jakob Nielsen. Although he's remarking on usability assessments in particular, his advice broadly applies to user testing, in general:[32]

> Some people think that . . . user tests should be reserved for the rare web design project with a huge budget and a lavish time schedule. Not true. Elaborate usability tests are a waste of resources. The best results come from testing no more than five users and running as many small tests as you can afford.

Later, Nielsen adds a sardonic caveat:

> The most striking truth . . . is that zero users give zero insights.

Testing each part of a learning engineering design may include validating assumptions—about your needs analyses, requirements, personas, scenarios and use cases, learning design elements, and prototypes—with people your design is intended to serve. Don't reserve testing for finished products. As the *Math Readiness* development process described in Chapter 3 demonstrated, it's important to test your design components early and often—even just the paper-based sketches.

AVOID THE "LAST MILE" PROBLEM WHERE YOU COLLECT DATA BUT DON'T USE IT TO INFORM DECISIONS OR ACTIONS (BECAUSE OF LACK OF TIME, EXPERTISE, OR SO ON)

When planning your testing activities, use the following questions to help guide your measurement approach:

- ❑ What features or functions are you testing?
- ❑ How precise (sensitive) do your measures need to be?
- ❑ Which stakeholder groups need to be included among participants?
- ❑ Have you identified an appropriately representative set of participants?
- ❑ How many people need to participate to generate sufficient data?
- ❑ What conditions (like the testing environment) might skew results?
- ❑ How closely does the testing context need to replicate the learning context?
- ❑ What assessment tools (like surveys or post-tests) do you need?
- ❑ Can you instrument the learning activity to collect relevant data?
- ❑ Are your assessment tools suitably valid and reliable?
- ❑ What ethical safeguards are needed? (See Chapters 7 and 17.)
- ❑ How will you analyze and use the resulting outcomes from the test?
- ❑ Have you left enough time to take action in response to the test results?

The qualitative and quantitative research methods discussed earlier in this chapter can be used for testing. Early in the design process, testing may involve lightweight approaches, like reactions surveys and focus groups; however, more mature prototypes and products will likely require stronger measures of their performance. For training and education contexts, Donald Kirkpatrick's four-levels evaluation model is a handy way to conceptualize learning assessment.[33] The model starts with easier to measure—but less reliable and potentially less impactful—targets, and then it progresses to more difficult to measure—but likely more valuable—ones:

1. **Reactions:** What did learners think? Did they enjoy the experience?
2. **Learning:** What did they learn? (Usually a pre/post-test combination)
3. **Behavior:** Did the experience affect future behaviors, like job activities?
4. **Results:** Was there a noticeable impact, like a company's performance?

USABILITY TESTING

Usability testing is one particular kind of end-user testing. It involves testing a product with representative end users to examine its human-system interface in order to identify problems in the design of the solution, uncover opportunities to improve or add features, and learn about the target population's behavior and preferences.[34]

Typically, usability testing involves a facilitator who asks participants to complete a series of tasks using the system. The facilitator (or their fellow team members) observes and records participants' behaviors, in particular noting anomalies from expected actions. The facilitator may also encourage participants to use a **"think aloud" protocol**, where they're asked to say whatever comes to mind while they're interacting with the system, such as "I can't find the menu option I'm looking for" or "that animation was cute." The facilitator may also ask or answer questions—although they must be careful to avoid inadvertently skewing the test results. Digital.gov from the US General Services Administration has open-access tips and training videos for conducting usability testing,[35] and the usability.gov site offers additional methods, templates, and examples.[36]

Usability testing is often combined with a reactions survey of some kind. One of the most frequently used is the **System Usability Scale (SUS)**. It's a "quick and dirty" questionnaire that collects end-user usability reactions about ease of use, satisfaction, and learnability.[37] The SUS has ten questions, and participants rate each item on a scale from one to five. (See Figure 12.10.)

Scoring the SUS takes some effort, because some of the questions are negatively worded while others are positively phrased.

- For odd-numbered items, subtract one from the user response.
- For even-numbered items, subtract the user responses from five.
- Add up the converted numbers per person and multiply that total by 2.5.

Multiplying the final score by 2.5 converts the range to 0–100 so that scores can be more easily understood. After calculating each participant's individual score, you can use basic statistical methods to find group outcomes, like mean, median, and standard deviation. In general, an overall (aggregate) SUS score for a system of 68 is considered above average, and scores above 80.3 are in the top 10 percent—those are A-quality systems.[38]

SYSTEM USABILITY SCALE

Score each item from 1 (Strongly Disagree) to 5 (Strongly Agree)
1. I think that I would like to use this system frequently.
2. I found the system unnecessarily complex.
3. I thought the system was easy to use.
4. I think that I would need the support of a technical person to be able to use this system.
5. I found the various functions in this system were well integrated.
6. I thought there was too much inconsistency in this system.
7. I would imagine that most people would learn to use this system very quickly.
8. I found the system very cumbersome to use.
9. I felt very confident using the system.
10. I needed to learn a lot of things before I could get going with this system.

FIGURE 12.10. SUS questionnaire

Pulling It All Together

This chapter introduced a broad toolkit of human-centered design techniques—and these only scratch the surface. But don't get overwhelmed. Remember, the goal of human-centered design is to understand the interactions among people and the other elements of the system in order to optimize human well-being and overall performance. Select the most relevant techniques that will help you achieve those goals. No single technique is required, and it's OK to adjust techniques to fit your needs and project constraints. Just remember that witty advice from Jakob Nielsen: While it's smart to be lightweight and efficient with human-centered design and testing activities, *zero* activities gives *zero* results. Integration of human-centered design is core to achieving learning engineering goals. ★

Endnotes

1 Figure 12.1 is adapted from Hughes, Ronda, ed. *Patient Safety and Quality: An Evidence-Based Handbook for Nurses*. Rockville, MD: Agency for Healthcare Research and Quality, US Department of Health and Human Services, 2008. http://research.policyarchive.org/21365.pdf

2 **USER-CENTERED DESIGN RESOURCES**

- The Interaction Design Foundation provides various design resources on topics such as user research, usability, UX design, and design thinking. These resources include tutorials, videos, and bootcamps with advice from experienced designers.
See: www.interaction-design.org
- The US General Services Administration provides overviews and how-to guides for designing good user experiences with software. See: www.usability.gov
- Conboy, Antony. "The User-Centered Design Process (UCD) - EXPLAINED FAST!!" Video, 4:46. December 12, 2019. https://youtu.be/4xeK9L7WmMM

3 **USER-EXPERIENCE DESIGN RESOURCES**

- As described in the User-Centered Design Resources, see www.interaction-design.org
- US General Services Administration. "User Experience Basics." Usability.gov. Accessed January 8, 2022. www.usability.gov/what-and-why/user-experience.html
- CareerFoundry. "What Is UX Design? - An Introduction (Full Guide)." Video, 8:23. March 4, 2021. https://youtu.be/ziQEqGZB8GE

4 **DESIGN THINKING RESOURCES**

- As described in the User-Centered Design Resources, see www.interaction-design.org
- IDEO U offers online courses and certificate programs in design thinking as well as other design-centric tools and processes. See: www.ideou.com
- Liedtka, Jeanne. "Why Design Thinking Works: It Addresses the Biases and Behaviors that Hamper Innovation." *Harvard Business Review* September–October (2018): 72–79. https://hbr.org/2018/09/why-design-thinking-works

5 **HUMAN-SYSTEMS INTEGRATION RESOURCES**

- Pew, Richard W. and Anne S. Mavor, eds. *Human-System Integration in the System Development Process*. Washington, DC: The National Academies Press, 2007. https://doi.org/10.17226/11893
- The US Department of Defense also offers courses in human-systems integration. Refer to the Defense Acquisition University's listing of resources. See: www.dau.edu/tools/se-brainbook/Pages/Design%20Considerations/Human-Systems-Integration.aspx
- The National Academies. "Human-Systems Integration." Video, 23:04. 2018. https://vimeo.com/258880061

6 **DESIGN JUSTICE RESOURCES**

- The Design Justice Network offers resources and conducts events for those practicing the design justice principles. See: https://designjustice.org
- Design Justice adopts an activist approach to design, focusing on traditionally underserved communities. It challenges the extent to which universal principles are valid in understanding the diverse needs of users. Sasha Costanza-Chock's book provides a comprehensive review of theories and issues in design.

- Costanza-Chock, Sasha. *Design Justice: Community-Led Practices to Build the Worlds We Need.* Cambridge, MA: MIT Press, 2020. https://doi.org/10.7551/mitpress/12255.001.0001

7 PARTICIPATORY DESIGN (ALSO CALLED CO-DESIGN) RESOURCES

- For a list of readings on participatory design, See:
  - Lampe, Cliff. "Readings on Participatory Design." *Medium* (2019). https://medium.com/@clifflampe/readings-on-participatory-design-e006ed21a91c
- DiSalvo, Betsy, Carl DiSalvo, Elizabeth Bonsignore, and Jason Yip, eds. *Participatory Design for Learning: Perspectives from Practice and Research.* New York: Routledge, 2017.

8 LEARNER-CENTERED DESIGN RESOURCES

- "Learner-Centered Design: The Secret of Creating Engaging eLearning Experiences." SH!FT. Last modified 2014. www.shiftelearning.com/blog/bid/345394/4-steps-to-becoming-a-learner-centered-elearning-professional
- Quintana, Chris, Namsoo Shin, Cathleen Norris, and Elliot Soloway. "Learner-Centered Design: Reflections on the Past and Directions for the Future." In *The Cambridge Handbook of the Learning Sciences,* edited by R. Keith Sawyer, 119–134. 2nd ed. Cambridge: Cambridge University Press, 2014. https://doi.org/10.1017/CBO9780511816833.020

9 LEARNING-EXPERIENCE DESIGN RESOURCES

- LXD.org is a community hub for learning experience designers. See: https://lxd.org
- Gutierrez, Karla. "Learning Experience Design: An Overview and 11 of the Best Resources." SH!FT. www.shiftelearning.com/blog/learning-experience-design-best-resources

10 UNIVERSAL DESIGN FOR LEARNING (UDL) RESOURCES

- CAST (which once stood for Center for Applied Special Technology) is a nonprofit education research and development organization that created the Universal Design for Learning framework and UDL Guidelines. CAST provides tutorials and resources for inclusive and accessible design for learning. See: www.cast.org
- Meyer, Anne, David H. Rose, and David Gordon. *Universal Design for Learning: Theory and Practice.* Wakefield, MA: CAST, 2014. http://castpublishing.org/books-media/udl-theory-and-practice

11 DESIGN-BASED RESEARCH

- Barab, Sasha. "Design-Based Research: A Methodological Toolkit for Engineering Change." In *The Cambridge Handbook of the Learning Sciences,* edited by R. Keith Sawyer, 153–170. 2nd ed. Cambridge: Cambridge University Press, 2014. https://doi.org/10.1017/CBO9781139519526.011
- Research–practice partnerships often use design-based implementation research to adapt, mix, and merge curricula and resources for use in particular venues. For more information on these practices, including other readings and case studies, see:
  - College of Education. "Research-Practice Partnerships and DBIR." University of Washington. Accessed January 8, 2022. www.education.uw.edu/slmi/research-practice-partnerships-and-dbir
  - School of Education. "Design Based Implementation Research." University of Colorado Boulder. Accessed January 8, 2022. www.colorado.edu/research/learn-dbir

12 Refer to the design-based research resources cited above:

- Barab, "Design-Based Research," 153–170.
- Quintana, Shin, Norris, and Soloway. "Learner-Centered Design," 119–134.

13 "Transcend Store: Designing for Learning Resources." Transcend. Accessed January 8, 2022. www.transcendeducation.org/store

14 "Design Mindset CARDS." InGlobal Learning Design. Accessed January 8, 2022. inglobal.org/design-mindset-cards

15 "Tools for Change." Co-Designing Schools Toolkit. Accessed January 8, 2022. www.codesigningschools.com/toolkit-appendix

16 Balanced Scorecard Institute. "Basic Tools for Process Improvement, Module 4: Affinity Diagram." In *Handbook for Basic Process Improvement.* https://balancedscorecard.org/bsc-basics/articles-videos/process-improvement-tools

17 Blomkvist, Stefan. "The User as a Personality." In *Using Personas as a Tool for Design.* Position paper for the course workshop "Theoretical Perspectives in Human-Computer Interaction" at IPLab, KTH. 2002. www.csc.kth.se/~tessy/Blomkvist.pdf

18 **PERSONAS RESOURCES**

- US General Services Administration. "Personas." Usability.gov. Accessed January 8, 2022. www.usability.gov/how-to-and-tools/methods/personas.html
- Chronister, Michelle. "Using Personas to Better Understand Customers: USA.gov Case Study." Digital.gov. Last updated April 6, 2015. https://digital.gov/2015/04/06/using-personas-to-better-understand-customers-usa-gov-case-study
- For examples of some personas see:
  - Daniel, Kendrick. "Personas 101." Digital.gov. Last updated January 9, 2015. https://digital.gov/2015/01/09/personas-101

19 US General Services Administration. "Use Cases." Usability.gov. Accessed January 8, 2022. www.usability.gov/how-to-and-tools/methods/use-cases.html

20 Pew and Mavor, *Human-System Integration in the System Development Process*, 191.

21 Robertson, Suzanne, and James Robertson. *Volere Requirements Specification Template*. 16th ed. London: Atlantic Systems Guild Limited, 2012.

22 Shakman, Karen and Sheila M. Rodriguez. *Logic Models for Program Design, Implementation, and Evaluation: Workshop Toolkit*, 9. Washington, DC: U.S. Department of Education, Institute of Education Sciences, National Center for Education Evaluation and Regional Assistance, Regional Educational Laboratory Northeast & Islands, 2015. http://ies.ed.gov/ncee/edlabs

23 Shakman and Rodriguez, *Logic Models for Program Design, Implementation, and Evaluation.*

24 Shakman and Rodriguez, *Logic Models for Program Design, Implementation, and Evaluation,* B-1.

25 **CONJECTURE MAPPING RESOURCES**

- Sandoval, William. "Conjecture Mapping: An Approach to Systematic Educational Design Research." *Journal of the Learning Sciences* 23, no. 1 (2014): 18–36. https://doi.org/10.1080/10508406.2013.778204
- "Conjecture Map." EduTechWiki. Last modified October 30, 2019. http://edutechwiki.unige.ch/en/Conjecture_map

- Lee, Victor R., Mimi Recker, and Abigail L. Phillips. "Conjecture Mapping the Library: Iterative Refinements Toward Supporting Maker Learning Activities in Small Community Spaces." In *Rethinking Learning in the Digital Age: Making the Learning Sciences Count, 13th International Conference of the Learning Sciences, London, June 23–27, 2018*, edited by Judy Kay and Rosemary Luckin. www.isls.org/icls/2018/icls2018.com/index.html

26 Ideo.org. "Explore Your Theory of Change." Design Kit. Accessed January 8, 2022. www.designkit.org/methods/explore-your-theory-of-change

27 Friis Dam, Rikke and Teo Yu Siang. "Design Thinking: Get Started with Prototyping." Interaction Design Foundation. Last modified 2021. www.interaction-design.org/literature/article/design-thinking-get-started-with-prototyping

28 Rubin, Jonathan. "Design Sketching: The Easiest Prototype Method Ever." Digital.gov. Last modified August 8, 2014. https://digital.gov/2014/08/08/design-sketching-the-easiest-prototype-method-ever

29 Kopp, Brandon. "Making Prototypes with Tools You Already Have." Digital.gov. Last modified December 19, 2014. https://digital.gov/2014/12/19/making-prototypes-with-tools-you-already-have

30 US General Services Administration. "Prototyping." Usability.gov. Accessed January 8, 2022. www.usability.gov/how-to-and-tools/methods/prototyping.html

31 Ideo.org. "Rapid Prototyping." Design Kit. Accessed January 8, 2022. www.designkit.org/methods/rapid-prototyping

32 Nielsen, Jakob. "Why You Only Need to Test with 5 Users." Nielsen Norman Group. Last modified March 18, 2000. www.nngroup.com/articles/why-you-only-need-to-test-with-5-users

33 Kirkpatrick, Donald L. and James D. Kirkpatrick. *Evaluating Training Programs*. 3rd ed. San Francisco: Berrett-Koehler Publishers, 2006.

34 Moran, Kate. "Usability Testing 101." Nielsen Norman Group. Last modified December 1, 2019. www.nngroup.com/articles/usability-testing-101

35 Digital.gov from the US General Services Administration has open-access tips and training videos for conducting usability testing. See: https://digital.gov/topics/usability-testing

36 Usability.gov offers additional methods, templates, and examples. See: www.usability.gov

37 US General Services Administration. "System Usability Scale (SUS)." Usability.gov. Accessed January 8, 2022. www.usability.gov/how-to-and-tools/methods/system-usability-scale.html

38 Sauro, Jeff. "Measuring Usability with the System Usability Scale (SUS)." MeasuringU. Last modified February 3, 2011. https://measuringu.com/sus

COLLECT

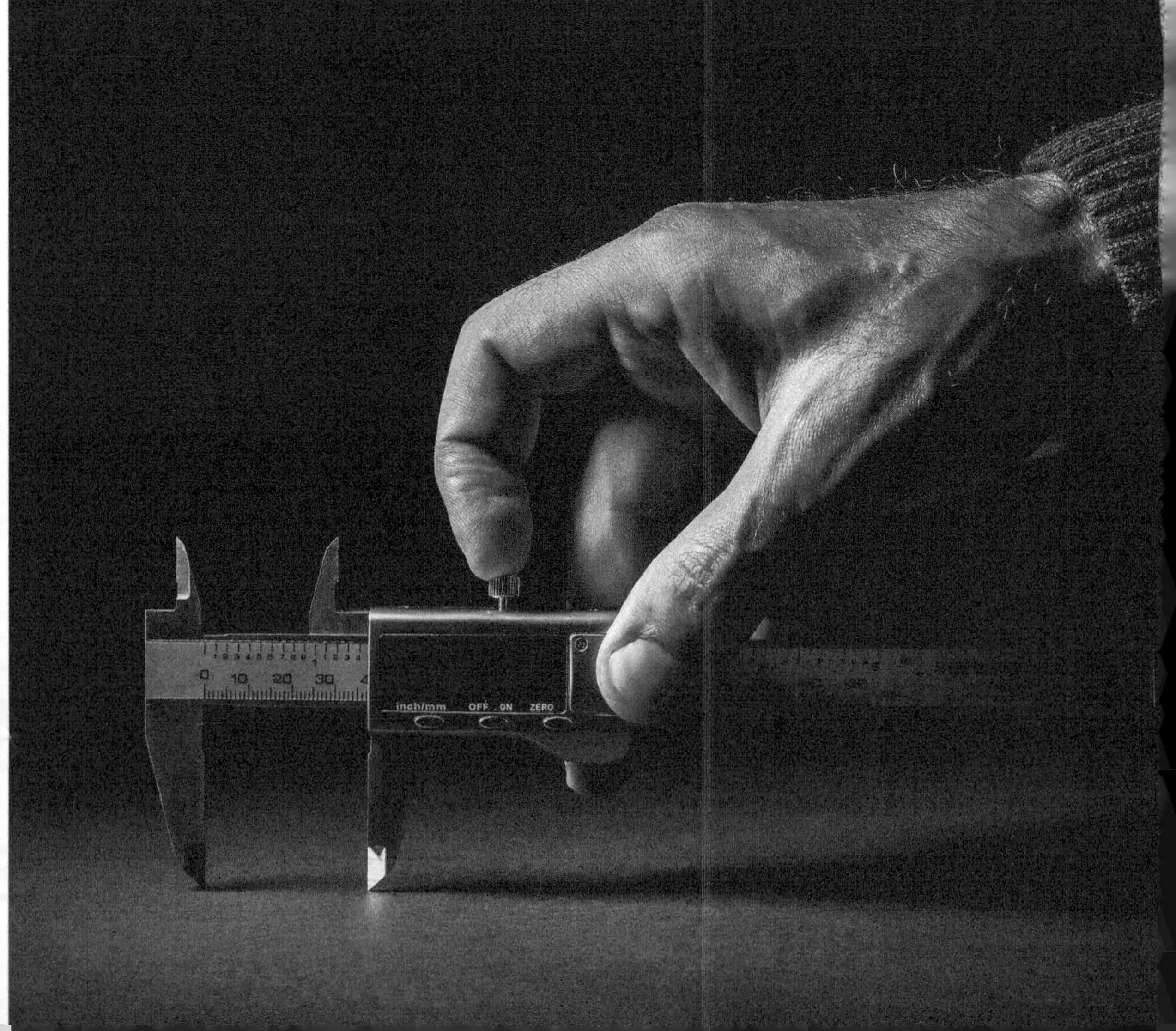

CHAPTER 13

Data Instrumentation Tools

by Erin Czerwinski, Jim Goodell, Steve Ritter, Robert Sottilare, and Khanh-Phuong Thai

This chapter provides process tools for deciding what data to collect and for designing instrumentation for the collection of those data. It supports practical application of concepts introduced in Chapter 5, Learning Engineering Uses Data (Part 1): Instrumentation. This chapter also includes references to standards-based open-source software resources for instrumenting learning experiences.

In Chapter 5 we examined the essential role of data collection in the learning engineering process. Instrumentation design and implementation are integral for this. During the creation phase we're not only creating learning experiences and things that impact the conditions for learning but also determining the data we'll use to inform iterative improvement of those products. This might mean designing and developing new sensors or new data pipelines—new ways of capturing, processing, and tagging collected data to help us answer questions. Other times, the necessary data are already captured by a learning platform, and we just need to confirm that they're being analyzed and used in meaningful ways.

START WITH THE QUESTION, "What do we want to learn from the data?"

One approach to answering that question is to consider the first or next implementation of our learning engineering creation as a research trial. Are we testing one possible solution against the status quo? Or are we testing two or more variations? We should have an idea about the desired outcome, that is, a theory based on the learning sciences and/or a hypothesis based on what we know about the specific challenge. This research trial will test our hypothesis or compare two or more options for meeting the challenge.

The next question is, "What are the possible ways we can test that theory or outcome using data?" We don't need perfect measures, only indicators. The most accurate way to measure a student outcome on a five-minute learning experience may be pre- and post-tests that take twenty minutes each. However, we don't have that luxury in most cases—nor do we typically have laboratory-like conditions in which to finely control the testing. Often instrumentation and sensors need to be unobtrusive and suitable for ecological (real-world) conditions. Is there another way that we can capture enough data to test our creation(s) with little or no additional work for learners and teachers?

We might ask, "Are sensors and a pipeline already in place?" Sometimes a learning platform or learning management system already logs learner interactions and outcomes. If not, we ask, "What resources do we have to create the needed sensor(s) and pipeline?" If the data collection mechanisms aren't already in place and we don't have the technical resources to develop new mechanisms from scratch, then there may be some open-source tools or creative approaches that could work. The following tools are designed to help in this process.

Data Instrumentation Decision Tool

Complete for each question that you want the data to answer:

- ❑ **Question:** What's the question to answer? Who wants to know? Why?
- ❑ **Method:** How can we answer this question using data? What trial or research methods should be used? What analysis techniques? How can we measure unobtrusively?
- ❑ **Metrics:** What do we need to calculate from the data to answer the question?
- ❑ **Data Elements:** What data elements must be collected at what grain size for the metric and analysis?
- ❑ **Sources:** Are the sensor(s) and pipeline already in place to collect the needed elements? If not, what are our options for creating the instrumentation?
- ❑ **Quality:** What assumptions do we have about the quality of data from the existing sources? Can we check those assumptions, for example, with data profiling tools? Was the instrumentation intended for a different purpose? Does the quality hold up for the new purpose and metrics? Are there other aspects of quality that will impact its use for this new purpose?

xAPI: Getting to the Data

As discussed in Chapter 5, Learning Engineering Uses Data (Part 1): Instrumentation, the Experience Application Programming Interface (xAPI) is an open-source data standard that helps learning engineers instrument sensors to get interoperable, granular, context-rich, and semantically linked data out of them. In practice, xAPI includes three main parts: coded statements (like the one below) that are written into your learning technology, a learning record store (a data store you implement) to catch and validate the xAPI outputs, and xAPI Profiles that help us have consistency in our data elements and terminology across different experiences and systems.

EXAMPLE xAPI STATEMENT IN JSON


```
{
"actor": {
   "objectType": "Agent",
   "name": "Ann Advisor",
   "mbox_sha1sum": "BF4479FD4A834CFC4033C40AB58F5DBBACC599BB"
 },
"verb": {
   "id": "https://w3id.org/xapi/dod-isd/verbs/advised",
   "display": {
             "fr": "conseiller",
             "en-US": "advised"
      }
 },
"object": {
   "objectType": "Agent",
   "name": "A. Learner"
   "mbox": "mailto:pojulgnatt@abcde.com",
 },
"timestamp": "2021-11-09T11:20:32.321-05:00"
}
```

FIGURE 13.1. An example xAPI statement for an event where "Ann Advisor" (actor) "advised" (verb) "A. Learner" (object). See also the Yet Analytics xAPI Statement Validator at http://yetanalytics.github.io/xapi-schema-demo

And the figure below shows an example web page instrumented with xAPI.

```
1. <head>
2.    <!-- Get reusable scripts that hide the complexity -->
3.    <script type="“text/javascript” src=“./js/jimsxapiwrapper.js”></script>
4.
5.    <!-- Script sets variables, calls scripts to format, sends Statement -->
6.    <script>
7.    function send_statement(value){
8.        var conf = {
9.            “endpoint” : “https://lrs.adlnet.gov/xapi/”,
10.             “auth” : “Basic ” + toBase64(“xapi-tools:xapi-tools”)
11.             };
12.         ADL.XAPIWrapper.changeConfig(conf);
13.
14.         // Set values and set up xAPI Statement in the right format
15.         var actorName = “Your Name Here”; // Change to your name or alias
16.         var actorMail = “mailto:Tester@example.com”;
17.         var verbId = “http://example.com/xapi/interacted;
18.         var verbDisplay =  “interacted”;
19.         var objectId = “http://example.com/button_example”,
20.         var resultResponse = value; // “value” is name button clicked
21.     // Call a function to construct the xAPI statement behind the scenes
22.         var statement = GOODELL.XAPIWrapper.setupSimpleStatement();
23.
24.         // Dispatch the statement to the LRS
25.         var result = ADL.XAPIWrapper.sendStatement(statement);
26.     }
27.     </script>
28. </head>
29.
30. <body>
31.     <!-- “name” is optional “response” + (actor) (interacted) (button) -->
32. <p>Instrumentation is easy.</p>
33.     <button type=“button” name=“True”
                    onclick=“send_statement(this.name)”>True</button>
34.     <button type=“button” name=“False”
                    onclick=“send_statement(this.name)”>False</button>
35. </body>
36. </html>
```

FIGURE 13.2. Adapted from Anthony Altieri's 2017 Learning Solutions article. Example results at http://adlnet.github.io/xapi-statement-viewer.

NOTES: This uses functions in lines 22 and 25 to call a separate script file (jimsxapiwrapper.js) loaded in line 3 to minimize the code needed in the web page. This is a simplified example for illustration purposes. In real implementations the basic authentication used here would be replaced with more robust security protocols.

Instrumentation in Commercial Platforms

USING DATA THAT ARE ALREADY COLLECTED BY AN ONLINE PLATFORM TO ANSWER SOME QUESTIONS

Most learning management systems already collect information about the learning activities a learner launches, times assignments are submitted, assignment scores, and other basic interactions. These platforms also log information about usage of the system and resources within the system. Those data may or may not include the details needed to answer all of your learning engineering questions—but that information may be able to answer some questions. Be careful when using data from instrumentation designed for a different purpose; the data labels may suggest meaning that wasn't intended, like in the story in Chapter 5 where the use of "SUCCEED" made sense to the software developers but the learning analytics team interpreted it differently. In any case, it's good to know what data are already available before developing new instrumentation.

GOOGLE CLASSROOM CONNECTOR FOR K-12

The Google Classroom Connector, by InnovateEDU, is a free and open-source data extraction tool for any school district that uses G Suite for Education. No external software or application is needed. Using the connector, Google Classroom data are loaded into Google BigQuery, a fully managed data warehouse within Google Cloud. BigQuery allows you to analyze data using SQL, and it provides the option to connect to popular business intelligence reporting tools such as Data Studio, Tableau, Power BI, or Looker. This allows districts to create data dashboards or reports using up-to-date Google Classroom data, for instance, to provide insights into student engagement and performance.[1]

LEARNING MANAGEMENT SYSTEMS AND LEARNING PLATFORMS

Each commercial learning management system (LMS) has its own approach to making internal data available in analytics tools or for visualization in the platform's own tools. Commercial vendors may have proprietary logging, use instrumentation standards such as Caliper, xAPI, or a mix of the two. The scope of the data is largely determined by the functions within the system. For example, some online assessments may be automatically scored but the detailed data about a learner's interaction with a specific assessment item and metadata about that item may not be available. If your team is engineering or curating learning activities for delivery in a specific learning management platform, you can start by identifying the data that are already being and are available to you.

WEB LOG ANALYTICS

At a minimum, learner interactions with anything hosted on a website can be collected from web logs and analyzed using tools like Google Analytics. Web log files are automatically created by web servers. These logs record website hits, such as document or image views, and contains information about who visited a site, where they came from, and what they did on it. However, these logs probably don't have enough detail to answer most learning engineering questions.

ASSISTMENTS AND E-TRIALS

Worcester Polytechnic Institute's ASSISTments is a forever-free online platform for assigning and assessing math homework. ASSISTments was developed and proven effective under federal grants. The efficacy research was conducted in middle school mathematics, but the platform has been used at other grades, including higher education, and for other academic subjects. In 2017, MIT researchers called ASSISTments one of the two most promising technology-based interventions in the US K-12 education system. In 2020, the What Works Clearinghouse funded a study to figure out what distance learning tools were effective, and ASSISTments was deemed to be one of three—out of the over nine hundred reviewed.[2] ASSISTments is used by more than 20,000 teachers and their 500,000 students in addition to researchers studying pedagogy and learning.

E-TRIALS (Ed Tech Research Infrastructure to Advance Learning Science) is a joint project between The ASSISTments Foundation and Worcester Polytechnic Institute that leverages ASSISTments to support researchers to create randomized controlled trials that strengthen the science of learning. New infrastructure, funded by Schmidt Futures, is being developed to reduce the cost and increase the volume of studies conducted using ASSISTments. While it was originally developed with a focus on learning sciences and educational research, E-TRIALS could be used for A/B testing and randomized controlled trials of EdTech products, online learning activities, or instructional content.

xAPI LEARNING COHORT

The xAPI Learning Cohort is a free, vendor-neutral twelve-week project-based team learning experience. Participants form teams based on shared interests and work together on an xAPI project. xAPI Cohorts run twice a year in spring and fall with weekly all-group web meetings. See xapicohort.com.

INSTRUMENTATION STANDARDS

Some commercial platforms may use standardized data formats and interfaces. That's a good thing! Standards make extracting data easier, so it's worthwhile to look for (or to build) systems that use interoperability standards, such as:

- xAPI (see the simple example in this chapter)
- OpenSimon tools (if a course is on the OpenSimon platform)
- Caliper (if a course is on an LMS using LTI and Caliper standards)
- Human Performance Markup Language (for fine-grained measures in certain training domains)

It's best to look for systems that use published standards created by voluntary consensus standards bodies, such as the Institute of Electrical and Electronics Engineers Learning Technology Standards Committee, the World Wide Web Consortium, the Simulation Interoperability Standards Organization, or the International Organization for Standardization. These organizations plan, develop, establish, and coordinate standards using agreed-upon procedures, and importantly, they maintain the standards through regular governance. They also adhere to principles such as openness, balance of interest, and due process.[3] ★

UPGRADE

UpGrade is a free open-source, dashboard-based web service that facilitates designing and deploying randomized A/B tests and fair comparisons of learning experiences in educational software. The tool allows developers of educational software and online learning experiences to define and run A/B tests to explore what works best for supporting the most effective learning outcomes. Information, guides, and source code are available at www.upgradeplatform.org.

Endnotes

1 InnovateEDU. "Google Classroom Connector." Landing Zone. Accessed April 21, 2021. www.landingzone.org/google-connector

2 Sahni, SD, JR Polanin, Q. Zhang, LE Michaelson, S. Caverly, ML Polese, and J. Yang. *A What Works Clearinghouse Rapid Evidence Review of Distance Learning Programs* (WWC 2021-005REV). Washington, DC: US Department of Education, Institute of Education Sciences, National Center for Education Evaluation and Regional Assistance, What Works Clearinghouse. https://eric.ed.gov/?id=ED610886

3 "Promoting Innovation, Competition, and Economic Growth: Principles for Effective Domestic and International Standards Development." National Institute of Standards and Technology (NIST), US Department of Commerce, February 9, 2012. www.nist.gov/speech-testimony/promoting-innovation-competition-and-economic-growth-principles-effective-domestic

4 Closing quotation from Park, Robert E., Wolfhart B. Goethert, and William A. Florac. *Goal-Driven Software Measurement. A Guidebook.* Pittsburgh: Software Engineering Institute, Carnegie Mellon University, 1996. https://resources.sei.cmu.edu/asset_files/Handbook/1996_002_001_16436.pdf

In goal-driven measurement, the primary question is not "What metrics should I use?" but "What do I want to know or learn?"

– *Goal-Driven Software Measurement*[4]

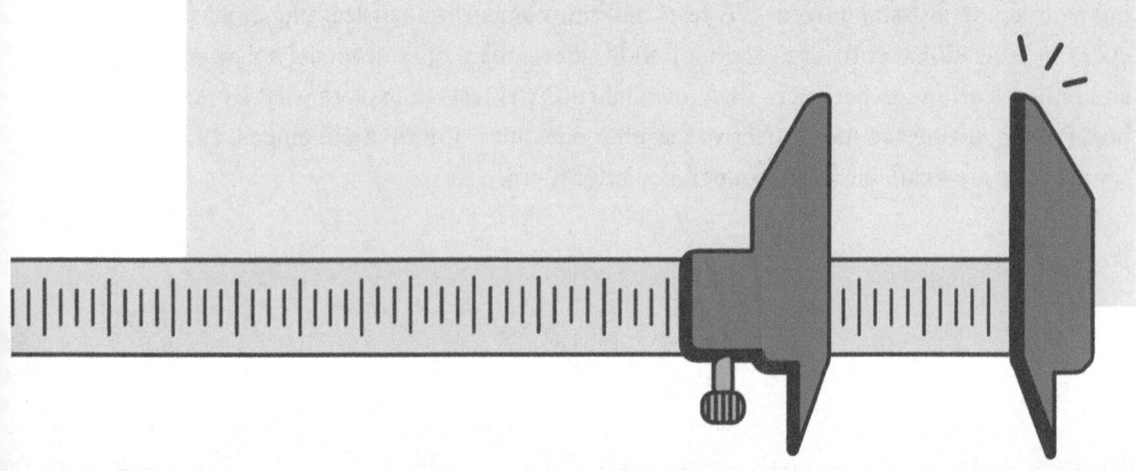

CHAPTER 14

Software and Technology Standards as Tools

by Jim Goodell, Andrew J. Hampton, Richard Tong, and Sae Schatz

This chapter gives a high-level map of current concepts from computer science, computer engineering, and software engineering relevant to learning engineering. It also covers technology and data standards used by engineers for scalable interoperable learning solutions.

The most scalable and impactful learning engineering endeavors leverage software engineering and computing technology. Examples featured in this book such as Duolingo and edX have a global scale, only possible due to modern software and telecommunications. Great advances in human-computer interface design, artificial intelligence, distributed computing, and distributed identity are being applied to revolutionize learning at scale.

Learning engineering also addresses challenges that go beyond EdTech. For example, learning engineering may be applied to re-engineer entire school systems using principles such as modularization, human-centered design, and social systems design. In these cases, solutions may focus on optimizing social structures, physical spaces, and human-centric practices, but the process will likely use data analytics and computer-aided design and may incorporate some technology elements in the final solution. In other words, nearly all learning engineering challenges will involve technology at some point, so it's important for all members of a learning engineering team to have a baseline level of understanding about these concepts.

The following reference is intended mainly for those without a background in computer science or software engineering. It's intended to build awareness of the technical tools available to support learning engineering solutions. This list reflects a point in time and will need to be updated as new technologies and approaches emerge.

Software Design and Development

Software engineering is valuable for learning solutions at scale. Also, as covered in Chapter 4, engineers can create complex systems of systems through modularization (a LEGO-brick approach to software). It's important to understand which software approaches that will enable—or block—long-term goals like modularization.

Software *designers* define how applications will look and function. They might use diagrams, like those described by the Unified Modeling Language, to plan and communicate how a system should work. However, although they're usually experts in computer science, software designers don't build the designs they create. Instead, software *developers* are responsible for turning those designs into reality using markup, scripting, and/or programming languages.

Markup languages, such as hypertext markup language (HTML) and extensible markup language (XML), are used to add metadata to a file. For example, HTML includes markup that specifies the placement of design elements on a web page, and XML is used to define structure (in other words, data about the data like naming the author of a web page) in data or documents. Markup languages are both human and machine readable. Because markup is used to annotate documents, it's considered *presentational* rather than *algorithmic,* so implementing markup isn't technically considered programming.

Programming languages include rules, commands, and syntax, which are used to write machine-readable algorithms that a computer compiles or interprets. Most software applications are written using human-readable (albeit complex) language that's then converted into machine-level or binary language (0s and 1s) for the computer. Popular programming languages include Java, C, C++ ("C plus plus"), and C# ("C sharp").

Scripting languages are a subset of programming languages. They're typically used in online applications to send instructions to another program. A key characteristic of scripting languages is that they're *interpreted* rather than *compiled.* That means a separate machine-readable file isn't created before run time; instead, they're processed line by line, just-in-time. This gives more flexibility but is often a bit slower and less robust. Popular scripting languages include Python, Ruby, PHP, SQL, and JavaScript (which sounds like it's the same as Java but isn't).[1]

There are several different programming paradigms, which refer to the frameworks, patterns, and styles of software development. Two common paradigms

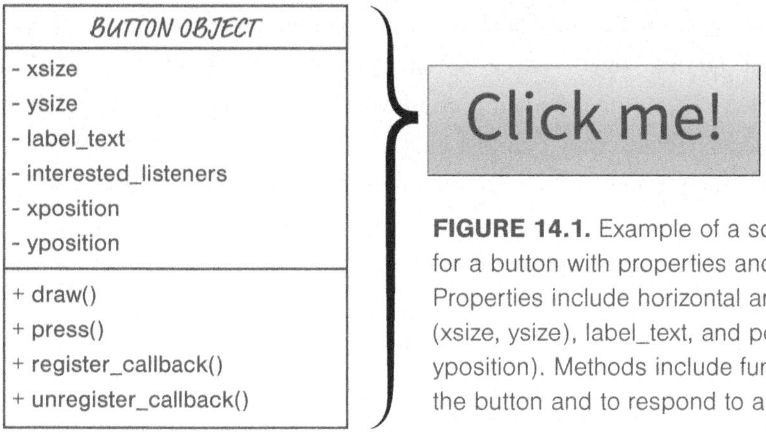

FIGURE 14.1. Example of a software object for a button with properties and methods. Properties include horizontal and vertical size (xsize, ysize), label_text, and position (xposition, yposition). Methods include functions to draw the button and to respond to a button press.

are procedural and object-oriented programming. **Procedural programming** specifies the sequence of steps to reach a desired state, and for that reason, it's sometimes called linear programming. Procedural programs also include procedures (sometimes called functions or modules) that encapsulate certain steps into repeatable recipes that are called by the code. In contrast, **object-oriented programming** uses software *objects* that contain both data and coded functions. Basically, each object is like a miniature program that includes a blueprint, and then you can create as many instances of that blueprint as you'd like. For example, you might have an object called "math_problem" that includes all of the typical properties (such as instructions, problem, answer, and steps) and methods (such as displayProblem, checkAnswer, and giveHint) of an algebra question. Then, rather than write code for each math problem, you could just create new questions from your "math_problem" class. Figure 14.1 demonstrates a basic software object with properties and methods.[2]

If you're not a software developer, then it's probably not important for you to understand the different programming paradigms; however, it's useful to know that they exist and that they influence design considerations, such as **composability** (how different components can be assembled, like LEGO bricks) and **extensibility** (the extent that software can be extended in the future, without too much difficulty).

OPEN-SOURCE SOFTWARE

Open-source software is released under a permissive license, so that the copyright holder grants others the right to see the uncompiled source code and often includes rights to use, study, change, and distribute the software. The rights granted under open-source software licenses vary. Open source doesn't always mean free and unlimited use, so check the license to be sure the rights you need are granted.

Using good quality open-source software, like the OpenSimon Toolkit featured in Chapter 13, can give learning engineering teams a head start on their development projects because they can just customize the code rather than starting from scratch. Plus, many popular open-source products have been heavily resourced or significantly developed over time. For example, in the case of the OpenSimon Toolkit, it was developed with millions of dollars of funding and informed by over a decade of research.

In some cases, open-source communities aren't developing whole software packages but are instead creating the building blocks of future learning systems. For example, Experience Application Programming Interface (xAPI) standards, xAPI compliance test suites, and supporting technologies are offered as open source through IEEE Standards Association's OPEN program and the US Government's Advanced Distributed Learning (ADL) Initiative.[3]

Open-source software may seem like a golden ticket, but while it does have a lot of benefits, it isn't technically free. Or rather, as former Sun Microsystems chief executive Scott McNealy once quipped, "Open source is free like a puppy is free."[4] In other words, it requires care and feeding. In practice, that typically means participating in an established open-source community to help maintain the code, flag bugs, or recommend features. For brand-new open-source projects, it could mean building that community from the ground up.

For learning engineering teams, it's important to understand the opportunities and trade-offs of open-source software. At their best, however, healthy open-source communities can accelerate innovation and help learning engineering teams develop their own solutions more efficiently.

DON'T CONFUSE OPEN SOURCE WITH OPEN ARCHITECTURE:

★ OPEN SOURCE = COPYRIGHTS

★ OPEN ARCHITECTURE = MODULAR DESIGN

SOFTWARE ARCHITECTURES

A **software architecture** describes the pieces of a software system (or system of systems), how each behaves, and how they interact. Just like there are different programming paradigms, there are different software architectures. It's important to choose an architectural design that will support your desired "-ilities" (or software quality attributes), such as composability and extensibility, mentioned above.

Web-based architectures (such as for online

learning) make use of web standards (such as HTML) and internet-connected systems (such as web browsers and mobile devices). Modern web-based applications are also built in modular ways, using data and interface standards that make it easier to accommodate new content, software, and learning scenarios. Modular designs that use publicly available software interface standards (versus one-off or proprietary interface designs) let you add or remove software elements—like LEGO bricks. These are called **open systems architectures** or modular open systems approach (MOSA) architectures.

Modern software best practices recommend using modular, versus monolith, designs. Modular architectures divide each major function into its own small code base or microservice. In contrast, monolithic architectures tightly intertwine all of the components, making it more difficult to change, remove, or add features. For learning engineers, the shift from monolithic to modular design can be seen in the evolution of learning management systems (LMSs). Functions that used to be built into a single, monolithic LMS are being separated into plug-and-play software elements. Modular architectures better support continuous innovation and prevent lock-in to specific platforms, pedagogies, learning contexts, or vendors.

Many web-based systems use a **REST architectural style**. REST stands for REpresentational State Transfer. REST leverages the hypertext transfer protocol (HTTP)—the standard communication protocol used by web browsers—to allow systems to access and manipulate web resources through predefined rules. Learning engineers might use RESTful **web services** for data storage and retrieval, translation, search and discovery, data visualization, and so on. RESTful architectures support modular web-based architectural designs, as recommended above. Also, the software examples featured in this book use REST, as do many of the featured instrumentation standards such as xAPI. (See Chapter 18.)

RESTful architectures leverage the World Wide Web infrastructure to send and receive messages, including between different microservices or between a learner's local device and an app or a cloud-based web service.

Modern web-based architectural best practices often call for the use of **linked data**.[5] As its name implies, linked data connects information from one system to another using World Wide Web protocols. However, unlike typical hypertext-based websites, linked data also includes some specific requirements to make the connected data better suited for machine-processing, such as using controlled vocabularies expressed in standardized formats. (Controlled vocabularies are sets of authorized terms or phrases that limit and define what tags can be used.)

Consider this example for how you might use linked data. Imagine you're creating a competency-based learning outline for a postsecondary computer programming course. Rather than coming up with all of the competencies yourself—and then updating them each semester as technology evolves—you could connect to a linked open data set, like the US Department of Labor's O*NET.[6] This would allow you to reference predetermined tasks, skills, knowledge, and other characteristics for computer programmers. The overall framework, and each of the elements in it, is referenced using a Uniform Resource Identifier (URI). URIs are global identifiers that give unique names to everything on the web. Using linked data not only saves time; it also facilitates shared understanding. In our example, tagging the different modules of your course with the standardized O*NET competencies would make it easier to compare or integrate that curriculum with similar learning content.

JSON-LD is a popular format for encoding linked data on the web. It's based on the widely used JavaScript Object Notation (JSON) format, which is a low-overhead alternative to XML. JSON is an open standard for file and data interchange that uses human-readable text to store and transmit machine-readable data objects. It supports attribute-value pairs, arrays of data objects, and any other data that can be serialized into text strings. It's commonly used to structure data for storage or transfer, for instance, between local and cloud components of distributed web applications. The *LD* in JSON-LD stands for Linked Data.[7] In the O*NET example, you could have used JSON-LD to link the O*NET competencies into the metadata of your course. The instrumentation standard xAPI also uses JSON formatting, and xAPI Profiles use JSON-LD @context files to specify design patterns for instrumentation and to link to controlled vocabularies.

It's increasingly common for apps to use JSON-LD to leverage the power of linked data, and using linked data is a best practice for modern web-based architectures—particularly for data-heavy applications. So, whether or not you're the "technology person" on your team, it's important to understand these general concepts so you can look for opportunities to link or exchange messages externally.

Applications that produce a high volume of data continuously over a period of time have additional architectural considerations. For example, an intelligent tutoring system that incorporates clickstream monitoring might produce thousands of messages per second.[8] Traditional point-to-point architectures (where each data packet is sent to each software service that might need to use it) will have too much lag under the strain of all that streaming data. Instead, a **streaming data architecture** is required.[9] Streaming data architectures are specifically designed to handle high volumes and velocities of data from multiple sources, and they allow you to process those data immediately—which is useful for, let's say, personalizing a learning experience in response to observed clickstream behaviors.

Streaming architectures aren't the only solution to processing large-scale learner data in real time (although they are the most robust solution). The more important point is that the amount of data, analysis/response time frame, and scale of your learning system all affect architectural considerations. Take these factors into account early in the design process to avoid issues with lag or scalability later.

DESIGN PATTERNS

Design patterns are established templates that improve the efficiency of software development, the quality and maintainability of code, and allow for new team members to quickly contribute to a project.

As introduced in Chapter 4 and shown in Chapter 9, **design patterns** are repeatable solutions to commonly occurring engineering problems. Essentially, they're templates of established best practices that improve the efficiency of development as well as the quality and maintainability of code. Design patterns also promote shared understanding and a common language among teams. Software engineers use design patterns so that everyone on a team can work together for consistent coding approaches based on known architectural patterns.

Design patterns can also apply to learning engineering. Most obviously, the technology-focused portions of a design can use software design patterns to aid their development processes. Beyond that, entire learning engineering teams can develop design patterns that incorporate concepts from the learning sciences and human-centered design disciplines in addition to the technological actions. Approaching learning engineering challenges in this way helps integrate the *engineering* and *science* components into more repeatable and scalable processes.

Data and Data Architectures

Data-driven decision-making is, by definition, part of learning engineering. Various database architectures and platform types address different kinds of learning engineering challenges.

Data architectures address the structure of data and the capabilities of associated data platforms. Data platforms are the various components required to acquire, store, prepare, deliver, and manage your data (along with the requisite security).[10] Most data platforms include one or more databases, including relational databases (for example, built using SQL) and/or non-relational or NoSQL databases (such as object databases, graph databases, document stores, key/value stores, triple/quad stores, and hybrid platforms). The different database types each have strengths and weaknesses. For instance, SQL needs predefined schema and structured data, while NoSQL can handle dynamic schema and unstructured data. The different database types also scale and perform differently, depending on how they're accessed and how data are structured within them.[11] For example, object databases are a convenient choice for applications built using object query languages, and they can handle complex relationships between objects. Meanwhile, graph databases excel at managing highly connected data and complex queries where the relationships between data elements are as important to the data elements themselves.

Structured data follows predetermined patterns, which make it easily searchable. For instance, a spreadsheet that includes students' names, email addresses, and test scores in well-defined columns is an example of structured data. In contrast, **unstructured data**, including most audio and video files, has more variations and few (if any) predefined controls. Some types of data fall in between these two concepts, and those data sets are called semi-structured. For example, if you collected all of the emails sent by a class of students over a semester, that set of emails would have some internal structure (like to, from, date stamps, and other metadata), but most of the emails' contents wouldn't adhere to a formal pattern.

Data lakes are repositories of raw data. They're places to store all different kinds of data—structured, semi-structured, and unstructured—in a single place "as is." They're specifically designed to store, process, and secure large amounts of diverse data.[12] The data from a data lake, or from other unstructured or semi-structured repositories, will need to be transformed before it can be effectively analyzed. This process is typically called data wrangling (or data munging), and it includes steps like discovery, structuring, cleaning, and validating the data.[13]

Systems often employ multiple methods that transform data into other structures for different purposes. Raw log data may be collected in a *triplestore* (a set of three entities encoded as a subject–predicate–object statement), then those data may be transformed and cleansed into another triplestore for analytical processing. Then, facts from those data may be transformed into a normalized operational data store for learner progress tracking and transformed once again to a *denormalized* data warehouse (that is, a database where redundant data, like duplications in different tables or version histories, are added back in) for enterprise analytics and reporting.

Learning engineering teams will work with data—and often data at large scales. These teams will need skilled *data engineers* to help design the data platforms and pipelines to collect, transport, store, and transform the data. Teams will likely also need *data scientists* who study sophisticated ways to extract meaningful insights from large data sets, like through modeling and advanced algorithms. Or, instead of full data scientists, teams with less complex analysis requirements may be able to work with *data analysts,* who are typically skilled in data cleaning, statistical analyses, and visualization tools.

DATA AND SOFTWARE INTEROPERABILITY STANDARDS

Standards are published documents that describe agreed-upon data or software features like structure, definition, transmission, tagging, and use.[14] By using standards (versus proprietary or one-off designs), you increase the interoperability of your data and systems, which will make it easier to scale your learning solutions. Data and interface standards also support modularization, as discussed in the Software

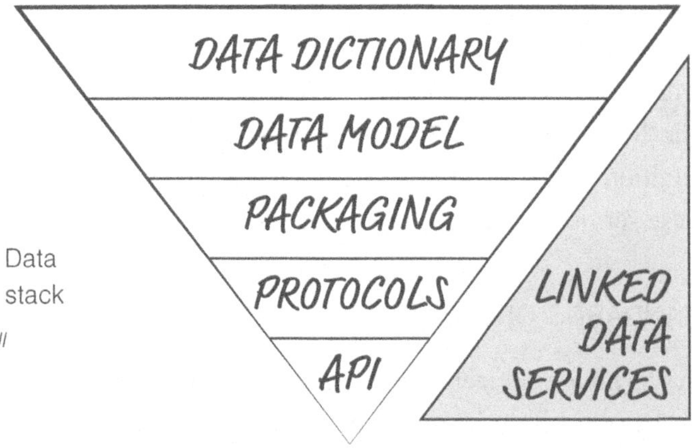

FIGURE 14.2. Data interoperability stack

CC-BY Jim Goodell

Architecture section above and in Chapter 4, Learning Engineering is Engineering. In other words, using data and interface standards can help learning engineering teams build learning ecosystems comprised of diverse learning technologies that "plug and play" with each together.

Interoperability isn't achieved by a single standard. It takes multiple layers of standards—often collected from different standards organizations—to achieve interoperability. Figure 14.2 shows layers in the data interoperability stack. At different levels within this conceptual model you may need standards for the following:

- **Data Vocabulary or Dictionary:** Standards that define the meanings and allowed values for data elements.
- **Data Model:** Standards that define entity definitions and entity relationships.
- **Data Serialization:** Standards that identify concrete data structures and formats to support transport between systems. For example, a standard might define a specific schema or binding using a specific serialization protocol or format like JSON-LD.
- **Data Protocols:** Standards by which data may be exchanged. Protocols are generalizable procedures (or systems of rules) that enable data exchange. Examples include packaging protocols, such as JSON, and communications protocols, such as HTTP and REST.
- **Application Programming Interfaces (APIs):** APIs are the software interfaces that allow applications to communicate with each other and exchange data. Standard APIs are specified using standard protocols (like REST), and they identify the specific types of data that may be transmitted, what commands are used to send and receive data, and how data transfers are confirmed.
- **Linked Data Services:** Linked data takes many forms, such as competency framework repositories, distributed identity, and certificate authorities for credentials. Correspondingly, linked data services provide access to those data; for example, a service might provide a machine-readable competency definition or verification of someone's encrypted distributed identity token. These services support interoperability and modular systems.

DATA STANDARDS ORGANIZATIONS

Although learning engineers won't need to become experts in all of the relevant standards, learning engineering teams working on technology-heavy or large-scale

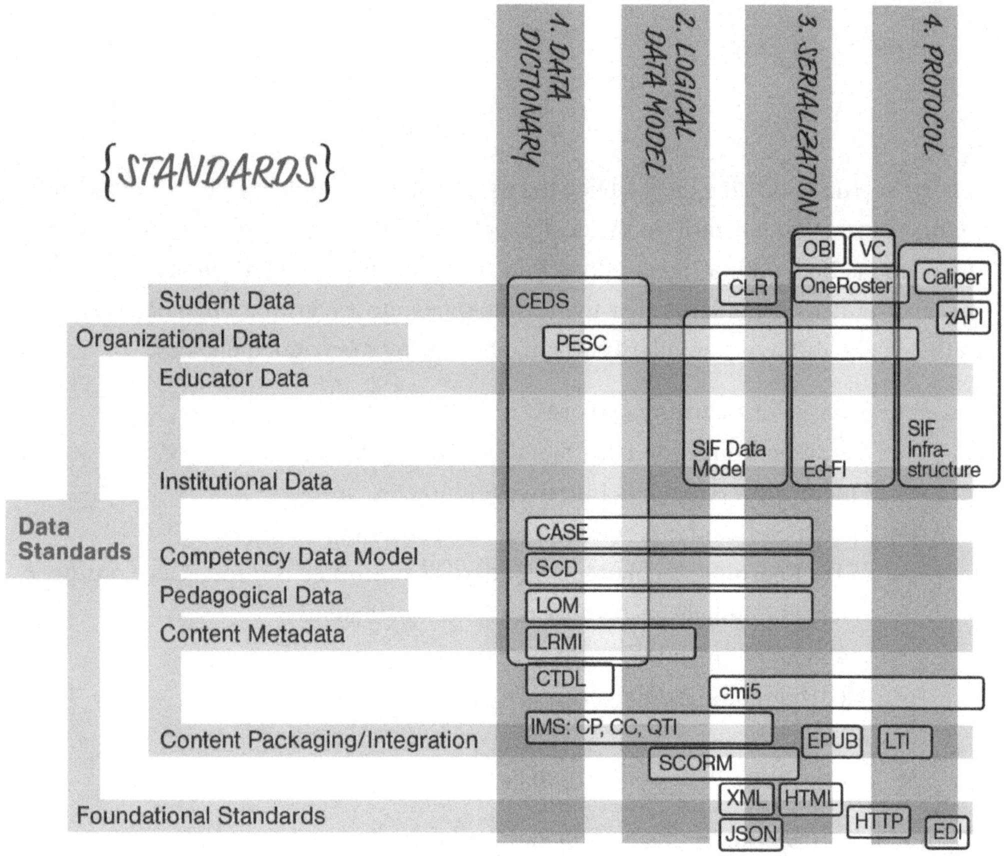

- **Caliper:** Protocol for transmitting and collecting learning events for later analysis
- **CASE–Competencies & Academic Standards Exchange:** Standard for competency frameworks
- **CEDS–Common Education Data Standards:** Data dictionary and logical data model for education
- **cmi5**–Integration of SCORM-like and xAPI capabilities
- **CLR–Comprehensive Learner Record:** For secure and verifiable learning and employment records
- **CTDL–Credential Transparency Description Language:** Rich description of credential resources
- **EDI–Electronic Data Interchange:** Older transmission standard for student transcript data
- **LRMI–Learning Resource Metadata Initiative:** Metadata for learning resources and their relationship
- **HyperText Transfer Protocol:** Standard protocol for transmitting content and data on the internet
- **Ed-Fi APIs**–Enable data exchange in K-12, such as assessment and demographic information
- **EPUB for Education:** A profile of the EPUB standard for digital books targeted at education
- **IMS CC–IMS Common Cartridge:** Content packaging standard for course materials
- **IMS CP–IMS Content Packaging:** Format for packaging content and associated metadata
- **IMS QTI–IMS Question and Test Interoperability:** Content packaging for assessment items and tests
- **JSON–JavaScript Object Notation:** A lightweight text-based format for data interchange
- **LOM–Learning Object Metadata:** Schema for metadata that describes learning objects and resources
- **LRMI–Learning Resource Metadata Initiative:** Metadata for learning resources and their competencies
- **OBI–Open Badge Infrastructure:** A format for communicating skills and achievements
- **OneRoster:** Protocol and format for secure exchange of class roster information between applications
- **PESC–Postsecondary Electronic Standards Council:** Offers a set of educational standards
- **SCD–Sharable Competency Definition:** Standard for competencies and frameworks
- **SCORM–Sharable Content Object Reference Model:** A format for publishing digital resources for LMSs
- **SIF Data Model:** Data model for representing and transmitting educational information
- **SIF Infrastructure:** Protocol for transmitting educational information
- **VC:** Verifiable Credentials (W3C)
- **xAPI–Experience API:** A protocol for reporting learning activities and student experiences
- **XML–EXtensible Markup Language:** Common format for representing digital content and data

FIGURE 14.3. Matrix of learning technology standards, organized by their data categories and the layers they affect in the interoperability stack efforts should seek out expert advice to ensure that a full and appropriate set of standards is incorporated early in the design process. There are numerous standards organizations that work diligently to define and maintain software, data, and all sorts of other industry standards. For the technologies most learning engineering teams will use, the following standards organizations offer many good choices:

- Access for Learning (a4l.org)
- Common Education Data Standards (ceds.ed.gov)
- Dublin Core Metadata Initiative (dublincore.org)
- HR Open Standards Association (hropenstandards.org)
- IEEE Learning Technology Standards Committee (sagroups.ieee.org/ltsc)
- Internet Engineering Task Force (ietf.org/standards)
- IMS Global (imsglobal.org)
- MedBiquitous (medbiq.org)
- PESC (pesc.org)
- World Wide Web Consortium (w3c.org)

Additionally, there are de facto data standards, created and popularized by widely used systems such as from LearnLab.org, DataShop, and the Credential Engine. Also, regional initiatives, such as the European Blockchain Services Infrastructure (digital-strategy.ec.europa.eu/en/policies/ebsi), are influencing international standards. Figure 14.3, derived from edmatrix.org, shows a sample of learning technology standards by interoperability layer and data domain.[15] (This matrix was created by contributors to EdMatrix and coordinated by Brandt Redd.)

Cloud Computing

Cloud computing allows for more rapid and iterative development and deployment. Instances of prototypes, apps, or web services can be spun up in days (rather than months) on platforms that can be instantly provisioned. Cloud infrastructure is also scalable with redundancies that reduce the risk of any single point of failure.

Cloud computing refers to interconnected servers (hardware/software resources) that deliver services over the internet. Servers—whether the traditional kind or cloud computing—are the computers on which distributed software applications run. (Unless a piece of software runs entirely on an end user's personal computer, then one or more servers need to be used.)

Cloud computing facilitates the on-demand availability of computer resources. So, instead of buying an entire hardware server, which you might only use for eight hours a day, you can acquire cloud-based resources as you need them. Cloud environments scale to meet growing or shrinking needs. Commercial cloud providers (such as Amazon Web Services, Google Cloud, or Microsoft Azure) also offer many tools and features, like built-in analytics engines and cybersecurity. Such services facilitate more rapid software development and implementation, and they minimize risk. Cloud computing also better supports streaming data architectures, which often require scalability and significant computing power.

Due to its scalability, flexibility, security, and other benefits, cloud computing is well suited to support technology-based learning. However, software designed for cloud environments should use different components and architectural patterns than applications built for legacy client-server (or client-only) architectures. Hence, it's important to make decisions about cloud environments early in the design process. Similarly, for project planning, it's useful to understand the associated cost model. Rather than pay for a piece of hardware once, commercial cloud providers often use usage-based pricing models. These tend to be much less expensive than traditional (non-cloud) server options, but they grow more costly as demand increases. That means it's important to plan ahead for things like the number of concurrent end users and scale of data being produced, analyzed, and stored.

Internet of Things

IoT is one of the emerging technologies supporting the modern distributed learning ecosystem. These network-connected devices can serve as *sensors* that collect relevant data as nodes in a distributed architecture. There's a growing need for learning engineers to develop software and systems that utilize IoT systems.

The **internet of things (IoT)** is a network of physical objects embedded with sensors, software, and computing technologies for the purpose of connecting and exchanging data over the internet. For example, instrumented medical tools (such as smart infusion pumps, electronic medical mannequins, and environmental spatial sensors) could be used to unobtrusively collect data about medical students' performance on a training scenario. (This data could then be streamed to a networked software analysis application, likely on a cloud server, to be analyzed and acted upon, such as by delivering real-time feedback.) There are countless potential uses for IoT systems for learning engineers—from instrumenting communications devices to inform military team training to using them to enhance the experience of a children's museum.[16] It's important for learning engineering team members to realize that learning technologies have moved beyond online platforms and client-side software apps. Increasingly, just-in-time learning is being facilitated by intelligent things like smart speakers with natural language processing and other technological devices distributed throughout learners' environments.

Human-Computer Interaction

Good human-computer interaction is a critical requirement for effective learning technologies. This broad field affects all technology-enabled learning interactions, including their usability, data instrumentation, and personalized learning features.

Human-computer interaction (HCI) is a transdisciplinary field addressing the interaction between humans and information technology.[17] These interactions might include traditional interfaces, like mouse and keyboard, as well as newer ones, such as natural language ("Hey Alexa"), gestures and haptics (touch), and virtual and augmented reality (or collectively extended reality). HCI also involves user interface design, and it examines how different behaviors, norms, and structures form around human-system interactions. For instance, subfields and areas of study include:

- Social computing
- Affective computing
- One-to-one computing where every learner has their own device(s)
- Inference modeling (see Chapters 6 and 19)
- Neurophysiological sensors, such as electroencephalograms (EEGs) and other brain-computer interfaces, eye trackers, and heart-rate monitors

As the list above implies, HCI also incorporates nontraditional interface methods. This is particularly applicable to learning engineering to help inform data-informed decisions. Instrumented learning experiences are a primary method used to collect data. **Instrumentation** involves hardware and software sensors and data pipelines that support the collection of learner experience data. Hardware sensors might include wearables and IoT devices. Software sensors may be built into learning platforms or online activities, such as within online simulations or game-based learning. These concepts are discussed in detail in Chapters 5 and 13.

Federated and Distributed Identity

Decentralized identifiers enable verifiable, decentralized digital identity. This can support self-sovereign learner records that give learners (and parents and guardians of minor learners) greater levels of access and control over their own data, enabling life-long learning free from institutional data silos.

All of the data—and diverse data sources—used for a learning engineering solution create a problem: How do we know which data packages belong to which learners? A single LMS might assign a unique User ID for each learner, but this quickly becomes cumbersome when using multiple data streams from different sources. For example, a single learning experience might easily include activities delivered from an LMS, a separate simulation-based learning experience, a microlearning mobile application for reinforcement during downtime, and a third-party testing application—and this doesn't even account for the various software and hardware sensors that might be added.

Federated and distributed identity methods store a person's (or organization's) electronic identity across multiple distinct identity management systems. A special type of federated identifier, the **decentralized identifier (DID)**, has been designed so that it may be decoupled from centralized registries, identity providers, and certificate authorities. In other words, DIDs enable each person (or other entity) to have a single, verifiable, machine readable User ID across systems.[18]

In addition to supporting multiple apps within a single learning experience, DIDs also help enable the integration of data across different learning experiences, for instance, in the form of a learner-owned learning wallet or universal learner record. Using DIDs helps learning engineering solutions become part of the larger ecosystem of learning, creating opportunities for learners and fellow learning engineering teams to build a data-driven network of life-long learning experiences.

Analytics

Learning analytics are central to learning engineering, both for decision-making about the process as well as for software-based feedback loops.

Analytics, or the systematic computational analysis of data, is central to the investigation phase of the learning engineering process introduced in Chapter 1. **Learning analytics** is the use of "data mining, machine learning, natural language processing, visualization, and human-computer interaction approaches among others to provide educators and learners with insights that might improve learning processes and teaching practice."[19] Learning analytics capabilities may be integrated as standalone applications that are used after a learning event, such as in the Kaplan worked problems example in Chapter 6. They can also be integrated into real-time operations, for instance, built into cloud-based streaming architectures or incorporated directly into a software system, such as an adaptive engine in an intelligent tutor to provide just-in-time feedback to learners, as described in the Generalized Intelligent Framework for Tutoring example in Chapter 5.

Learning analytics is a broad and growing discipline, and many of its techniques are discussed in more detail in Chapters 6 and 18, and the open-access *Handbook of Learning Analytics* provides a scholarly primer.[20] For this chapter, it's most important to understand that learning analytics don't simply "happen." In addition to making decisions about how to instrument, stream, and store learning data, appropriate algorithms are needed to process those data. Software considerations—such as the source or sources of data, data formats, software architectures, and the use of cloud computing—all influence which algorithms can be effectively used.

Artificial Intelligence

Some of the most impactful advances in learning technology involve AI and specifically machine learning. For example, promising advances in *deep knowledge tracing* are allowing systems to make accurate inferences about learner mastery, and machine learning capabilities like natural language processing and computer vision are revolutionizing human-computer interfaces for learning.

AI simulates facets of human intelligence in machines, such as problem solving or image recognition.[21] **Machine learning** is one kind of AI. It gets computers to act without being explicitly programmed. Instead, it uses data to train an algorithm to recognize patterns. "In the past decade, machine learning has given us self-driving cars, practical speech recognition, effective web search, and a vastly improved understanding of the human genome."[22] Duolingo uses machine learning and large data sets to train its spaced-repetition algorithm that predicts when learners should practice a word while language learning.

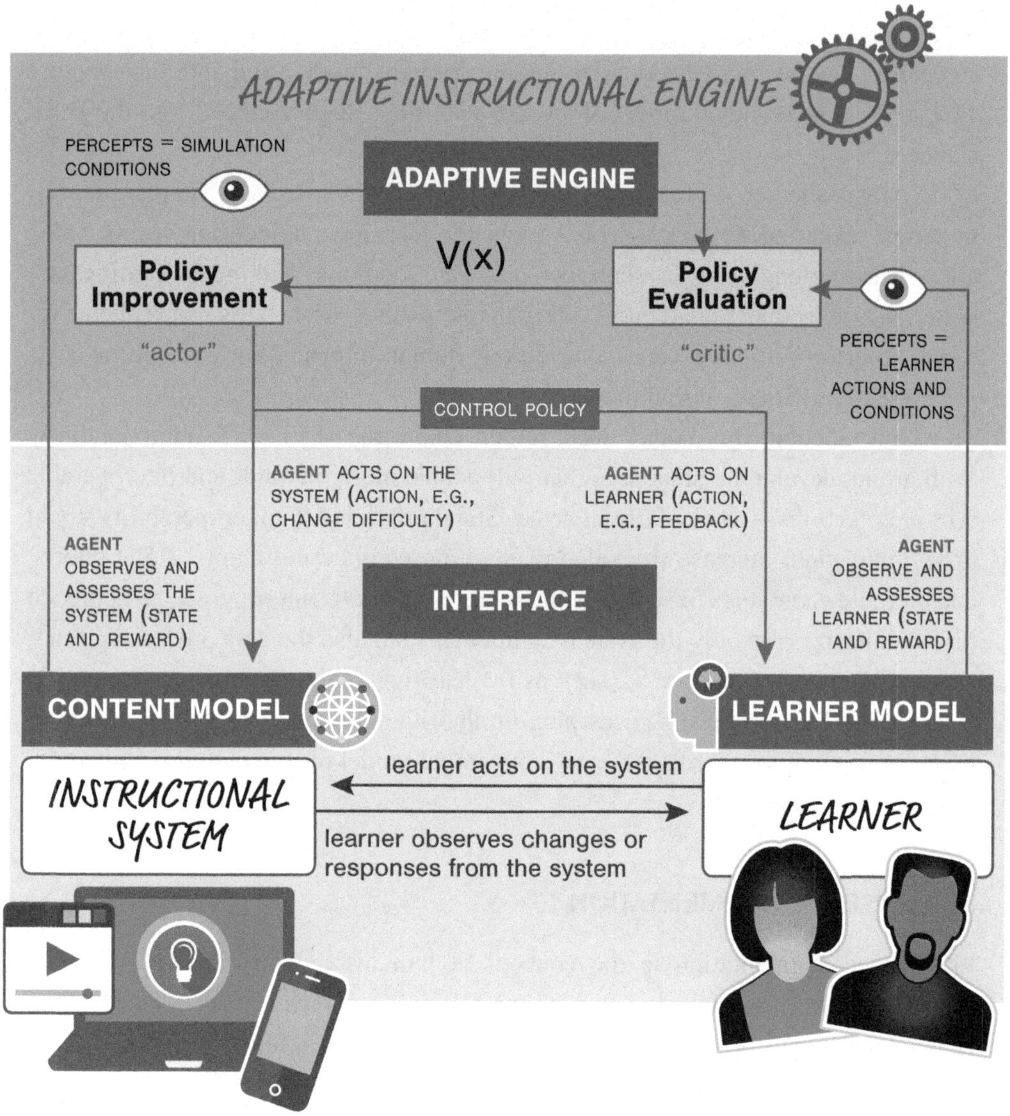

FIGURE 14.4. Model of an adaptive instructional system from the AIS Consortium

ADAPTIVE INSTRUCTIONAL SYSTEMS

Adaptive instructional systems (AISs) use AI and user modeling to determine what to teach, when to teach it, and which methods of instruction to use. For example, intelligent tutoring systems are one kind of AIS.[23]

Bob Sottilare, coauthor of Chapter 5, developed the Generalized Intelligent Framework for Tutoring, and he leads the AIS Consortium.[24] Other coauthors developed AISs and authored the IEEE's Standard for the Classification of Adaptive Instructional Systems. That standard classifies components of AISs into four categories: learner model, adaptive engine, content model, and interface. Figure 14.4 shows a generalized model of an AIS with the category labels from the IEEE standard.[25]

AISs, whether sophisticated intelligent tutors or relatively simple adaptive hypertext experiences, are essential tools for learning engineering teams. AISs allow learning engineers to scale personalized solutions, leading to significantly better outcomes than nonadaptive alternatives. At their best, AISs can replicate (or even outperform in a few cases) one-on-one human tutoring, but without the costs or physical limitations of that model.[26]

Jim Goodell, this book's lead author, chairs the IEEE AIS Interoperability Workgroup, developing standards that will enable more modular and interoperable AIS architectures—particularly at scale. Standards for AIS interoperability could drive innovation, increase the value of learning engineering teams' R&D efforts, and promote economies of scale fueling more innovation. Jim proposes an approach that modularizes not only the system components but also the data processing functions within and between AISs, such as the learning analytics methods featured in Chapter 18. This framework uses plug-in algorithms and linked data concepts as part of a stack of standards. An early conceptual model of this plug-in architecture is shown in Figure 14.5.

INTELLIGENCE AUGMENTATION

Intelligence augmentation is the concept of humans and artificially intelligent software agents working together to perform some task. That task could be helping the human learn something or otherwise augmenting the human's skills to accomplish tasks more effectively than either the person or AI agent could do on their own. It's likely that more and more of the work that humans do will be augmented by intelligent software agents. Time spent *learning* versus time spent *doing* will increasingly overlap. People will learn while doing, and the lines will blur between task automation and learning engineering. There could be a growing role for learning engineering to create and optimize learning experiences within the context of *learning while doing* with intelligence augmentation playing the roles of teacher, coach, mentor, peer, and assistant. ★

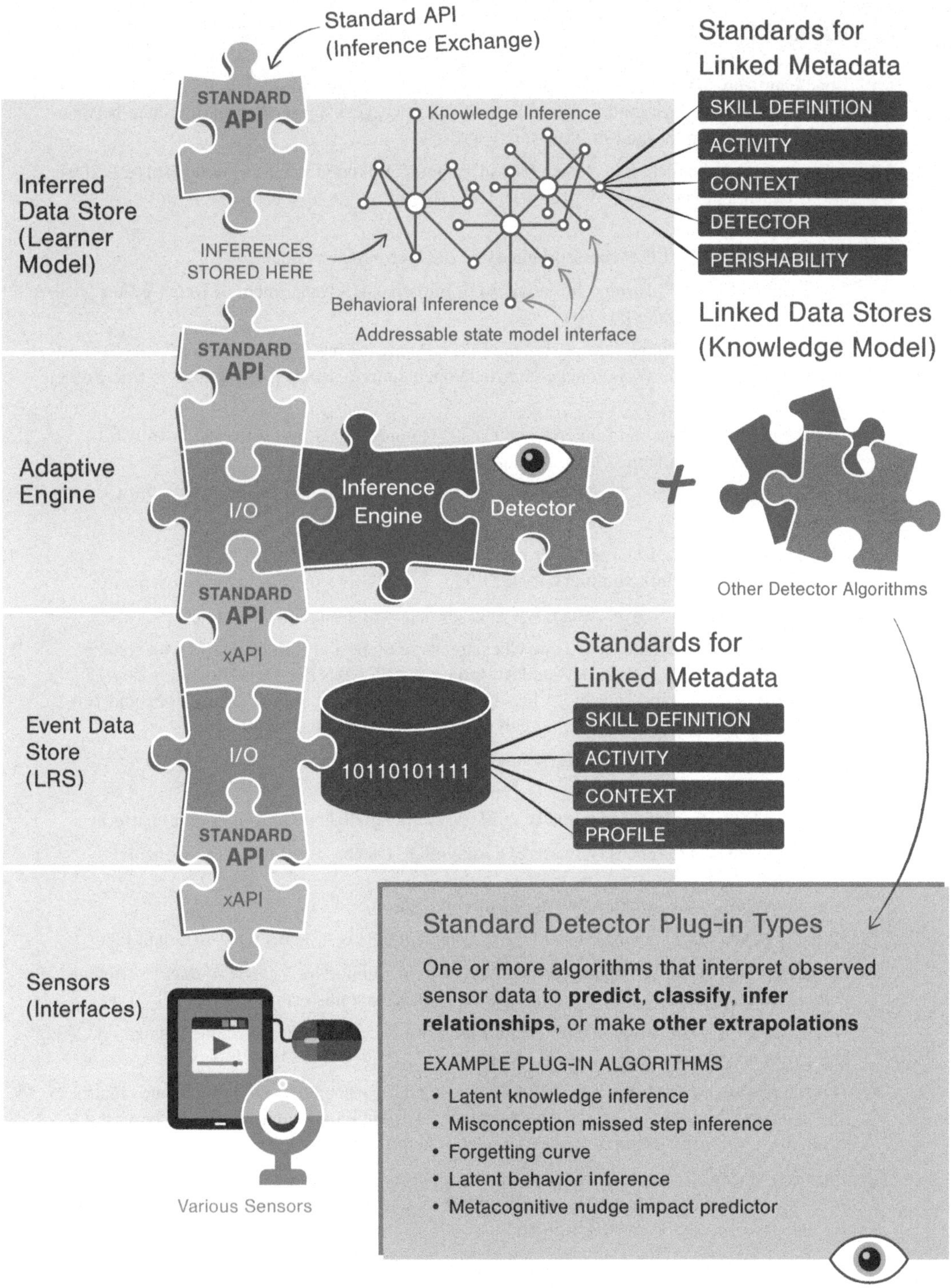

FIGURE 14.5. Modularized AIS Interoperability Framework

Endnotes

1 Upadhyay, Anu. "Difference Between Programming, Scripting, and Markup Languages." Geeksforgeeks.org. Last modified January 6, 2020. www.geeksforgeeks.org/difference-between-programming-scripting-and-markup-languages

2 Adapted from Pulkkinen, Esa. "UML Class Example." Wikimedia. Last modified July 31, 2004. https://en.wikipedia.org/wiki/Object-oriented_programming#/media/File:Oop-uml-class-example.png

3 "IEEE SA OPEN." IEEE. Accessed January 8, 2022. https://saopen.ieee.org

Advanced Distributed Learning Initiative. ADL Initiative, US Department of Defense. Accessed January 8, 2022. https://adlnet.gov

4 Donoghue, Andrew. "Open Source 'is Free Like a Puppy is Free', Says Sun Boss." ZDNet. Last modified June 8, 2005. www.zdnet.com/article/open-source-is-free-like-a-puppy-is-free-says-sun-boss

5 "What Are Linked Data and Linked Open Data?" Ontotext, 2021. www.ontotext.com/knowledgehub/fundamentals/linked-data-linked-open-data

6 "O*NET Resource Center." US Department of Labor. Last modified November 16, 2021. www.onetcenter.org

Also refer to the O*NET Computer Programmers competency framework: www.onetonline.org/link/summary/15-1251.00

7 "What is Linked Data?" W3C. 2015. www.w3.org/standards/semanticweb/data

8 Rozestraten, Hugo. "Create Real-Time Clickstream Sessions and Run Analytics with Amazon Kinesis Data Analytics, AWS Glue, and Amazon Athena." AWS Big Data Blog, February 17, 2019. https://aws.amazon.com/blogs/big-data/create-real-time-clickstream-sessions-and-run-analytics-with-amazon-kinesis-data-analytics-aws-glue-and-amazon-athena

9 Dunning, Ted, and Ellen Friedman. *Streaming Architecture: New Designs Using Apache Kafka and MapR Streams*. Sebastopol, CA: O'Reilly Media, Inc., 2016.

10 "What is a Data Platform?" MongoDB. 2021. www.mongodb.com/what-is-a-data-platform

11 Keshari, Kislay. "Differences Between SQL & NoSQL Databases—MySQL & MongoDB Comparison." *Edureka,* April 16, 2019. https://medium.com/edureka/sql-vs-nosql-db-5d9b69ace6ac

12 "What is a Data Lake?" Google Cloud. https://cloud.google.com/learn/what-is-a-data-lake

13 Stobierski, Tim. "Data Wrangling: What it is & Why it's Important." *Harvard Business School Online,* January 19, 2021. https://online.hbs.edu/blog/post/data-wrangling

14 "Data Standards." US Government Federal Enterprise Data Resources. Accessed January 8, 2022. https://resources.data.gov/standards/concepts

15 The contributors to EdMatrix advocate for open-stand.org principles, and the standards matrix in this chapter is licensed under a Creative Commons Attribution 4.0 International License. It was originally developed by Brandt Redd with a lot of help from friends.

16 Torrance, Megan. "Adventures in the xAPI: The Ann Arbor Hands-on Museum Project." *Learning Solutions,* April 2, 2015. https://learningsolutionsmag.com/articles/1665/adventures-in-the-xapi-the-ann-arbor-hands-on-museum-project

17 "Human-Computer Interaction: Your Constantly-Updated Definition of Human-Computer Interaction and Collection of Topical Content and Literature." Accessed January 8, 2022. Interaction Design Foundation. www.interaction-design.org/literature/topics/human-computer-interaction

18 "Decentralized Identifiers (DIDs) v1.0: Core Architecture, Data Model, and Representations." W3C. Last modified August 3, 2021. www.w3.org/TR/did-core

19 Pechenizkiy, Mykola. Introduction to *The Handbook of Learning Analytics. Society for Learning Analytics Research (SoLAR),* edited by Charles Lang, George Siemens, Alyssa Wise, and Dragan Gašević, no page numbers, introduction page 9. 1st ed. SoLaR, 2017. https://solaresearch.org/wp-content/uploads/2017/05/hla17.pdf

20 Lang, Charles, George Siemens, Alyssa Wise, and Dragan Gašević, eds. *The Handbook of Learning Analytics. Society for Learning Analytics Research (SoLAR).* 1st ed. SoLaR, 2017. https://solaresearch.org/wp-content/uploads/2017/05/hla17.pdf

21 Manning, Christopher. "Artificial Intelligence Definitions." Stanford University. Last modified September 2020. https://hai.stanford.edu/sites/default/files/2020-09/AI-Definitions-HAI.pdf

22 Ng, Andrew. "Machine Learning." Coursera. www.coursera.org/learn/machine-learning

23 Brusilovsky, Peter, and Christoph Peylo. "Adaptive and Intelligent Web-based Educational Systems." *International Journal of Artificial Intelligence in Education* 13 (2003), 156–169.

Schatz, Sae, Cynthia Oakes, Jeremiah T. Folsom-Kovarik, and Rhianon Dolletski-Lazar. "ITS+ SBT: A Review of Operational Situated Tutors." *Military Psychology* 24, no. 2 (2012): 166–193.

24 Sottilare, Robert. "Adaptive Instructional Systems Consortium." AIS Consortium. Accessed January 8, 2022. https://aisconsortium.com

25 Sottilare, Robert. "Innovative Adaptive Instructional Solutions" Video, 55:17. AIS Consortium. https://youtu.be/7D-89ybPHUI

26 Fletcher, J.D. and James A. Kulik. Effectiveness of Intelligent Tutoring Systems: A Meta-Analytic Review. *IDA Research Notes,* 2017. www.ida.org/-/media/feature/publications/w/we/welch-award-2017---effectiveness-of-intelligent-tutoring-systems-a-meta-analytic-review/1-effectivenessits.ashx

INSPIRE
1872

CHAPTER 15

Tools for Learner Motivation

by Laura Casey, Diana Delgado, Jim Goodell, and Prasad Ram

This chapter discusses learner motivation, one of the most important—yet often overlooked—elements to successful learning. A tool later in the chapter offers categories of motivational variables and suggestions for motivating operations.

Chapter 1 presented the learning engineering process, which starts with understanding the challenge. This includes recognizing that learners and teams are contextually situated and also that learning challenges often involve motivation. Learner motivation impacts engagement and may be heavily influenced by the context and culture of the learning environment. This is highly personal. Each learner is motivated by different things at different times. In examining motivational variables, it's useful to understand how they impact learners differently and in different types of activities.

Learning requires effort and engagement from learners, and behavioral science gives insights into the core drives that motivate productive (or nonproductive) behaviors. Generally defined, a **motivating event** is one that momentarily alters the value of a motivational variable by making it more or less desirable. Consequently, and by virtue of this value-altering effect, the behavior associated with that reinforcer will be directly affected; that is, it will be more or less likely to occur.[1] **Motivating operations** can also affect motivational variables beyond a single learning activity; for example, a particular motivational strategy may help learners developing more productive attitudes, long term.

MOTIVATING OPERATIONS are deliberate actions to adjust features of a learning environment or a learning experience in ways that lead to productive learning behaviors. These include learner-initiated and externally initiated actions.

Motivating operations can be taken by any person or automated system, and these operations can apply to any kind of motivating variable. Learning engineering teams apply a variety of motivating operations to adjust motivational variables to increase the probability learners will engage in learning activities and in productive learning behaviors that increase the probability of productive learning.

Chapter 2 examined the Knowledge-Learning-Instruction Framework (KLI) having *external* instructional events and assessment events that may lead to *internal* learning events. We can add to that model "motivational events." In the field of psychology, motivation has been understood as being either *intrinsic* (for example, natural curiosity) or *extrinsic* (for example, obtaining a good grade) depending on whether the source of motivation is internal or external; however, we purposely avoid this distinction. Attempting to classify motivating variables as intrinsic or extrinsic may not only lead us to a historically unresolved debate but also seems theoretical and pragmatically unnecessary. Instead, we suggest an action-oriented focus.

Use the table in Figure 15.1 to consider strategies for learner motivation. For each motivational category, what variables and corresponding motivational operations might be useful? The example given is for the category of "autonomy." In it, we want to activate the motivational variable "choice" with the motivating operation of allowing learners to "select the topic of a problem-based learning activity." Multiple motivating operations may be employed within a single category, and you'll probably need several techniques to account for different learners' personalities and circumstances. As you plan your motivating operations, also think about how you'll implement them. For example, when will you deliver them (the timing), and how will you verify that they've successfully tapped into learners' core drives?

Each of the categories in the table is briefly summarized below:

- **Autonomy:** Learners motivated by autonomy value independence or freedom. For example, they're more likely to be engaged when given the ability to choose the path, pace, or features of their own learning.
- **Competence:** Learners motivated by competence value what they know and can do. They find satisfaction in academic achievements. This intrinsic factor might be activated by making learners' progress more visible to them.
- **Value:** Learners can be motivated by something they perceive as valuable and that they'd like to have. It might be social value (belonging, being recognized as a significant member of a community, or being appreciated by others for who they are). Or value could mean earning tangible rewards that lead to a sense of ownership and possession. This can be activated by some forms of

MOTIVATING OPERATIONS (STRATEGY) WORKSHEET

CATEGORY	VARIABLE	MOTIVATING OPERATION
Autonomy	*For example:* CHOICE	*For example:* LET LEARNERS SELECT THE TOPIC FOR A PROBLEM-BASED LEARNING ACTIVITY
Competence		
Value		
Meaning and Purpose		
Avoidance		
Unpredictability		
Scarcity		

FIGURE 15.1. Tool for considering motivational approaches

social learning as well as some of the more stereotypical game mechanics such as points and leaderboards.

- **Meaning/Purpose:** Learners are motivated by a sense of meaning—a purpose or higher calling. They're motivated to work hard when the results of that work make a difference. They find satisfaction in helping others and being recognized as a value to others. This can be activated through project-based learning, especially in projects that contribute to a local or global cause.
- **Avoidance:** Learners motivated by avoidance will work hard to prevent losing something they've earned. For example, Duolingo uses *streaks,* which are the number of days in a row you've completed a lesson. Each day that you complete a lesson your streak increases. As the streak grows the sense of loss in missing a day also grows. This can be a powerful motivator for some learners.
- **Unpredictability:** Learners are motivated by unpredictability that makes learning experiences more interesting or gives them unexpected rewards. For example, hidden messages, images, or features in electronic media, commonly know as Easter eggs, can be embedded in a lesson or activity.
- **Scarcity:** Learners are motivated to have or experience things that not everyone can readily possess or experience. The rarer the possession, the greater its perceived value. For example, schools with dress codes might motivate students by offering a rare "dress down day" when some students get to wear sweat pants instead of the formal uniform.

Motivation Across Levels of Life-Long Learning

Chapter 4 presented engineering control theory principles, open-loop, and closed-loop systems, and how these principles apply to adaptive systems of feedback to learners. These same principles apply to motivational feedback. Just as there are multiple levels of feedback for instruction (as shown in Figure 15.2), motivational feedback (motivating operations) may also occur at these multiple levels.

Motivating operations can have an immediate effect upon a particular form of behavior or can exert an influence over more complex classes of behavior that extend over longer periods of time. Providing feedback, enthusiastic praise, or access to preferred items or activities are often used as immediate, short-term motivators. Over time, these short-term motivators can also increase the likelihood of engaging in activities over larger units of time; for example, a student who receives appropriate praise and descriptive feedback may feel better about going to school, attending

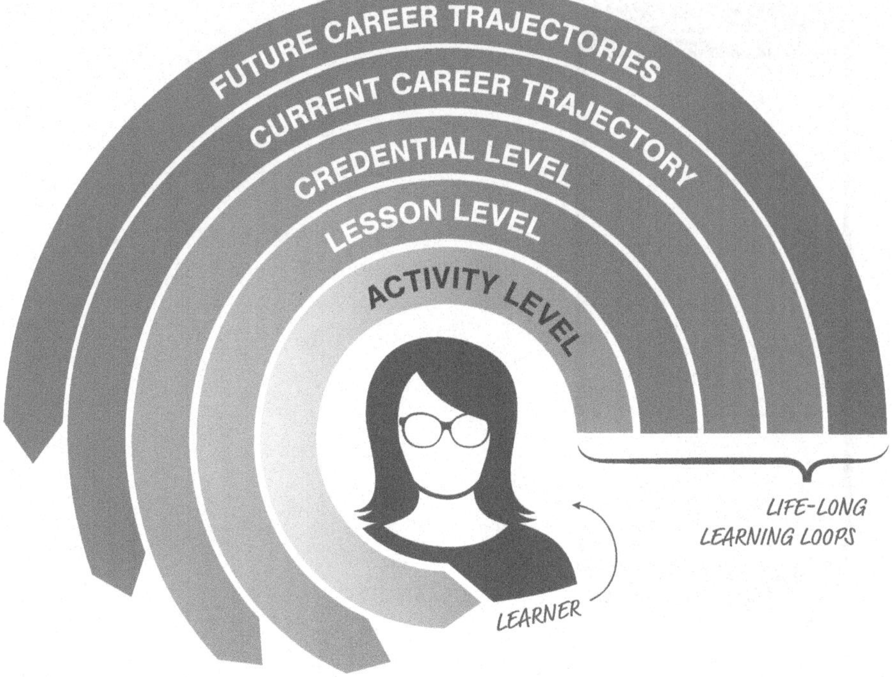

FIGURE 15.2. Motivational operations can occur and influence multiple time frames of learner motivation

a class, participating in a daily activity, reading a book, or working on a long-term project. Longer-term motivators include dashboards and maps that let learners visualize their progress toward learning goals, credentials, and career goals. (An example of this is show in Figure 15.3 from Gooru Navigator.) Learners are also motivated when they can see that goals are attainable. They may be motivated by some level of autonomy over their paths or by a sense of ownership, knowing that their learning path is customized for them.

Data-Driven Motivating Operations

Chapters 5 and 6 examined how data from instrumented learning activities may be used to predict when a learner is bored, frustrated, or engaged in nonproductive behaviors. Similarly, learning analytics may be used to predict which motivating operations will be most effective for which learners in which contexts.

Predicting the impact of motivational operations is challenging because the effect of motivational variables (also known as reinforcers) changes based on

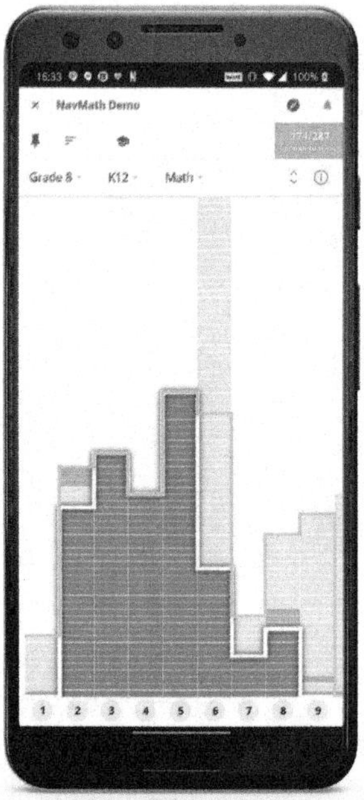

FIGURE 15.3. Gooru Navigator provides GPS-like guidance to learners. This may motivate some learners who want to visualize their competence or have a sense of autonomy over their learning.

learners' context. For example, points earned in a game are more likely to maintain an individual's behavior of playing the game, *if* the desired goal is within reach, such as beating a competitor or leveling up. Similarly, the value of obtaining good grades may fluctuate over time depending on motivating and demotivating factors and may be influenced by personal values. A particular learner who frequently receives good grades independently of their effort, may be less motivated to work hard on an assignment, while another student may put in a full effort, whether based on an intrinsic work ethic or in fear of a decrease in grade point average. Therefore data-driven decisions about the application of motivational operations should attempt to factor in contextual and learner data. In the same way that knowledge inference models use prior learner performance data, motivational variable predictors could use data from prior observations of levels of engagement and behaviors that occurred with variations of motivational variables. (See Chapter 18 for more details on such analyses.)

LEARNER IDENTITY

Motivation is one aspect of a learner's identity. We need to understand a learner against a learning space structured as a progression of competencies. This covers all aspects of learning—cognitive and behavioral, both covert and overt. Competency frameworks need to be extremely thorough, and they should be linked to diverse

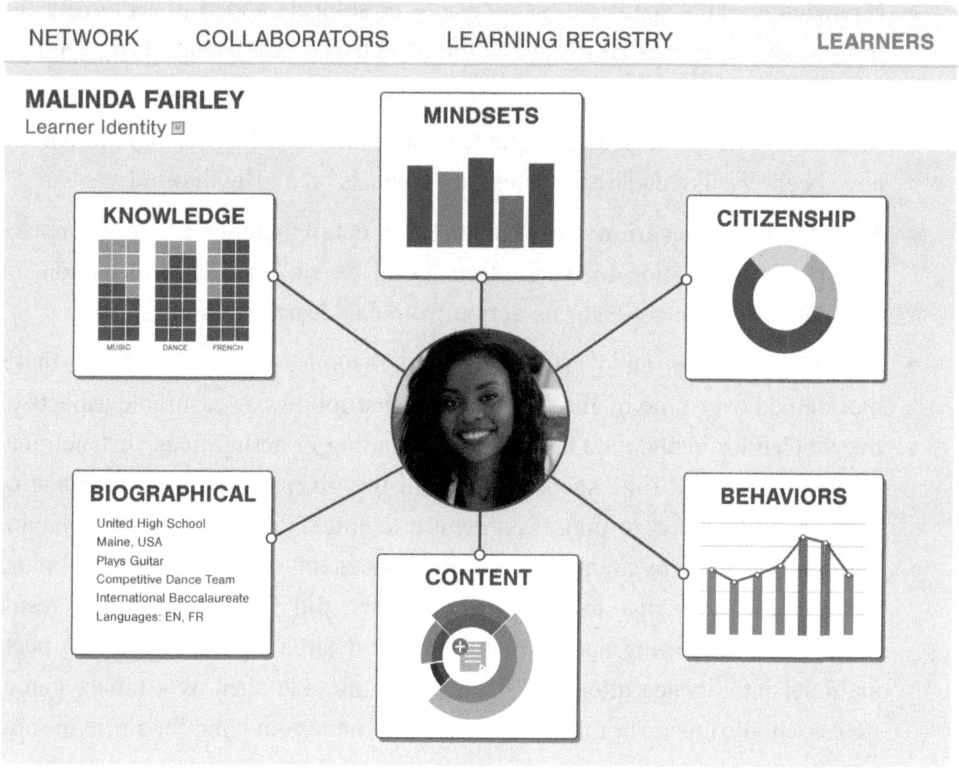

FIGURE 15.4. A model of learner identity may be captured as data structured as a progression of competencies covering all aspects of learning–cognitive and behavioral, both covert and overt

learning activities ranging from off-line tasks such as projects, essays, and proofs to digital activities such as videos and simulations. Learner mastery by competency should be detailed across all elements of learning, depth-of-knowledge, and decay functions (to represent the time to refresh the learner on the competency), and competencies should be mapped to local norms such as state standards and courses.

A very coarse representation of learner identity has limited use; for example, 3.5 GPA, B+, or 78% doesn't provide adequate information about learners to support them. Learner identity must be established for each of the competencies across the entire learning space (sparse matrix). Learner identity for each competency can be grouped into dimensions, and each dimension can have many attributes. For instance, a learning identity may include the dimensions below:

- **Vitals:** This includes biographical data and summary data across all other elements to provide a quick understanding of the learner.

- **Knowledge:** This spans across a variety of subjects and courses during the lifetime of the learner. Skills are captured as part of knowledge as a "depth of knowledge" level encoding.
- **Mindsets:** Factors such as grit, perseverance, self-confidence, and motivation have been discussed. There's often an emphasis on a growth mindset.
- **Motivational Operation:** This is an event or detail that increases or decreases a learner's motivation to work often based on satisfaction, deprivation, or consequence of an action or no action from past learning experiences.
- **Behavior:** This is an overt, measurable response to an antecedent that's maintained over time by the consequence that follows. Measurable aspects of overt behavior include the latency in responding or acting to an instructional cue or antecedent, time spent engaged in the given task, and percentage of correct and incorrect responses on items attempted. Predicting future behavior is often best done by an analysis of the antecedent, the modus operandi, and the consequences that followed. Specifically, did the consequences result in the learner gaining access to his or her desired function (teacher, peer, artificial intelligence attention; access to a tangible such as a tablet, game, recess, candy, music, or tokens; escape from the task at hand for a brief period or longer, such as asking for a break or time away, or a sensory response).
- **Other dimensions and attributes:** These can include higher-order thinking, context, and so on.

Role of Motivation in Gamification

In recent years more and more education and training contexts are integrating game-like activities into instructional routines,[2] and studies in game-based learning have shown that it increases learning performance. Game mechanics, or rules of interaction, can be introduced into any learning context without making the activity a game.

Some of the reasons learners engage with and enjoy gamification are that it can provide feedback on performance, fulfill learners' needs for recognition, and promote goal setting. In a nutshell, putting learning activities into a game format allows for the design of an environment that guarantees the success of the learner. However, fully realized gamification to improve motivation requires good instrumentation (see Chapter 5) and a clear representation of learner identity.

Because behavior is dynamic and complex, effective motivating factors are likely to change over time—both in general and in gamified activities. A learner may value participation and social recognition one day, while on a different day they may value listening to others or simply interacting non-socially with learning materials. Strategy games or games that involve role-playing with others may target different types of motivations. Consequently, it's useful for learning engineers to have a toolkit of gamification operations to draw from. If we consider the learning modality of an online game, Zachary Morford and his colleagues[3] describe the following as elements of gamification that are likely to increase game-playing behavior and maintain learners' engagement:

- Gamification may provide learners with the option to choose between learning modalities. By doing so, learners acquire control over the actions needed to access consequences and outcomes and to achieve goals aligned with values.
- Game environments may allow for immediate contact with the consequences of a learner's behavior, in environments where those consequences wouldn't be easily accessible.
- High variation in learning environments and materials decreases habituation (that is, decreased responding due to repetitive or prolonged exposure to a source of stimulation). For example, while a long lecture given in a monotone voice is likely to decrease students' attention, the elements of novelty, variation, interaction, or even physical activity (as often involved in game-playing) are likely to sustain longer periods of their engagement.
- When rewards or other positive outcomes are arranged to be delivered in ways that are unpredictable to the learner, a more stable and constant pattern of game-playing is typically observed versus when all outcomes follow a predictable pattern. For example, it's known that when response-dependent rewards are scheduled to be delivered after a variable time interval (not known to the learner), responses associated with that reward are likely to show a more persistent pattern of responding over time.[4]
- Contacting a variety of highly valued reinforcers while playing a game increases the overall likelihood of game-playing behavior and thus exposure to and contact with the learning materials.
- Because coercive strategies are absent from the learning experience, learning becomes a pleasant experience rather than an aversive one. While traditional approaches to education often involve doing things to avoid a negative consequence (studying to avoid a bad grade or doing homework to avoid a

reprimand),[5] games are self-initiated and maintained by both immediate reinforcers and by the long-term natural reinforcers of the learning process (which are value-oriented). In gamification, letter grades associated with passing or failing can be replaced by words that are indicative of continuing progress such as novice, apprentice, and expert.[6] Gamification blurs the stark work/play distinction that characterizes the former as a non-desirable activity that the learner seeks to avoid or escape, and the latter, as a highly desirable activity that the learner seeks out. Even low probability actions that a learner may not spontaneously initiate in real life (such as leading social interactions with peers or writing a descriptive narrative about a topic) may be more likely in a role-play situation or as an element of a game.

Another motivational aspect that accounts for the increased engagement of learners who are exposed to gamification is that games afford the possibility to apply (and evaluate) integrated skills in relevant contexts. Instructional activities designed to resemble a game may include objectives that integrate skills from different subject matters. Solving a problem may entail, for example, interacting in a simulated situation that requires math, science, and art skills. Also, a gamified approach that includes situations that resemble real-world challenges may facilitate the generalization of the acquired skills to different contexts and settings. By making the learning experience useful and relevant, such games aren't only continuously motivating but can also be ecologically valid. Finally, by accessing learners' progress in the relevant skills and objectives, gamified experiences can positively impact learners' motivation. Viewing user-friendly visual representations of their performance is often an effective reinforcer and an immediate indicator of learners' success.

Big 'M' and Small 'm' Motivators

As discussed earlier, learners have short-term (getting through an assignment or activity) and long-term (completing a course or credential) motivations. It's erroneous to assume all learners are driven to do well for the sake of finding a purpose or meaning in life. While some may be in search of learning for sake of learning, others are seeking a diploma, a trade, college admission, or gainful employment. Understanding and identifying the kinds of things that motivate people is a first step in identifying what motivating operations might be employed.

CATEGORIES OF HUMAN MOTIVATION

Across business and academic domains there are multiple perspectives on how to classify human motivation. (The motivational categories provided earlier in this chapter and shown in Figure 15.1 represent just one approach to the categorization of motivation.) Daniel Pink discusses the puzzle of motivation and distills it to autonomy, mastery, and purpose.[7] Daisy Yuhas in a *Scientific American* article identified three critical elements for sustained motivation:[8]

- Autonomy: You gain motivation when you feel in charge
- Value: You stay motivated when you're true to your beliefs / values
- Competence: Through work and growth you gain a sense of competence

Patrick C. Friman identified six sources of motivational reinforcement:[9]

- Personal growth: Achievements show progress; increase self-confidence
- Giving: Naturally reinforcing effect of contributing to others' well-being
- Belonging: Acquiring a sense of connection with others or belonging
- Significance: Acquiring a sense of being valued and recognized by others
- Certainty: Having control that something will happen reliably
- Uncertainty: Excitement of something yet to happen, an unknown outcome

Finally, Yu-kai Chou's Octalysis framework lists eight gamification core drives:[10]

- Empowerment
- Accomplishment
- Ownership
- Social Value
- Meaning
- Unpredictability
- Scarcity
- Avoidance

Five of Chou's categories are what he calls "white hat gamification," for example, motivators about conditions people desire, and three of Chou's categories are what he calls "black hat gamification," for example, categories of conditions that people tend to avoid. It isn't necessarily bad to use these negative motivators. For example, an award is considered valuable because of scarcity; an award that's plentiful, that everyone receives, may not be as much of a motivator. Another example is unpredictability; a learning game with Easter eggs that learners can discover may motivate them to play longer. The following table provides a crosswalk of the categories from these four different sources. (See Figure 15.5.)

Even though behavioral scientists and authors have different ways of classifying motivational factors, there are overlaps in these frameworks. For example, the definitions of significance, meaning, and purpose are separate labels for similar concepts in three of the frameworks. It's not so important which labels are chosen. Rather, it's critical for learning engineering teams to consider the full range of relevant variables and to develop strategies that address them with motivating operations within a learning engineering solution. ★

Human Motivator Categories

Friman[11]	Chou[12]	Pink[13]	Yuhas[14]
Positive Motivators			
Certainty	Empowerment	Autonomy	Autonomy
Personal Growth	Accomplishment	Mastery	Competence
	Ownership		Value
Giving	Social		
Belonging			
Significance	Meaning	Purpose	
Negative Motivators			
	Avoidance		
Uncertainty	Unpredictability		
	Scarcity		

FIGURE 15.5. Crosswalk of four human motivator frameworks

Endnotes

1 Michael, Jack and Caio Miguel. "Motivating Operations." In *Applied Behavior Analysis*, edited by John O. Cooper, Timothy E. Heron, William L. Heward, 374–391. 2nd ed. NJ: Merrill Prentice Hall, 2007.

2 Corbett, Sara. "Learning by Playing: Video Games in the Classroom." *The New York Times Magazine,* September 19, 2010. www.nytimes.com/2010/09/19/magazine/19video-t.html

3 Morford, Zachary H., Benjamin N. Witts, Kenneth J. Killingsworth & Mark P. Alavosius. "Gamification: The Intersection Between Behavior Analysis and Game Design Technologies." *The Behavior Analyst* 37, no. 1 (2014): 25–40. https://doi.org/10.1007/s40614-014-0006-1

4 Cooper, John O., Timothy E. Heron, and William L. Heward. *Applied Behavior Analysis.* 3rd ed. Hoboken, NJ: Pearson Education, 2019.

5 Michael, Jack. "A Behavioral Perspective on College Teaching." *The Behavior Analyst* 14, no. 2 (1991): 229–239. https://doi.org/10.1007/BF03392578

6 Corbett, "Learning by Playing."

7 Pink, Dan. "The Puzzle of Motivation." TEDGlobal 2009. Video, 18:23. July 2009. www.ted.com/talks/dan_pink_the_puzzle_of_motivation

8 Yuhas, Daisy. "Three Critical Elements Sustain Motivation: When It Comes To Cultivating Genius, Talent Matters, But Motivation May Matter More." *Scientific American,* November 1, 2012. www.scientificamerican.com/article/three-critical-elements-sustain-motivation

9 Friman, Patrick. 2020. "Metaphysical Sources of Reinforcement." Presentation at the *Behavior Analysis Association of Mississippi Convention, Mississippi, November 2–5, 2020.*

10 Chou, Yu-kai. *Actionable Gamification: Beyond Points, Badges and Leaderboards.* Createspace Independent Publishing Platform, 2015.

11 Friman, "Metaphysical Sources of Reinforcement."

12 Chou, *Actionable Gamification.*

13 Pink, "The Puzzle of Motivation."

14 Yuhas, "Three Critical Elements Sustain Motivation."

REALIZE

CHAPTER 16

Implementation Tools

by Jodi Lis, Jessie Chuang, and Jordan Richard Schoenherr

This chapter further unpacks the implementation phase of the learning engineering process presented in Chapter 1. This chapter includes a checklist for implementation of a learning engineering solution.

Learning engineering doesn't end with the completion of a product, process, or pedagogy. Once developed, the creation must be implemented within specific environmental contexts. Prior to releasing the engineered solution "into the wild," the learning engineering team must consider the specific deployment strategies along with how data will be collected and used to inform iterative improvement of the solution. Implementation issues are considered as implementation planning during the creation stage of the learning engineering process and then during implementation stage other issues that couldn't have been anticipated at the time of design need to be addressed.

This chapter includes an implementation framework (in the form of a checklist) that outlines considerations for learning engineering teams when planning and managing (or monitoring) the implementation phase. Ultimately, the effectiveness of any learning engineering solution is dependent on the people and organization in which it's deployed. It's up to learning engineers to ensure that all reasonable steps have been taken during the creation phase to ensure that a solution can be adapted to all relevant learning contexts. This often means the development of implementation resources, an implementation plan, and/or an implementation guide. The nature of these resources depend on the project and factors such as the complexity of the work needed to successfully implement the innovation.

The following tool contains a summary of the domains that should be considered for implementation and a list of key questions for consideration. We also provide some illustrative examples to demonstrate the kinds of considerations that can be relevant in the context of learning engineering.

Implementation Considerations Framework	
DOMAINS	*QUESTIONS*
1. Policies and Strategy	• What are the relevant policies in the context of the implementation? • What are the relevant strategies in the context of the implementation?
2. Budget	• Is adequate funding available for implementation? • If full funding isn't available now, should it be rolled out over time, starting with a more limited scope or population?
3. Material Resources	• Are adequate resources in place for implementation?
4. Leadership and Organizational Capacity	• How will the leadership support the roll-out, implementation and evaluation of the product? • Does the organization have the human resource talent needed to support the implementation?
5. Team	• What roles and expertise are needed to manage, support, monitor, and implement the solution (such as, administrative support, program coordination, technology, data management)? *See Chapter 10, Tools for Teaming*
6. Technology	• What technologies are required to respond to the challenge? *See Chapter 14, Software and Technology Standards as Tools*
7. Operationalization	**Deployment and Delivery** • What's the process to integrate the solution into the existing culture? • What's the process to integrate it into the existing environment? • What is the process to deliver the product to the users? **Commitment and Support** • What's the strategy to demonstrate the product is beneficial / useful? • What's the process to manage changes in process and behavior needed for effective implementation? **User or Learner** • What preparation is needed for users to engage with the solution? • What support is provided to the user? **Professional Development and Mentorship** • Is professional development needed for those supporting learners? • If professional development is needed, how will that be provided? • Will support be provided within the organization? • Are external parties required?

Implementation Considerations Framework	
DOMAINS	*QUESTIONS*
8. Instrumentation	• What is the process to identify, collect, monitor, review, and document data (stakeholder perceptions, learning, usage patterns) during implementation? • Is the instrumentation developed during the Creation phase to collect data fully deployed and operational? *See Chapter 5, Learning Engineering Uses Data (Part 1): Instrumentation*
9. Investigation During Implementation	• What qualitative and quantitative variables will be monitored during implementation? • How will the data be analyzed, interpreted, and represented? • To what extent do they represent industry standards or best practices? • How might these analyses inform future Challenge phases and iterative improvements and cost-benefit analysis regarding the future of the product? *See Chapter 6, Learning Engineering Uses Data (Part 2): Analytics*
10. Ethics	• Does the implementation process comply with organizational, regional, national and international standards, for example, data privacy, consent, anonymity, and confidentiality? • Have ethical considerations beyond compliance been considered? • What ethical dimensions have been evaluated? • How have trade-offs and conflicts of interests been addressed? *See Chapter 7, Learning Engineering is Ethical* *See Chapter 17, Ethical Decision Tools*
11. Scale-up and Sustainability	• What is the current scale of implementation? • What plans or strategies are established for scaling up? What are the associated costs (human, financial, social capital) of scaling up? • What foreseeable problems are likely to occur? What are the strategies in place for risk assessment and management?

FIGURE 16.1. Learning engineering implementation checklist

Implementation Considerations Framework Examples

1. POLICIES AND STRATEGY

What are the policies/strategies to support the implementation?

A solution should support and comply with local or organizational policies and strategies. It could be to achieve an objective in the strategy, work toward an overarching goal, or extend the strategy beyond its initial purpose. In the example described below about e-learning in Zambia, e-learning is a pillar in Ministry of Health's eHealth strategy. The e-learning initiative worked toward achieving the goal of that pillar. In Chapter 5, Learning Engineering Uses Data (Part 1): Instrumentation, sensors were used to encode communication and determine how well a team followed communications protocols. Precise communication was essential for the safety and work of the team. The investigation involved complying and aligning with policies and strategies such as the US Army's communication strategies, security and privacy policies, and technology procedures.

2. BUDGET

Is adequate funding available for implementation for sustained use? Budgeting will include human resources, technical resources and other materials, training, implementation, monitoring, and scale-up.

Any solution must be budgeted adequately. Consideration must be given to how much funding is needed, where the funding will come from, and if the funding will be stable and available. Also, if you plan to scale up a solution, then future cost must be considered. There are many instances in which the funding is available to develop, test, and pilot a solution but the scale-up and expansion of the solution isn't thought about until it's too late. Budgeting for the creation stage is only part of putting a solution into practice. It's important to consider what funding may be required and if the source of funding will be stable past the research or pilot phase to scale the solution and add more users.

The objective of Open edX, the open-source software platform described in Chapter 4, Learning Engineering is Engineering, was to build a learning platform using a broad range of robust, effective learning techniques. From its inception the plan was for the platform to scale to support thousands of courses and reach millions of students. Attention was paid to making course creation effective yet economical with low investment.

It's been estimated that the cost of content and platform development of the original Open edX platform and first course were roughly a half-million dollars. Beyond the cost to develop and deploy the platform, the team also calculated the return-on-investment to scale Open edX: $1 in per-student cost or benefit equals roughly $1000 per course when assuming an average of 1000 students per course, and $1 in per-course cost or benefit equals roughly $1000 per platform. The financial plan worked. Open edX became the learning technology behind edX, the online learning platform co-founded by Harvard and MIT, and Open edX has since evolved to support higher education, enterprise, and government organizations.

3. MATERIAL RESOURCES

Are resources in place for the product for implementation?

Material resources, consumables, and other accessories may be required for the solution. These are in addition to the technology and human resources. In Chapter 1, Learning Engineering is a Process, virtual reality equipment for a class at MIT was required for the solution. Were there enough headsets for the amount of students in the classroom? Budgeting and procuring them was essential. Without the headsets, there would've been no solution.

A simulation environment in a medical school in Chapter 3, Learning Engineering is Human-Centered, and Chapter 7, Learning Engineering is Ethical, allowed medical students, student nurses, and others to learn surgical and clinical skills by practicing them without risking the safety of live patients. The lab required a set-up with a vast range of material resources. In the operating room simulations, learners performed the roles of nurse, anesthetist, and other clinicians on a simulation mannequin placed on a gurney in the room with vital signs displayed on monitors along with the rhythmic beeps of the simulated patient's pulse. Technicians and educators sat behind a one-way mirror voicing the mannequin and running through a crisis situation by changing the simulated patient's vital signs. In multipurpose training spaces, students moved around in groups of five or six to different simulation stations learning skills on tools and resources ultrasound and laparoscopic trainers, intubation, whole or parts of cadavers, and simulated tissue. The point is:

When planning the intervention, ensuring that material resources and consumables are available and working properly are essential to the solution.

4. LEADERSHIP AND ORGANIZATIONAL CAPACITY

How will the leadership support the roll-out and implementation of the product?

With any new approach or solution, leadership is needed to support, implement, and encourage new, different, innovative, and nontraditional methods. Change management is a key ingredient in learning engineering.

An example of how leadership enables research, testing, and change is offered in Chapter 5, Learning Engineering Uses Data (Part 1): Instrumentation. As chief learning officer at Kaplan, Inc., Bror Saxberg and his team had questions on what was happening around the learning that the current science couldn't answer. The research lacked evidence about what worked for their specific student population and within the context of their delivery model. To test the impact of their interventions on student learning and implement the best approaches at scale, the chief learning officer, the vice president of measurement and evaluation, and other members on the learning team created a research pipeline for their own experiments to accumulate credible evidence about what measurably improved learning outcomes for their students. In this example, the leadership made the human resources available and developed the organizational capacity for the research pipeline. Without the support and resources provided by the leadership, they couldn't have been successful.

5. TEAM (HUMAN) RESOURCES

Who's on the team to manage, support, monitor, and implement the product (program coordination, IT, data management, and other needs)? What are their roles?

Learning engineering can be a team sport, as described in Chapter 10, Tools for Teaming. The team that produced the game in Ghana from Chapter 3, Learning Engineering is Human-Centered, had many players. (See Figure 16.2 for a summary of stakeholders by phase.) Leti Arts, the gaming company, was involved throughout the learning engineering process. The roles on the team included a project manager, a creative director, game programmers, developers, illustrators, and sound experts.

The international development organization that contracted Leti Arts had a project manager and technical experts to create, implement and investigate the solution. Government officials from the Ghana Ministry of Health and Ghana Health Services along with representatives of health organizations and medical associations were involved in the creation and implementation phases.

	CREATION	IMPLEMENTATION	INSTRUMENTATION	INVESTIGATION
Leti Arts team	x	x	x	x
International organization managing the project	x	x	x	x
Government, Ministry of Health, Ghana Health Services	x	x	x	
Local health organizations	x			
Medical profession associations	x	x		
Peer educators from the community	x	x		
MSM population	x	x	x	

FIGURE 16.2. Leti Arts example showing different teams during different phases

Peer educators from the community implemented the game. They learned how to integrate the game into the training and assistance that they provided to the community. They supported and introduced the game to the target population. For the investigation, instrumentation was built into the scenarios. The Leti Arts team gathered the data and prepared reports for the project team. The project team reviewed the decisions made in the scenarios with the peer educators and noted the areas in which further reinforcement would be helpful. That information from the investigation was also incorporated into other outreach strategies.

6. TECHNOLOGY AND INFRASTRUCTURE

What tools and processes are needed?

Wikipedia defines technology as "the sum of techniques, skills, methods, and processes used in the production of goods or services." The case studies throughout this book all include a form of technology, from a donkey cart in West Africa described in Chapter 1, Learning Engineering is a Process, to complex software such as adaptive learning systems used by the US Army in Chapter 5, Learning Engineering Uses Data (Part 1): Instrumentation, to designing learning for two- and three-year-old children in Chapter 3, Learning Engineering is Human-Centered. The technology may be a single solution or may include an interoperable solution of several platforms and applications. Implementation focuses on how to build and operationalize these technologies and other components needed for the solution.

7. OPERATIONALIZATION

What is the process for the solution to be integrated into the existing culture and learning environment?

The answer to this question requires its own learning engineering processes and sub-process cycles. Every implementation context may be different, have unique challenges, and require different approaches, plans, and solutions to problems.

See example: Zambia case study below.

8. INSTRUMENTATION

What's the process to identify, collect, monitor, review, and document data (stakeholder perceptions, learning, usage patterns) during implementation?

The early phases of the learning engineering process (understanding the challenge and the creation phase) include determining what questions to answer and developing a system to gather that data, for example, the instrumentation. A focus of the implementation phase is to ensure that the data sources are accessible and the systems are working to collect and review the data.

A scenario in Chapter 6, Learning Engineering Uses Data (Part 2): Analytics, illustrates how a team at Edmentum reviews and interprets analytic results from a formative assessment. Edmentum has learning engineers in their company who are well-versed in learning sciences, data sciences, and psychometrics, but most importantly, can drive the overall learning engineering process. The process to collect, monitor, and review data is ongoing as products and content are implemented in the field. As data are collected and insights gained, new cycles of the learning engineering are initiated. These processes include various team members, who ask the following kinds of questions:

- **Learning engineer** asks what are the potential causes of the result and what additional analyses should be done and actions should be taken.
- **Learning designer** asks if there's evidence that instruction could lead to confusion, is chunked properly, or has distracting elements; and they may recommend other pedagogical methods.
- **Content and assessment developers** ask if the content and assessment are aligned so that the construct taught is the construct measured.
- **Psychometrician** asks if the passing score is set properly to distinguish between learners who have mastered the content and those who haven't and if there's evidence of multiple correct responses or if students are disengaged.
- **Implementation consultant** asks if there's evidence that teachers may be implementing the system in an unintended way or if there's anything within the context or setting that's unusual.
- **Software engineer** asks if there's an error in the calculation of a pass.
- **User experience or user interface designer** asks if there's evidence of construct-irrelevant variance or additional ways to engage learners.

9. INVESTIGATION DURING IMPLEMENTATION

Instrumentation developed during the creation phase will collect data during the implementation phase. The team must monitor data collection to ensure everything is working. The team may monitor metrics and do analysis during the implementation phase to inform mid-implementation course corrections, define challenges for iterative improvements, and inform future decisions about the product. These metrics will differ depending on the product, implementation context, and organization.

What do we want to know? What question do we want to answer about the impact? Based on the question, what data do we need? What are the qualitative and quantitative variables? Are we collecting the data we need to answer key questions? Sometimes questions are answered with predefined metrics and methods. Other times, important features and new questions are discovered through data mining.

Based on interviews with several private sector companies, Jessie Chuang, vice-chair of IEEE's Industry Connections / Industry Consortium on Learning Engineering (ICICLE) and chair of Corporate Special Interest Group, identified the following metrics that companies often care about monitoring during the implementation of solutions:

- Engagement
- Empowerment of employees
- Transformation
- Employee well-being
- Experience and satisfaction
- Diversity and inclusivity
- Personalized learning

In the Introduction Chapter, What is Learning Engineering, we described how Duolingo looks at metrics. For every design decision the Duolingo team makes, they consider multiple metrics of success. Those metrics include measures of learning, measures of user engagement, and how user interactions impact the company's bottom line. They know that to continue to provide free language learning to millions of people around the world they need to stay in business. This means that every decision is a balance between these metrics. They run controlled experiments for almost everything that they change. If they can improve one metric without hurting the others, they do it.

10. ETHICS

Consequences of the solution may arise that couldn't have been known or predicted in the creation of the solution and instrumentation. It'll be important during implementation to periodically evaluate how the solution is being implemented and the data being collected.

- Do the development and implementation processes comply with organizational, regional, national, and international standards, for example, data privacy, consent, anonymity, and confidentiality?
- Have ethical considerations beyond compliance been considered?
- What ethical dimensions have been evaluated?
- How have trade-offs and conflicts of interests been addressed?

Chapter 7, Learning Engineering is Ethical, describes several approaches to ethical sense-making and provides examples of ethical frameworks. Also, the ethics decision tool in Chapter 17, Ethical Decision-Making Tools, is a matrix for ethical design. The matrix has domains to consider and review when designing and implementing the solution. As the solution is being implemented it's important to remain vigilant about how the processes are developed, how the solution is being used, and how data are collected, tracked, and applied.

11. SCALE-UP AND SUSTAINABILITY

What's the plan for the desired scale of implementation?

The intervention may be intended only for a small audience of learners for research, or it could be piloted with the intent of scaling to support people globally. If the plan is to scale the solution, a scaling strategy should be thought about at the inception and established throughout the implementation process. Strategies must be implemented for risk assessment and management. Open edX was planned from the inception to scale to thousands of courses and millions of users. Duolingo continues to scale to more users. The solution in Zambia, illustrated in the following case study, was designed to scale across the country.

Case Study

HEALTH WORKER E-LEARNING TO SCALE IN ZAMBIA

A viable, trained and experienced health workforce is essential to provide quality service delivery. In Zambia, a project funded by the US Center for Disease Control and Prevention (CDC) invested in the education of health workers to improve their competence in clinical areas from 2016–2020. The project used a blended learning approach including e-learning and on-site mentorship to train the health providers. An international health organization supported the Ministry of Health to implement the project.

IMPLEMENTATION CONSIDERATIONS	
1. Policies and Strategy	E-learning is a pillar in the Ministry of Health's (MOH) National eHealth Strategy. It was identified as an approach for continuous personal development to improve health worker's competence. In 2016 when the project began e-learning wasn't commonly used as a training method. The MOH didn't have a learning management system (LMS), and there was no office in the MOH that managed e-learning. The project supported the strategy by deploying a learning platform, developing courses, incorporating e-learning into their continuous professional development and building capacity in the ministry to use digital learning tools.
2. Budget	The intervention was a component in an HIV project funded by the US CDC from 2016 to 2020. An international health organization was contracted to manage it. CDC is continuing to support the hosting and other components after the completion of that project. As e-learning was a new activity for the MOH budget, they're identifying mechanisms to fund it.
3. Material Resources	Many health workers didn't have mobile devices with the specifications needed for the LMS mobile application. The project procured tablets and preloaded them with the learning app and content. A process was developed for distribution to the health workers. Technical support was provided by the project and MOH IT staff. The tablets were returned to the project after completion for redistribution to the next cohort of learners.
4. Leadership and Organizational Capacity	Leadership consisted of MOH officials, project staff, and staff from CDC, the donor who provided the funding for the intervention. The project collaborated with the Ministry throughout the process to build capacity within the government to transition the activity to them.
5. Human Resources and Team	Implementing e-learning as a new tool in capacity building involved a learning engineering team. The team consisted of project staff who orchestrated and managed every stage of the learning engineering process, MOH officials at the national and district levels, health associations, IT experts at the MOH, subject matter experts, health training institutes, and a monitoring team. The project contracted out the development of the courses and deployment of the LMS. That team included the instructional designer, project manager, technical staff for the learning platform and experts for graphics, multimedia, e-learning authoring and voicing. At the end of the project, the management of activities and administration of the learning platform was transitioned to a university teaching hospital. They are managing and implementing telementoring and other digital learning activities for health workers.
6. Technology	The project procured tablets for the e-learning. The courses and additional reference materials were loaded on tablets using an off-line mobile solution. An off-line solution was essential because many facilities had no or limited internet connectivity. Courses were downloaded onto the tablet and could be taken off-line.

IMPLEMENTATION CONSIDERATIONS

7. Operationalization

Commitment and Support: The project worked the IT department, the health workforce department, and clinical areas at national, regional, district, and community levels of the MOH. Through workshops, site visits, and meetings the Ministry's capacity and understanding of e-learning and blended learning grew. The Ministry came to support and promote e-learning. The leadership at the Ministry sent official announcements and letters to all health workers in the country to take the courses for continuous professional development and licensure. Health workers were excited to have the opportunity. They liked the engagement and found the courses useful and applicable to providing services. E-learning has become an integral point of professional learning at the MOH.

Integration: A blended learning approach was used, consisting of e-learning, on-site mentorship, and a WhatsApp community of practice. Interactive, case-based courses in HIV, TB, and maternal and newborn health were developed. They complemented clinical skills practice during on-site mentorship, which learners continued to receive. WhatsApp was used to communicate, share information, and ask questions. Expert clinicians provided guidance and advice via WhatsApp. Through these activities, the health providers gained new skills and improved the quality of services delivered.

Professional Development: Selected experienced providers from district training teams served as mentors. Workshops were held to introduce e-learning first to the mentors. Using technology for learning was new to them. They learned how to incorporate it into their mentoring processes and use it to enhance their skills. The mentors also learned how to use the learning application and tablets.

Learners Use and Support: After the mentors in the designated cohort learned the blended learning approach and use of the learning application, they trained health workers whom they mentored how to access the e-learning on the tablets that were distributed to health providers. The health providers took the courses on their own time over two months. They also referred to the e-learning and other documentation on the tablet for reference when managing patients. The learners continued to receive on-site mentoring and received continuous development points when they completed the courses.

Delivery: The project worked in three regions of the country. Regions had several districts. Implementation started with one cohort of thirty health workers on one district, then increased to two-hundred health workers in three districts in 2017. The MOH rolled out the courses nationwide in 2019, and by 2021 over ten-thousand health workers registered for the courses.

IMPLEMENTATION CONSIDERATIONS	
8. Instrumentation	The objective of the intervention was to improve the competence of health workers in clinical areas. The learning was tracked and monitored using data from the learning platform, mentoring checklists that the mentors and health workers used during site visits at the facilities, observation examinations on clinical skills, and facility data to track the performance improvement in delivery of services for HIV and tuberculous. Noting topics within the clinical areas that weren't improving, adjustments were made within the training and mentoring.
9. Investigation During Implementation	Data collected during implementation suggested that e-learning improved service delivery in two ways. Training previously involved sending workers on workshops off-site, which took the providers away from their clinics. The prior approach was also expensive and ineffective, as workers retained very little of the information delivered. The design, approach, and delivery of the e-learning improved learning experiences with health workers gaining and retaining new knowledge and skills. The blended learning increased the number of HIV and TB sites in districts that could provide clinical care to areas that previously didn't have it. In keeping with the iterative learning engineering process, the team acknowledged both successes and remaining challenges. The challenges: health worker shortages remain common, and education and training of health workers is under-invested. As a result, the country began exploring and expanding other approaches such as telementoring for training and telemedicine to improve access and quality of care. The iterative learning engineering process can be applied to the creation and implementation of these other approaches.
10. Ethics	Data collected on building capacity among health workers followed the considerations and policies in place by the MOH.
11. Scale-up and Sustainability	From the onset, this five-year project was funded for its full five years, with a plan to transition the activity to the government upon completion. The project worked in conjunction with MOH officials at the national and district levels, national health worker councils and associations, IT experts at the MOH, subject-matter experts, health training institutes, and other stakeholders throughout the period of intervention. In the last year of the project, a series of meetings was held to finalize the transition. An example of one of these decisions was the administration and management of the LMS. It will initially continue to be hosted by an outside contractor, with the plan to move the platform to a local Zambian vendor to manage and maintain it in the future. The activities are now led by the university teaching hospital, which was already involved with other digital education activities.

★

CHAPTER 17

Ethical Decision-Making Tools

by Jordan Richard Schoenherr and Jodi Lis

This chapter builds on the concepts presented in Chapter 7 and offers a decision process tool to guide practitioners in an ethical practice of learning engineering.

Learning engineering is a value-laden process. Learning engineers must consider the ethical affordances of instructional design and assessment in addition to technical affordances. Values and ethics must inform all phases of the design and implementation process. Although some value-based checklists are available (for example, Carnegie Mellon University's *Designing Ethical AI Experiences: Checklist and Agreement*), learning engineering requires questions that are specific to the design process. Consequently, this chapter presents an ethics assessment instrument. These tools have been developed to be complementary. The Sense-making Ethical Evaluation Matrix for Ethical Design (SEEM-ED) reflects a bottom-up approach that learning engineers can use when developing products and processes. SEEM-ED assumes that there are two relevant dimensions to ethical assessment: (1) ethical principles and (2) the stage of the learning engineering process.

Numerous ethical principles can inform the learning engineering process. Principles can be found in codes of conduct as well as legal standards. Codes tend to provide high-level values that might not be clearly specified for a specific learning engineering context. Legal standards reflect minimal standards associated with compliance rather than more complex, dynamic ethical concerns. Consequently, ethical sense-making requires that we consider the ethical affordances, disaffordances, and dysaffordances of a design—how a design assists users and how the design can impede or discriminate against users. This requires considering technological affordances as well as social and mental processes. These topics are reviewed in more detail in Chapter 7.

SEEM-ED is a design assessment instrument for developers that asks specific questions about the design and addresses features of the ethical sense-making process. SEEM-ED assumes that ethical principles can be translated into specific questions of values and ethics. It additionally assumes that these questions should be asked throughout the learning engineering process during the identification of challenges, the iterations of the design process, the implementation of a design, and through later investigation. Moreover, we must consider how related and complementary designs compete and cooperate in sociotechnical systems (Chapter 3).

A demonstration of the SEEM-ED approach is provided in Figure 17.1. Here, we adopt the principles of the American Psychological Association to address issues related to teaching, research, and practice. These principles should then be used to inform each stage of the learning engineering process.

A crucial feature of the SEEM-ED approach is that it doesn't reflect a simple checklist. At a quantitative level, each question is assessed in terms of a continuum of responses. At a minimum, evaluation should use a three-point scale (represented below as Yes, Maybe, and No); however, a five-point scale (for example, Strongly Disagree, Disagree, Neither Agree nor Disagree, Agree, and Strongly Agree) would provide a greater level of precision. At each stage, a representative group of stakeholders should use the instrument to provide their ratings and responses independently. These responses can then be averaged to obtain an overall score on each dimension. If there are concerns about social influences, this process should be conducted anonymously.

At a qualitative level, learning engineers and stakeholders should be able to articulate coherent responses to each question such that more questions are raised. Below each of the ratings, follow-up question(s) are presented. Each of these questions requires that the evaluators consider deeper questions and responses to social and ethical issues.

When using the scale, learning engineers and stakeholders involved in participatory design *should* experience uncertainty such that the scale identifies ethical vulnerabilities in the design process. As we progress through the learning engineering process, more questions and greater specificity in the kinds of questions and answers suggest that SEEM-ED is being used effectively. All stakeholders should gain a better idea of the trade-offs between design approaches in terms of functionality and value. ★

Sense-Making Ethical Evaluation Matrix for Ethical Design	
1. FIDELITY AND RESPONSIBILITY	
Will the product/process promote trust in users and the general public? How will you assess trust/confidence in the product/process?	Yes/Maybe/No
Have local regulations (laws, policies, guidelines) been reviewed and incorporated into the design? How have experts in these domains been engaged?	Yes/Maybe/No
Have users and other stakeholders been consulted? Are there any accessibility issues that might limit this process?	Yes/Maybe/No
Does the design comply with relevant codes of conduct (for example, IEEE)? How have codes and guidelines been identified?	Yes/Maybe/No
Are there conflicts of interests? Conflicts between codes, laws, and police? How are they resolved?	Yes/Maybe/No
Have material, financial, and human resources been used efficiently? How have these measures been selected?	Yes/Maybe/No
2. INTEGRITY	
Have developers/designers clearly shared their competencies and limits? What barriers to knowledge translation are possible?	Yes/Maybe/No
Have any intentional or unintentional errors or biases been corrected? How have corrections been reported/addressed?	Yes/Maybe/No
Have the features of the product/process been represented accurately? How have you ensured that users understand these features?	Yes/Maybe/No
Have only those parties contributing to the design been acknowledged? What criteria were used to determine contributorship?	Yes/Maybe/No
Have all parties contributing to the design been acknowledged? How have parties been acknowledged? Are different criteria used for each group?	Yes/Maybe/No
3. BENEFICENCE AND NONMALEFICENCE	
Are there foreseeable short- and medium-term harms and benefits? What risk management framework and mitigation strategies have been used?	Yes/Maybe/No
Are there foreseeable long-term harms and benefits? What risk management framework and mitigation strategies have been used?	Yes/Maybe/No
Do users understand the harms/benefits? How have harms/benefits been communicated to users? Which individuals, communities, and governmental organizations have been involved?	Yes/Maybe/No

Sense-Making Ethical Evaluation Matrix for Ethical Design	
Have the real, perceived, and potential risks been assessed? Which stakeholders and experts are engaged? Are they a representative group?	Yes / Maybe / No
Have users' experiences be assessed in the long term? How have these measures been identified? What kind of risk models will be used?	Yes / Maybe / No
4. JUSTICE	
Will the harms / benefits be distributed equally among users and nonusers? How have the user and nonuser population been identified? How will you address trade-offs between groups? How have these been justified?	Yes / Maybe / No
Will benefits / harms be shared in all geographic regions in which the product / process operates? Why will these regions be affected? How have geographic boundaries been identified?	Yes / Maybe / No
Is the product / process accessible? What are the solution's affordances, disaffordances, and dysaffordances?	Yes / Maybe / No
Are users' rights protected by the design of the product / process? What legal/ethical frameworks have been used? How have you assessed "rights" in the context of this project?	Yes / Maybe / No
Are users' rights potentially threatened by the design of product / process? Are there alternative designs that might limit potential threats? Have stakeholders' experiences and perceptions been used to inform the design process?	Yes / Maybe / No
Will user / nonuser rights differ depending on the geographic region? How will you address regional differences? How will you communicate these differences to users?	Yes / Maybe / No
5. RESPECT FOR PEOPLE'S RIGHTS AND DIGNITY	
Does the product / process protect users' rights to privacy / confidentiality? How have you assessed privacy? How has confidentiality/anonymity been preserved in the data?	Yes / Maybe / No
Does the design team have ethics education, training, and experience? How much experience and in what context was knowledge acquired? Is it appropriate to the user population and geographical region?	Yes / Maybe / No
Would / will any feature adversely affect the self-determination of the user? How have you assessed users' awareness of the consequences of using the product / process? How have users been informed / educated?	Yes / Maybe / No

FIGURE 17.1. Sensemaking Ethical Evaluation Matrix for Ethical Design

The SEEM-ED matrix is not meant to be an exhaustive list of questions. Rather, these questions represent a starting point. A critical aspect of using the SEEM-ED approach requires that all stakeholders contribute to the development of relevant ethical questions.

CHAPTER 18

Data Analysis Tools

by Erin Czerwinski, Tanvi Domadia, Scotty D. Craig, Jim Goodell, and Steve Ritter

This chapter builds on the concepts from the foundations Chapter 6 on data analysis. It provides a learning analytics process model and discusses a few other analysis methods and tools.

This chapter begins with an overview of the learning analytics process model. It's a guide to the kinds of analytical methods used to answer different kinds of questions. These methods may be used within a system for feedback to the learner, to people supporting learners, and to the engineering team to inform iterative improvements to engineered solutions. Following this, information about the OpenSimon Toolkit and learning curve analysis is included.

Learning Analytics Process Model[1]

In learning engineering, data analytics are part of an experimentally driven learning sciences approach to iterative improvement. Data analysts on a learning engineering team help to develop A/B tests to compare various learning conditions, collecting new experimental data. They also work with others who are experts in the subject matter, implementation context, and learning sciences to interpret and answer "why" questions that the data alone can't answer. Just like the learning engineering process is iterative, the learning analytics process may be iterative. Analysis begins with a question and may result in answers and follow-on questions. The following subsections describe that iterative process. Each corresponds to part of the learning analytics process model in Figure 18.1—starting from the top.

The learning analytics process model is a synthesis of concepts from Ryan Baker's Massively Open Online Textbook (MOOT), which is made up of a series of videos and links to the related edX course. The model can be used as a framework

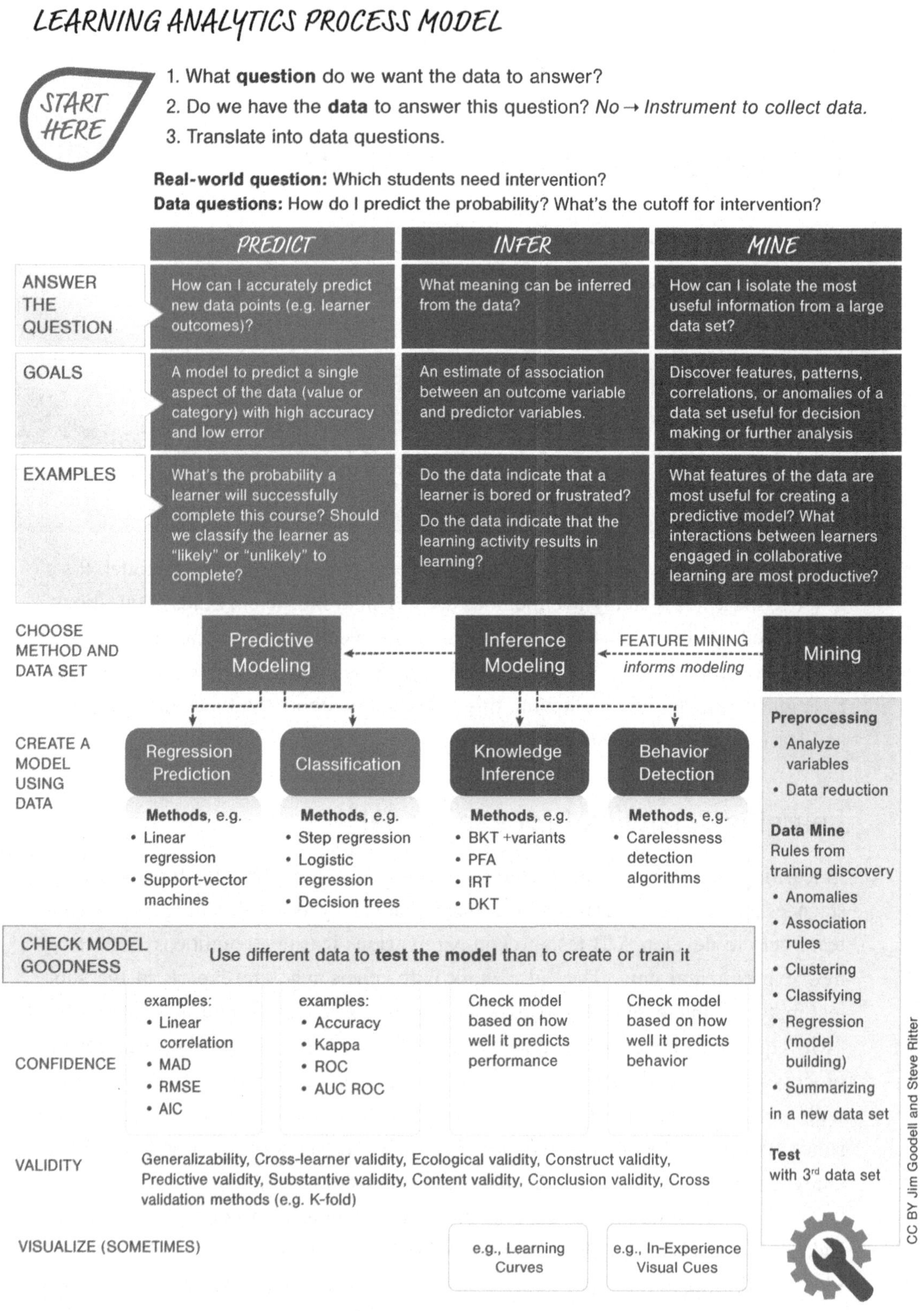

FIGURE 18.1. Learning Analytics Process Model

for use by those doing the analysis and by others on the learning engineering team who want to understand the kinds of analysis that might be applicable. For a deeper dive into these topics see Ryan Baker's MOOT (as well as his MOOC).[2]

Start with a Question

The process starts by identifying a real-world question that the team hopes the data can help them answer. Often learning engineering involves experimentation, so the question might be, "Does learning work best under treatment A or treatment B?"

Translate the Question into a Data Question

The real-world question must be translated into a data question. In Chapter 6 we looked at a simple hypothetical example where the real-world question might have been written as, "What number of test prep worked examples should a student experience to score highest on the LSAT?" A translation of that question might be, "Given data from previous trials where students experienced zero, eight, or fifteen worked examples before taking a post-test and using the scores from those post-tests, can we predict the scores of students exposed to other numbers of worked examples?" In other words, "Can we predict the number of worked examples likely to result in the highest score?"

Do we have the data needed to answer the question?

This isn't a simple question. What we're really asking is:

1. Do we have data that can give us *an* answer or insight?
2. Are the data sufficient to give us an answer with some level of certainty?
3. If not, will it be enough to give any value or insight for future iteration?

> If you know almost nothing, almost anything will tell you something.
> – Douglas W. Hubbard[3]

For the example from Chapter 6 we might have said that the data are insufficient to predict with any level of certainty. With just three data points (two if we consider one of the data points was zero worked examples), limited number of participants, and the reported margins of error from the original study, we won't be able to get an accurate prediction. However, it might be worth doing just to gain some insights about what additional experiments might be needed in a next iteration.

Is more instrumentation or experimentation needed?

If the data aren't sufficient to completely answer the question you might ask what additional data are needed and how can you collect them. This might spawn a new subproject to develop new instrumentation. Sometimes new experiments need to be designed, and sometimes it's just a matter of collecting more of the same.

Based on the question, what kind of analysis is needed?

Look at the table near the top of the Learning Analytics Process Model with the headings Predict, Infer, and Mine. Which of these analytics methods is most appropriate for your data question? Are you trying to forecast something that might happen in the future, such as the likelihood of a student passing a course? (If so, use predictive modeling.) Are you trying to uncover unobservable or latent factors, such as whether a learner is trying to game the system based on their interaction with it? (If so, use inference modeling.) Or are you trying to uncover patterns in a large data set, such as whether certain test questions show bias for learners from particular backgrounds. (If so, use data mining.)

What analysis technique should I use?

For each category of analysis there are sets of methods that might be applied. These methods are also called analysis or modeling techniques. Our example from Chapter 6 used a kind of linear regression or curve-fitting. That falls into the "regression prediction" category. In that case, the curve was modeled as a quadratic equation. If we wanted to predict which students in a data set might answer a problem correctly given previous answers to similar questions we might use "classification" techniques. The subsections below outline some common modeling techniques.

PREDICTIVE MODELING

The goal of **predictive modeling** is to develop a model that can infer a single aspect of the data (called a "**label**") from some combination of other data. It may be used to make predictions about the future; for example, Duolingo uses a model to predict whether a learner will be able to translate the French phrase *le chapeau rouge* into the English phrase *the red hat.* Predictive modeling may also be used to make inferences about the present, such as predicting if a student is bored during an activity. Or it could be used to evaluate a design, such as predicting what scores a set of learners might get on a post-test based on various design options.

- **Regression Prediction:** A model that predicts a number is called a "regressor" in data mining. The overall task is called **regression**. To build a regression, start with a data set where you already know the answer—called the **training label** because it's used to train the model. Associated with each training label record are other variables, called **features** in data mining. The goal of regression is to find which features, in what combination, can predict the label's value.
- **Classification** is used to predict things that aren't numbers, such as the answer to a yes-or-no question. Instead of a number, the label is one of a set of categories (a **classifier**). This is the same as regression prediction except we add one or more thresholds; for example, we could say the answer is "yes" when a given score is greater than 0.5 and "no" when the variable is less than or equal to 0.5.

INFERENCE MODELING

The goal of **inference modeling** is to estimate an association between an outcome variable and a predictor variable. In other words, it's used to understand the relationship between x and y.

- **Knowledge Inference:** The goal of knowledge inference is to estimate a person or group of people's knowledge, skills, or abilities to give feedback to learners, instructors, and other stakeholders—including the learning engineering team—so they can make the learning conditions better. It's also called *latent knowledge estimation,* where **latent** means that something isn't directly measurable (such as confusion or boredom).
- **Behavior Detection:** Automated models can use log data (such as clickstream data from an online activity) to infer a learner's behavior. This can help us understand how different behaviors affect learning, which is useful for iterative improvement as well as for adaptive systems that respond to behaviors to improve learner success.

MINING

The goal of **mining** is to discover features, patterns, correlations, or anomalies of a data set that are useful for decision-making or further analysis, for example, which features of an instructional design correlate to desired outcomes. (The word "discover" implies that mining is more of a method for science than engineering, but especially when combined with other techniques these methods can be a valuable part of making data sets useful for answering specific engineering questions.) Mining techniques include, but aren't limited to, the following:

- **Relationship Mining:** The goal of relationship mining is to discover variables that are related to one another within sets of many variables. Relationship mining is also key to big data reduction, that is, reducing the number of variables and size of the data set while keeping the relevant information needed to answer the question.
- **Correlation Mining** is used to find substantial linear correlations between variables. Remember, though: Correlation doesn't mean causation!
- **Causal Mining** is used to infer causality, as in *x* causes *y*.
- **Association Rule Mining** is used to find simple if/then rules in the data set. For example, if a learner does *x*, they're likely do *y*. This is useful for finding unexpected connections and generating hypotheses.
- **Sequential Pattern Mining** is used for finding patterns over time. For example, if a person reads a book on learning engineering now, how likely is it that person will take a class on education data mining later?
- **Network Analysis** is used for finding connections and their relative strengths, such as in social networks.

How good is my model?

For prediction and inference modeling the next step in the process is to test how good the model is using different data sets than those used to create the model. Machine learning experts call this "model goodness" and recommend using techniques that test confidence and validity of a model.

CONFIDENCE

Confidence is about how much you can trust that a prediction will be accurate. A learning engineering team might use classification as described above to predict *yes,* a design decision is likely to improve learning, or *no,* it likely won't. But a *yes* with only a 50.1% confidence is not as good as a *yes* with a 99% confidence. A learning engineering team might decide to adopt a design decision that's predicted to work only if the confidence is over a certain percentage.

Design decisions or interventions can have potential benefits and potential risks. So decisions about whether to act can be made using a cost-benefit analysis. It's important to consider, for example, "What's the cost of an incorrectly applied intervention or design decision?" along with "What's the potential benefit of a correctly applied intervention?" We might be less likely to apply a design decision that could do a lot of good if there's also a good chance that it might do harm if incorrectly applied or applied under certain conditions. In this case, analysis can suggest when it's safe to apply a stronger but riskier approach and when to revert to a weaker but safer one.

VALIDITY

Validity refers to the extent to which a model reflects what you meant it to model. For example, if a model is meant to analyze a learner's level of understanding, but instead it inadvertently measures (or is affected by) their engagement level, then that model wouldn't be particularly valid for its intended use. There are multiple dimensions to consider when testing for validity, including the following:

- **Generalizability:** Does your model (developed with data from one set of conditions) transfer to a new context in which you want to use it?
- **Cross-Learner Validity:** If you developed a model to detect learner frustration using data from three learners, will that model still work for other learners in your target population?
- **Ecological Validity:** If you built a detector in a lab setting will it still work in real-life education and training environments?
- **Construct Validity:** Does the model behave in a way consistent with theoretical hypotheses?
- **Predictive Validity:** Does the model accurately fit existing data as well as future data? For example, if you built a linear model that predicts the

relationship between hours studied (from 0 to 10 hours) and post-test scores, does the model accurately predict the outcomes of new data, such as the post-tests scores of learners who studied for 15 hours?

- **Content Validity:** Does the model cover the full intended scope, such as the full range of predicted behaviors or indicators of learner states? Are there other indicators that should be considered?
- **Conclusion Validity:** Are your conclusions justified based on the evidence?

Will it be helpful to visualize the outputs?

There are times when visualizing data is the best way to spot features for decision-making. For example, the learning curve analysis discussed below shows an example where we expect to see the error rate go down over time as students learn, but a visualization of the data shows a point in time where the error rate jumped. That's a case where the anomaly is much easier to see on a graph than by looking at numbers.

OpenSimon Toolkit

Carnegie Mellon University (CMU) has packaged its educational technologies developed through decades of educational research into a toolkit for conducting learning engineering. These tools support learning design through analysis and iterative improvement. Two of these tools support data analytics.

DataShop[4] is first an open online repository of over 3,000 EdTech data sets. It's also an online tool for analysis of log data from learning activities. It can be used to perform various analyses for visualization and modeling of learning data like the learning curve analysis shown in Chapter 6 where CMU could visualize the learning, or lack thereof, taking place in its first-year math course. These analyses also provided key information about which skills students needed more practice with, as well as where there were holes in the analytics being collected.

LearnSphere[5] provides a learning analytics infrastructure within the OpenSimon Toolkit. This infrastructure provides the ability to perform repeatable custom analysis methods, and stores learning analytics data in a standard format that can be analyzed using DataShop. LearnSphere was designed for educational research and includes access to anonymized research data sets from multiple platforms via its portal.

Learning Curve Analysis

ITERATIVE IMPROVEMENT USING OPEN LEARNING INITIATIVE INSTRUMENTED COURSEWARE

Learning curve analysis can be used to infer whether a student is receiving sufficient practice for a skill or if there are potential problems with the instructional or assessment content tied to a specific skill.

The **Open Learning Initiative (OLI)** at CMU offers courseware with content that is instrumented to collect learner data, along with its semantic context. Rather than analyzing page views and time on task, which are proxies for information about how the students are learning, OLI collects data on user selections to answer questions and respond to activity interactions that are carefully designed and tagged to the learning objectives and skills (also known as sub-objectives or knowledge components) for the purpose of measuring learner mastery toward the stated learning outcomes. These data drive important feedback loops, delivering data back to the students, the instructors, learning designers, and the learning science community (as this anonymized data are collected in large data repositories such as DataShop and LearnSphere). Instructors use these data, reporting to a dashboard in the OLI interface, to drive classroom discussions based on which skills might be difficult to learn for the majority of the students.

The skill tagging later helps the course developers, in the aggregate, gain more insight into the learning design of the course. After the course has been completed by students in any given course cohort, OLI can export the data to DataShop, the world's largest repository of learning interaction data. DataShop can provide a visualization of the data, providing the simplest form of analysis with learning curves.

Learning curves represent the amount of mastery over each skill. Learning curve analysis is a kind of knowledge inference. When viewing a learning curve, the *x*-axis represents the number of opportunities against a given skill, and the *y*-axis represents the aggregated error rate for all the students of that data set. Ideally the error rate should decrease with each opportunity, which means that the curve always should slope downward. It's expected that the more that students practice with a given outcome, the more adept they'll become at that skill, and therefore have fewer errors on problems targeting that skill.

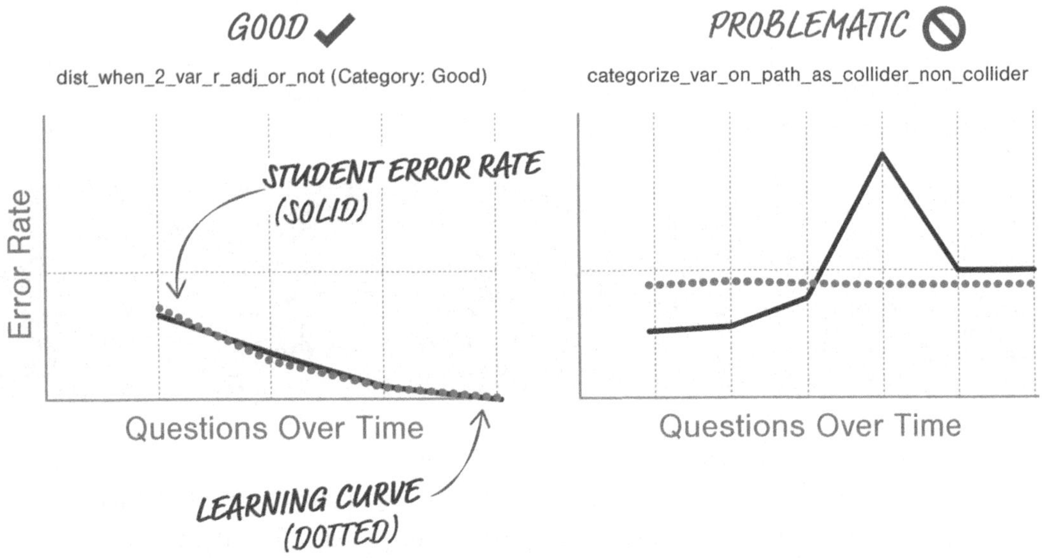

FIGURE 18.2. Example learning curves, illustrating a good and a problematic skill in a graphical causal modeling course delivered by OLI courseware

CC-BY Carnegie Mellon University

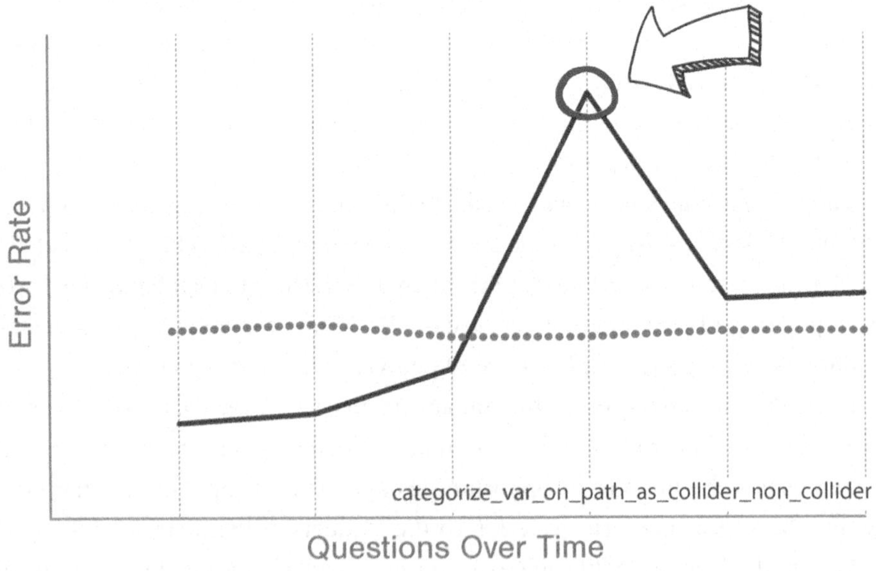

FIGURE 18.3. Example learning curve representing a problematic skill in a graphical causal modeling course delivered by OLI courseware

CC-BY Carnegie Mellon University

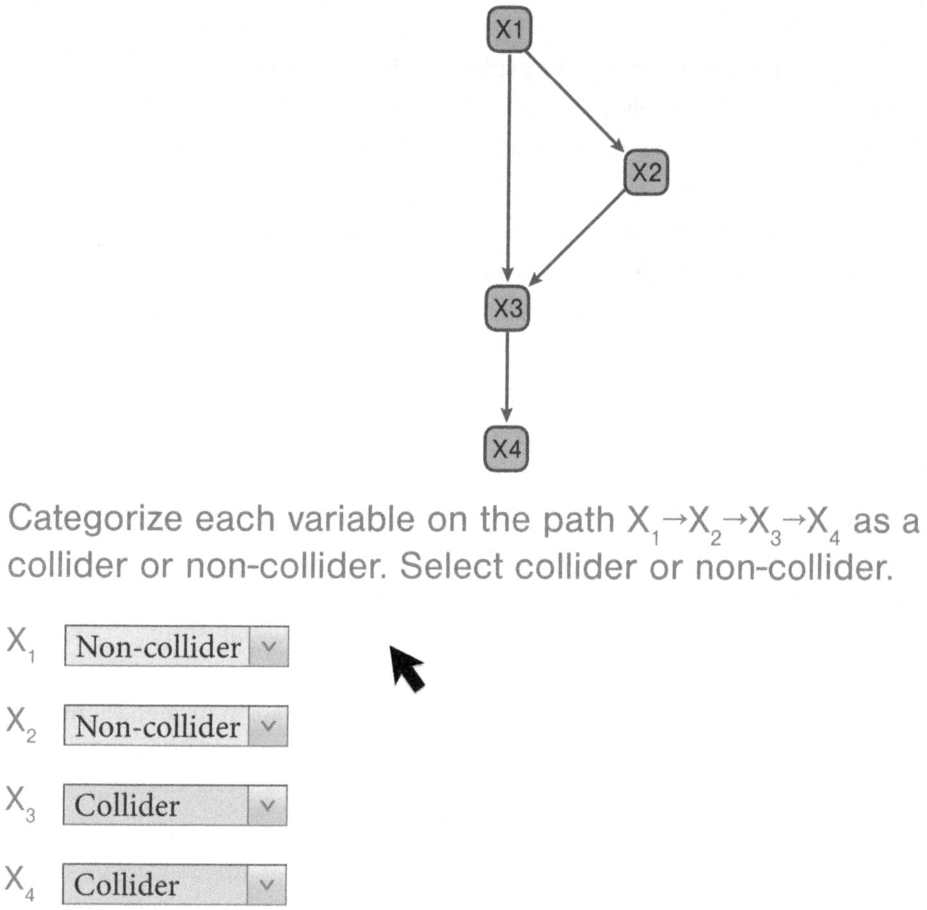

FIGURE 18.4. Viewing a problematic question as part of learning curve analysis for instructional/assessment content

Learning curve analysis can tell us about how students are doing and can be used to uncover problems with instructional content. For a particular skill, if the learning curve doesn't slope downward or shows upward spikes, it might represent some problem within the learning design for that skill.

Figure 18.2 shows an example from a course on graphical causal modeling. In this example, the curve on the left is an example of a good learning curve, and the one on the right is a problematic learning curve. As seen in Figure 18.3, the problematic learning curve from the right side is for the skill with the identifier "categorize_var_on_path_as_collider_non_collider." From looking at the learning curve graph, it appears there are a total of six questions in the courseware providing practice and assessment against this one skill.

DataShop offers the ability to explore further and expose more of the data for any given point in the graph, offering functionality for the user to click on the point at the spike in the learning curve, taking the user directly to the question where the spike occurred.

In the example provided, Figure 18.4 shows the question related to the spike shown in the problematic learning curve above. As you can see, the issue is caused by the third item in this set of questions that asks students to categorize X3 as a "collider" or a "non-collider." We can try to understand where students specifically encountered an obstacle by further viewing a table from DataShop, as shown in Figure 18.5. It summarizes the answer options and the numbers of students who selected each as well as the feedback associated with each option.

Upon further examination of the feedback for X3, as shown in Figure 18.6, there is mention about a "mediator," which isn't mentioned at all in the list of skills being analyzed. This observation could lead one to conclude that "identifying a collider" and "identifying a mediator" are potentially two different skills.

A learning engineering data-driven decision from this analysis might be to define a separate sub-skill "identify the mediator" as a separate knowledge component to be practiced and assessed. Practice problems for this separate skill would then be developed and included in the online course model.

In this case, the course developers added "Identify the mediator" as a skill in the course and added practice questions for identifying mediators to the course as scaffolding toward mastery of the "categorize_var_on_path_as_collider_non_collider" skill. In the subsequent implementation of the course, the learning curve analyses for the "categorize_var_on_path_as_collider_non_collider" skill were found to be "good" learning curves, and the learning curve analyses related to the new skill "identify_mediators" also were found to be "good" learning curves.

In another case, Carnegie Learning used learning curve analysis to discover ways that students think about solving linear equations. Their MATHia software teaches students to solve linear equations, including those of the form $ax = b$ (such as $3x = 5$). A learning curve shows that students make fewer errors as they gain experience with such equations. But a close analysis of the learning curves may show "blips." The blips may represent cases where equations that might seem similar to an expert are seen as different by students.

For example, suppose the software gave students a set of equations that solve to an integer, such as $2x = 6$, $3x = 12$, $4x = 8$, and so on. Students will likely get better at solving such equations, showing a learning curve where errors are reduced over time. If these students next encountered an equation that's superficially similar but

Evaluation	Number of Observations	Answer	Feedback/Classification
Correct	9 (81.82%)	<material> Non-Collider </material>	<material>Correct. X1 is not a collider because it only has one edge connected to it.</material>
Incorrect	2 (18.18%)	<material> Collider </material>	<material>Incorrect. X1 cannot be a collider because X1 only has one edge connected to it. Remember, a variable is a collider if two edges point into it.</material>
Evaluation	**Number of Observations**	**Answer**	**Feedback/Classification**
Correct	4 (36.36%)	<material> Non-Collider </material>	<material>Correct. X3 is not a collider since it is a mediator, and all mediators are non-colliders.</material>
Incorrect	7 (63.64%)	<material> Collider </material>	<material>Incorrect. X3 cannot be a collider since it is a mediator, and all mediators are non-colliders. Remember, a variable is a collider if two edges point into it.</material>

FIGURE 18.5. Answers and student responses from the learning curve analysis

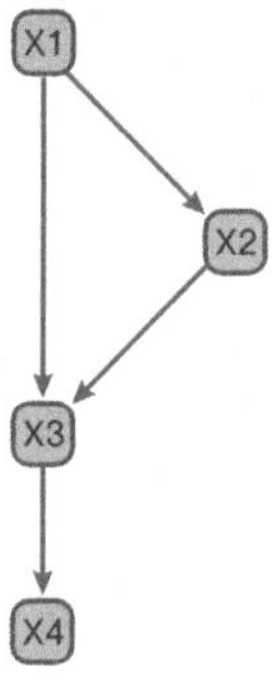

Categorize each variable on the path $X_1 \to X_2 \to X_3 \to X_4$ as a collider or non-collider. Select collider or non-collider.

✓ Correct. X1 is not a collider because it only has one edge connected to it. X

✓ Correct. X2 is not a collider since it is a mediator, and all mediators are non-colliders. X

X Incorrect. X3 cannot be a collider since it is a mediator, and all mediators are non-colliders. Remember, a variable is a collider if two edges point into it. X

X Incorrect. X4 cannot be a collider because X4 only has one edge connected to it. Remember, a variable is a collider if two edges point into it. X

FIGURE 18.6. Viewing answer options and feedback as part of learning curve analysis for instructional/assessment content whose answer isn't an integer (such as $2x = 7$ or $3x = 8$), the learning curve is likely to show an increase in the error rate for those equations. The reason is that students can solve an equation like $2x = 6$ by thinking "two times what number is six"? But few students can apply this thought process to an equation like $2x = 7$ ("two times what number is seven?"). In learning science terms, the knowledge required to solve $ax = b$ equations where the answer is an integer doesn't transfer to the case where the answer isn't an integer. Paying attention to learning curves can reveal subtle ways that students think about problem solving. ★

Endnotes

1 CC-BY Jim Goodell and Steve Ritter. Informed by:

- Glen, Stephanie. "Inference vs Prediction in One Picture." *Datasciencecentral,* May 10, 2020. www.datasciencecentral.com/profiles/blogs/inference-vs-prediction-in-one-picture
- Baker, Ryan S. *Big Data and Education.* 6th ed. Philadelphia, PA: University of Pennsylvania, 2020. www.upenn.edu/learninganalytics/MOOT/bigdataeducation.html
- Fayyad, Usama, Gregory Piatetsky-Shapiro, and Padhraic Smyth. 1996. "From Data Mining to Knowledge Discovery in Databases."*AI Magazine* 17, no. 3: 37–54. https://doi.org/10.1609/aimag.v17i3.1230

2 Baker, *Big Data and Education.*

3 Hubbard, Douglas W. *How to Measure Anything: Finding the Value of Intangibles in Business.* Hoboken, NJ: John Wiley & Sons, 2014.

4 "Welcome to DataShop, the World's Largest Repository of Learning Interaction Data." LearnLab, the Pittsburgh Science of Learning Center. Last modified October 31, 2021. https://pslcdatashop.web.cmu.edu

5 "LearnSphere: A Community Data Infrastructure to Support Learning Improvement Online." Carnegie Mellon University, Last modified 2018. http://learnsphere.org

VISION AND COMMENTARY

A SHORT STORY ABOUT LEARNING ENGINEERS IN THE FUTURE

IMAGINE

CHAPTER 19

The Future World with Learning Engineering: A Story

by Sae Schatz and JJ Walcutt

This chapter weaves together five stories from a not-too-distant future where learning engineering has become the norm. This is a fictional narrative of what might become—created for our shared insight and, hopefully, enjoyment!

Imagine sometime in the future. Technology and globalization have driven disruptive change across the world. The intelligence augmentation economy is in full swing, and just like the industrial and service economies before it, this new paradigm has fundamentally transformed the nature of work, life, and learning.

Information has become ubiquitous. Jobs that once required specialized subject-matter expertise are now being filled by less expert—but highly adaptable—people augmented with high-performing intelligent agents. The value of lower-order knowledge and skills has diminished, replaced by an increased emphasis on more transcendent capabilities such as continuous learning, systems thinking, creativity, distributed teamwork, and a breadth of knowledge literacy.

Schools are no longer the primary gatekeepers of knowledge. Learning and working happens anywhere and everywhere—in virtual and physical spaces and across a shifting landscape of organizations, platforms, and social constructs. The lines have blurred between education, training, working, and participating in society. Words like "curriculum" and "teacher" have taken on different meanings, given the range of autonomous, application-oriented, and adaptive learning approaches now regularly used. Similarly, the purpose of primary and secondary schools has shifted away from an outmoded information-centric model to one focused on preparing students for life-long learning, global citizenship, and human-machine collaboration. Schools try to help students develop a working familiarity of as many areas as possible, along with the mental models needed to connect concepts across disciplines, adeptly address novel challenges, navigate an interconnected information-dense environment, and participate as ethical contributors within society.

Alternative forms of learning and development, including self-directed, experiential, and just-in-time learning in the flow of work have also become commonplace. Across this tapestry of experiences, individuals demonstrate their mastery through verified credentials aligned to competencies. Competencies have become a currency of sorts. They're held in individuals' digital wallets and used for a variety of learning and working purposes such as discovering relevant educational opportunities, connecting potential employees to employers, and evaluating organizational talent management needs.

In this new world, global learning engineering teams work together with intelligent agents, communities of learners and other stakeholders, human and AI learning coaches, implementation teams, and big data analysts to co-create the tools and conditions for optimal life-long learning. This chapter follows the story of five team members from different functional domains and geographical regions as they collaborate on learning engineering tasks. These stories aren't meant to comprehensively depict learning engineering in the future. They're just one slice of life from one particular team that might someday exist.

[1]

Arun's Story

Arun looked up from his bank of monitors. Above them, he could see rain pelting his office window. Normally, it showed an impressive view of Bengaluru's bustling National Highway 44, but today Arun could only see the gray smudges of an afternoon downpour. He sighed and turned back to his work. It was nearly 5 p.m., but the thought of commuting home in that weather slowed his feet. *Well,* he thought, *may as well stay a bit later and hope for a break in the storm.*

Arun worked in the analysis division at Chakrabarti-Dhav Infotek. His team specifically focused on global trends and insights reporting. Businesses paid good money for their forecasts. The finance and entertainment reports were most popular, but their reports on emerging learning and development targets also had a dedicated following. Years ago he would have expected only schools and universities to be interested, but in this age of life-long learning, businesses and NGOs accounted for the report's largest customer base.

A dialog box on Arun's console was flashing, bringing his attention back to the screen. The blinking indicator meant the data reduction algorithm had finished processing. He'd planned to finish his data wrangling work tomorrow, but with the weather looking like a monsoon outside, he may as well handle it now.

Arun clicked the confirmation button to proceed, and a visualization filled his screen. On the left, ranked-ordered lists of popular topics appeared. Icons next to each item showed the topic's popularity over time along with a summary of the typical sentiment felt toward it. On the dashboard's right side, a world map glowed with colorful overlays illustrating regional differences, and with a few clicks, he could explore other filters, like demographic or temporal overlays.

Arun moved his cursor down the list as he reviewed it. Immediately, his eye was drawn to the line, "First successful Mars walk." Like many around the world, Arun was captivated by the inaugural human spaceflight to Mars. He'd followed the astronauts' vlog and had tuned into the live (or, rather, three and a half hours delayed) stream of the crew's first steps on the red planet. The world's interest in the Martian mission wasn't surprising, although he hadn't expected the topic to be trending so vigorously after this many weeks. He clicked through to examine it in more detail. Its emotionality quotient looked good—broadly positive and with a moderately high excitement level across demographic groups. This trend seemed to have across-the-board staying power. Closing out that dialog box, Arun confirmed the trend's inclusion, formally adding it to his report.

Returning to the master list, Arun clicked through several more items, reprioritizing or eliminating entries all together—like the new K-pop sensation W1$H Girls Magic. Among certain demographics, that K-pop band was far and away the most popular trend, but its sentiment was all wrong for this particular report. The emotionality magnitude was running near the ceiling, and Arun knew from experience that pop-culture fads with that sentiment profile tended to create distractions rather than hooks when it came to instructional settings.

After finishing the popular trends list, Arun turned to the scholarly trends window. The algorithm sifted through the previous month's academic publications to create a summary of the most popular topics, latest breakthroughs, or leading indicators of new science and engineering findings. He brought up a different view, a dashboard showing a dense network diagram with clusters of interconnected dots representing the relationships and frequencies of different topics. Working with his AI decision-support bot, Arun sorted through the trends, adding the most relevant ones to this month's report and culling those he deemed less viable.

A couple of hours later, Arun was done. He'd sorted through the popular and scholarly trends and was ready to add the crowdsourced Experts Pool™ opinions, a unique selling point his company offered. The expert panel for this report included a group of verified learning engineers who'd had the opportunity to review and comment on trends using Delphi-style techniques and a private (human-with-AI moderated) online discussion board. They received full access to the trends data at no cost, and in turn, Chakrabarti-Dhav Infotek benefited from their human-centered, context-specific, and data-informed practices and expertise.

But the real secret sauce in the Experts Pool™ came from the company's integrated testing platform. Thousands of end-user learners received early access to the (sometimes experimental) learning experiences built from the report, and in return they shared their own backgrounds and experiences. Using natural language processing, Chakrabarti-Dhav Infotek was able to ingest their comments and use data-mining algorithms to uncover learner-centric insights. In recent years, the company had even established a dedicated user-testing and participatory design division based on this capability, and now that division supported learning engineering teams from around the world in A/B testing and iterative curriculum development.

Arun spent another hour scrolling through the experts' commentary online, while checking the summaries and recommendations supplied by the corresponding AI filtering app with the integrated end-user model. As he reviewed the material, Arun continued to nudge the parameters, causing his AI assistant to optimize the master trends list until it was up to Arun's standard. By incorporating the expert and learner opinions, along with AI-supported learning engineers like Arun, Chakrabarti-Dhav Infotek *Learning and Development (L&D) Trends Targets Report* was nearly 15 percent more accurate than their next successful competitor.

Human-algorithm teams for the win, Arun mused.

Outside, the sky had darkened from pale gray to a deep coal black. Night had fallen, and the rain hadn't slacked. Arun rang for a runner to bring him some food as he settled in for a long night. *No use in stopping now,* he thought. *If I get the report packaged tonight, then I can just take tomorrow off.*

As the last step, Arun checked the information quality of the aggregate list. The AI agent had already applied the Mägi-Yang filter, an algorithm named after two AI researchers who'd won a Turing Award for their work—their Trust DApp algorithm. It used a combination of explainable neural networks and distributed ledgers to provide a reliable estimation of an information source's validity and bias. It worked best when the source data came from stable organizations or people with patterns of trusted micro-transitions over time. It also worked well on high-volume data sets, like the one Arun was working with. The M-Y Trust DApp flagged several trends as possible sources of misinformation, incomplete, or misleading materials. Arun reviewed each warning, particularly the high-risk items. He also published the risk-by-topic list to the expert discussion board for their future feedback.

Like the information sources themselves, each of the reviewers in the Experts Pool™ also developed Trust Factors over time, based on the fairness and accuracy of their contributions to the group. Arun couldn't have mentally kept up with the different layers of reliability across topics, sources, and individual peer reviewers. Fortunately, the system calculated those weights for him, and the result was that his company's *L&D Trends Targets Report* was regarded as one of the most valid and reliable publications in its sector.

Finally, the data set was nearly complete. Arun double-checked its metadata. His software automatically tagged the package with the standard digital signatures—date, time, contributor codes, and so on. This included identifiers for the contributing algorithms, along with the aggregate MYTCO score (the Mägi-Yang Trust Coefficient) for the package. The metadata also included machine-readable pointers to the original data sources to show the lineage of the information used in the report, and it had human-readable tags for the topics included in the data set. These topical tags, like "astrophysics" or "game studies," referenced the Worldwide Wikiword, a community-maintained linked data set for disambiguating terms. Over time, Arun had discovered that he always needed to check those tags; invariably, he'd find one that was off. And it was just that case today. He chuckled to himself as he fixed the link to "Mars" away from "a caramel and nougat candy bar" to "fourth planet from the sun." It was times like this when Arun was reminded that he would always have a job, no matter how sophisticated his AI teammates became.

Finally finished, Arun pressed "publish," and smiled as the processing bar appeared on his screen. Pleased with his long day of work, Arun stretched and turned off his monitor. Outside, the rain had slowed, and miraculously, traffic on the NH-44 was light. He'd be able to make it home in half an hour—and he'd finished his work for the rest of the week too. It had been a good day.

[2]

Dahlia's Story

Dahlia nodded politely at her colleagues as she passed them in the hall. In one hand, she carried a steaming espresso, and in her other, she clutched her bulky coat. Dahlia always struggled this time of year, when the sun didn't rise until late in the morning. Blearily, she found her desk, situated near a window that looked onto one of Helsinki's many cobblestone streets.

Dahlia settled in, turning on her monitor and donning the oversized noise-canceling headphones she preferred. Her console came to life, and she logged in. Taking a sip from her mug, she clicked the icon for her Command Station app. It aggregated her work-related feeds into a single dashboard, including her email, assigned tasks, file update notifications, and filtered newsfeeds. Dahlia immediately noticed her team's thread for the national curriculum project. It showed several new file commits. Presumably, that meant they'd met yesterday's milestone gates. The project was the company's largest and most important contract, financed by the Finnish National Agency for Education. The curriculum focused on adaptive, mixed-mode skills development in a collaborative problem-solving context that required students to demonstrate cross-domain knowledge literacy. Before she could explore the updates more fully, though, a priority alert caught her attention. One of her automatic reminders had flagged "L&D Trends Targets Report update" at the top of her daily checklist. Clicking the alert launched a visualization app where she could explore the latest *L&D Trends Targets* data set.

Dahlia worked at a learning technology—or LTech—firm, one of several similar businesses in that burgeoning sector. Her own company was relatively small, just a few dozen employees. They balanced their size with a reputation for product excellence and through a network of worldwide partners, including the analytics firm Chakrabarti-Dhav Infotek, who'd produced this trends report. Through such partnerships, the learning engineering team for any given product effectively included members from multiple companies, backgrounds, and capability areas.

A few parts of the report immediately stood out to Dahlia. The excitement of the Mars mission continued to be high across all demographics. That was good. The national curriculum project team had already integrated those themes into several prototype lessons that were being evaluated through Chakrabarti-Dhav Infotek's user-testing platform, and she was pleased to see interest in the topic wasn't waning. Dahlia also noted some developing topics in bioengineering, health sciences, corporate finance, and popular arts. The forthcoming release of the e-Mersion 360°, the next-generation consumer-grade VR platform with high-fidelity onboard haptics and proprioception sensors, also topped the list. People were calling it "gadget of the year" and the "herald of a new reality." Whether that hype panned out, the system's popularity had catalyzed substantial interest in new media creation, and as a result, experiential immersive design had re-emerged as a hot topic. That was particularly great for Dahlia, because she could easily add elements of new media design into nearly every curricular package she created.

Dahlia specialized in designing packages for problem-based learning, or PBL for short, that integrated multiple topics from across different competency areas. For instance, her most recent deliverable bundled sustainable agriculture, introduction to the scientific method, public policy, and personal health into a package for secondary schools. Dahlia also had several L&D projects under contract for business-to-business (B2B) clients. Although they generally focused on workforce development, they still used PBL and other pedagogical approaches similar to the modules she built for schools and universities. Remembering this, Dahlia selected some of the demographic filters on her visualization app, examining the latest employee up-skilling developments in the *L&D Trends Targets Report.*

The right-to-repair movement had become popular across the commercial sector, and today, it was becoming common for large businesses to train their employees in basic maintenance skills. With that foundation, employees—assisted by their AI agents—could fix just about anything. Several industry reports showed that "troubleshooting literacy" helped businesses sustain software and equipment longer, and it increased productivity by shortening downtimes. As a result, just-in-time learning modules on various repair topics were flying off the digital shelves, and the PBL packages Dahlia designed were also popular. Her introductory modules helped workers build basic troubleshooting competences, creating a baseline that let them more effectively use the specific just-in-time packages when they needed them.

The firm where Dahlia worked, Oivallus, also had a team focused on microlearning curation. Of course, since the mid-2020s, microlearning businesses had become a dime a dozen. Anyone could search the web for whatever topic they wanted and find hundreds of automated websites offering microlearning "courses." In practice, typically, these were just strings of automatically assembled multimedia with computer-generated quizzes tacked on. Initially hailed as a revolution in learning, these microlearning aggregators had soon become jumbles of noisy content.

Development of the MYTCO score helped. As its use grew in popularity, it helped individuals find the most trustworthy resources. But just because an instructional video or how-to guide isn't biased or misleading, doesn't mean it's pedagogically sound or appropriate for all contexts. As a result, in the old days of crowdsourced microlearning, too many of these Frankenstein just-in-time-training packages were created. And even though they included all of the de facto concepts, the pieces were often too difficult to follow—like reading a book where different authors wrote each page without consulting with one another. This was especially problematic for schools developing knowledge literacies, which require coherent learning experiences—particularly at the introductory stages. And after several large-scale state-sponsored studies, it became clear that the low-effort microlearning platforms weren't really effective, at least from a learning outcomes perspective.

That's how Oivallus got its start. Their first successful product was a microlearning curation service that used human-supervised AI to verify and tag instructional resources with contextual relevance and pedagogical metrics, making it possible for both educational software and human teachers to assemble and sequence the content into semantically coherent curricular arcs. The algorithm Oivallus developed also automatically identified topical, contextual, and pedagogical similarity so that assembled strings of learning resources would function as integrated lessons rather than disjoint factoids.

Oivallus soon evolved from a software-centric startup to a learning engineering firm. They hired learning designers, including Dahlia, and found their niche in the intersection of applied AI and learning theory. Dahlia specialized in cognition and education. She worked closely with her more tech-savvy coworkers, and she relied on data sets, such as the *L&D Trends Targets Report,* and advanced software, like the Chakrabarti-Dhav Infotek user-testing and participatory design platform. With these tools, combined with iterative cycles of testing and analysis, Dahlia and her fellow Oivallus learning engineers were able to substantially enhance the effectiveness of the learning experiences they created, even across different contexts and for diverse learner populations.

It was time for Dahlia to get to work. She opened her latest assignment, a vocational project called Practical Piping, contracted by an industry group. It focused on new smart plumbing technologies. (*Who knew that was a thing?* Dahlia mused.) The learning engineering challenge this time was to train an entire industry on a brand-new plumbing technology. The project also incorporated several twenty-first century competencies, specifically metacognition and self-directed connectivism skills, and it included practical exercises organized around a space exploration theme. *Oivallus had been getting mileage out of the popularity of that Mars mission!*

Several hours passed. Dahlia lost herself in her work, until she was interrupted by a gentle tapping on her desk. Elliot stood there, with two other coworkers loitering expectantly near the door. They were heading down the café for a midmorning coffee. *Already?! The morning had been a blur!* she thought. With a start, Dahlia checked the time. It was already ten o'clock. That meant the workday would be ending soon in Singapore. Declining her team's invitation, she instead logged into the extranet chat and found her Pac-World Informatica contact. After a few polite texts to confirm the call, Dahlia joined a video-teleconference with Ehuang, her performance analytics point of contact.

Ehuang was a wiz at data science, and even better, she made the technobabble intelligible.

"This latest package we're making," Dahlia began.

"The plumbing one . . . ?"

"Yes, Practical Piping for Plumbing Professionals," Dahlia smiled at the ostentatious module name. "It's almost done, but I need to add in the instrumentation data hooks you created."

The company where Ehuang worked, a massive analytics firm based in the heart of Singapore's tech sector, had an agreement with Oivallus to collect and analyze data on the performance of its learning products. Every module Oivallus created included—what Ehuang called—paradata. It provided general inference tracking based on the module's access, use, and ratings. The higher-end products, like the PBL packages Dahlia designed, also included tailored impact metrics that tied into Pac-World Informatica's global network of data systems. These additional measures went over and above the learning effectiveness evaluations that Dahlia included in the curriculum. For example, Ehuang explained how some of the measures were included in the current package to tease out the profitability impacts of the training.

Dahlia always found it difficult to envision how such distal impacts could be correlated with specific interventions, like a single training program, but the specialists at Pac-World Informatica were masters of that kind of big data analysis as well as the instrumentation that made it possible. Ehuang would sometimes joke that their secret was "data farming" instead of "data mining."

"You have to plant the data seeds if you want the data fruits, *lah!*"

Over the next hour, Ehuang walked Dahlia through the package that Pac-World Informatica had sent over for the new plumbing curriculum. By the time their call ended, Dahlia was ready to do the project's pre-flight review.

The Practical Piping curriculum covered a set of three primary and five secondary competencies. It included three interrelated PBL activities (with the embedded impact measures from Ehuang) as well as integrated formative and summative assessments and AI-enabled student, mentor, and evaluator guidance, such as scaffolding recommendations, just-in-time nudges, and feedback templates. The package also included alternative pedagogical recommendations, adaptation pathways, and different presentation modes depending on whether it was used in a formal learning context (like a vo-tech school), a technology-aided blended one, or a self-directed learning situation.

Once the files were packaged, Dahlia clicked the "pre-flight check" button. Her mouse icon became a spinning animation, indicating the system was processing, and a few moments later, a dialog window appeared with a list of errors and warnings about the curriculum package. Dahlia reviewed them, accepting or fixing each as appropriate. Once satisfied, Dahlia clicked "approve" and then committed the Practical Piping package to her team's repository. Elliot would do the final quality control on it—including the crowdsourced user-testing facilitated by their partner Chakrabarti-Dhav Infotek—and then he'd send it off for the customer's review. Once they gave the greenlight, it would be disseminated across their partner organizations and vocational schools.

Dahlia smiled. That was one task done for the day. *After lunch,* she thought, *I'll review the team's update on our national curriculum project.*

[3]

Dominic's Story

Dominic tugged at his collar. He hated wearing a tie, especially when it was so hot out. It was nearly winter, but Austin still felt like a sauna. He fidgeted unconsciously. Normally, his in-office days at the CrownSoft Learning Systems Corporate HQ were the highlight of his workweek. He looked forward to the breakout groups and good-natured camaraderie among the Scrum teams—and the less formal dress code. But today wasn't business as usual; instead, Dominic was leading a special in-progress review with their important (VIP) clients from the Faang Academy.

He checked his watch again. Logically, he knew there was plenty of time, but these VIP ceremonies always made him inexplicably nervous. He took a breath and closed his eyes. Dominic considered his day; walking through his mental to-do list helped settle his jitters. First, he'd check in with Marko and Liz to make sure they were ready to show off the new content streaming server. It leveraged widespread interoperability standards to enable CrownSoft's curricular packages to flow seamlessly across different learning platforms, whether web browsers, mixed reality gear, pedagogical assistance apps, or some other emerging tech. CrownSoft had effectively abstracted the content from the hardware and software, a major coup in terms of efficiency and flexibility.

Next, he'd talk with Imani about her adaptive VR demo. CrownSoft had scored pre-release copies of the new e-Mersion 360° system, and Imani's team had wasted no time assembling an adaptive learning module for it. The lesson was built on a PBL package they'd gotten from their Finnish vendor. Dominic had tested it last week. *And what a marvel!* The system transported him to different "locations" around the world where he could work with people from other countries on problem-solving challenges, and it doled out in-game rewards for his actions. It had felt like a game and a vacation all at once, and beyond that enjoyment, he'd also picked up a new appreciation for cross-cultural skills and international affairs.

★ ★ ★

Later that morning, Dominic found himself in the CrownSoft development team conference room. He'd completed his to-do list hours before, and Mackenzie, the team's project coordinator, had the meeting logistics well in hand. She was just connecting the video feed to their colleagues in Helsinki when the VIP customers arrived. Through the etched-glass walls of the conference room, Dominic could see them in the atrium. He waved, and Kevin Tanaka made a friendly gesture in reply, as he and his companions turned toward the meeting room.

Mr. Tanaka was one of the executives at the Faang Academy, a private nonprofit school system that had spun out of a Silicon Valley conglomerate. The Academy began as a postsecondary vocational program, a bridge meant to prepare prospective workers to fill the high-tech roles those companies needed. Soon it expanded into a magnet school for secondary students. Over time, it grew even more: adding adult education for ongoing workforce development and incorporating younger and younger preparation programs. Eventually, the Academy became a fully integrated learning pipeline, stretching from primary school to workforce development. It also built public-private partnerships, and in coordination with government programs, was soon recognized as the first public-private K-to-Gray (kindergarten through life) school system.

The Academy's success could be attributed, at least in part, to its adoption of learning engineering principles. From its first days, the Academy focused on high-yield learning approaches. It championed proven learning science theories, employed iterative human-centered engineering design methodologies, and verified their impacts through ongoing performance assessments. Using the wealth of data science knowledge its parent companies had refined through e-commerce or digital media, the Academy also incorporated advanced learning analytics and constantly improved its offerings through experimentation and A/B testing. They also leveraged those data to support highly adaptive learning—what the Academy touted as educational "mass customization," a term borrowed from its commercial roots. Regardless of the nomenclature, the results were powerful. Academy programs showed effect sizes over 3.0, as compared to more traditional educational offerings.[1]

What's more, because the Academy began as a vocational program, it hadn't been constrained by the classic template of a multiyear degree. Instead, individual learners could identify the jobs or tasks they wanted to accomplish, then complete curricular blocks to build those competencies and earn associated microcredentials along the way. Over time, as the Academy expanded into K-12 educational offerings, including foundational requirements such as algebra, English, and a broad range of cross-domain knowledge literacy competencies.

Across sectors, Faang's competency-based approach untethered education and training from the time-in-seat model. It was also a key factor in personalizing each person's learning trajectory, making the Academy widely popular—from individuals and parents to companies and communities.

★ ★ ★

" . . . and with these inference engines, we fuse the different assessment pieces and parts to give us the holistic profile for the learner," Elliot Mäkinen was explaining through the video conference. The meeting was well into its third hour, albeit with a lunch break in the middle where Mackenzie had served up platters of street tacos—much to the delight of their out-of-town clients. Bellies sated and in high spirits after the morning's successful tech demos, the second phase of the meeting was progressing steadily. It featured CrownSoft's data engineering team and their partners at Oivallus, a boutique Finnish company expert in cognition and learning with advanced technologies.

This discussion was the main feature of the meeting, and despite himself, Dominic felt that familiar nervous energy creeping into his mind. For reassurance, he glanced at Mr. Tanaka, sitting at the head of the table. The VIP client was deep in discussion with Elliot and seemed genuinely absorbed in the conversation. In his earlier days, Mr. Tanaka had been an accomplished software engineer, and Dominic could tell the older man still enjoyed diving into the technical details. That was good. It boded well for this part of the meeting where Dominic's team planned to unveil the beta release of their Autodex 3.0 software.

Autodex had become the industry leader for 3E records—those digital wallets that individuals and organizations use to store, validate, and exchange data on their education, employment, and experience (the so-called 3Es). Autodex used distributed ledger technologies and standards-based interfaces to create a secure and trustworthy data exchange system. By a large margin, Autodex was the most popular application for this, but it wasn't the only app available. The data feeding into the Autodex was considered a public utility, so anyone could (theoretically) build applications and data exchanges on top of that stream. Several different 3E exchanges, sort of like different credit card companies and credit monitoring bureaus, were popular across the learning and development sector, and associated application programming interfaces (APIs) were standard on most devices.

Dominic's thoughts refocused as Mackenzie made a drum-rolling sound on the conference table. "And now, ladies and gentlemen," she said with a verbal flourish, "the thing you've all been waiting for: It's time for Dominic Morales to truly geek-out over data." A couple of the clients smiled, and Mr. Tanaka looked eager. Dominic got to his feet and gestured at the oversized display screen. On it, a video of the new Autodex upgrade had begun to play.

"Thanks, Mac, for that . . . flattering introduction." Dominic said with good-natured sarcasm. "And thanks to Elliot and our friends at Oivallus. With their latest set of composite assessments, we're getting a remarkable level of validity from today's L&D performance data. We're up to 92 percent reliability for identifying someone's digital signature, just from their routine clickstream interactions. That's almost eliminated K-16 cheating in Faang schools and apps. Also, the results of last quarter's testing in the Midwest vo-tech sector found a better than 80 percent correlation—consistently—between assessments embedded in our curriculum and downstream training transfer tasks."

The clients nodded politely. No doubt, they'd heard these statistics before. He was simply leading up to the big reveal, so Dominic continued.

"These are all incremental improvements. Important, meat-and-potatoes improvements, but not really *new,* you know? Schools and students have come to expect that level of rigor with our products. So where are their pain points?"

The video playing on the conference screen shifted to a set of graphs showing the results of CrownSoft's most recent consumer studies. Dominic touched the first graph, and it expanded to fill the monitor.

"For the third year in a row, businesses want more consumer confidence. A lot of workplaces are still hesitant to cut the cord. They're requiring applicants and workers to use an Autodex app, but still verifying personnel through legacy, manual means. This is a particular problem in these two factors, here." Dominic pointed. "First, third-party credentials. Although Faang Academy and a lot of other classic school systems have good name-recognition, which has built trust in our programs, our smaller partners don't benefit from that celebrity status."

"And institutional name-recognition isn't a pedagogical technique!" Dahlia quipped from the video feed, as she and Dominic had practiced in advance.

"The other issue," Dominic continued after pausing for some polite chuckling, "is the public competency sets Autodex uses." The Autodex software, like the software used by their industry competitors, leveraged open ontologies that were created from common definitions of competencies, accessible via linked data from APIs.

"The governance process for those public data sets is slow. And I mean sloooow—like Austin traffic before a three-day weekend. Which means we're starting out with stale or incomplete competency data. It's no surprise our consumers are skeptical of it. But we've fixed both of those issues in the latest Autodex release. Here's how . . . "

Dominic then launched into his well-rehearsed summary of the new features meant to improve consumer trust in the system's outputs. He walked through its updated data-lineage tagging and multitiered trust algorithms, along with the new user-experience features meant to better convey those trust quotients to end users. He also highlighted a new human-AI filtering algorithm meant to improve the currency and reliability of baseline competency data.

"We expect these enhancements to appeal to our employer end users and to help smaller schools or EdTech businesses. But what about individuals—the students and employees? We surveyed them too, and pretty universally, they want better self-directed learning."

Dahlia chimed in on cue. "Schools and businesses want this feature too. Schools are always eager to supplement their formal curriculum, and employers want their workforces up-skilled to the latest knowledge and skills. Meanwhile, individuals have a whole spectrum of reasons for wanting to learn." Remotely, Dahlia clicked through to the next graph as she described the different archetypes of self-directed learners.

"On the surface," Dahlia continued as she advanced the presentation to a new screen, "it seems like our main challenges are identification (of the desired competencies), access (on the right platform), and motivation (to make the activity intrinsically or extrinsically appealing). These are all real issues, but there's another factor: Learning skill—how effectively a student can teach themselves."

"The new algorithms in Autodex 3.0 include user-support for . . . " Dominic fumbled at the word and checked his notes, while Dahlia chimed in to help.

" . . . for metacognitive support. Formally, we call it self-regulated learning scaffolding."

"Yeah, thanks! Dahlia's talking about our new embedded pedagogical assistance algorithm. At CrownSoft, we've just been calling it 'Mentor in a Box.'"

The meeting continued on for a couple more hours, broken up by demos and coffee breaks. By the end of the day, Dominic felt exhausted but accomplished. He'd rather spend twelve hours coding than half a day in meetings. But it had been worth it. Mr. Tanaka and his team loved the new immersive learning modules, and they seemed to appreciate the Autodex 3.0 upgrades. In fact, Mr. Tanaka had already scheduled time for Dominic to brief the Faang Chief Learning Officer Council so they could begin planning its roll-out.

Ugh, another corporate meeting, Dominic mused. *Well, I suppose that's just the price of success!*

[4]

Ishimwe's Story

Ishimwe squinted at the midday sun beating down on her and the small group following behind her. She was leading them on a tour of the new Icyizere Hybrid School campus in Rwanda's Ngoma District. They were a curious sight strolling along the town's red-clay streets, each wearing business attire topped with fluorescent safety vests and hardhats. Ishimwe paused and gestured to a half-constructed building.

"This will be one of the multipurpose seminar buildings, and it's one of the hubs in the sensor network we discussed."

"Is this another community-built structure?" Shema Mugisha asked. The white-haired man walked with a cane, and he was the most elderly representative on the board of advisors. Despite the heat, he wore a button-up shirt and black suit jacket, adorned with a silver pin from his favorite philanthropy. It reflected the light like a miniature sun on his lapel.

"Yes!" Ishimwe replied. "Through our program, we supply the autonomous construction system that essentially prints the components, but we work closely with the community to assemble the actual buildings and design the campus layout. We also supply the smart sensors, so that the campus and portions of the city can be added to the IoT network. But again, we work with the community to design the specific features of each network. That means each region implements a different version of it."

"Most of the sensors are self-powered, a majority through solar energy here in Ngoma, and their connectivity is almost entirely wireless," Ishimwe continued, as she carefully stepped over a bundle of newly unfurled cables stretched out on the ground. "But we're also installing some high-performance structured cabling under the campus."

"Come, let me show you one of the completed seminar buildings, and we can see how the citywide sensors are supporting educational outreach." Ishimwe led the group to one of the nearby buildings.

Inside, much-needed shade and water bottles awaited. The group sat down at a table, which had been arranged for them in a partially completed classroom. All around, electrical wires and monitor mounts hung from bare walls, clearly awaiting the addition of video screens and other technologies. Ishimwe continued chatting with the board members, and after a few minutes, she described the various technologies that would soon be installed in the educational space. She also highlighted the back-end technology, including the underlying data fabric that would connect the various learning applications into an interoperable, holistic system of systems—a learning ecosystem. That ecosystem could incorporate a range of technologies, from common computers to mixed reality devices, mobile learning tools, and even embedded sensors. Together, these interoperable delivery platforms created flexibility, and they offered learners many different learning pathways, depending on their unique needs.

She continued, "We've found it's important to situate learning within the real lives of the students. For example, in this region, there's still a lot of traditional agriculture, and we use that in some lessons. The district-wide sensor grid monitors weather conditions, and then we use those data in modules related to climate, weather, and even students' own farming projects."

"This goes both ways too. We can bring the outside data into structured lessons, making those lessons more relevant to students. Conversely, we can take lessons out into the students' world. Thanks to our network upgrades, students have 6G connections anywhere in the district."

Ishimwe pulled a pair of augmented reality glasses from her bag and then showed how their embedded location sensors and computer vision could help situate lessons. She loaded a postsecondary biology module that her group had recently acquired from CrownSoft Learning Systems. Then, using the software's developer mode to spoof some of the context data, she showed how the glasses could detect different animals and plants, such as the slightly wilted eucalyptus leaf she produced for demonstration purposes. Once detected, the glasses could deliver anatomy or phytotomy in microlessons that were overlaid in the wearer's audio and visual channels. The software came as a part of a gamified package. It encouraged students to earn points by seeking out different species and then proving their biological knowledge of them. Microlessons in the package also accounted for the local environment, for example, incorporating geo-specific modules on invasive species if students happen to find non-native flora at a particular location.

The board of advisors seemed impressed, and their appreciation grew as Ishimwe reviewed the financial details. The ruggedized AR hardware had become cost-effective enough to provide up to two pairs for every student covered by their program.

"That's all quite good," Shema Mugisha said slowly. "You've made great progress in expanding educational access. You should be proud of this work, Doctor Mahoro," the elderly man continued, using Ishimwe's surname. "But I still worry about the digital *education* divide. Yes, we're rapidly closing the access gap, but I have seen many educational programs and many, *many* new educational tools. So, I know! I know there is more to the divide than technology. Simply increasing access to computers, networks, and"—he gestured toward the glasses—"other gadgets, that is not enough. Technology, alone, is not learning, and information, alone, is not education."

Ishimwe nodded and began to reply, but Mugisha kept talking over her. Clearly, he'd been mulling over this point for some time, and it was bursting to escape.

"I am no Luddite. I see the potential, but we need to also ensure the lessons are well made and well curated. We need semantic coherence in our curricula. All of the individual pieces need to come together so that they create quality learning. It is our job to produce students who have knowledge and learning literacy, who can *think,* and who can transfer that foundational knowledge out into the world. Ultimately, I worry about the hidden digital divide. I worry that some students will have unequal access to coherent and high-quality educational curricula—even as they get access to new electronics and libraries worth of information." Mugisha continued on his soapbox a bit longer, even referencing some graphs he'd prepared on his tablet.

"Mwami Mugisha," Ishimwe finally interjected, using the loquacious man's honorific title. "Thank you for your concern. It's clear you understand the depths of the challenge we face. I can assure you that we've learned from the past. Today's modernization efforts extend beyond a mere moment in time."

Mugisha nodded for Ishimwe to explain.

"One of the keys to our success is community outreach. We don't simply arrive with premade solutions from Kigali, Addis Ababa, or Geneva. The first phase of any development project starts months before even a single meter of dirt is moved. We work hand-in-hand with the local teachers and leaders. It's a human-centered design process. Together, we identify their city's needs and tailor the curriculum, technology grid, and construction to them. We also take special care to find community groups, like the Zaza Women's Center, so that we can make sure different voices are heard."

"Especially, we collaborate closely with educational professionals. For example, here in Ngoma, we've just completed the third cohort of teacher training. The training helps them learn to use new educational technologies, including the assistive AI coaches and all of the associated pedagogies," Ishimwe explained with a pointed tilt of her head toward Mugisha. "Once these systems reach an initial operational capacity, we leave a smaller team behind. They continue working with the community and maturing their processes iteratively. They also collect efficacy data, like what you're looking at here in the presentation."

Mugisha smiled. "Our investors from the World Bank and United Nations will be pleased."

"Yes, agreed . . . " another member of the board, Adola Abdullahi, interjected, her tone implying a forthcoming "but" at the end of her words. The shrewd businesswoman continued, "But what about the 'private' side of our public-private partnership? We can all agree that expanding educational access is admirable, but we also need to consider our private sector investors. Doctor Mahoro, would you talk to us about the business case?"

"If you'll turn to page twelve on your tablet," Ishimwe responded, "you'll see initial results from our newest commercialization initiative, called the Pathways Network. It's still early, but we've established a network of schools and businesses that create sponsored educational opportunities as well as a business pipeline for both employers and students (or, as we like to say, 'future employees')."

"This says businesses have access to freemium subscriptions?" Abdullahi questioned as she examined the presentation on her tablet.

"That's correct. Businesses or business groups, like the International Chamber of Commerce, purchase licenses to join Pathways. Among other things, those subscriptions give them unique access to certified talent in places like rural Ngoma. This gives businesses the high-quality employees they desperately need and at a competitive rate in the global context."

"But what does *freemium* mean, here?"

"The license costs are on a sliding scale, depending on the other contributions an organization provides. For instance, some businesses sign up for our mentor program. They dedicate a set number of expert hours for group teaching and individual coaching. This actually serves our needs just as well as, if not better than, financial payments. It gives our students access to professionals who can help them understand how different lessons translate to workplace settings. And, as Mwami Mugisha will appreciate, the small-group sessions and personal mentorship prove extraordinarily valuable to the students. This is just one example. Businesses can contribute in several other ways, and ultimately, those that choose a full level of commitment pay nothing for their Pathways membership, at least monetarily."

"You said 'high-quality employees,'" Eric Kubwimana, one of the newest advisory board members, noted. "How are you determining that?"

"One of the options is to participate in our validation and accreditation program. Members assist with continuous content reviews and certifications as well as some individual assessments and credentialing work."

"The NGOs also support those programs," the venerable Mugisha observed.

"Can you tell us more about this?" Abdullahi asked, pointing at a new page on her table. Ishimwe noted where the woman was looking and then launched into another topic.

"You mean our AI-recommender system. It's the cornerstone of our learning ecosystem. It accounts for a variety of factors, from individuals' personal profiles in their Autodex to their physical context, teacher and mentor suggestions, and even the time of day or local weather. Students can access their personalized recommendations through an interface on either their AR glasses or personal computers, tablets, or phones. Teachers and educational cohorts have similar user interfaces, and if students lack the proper gear, they can go to one of these classroom huts, located around the region, which all have connectivity and public screens."

Ishimwe stood from the table, motioning for the others to do the same. "Actually, this is good timing. I want to show you how the smart interface on this system works in context. I've planned a little demonstration at the nearby irrigation station. When you get there, put on your AR glasses and enter this code. It will make the system think that you're Jan Alleman, a young man in the tenth grade who wants to be a civil engineer. When you arrive at the pumping station, you'll see how the AI-recommender suggests a variety of lessons, including some hybrid activities that incorporate multiple competency sets. Is everyone rested and ready? Good, let's head out."

[5]

Ehuang's Story

"... but in two years, our forecast predicts a shortage of professionals across your medical sector," Ehuang explained through the video conference to her audience on the other side of the world. She was one of the senior scientists at Pac-World Informatica (PWI), a world leader in data engineering and analytics. Her specialty was education and workforce data, and today, she was briefing the results of her most recent project. A consortium of civic leaders had commissioned PWI to gauge the health of their education, training, and employment indicators and to help them predict potential risks and opportunities.

"This result, which I report at a 90 percent confidence interval, shows a shortfall of 18 to 23 percent. Fortunately, we have recommendations for you." Ehuang pressed her screen, advancing the presentation to the next page. There, she drilled into several courses of action her team had prepared. These included proposals for educational apprenticeships and new vocational modules to help mitigate some high attrition rates they'd uncovered. Ehuang walked through several more projections. One showed how certain improvements to science programs in secondary schools would predictably improve their medical sector workforce along with jobs in other bio-related fields. They also discussed some mature vo-tech programs that the communities could implement.

"These vocational curricula are produced by a Finnish company called Oivallus. They partner with us, and we can help arrange for them to work with your school system, if you'd like. Also, a notable feature of the curricula is their embedded assessments, courtesy of PWI. These include the typical tests and evaluative simulations but also many stealth assessments, which have a significantly greater reliability and validity when used over time."

Ehuang also pitched a creative solution available from another one of PWI's partners. "It's called the Pathways Network. You purchase subscriptions, with a high majority of those proceeds directly supporting the program's operation, or you provide in-kind resources like some faculty service. Participation gives direct access to entry-level employees who matriculate through a rigorous program and receive certifications from a well-accredited board. This won't completely solve your worker shortage (because the graduates don't typically emigrate), but a portion of your at-risk jobs can be filled through telehealth. This means Pathway could be an ideal way to augment your local communities while also growing global connections."

Ehuang continued through the presentation, next reviewing several indicators tied to arts and humanities. She also shared some interesting correlations her team had uncovered about population wellbeing, worker sick days, and various arts programs. As she began to flip to the next digital page, one of the viewers, a woman whose screen name read *Mme Renée Bouchard* interrupted.

"Pardon me, but before we continue, could you address the gray section on that chart?"

The woman's eye had been drawn to a voided section of the visualization.

"This place has unavailable data. Although we can collect this data, it hasn't been integrated into the analysis because of privacy policies. This data could be useful, as it gives a more complete picture of primary education factors," Ehuang replied. "Actually, this is a good time to explain. You can see the 'more details' box near the bottom of your screens, *meh?* Click it and I will highlight something."

Ehuang pressed a spot on her display, making the presentation jump to the appendix. It showed a chart with cost figures and copious fine print. "This is the work-breakdown cost of our project. The green-colored portion, here, is overhead cost. The next section is the labor-hour cost, mostly for analysis and reporting. Look at the portions highlighted in blue. Those indicate the data usage fee. Around half of the report cost is used for microtransactions to the data owners. This fee doesn't apply to all data. Some of it comes at no cost from sensors in your own public infrastructure. Some other data was provided by your schools, at no cost to PWI. But individual data points—particularly those collected by PWI or its partners—each connect to a distributed ledger that records third-party uses of it. In return, PWI (or whomever uses that data) sends a very small payment back to the person who produced it—the student or worker, in this case."

"So, to answer Ms. Bouchard's question more fully: The missing data on the earlier chart is governed by privacy regulations that prevent us from collecting or analyzing it. But, if you wanted to, we could 'turn on' that data collection for students. You would need to gain their permissions and those of their legal guardian. And we'd need to provide micropayments to all who consent. Make sense, *meh?*"

"That does make sense," a man with a graying mustache remarked. His screen name read *Lucas Russell.* "How does this work with the Autodex service that we recently purchased for the public schools? Should we anticipate escalating costs as the program's implementation expands?"

"No," Ehuang said. "The data in Autodexes (or any brand of education, employment, and experience record) belongs to the individual owning that wallet, *lah.* So, there are no privacy restrictions or microtransactions for their own use of their own data. This has been codified in various self-sovereignty regulations, including several endorsed by your own nation. People must be allowed unfettered access to their own data."

"How does that work with schools and businesses? If someone is, let's say, a nurse at a regional hospital, does the hospital or the medical system have access to their records?"

Inwardly, Ehuang counted her blessings that Tan (their unit's legal and ethics officer) had required her to earn that credential in regional data regulations. Originally, she'd groused about the compliance training. She was a data scientist—not an attorney after all! But she had to admit, the training had paid dividends, especially in meetings like this.

"Yes and no," she replied to Mr. Russell. "Workers, for example, may freely provide data such as their earned credentials or their competency mosaic to their employer. But organizations may only access these freely for the benefit of that worker, such as hiring or development. And they may not store the employee's information outside of their Autodex without permission. But a hospital or health care system *may* access those data for, say, workforce planning or even for broader goals, such as scientific studies, if the data owner has set their privacy permissions accordingly and microtransitions are paid."

"So, if we'd like to identify high-potential junior medical workers, or others who we could up-skill into lower-density health care roles, would that be possible?" a different woman, marked as *Councillor Namid,* asked.

"In general, yes." Ehuang responded. "In fact, that's one of the most efficacious uses of such data, and it leads me back to some recommendations we had prepared. Shall we return to the main presentation?"

★ ★ ★

By the time the briefing had ended, Ehuang felt wrung out. It had only taken a few hours, but briefing clients across a video conference—at five o'clock in the morning, no less—was exhausting! Fortunately, she'd planned her workday wisely, blocking the rest of it for quiet data science tasks. Psychometrics and statistical computing were just the thing to soothe Ehuang. She stretched and flipped on the electric kettle, which sat on the other side of her small home office. Her dog, Ginger Bean, stirred on his little bed as she passed, exposing his furry belly in hopes of some pets, which Ehuang dutifully provided as she waited for the water to boil.

With a steaming tea in hand, she returned to her workstation and clicked the Command Station app. It brought up her assignments, reports, and team chatter. She had two tasks for the day, in addition to that early morning briefing. Her team had received a new job from a major athletic brand who wanted to create data-driven credentials for lifestyle activities, like mountain climbing or snowboarding. She and her team needed to identify the stealth assessment factors. She would create those classifiers by analyzing the data streams from the brand's wearable sensors. The company wanted to issue validated digital badges to people who wore their gear while accomplishing certain athletic feats, as logged by the smart apparel. It seemed like a complex task—but incredibly exciting! Ehuang couldn't wait to dig into it. But first, she had better clear out some of her backlog.

She owed one of her colleagues at Oivallus a follow-up. Ehuang had worked with Dahlia for years, and now counted the learning scientist among her friends, even though they had never met in person. Dahlia wanted to coordinate on the embedded assessments in their Finnish National Agency for Education project. It had something to do with connecting learning analytics from the K-12 curriculum to improved feedback for teachers and mentors. If it had been up to Ehuang, she'd have simply shown the faculty the educational data, but Dahlia insisted on creating something she called "scaffolded support." It tied into a decision support system Oivallus helped to maintain, and although Ehuang didn't understand the details, she could appreciate the need to validate the interactions between the data streams, teacher recommendations, and performance outcomes.

Ehuang checked the time on her computer. It was barely past 8:00 a.m., too early for Dahlia in Finland. That meant Ehuang could dive into that athletic sensor data, after all, at least for a few hours. This was going to be a fun day!

[6]

Conclusion

This chapter was written as a story to illustrate several themes. In Arun's section, we incorporated notions of data-driven learning analyses, human-AI teaming, social learning, crowdsourcing from both experts and learners, A/B testing, and trust. In Dahlia's section, we emphasized the critical role learning theory plays in building quality education and training interventions, and we touched on nonlinear learning concepts, competency-based learning, twenty-first century competencies, social and problem-based learning, semantic coherence, and the integration of multiple subjects into a single curriculum.

Dominic's section highlights the collaboration between pedagogical and technological experts as well as concepts such as credentials, AI mentors, personalized learning, and the integration of schooling and employment sectors. Perhaps most notably, this section also introduced the Autodex, a persistent record of someone's education, employment, and experience. Ishimwe's section builds on several learning technology topics, including augmented reality, network connectivity, AI-driven personalization, and the internet of things. Her section also extends the theme of blurred boundaries across educational, commercial, and geographical borders, and importantly, it highlights educational access and equity issues. Finally, Ehuang's section focuses on assessment, for both formal and informal learning contexts, and it references learning analytics, stealth assessment, data privacy, and self-sovereignty.

Taken together, these five stories emphasize the diverse, interdisciplinary teamwork needed for learning engineering. In the future, we imagine learning theorists working closely with technology developers, psychometricians, data scientists, business leaders, and community advocates—among many others. Similarly, we foresee an evolution in learning and employment, with both shifting toward anytime, anywhere modalities and moving away from artificial constraints such as age, location, and time.

Humans, by our nature, are always learning, but in the future, we imagine there will be mechanisms that allow individuals to earn credit for ubiquitous learning—even experiences like climbing a mountain. Informal learning will be captured through various data streams, possibly through stealth assessments running in the background, making it more measurable and accreditable. And when enough evidence has been demonstrated, someone may be able to earn inferred ranks in a competency or a verified credential, like a digital badge. Similarly, we would expect that many of these learning experiences would help reveal traditionally underrepresented factors, such as social or emotional capabilities, and that such valuable competencies will become more explicitly recognized in individuals' personal profiles.

Changing how education, employment, and experiences interact and are credited will, necessarily, also have large effects on today's formal learning institutions. For example, there will be a significant power transfer from teachers (today's classroom leaders) to students, who will be more empowered to pursue their own learning goals and definitions of success. In the intelligence augmentation economy, where new knowledge is created faster than it can be consumed, this learning-to-learn skill will be essential, along with other novel or reimagined twenty-first century competencies, such as collaboration, empathy, and creativity. Similarly, self-regulation and other metacognitive skills will grow in importance, as success in this self-driven, nonlinear, AI-supported life-long learning environment will depend so heavily on them.

Because this chapter focuses on the learning engineering process, the involvement of teachers and trainers was muted in the narrative. However, we anticipate that learning facilitators (of all flavors) will continue to fill important, albeit different, roles. Teaching methods, subject areas, technologies, and data-driven algorithms will change the character of their jobs. Their roles will evolve from "sage on the stage" (a more passive approach focused on information transfer) to "guide on the side" (an active mentor who helps scaffold knowledge and offer coaching across mental, social, emotional, and physical domains).

In addition to learning technology and technique, significant portions of our story focused on data. The big data revolution promises to have massive, paradigm-changing impacts on education and employment. This chapter paints an optimistic picture, but we've also hinted at the darker side of what's possible. For example, data-rich and AI-enabled contexts present opportunities to spread disinformation, create inequitable access to quality information, or misuse personal data. While we mustn't let these risks derail progress, we do have an imperative to address them. For example, what safeguards can the learning engineering community establish to ensure educational access and build internal safeguards against corrupt or degraded information? How can we quantify and validate *trust* in educational resources or manage the veracity and potential bias of data sources and analyses? Privacy and protection of data are other areas of concern, along with issues of self-sovereignty of one's own data. We will need to invest in intentional planning, policies, and governance to prepare for this dynamic worldwide system of systems.

We believe the capabilities described in this chapter are within reach. Each of the techniques and technologies exists in some form today (if not yet fully realized or deployed). Similarly, there is a real desire for quality formal and informal learning, improved measurement, data-driven analyses, and broad integration across global education and employment practices. So, the question isn't technical feasibility or motivation, rather the question is whether we can organize a practical, equitable, and sustainable learning engineering system. This is the challenge that we, the burgeoning learning engineering community, face. Will we rise to the challenge, navigating complex integrated systems, ethical conundrums, and wise governance? We have the tools if we're willing to commit to its success. The future of learning is our story to write. ★

Endnote

1 An effect size of 3.0 means that 99.9% of the experimental group outperformed the control group. In practice, it's essentially the highest effect size. Today, the best designed intelligent tutors can produce this effect size as compared to traditional training and education modalities. For example, see Kulik, James A., and J. Dexter Fletcher. "Effectiveness of intelligent tutoring systems: a meta-analytic review." *Review of Educational Research* 86, no. 1 (2016): 42–78. https://doi.org/10.3102/0034654315581420

About the Authors

Avron Barr

Avron Barr edited the seminal *Handbook of Artificial Intelligence* while at Stanford University and then co-founded Teknowledge, an early AI startup in Silicon Valley. As a consultant, he helps people understand, explain, and market cutting-edge software. Avron is an expert on the infrastructure needed to support AI-assisted learning. He chaired the IEEE Learning Technology Standards Committee and currently serves on the IEEE Educational Activities Board. He's had a life-long interest in how AI will change the way we know, the way we learn, and the way we teach.

Michelle Barrett

Dr. Michelle D. Barrett is Vice President of Research and Learning Engineering for Edmentum, where she leads initiatives in learning engineering, efficacy research, psychometrics and assessment design. After starting her career in education teaching middle and high school mathematics, Dr. Barrett has since held research, technical, and leadership roles at the Colorado Commission on Higher Education, the Colorado Department of Education, CTB/McGraw-Hill, Pacific Metrics, and ACT. She is published in the *Journal of Educational and Behavioral Statistics,* the *Journal of Educational Measurement,* the *International Journal of Artificial Intelligence in Education,* and *Psychometrika.* Dr. Barrett serves on the Board of Directors for the nonprofit organizations AIS Consortium and We Can Learn and chaired the IEEE Industry Consortium on Learning Engineering SIG on AI and Adaptive Technology from 2018 to 2019. Dr. Barrett earned her BS from Stanford University, her MEd from Harvard University, a graduate certificate in large-scale assessment from the University of Maryland, and her PhD from the University of Twente, Netherlands. She also holds certifications in Scaled Agile, Lean Six Sigma, and Pragmatic Marketing.

Erin S. Barry

Erin S. Barry, MS, is Assistant Professor in the Department of Military and Emergency Medicine at the Uniformed Services University (USU). She is a biomedical and biobehavioral scientist with expertise in research design, data management, statistical analyses, and assessment. Her role is to work on all aspects of leadership curriculum, assessment, and research and development to translate scientific materials and evidence to be effectively taught and disseminated. She serves as Principal Researcher for several studies of leadership that focus on individual characteristics, interpersonal dynamics, team building, and academic performance as predictors of leadership competence. Ms. Barry earned a BE in Biomedical Engineering from Vanderbilt University. She earned an MS in Biomedical Engineering from the University of Texas at Arlington. She has worked at USU since 2010 where her research has focused on traumatic brain injury, post-traumatic stress disorder, and leadership. In addition, she helps to mentor graduate and medical students with regard to research activities and is a leadership coach for faculty, staff, and students. She is currently working on her PhD in Health Professions Education focusing on leadership and followership within healthcare teams.

Laura Casey

Dr. Laura Casey is a professor in the Applied Behavior Analysis (ABA)/Special Education program at the University of Memphis. She earned her doctoral degree in Educational Psychology, a Master of Science in School Psychology, a Master of Arts in Community Counseling, and a Bachelor's in Psychology. She completed her doctoral intern at the May Institute with an emphasis in ABA and Positive Behavior Supports in the school. She is a board certified behavior analyst (BCBA), a nationally certified counselor (NCC), and a nationally certified school psychologist (NCSP). She has been the PI and Co-PI on multiple grants totaling over 6 million dollars. She has over 65 peer-reviewed publications and a leading book in ABA and early childhood. Dr. Casey teaches undergraduate and graduate courses in behavior analysis and autism, specializing in evidence-based practice, ethics, and assessment.

Jessie Chuang

With a background in science and engineering, semiconductor industry R&D, and consultancy experience with corporations on learning technologies and AI, Jessie believes that innovations flourish from the collaboration between parties in different domains, and has been dedicated to building interdisciplinary knowledge networks for big challenges, digital transformation, and open innovations. She co-founds Wise Ocean to help scaleups build the growth journey to scale up impact through strategic partnerships across boundaries. She is also on the Executive Board of IEEE IC Industry Consortium on Learning Engineering (ICICLE) and works on industry and corporate engagement for ICICLE.

Scotty D. Craig

Dr. Scotty Craig is an Associate Professor of Human Systems Engineering at Arizona State University and Director of the DoD Advanced Distributed Learning Initiative Partnership Laboratory at Arizona State University. He has a dual affiliation with the Ira A. Fulton Schools of Engineering and the Mary Lou Fulton Teachers College. Dr. Craig has expertise at the intersection of cognitive psychology, usability, and the science of learning (specifically learning technology). He has published widely in the intersecting areas of psychology, education, and technology. Dr. Craig's previously funded projects include grants and contracts from the Institute of Educational Sciences, Office of Naval Research, and several organizations within the US Department of Defense. He has served on the program committee for AIED, iFEST, and Cognitive Science and the editorial board for *Journal of Educational Psychology, Computers & Education (open), International Journal of STEM Education,* and the journal *Technology, Mind, & Behavior.* He has also guest edited volumes for the *International Journal of Learning Technology, International Journal of STEM Education,* and *Journal of Research on Technology in Education* and edited three books: *End-User Considerations in Educational Technology Design, Tutoring and Intelligent Tutoring Systems,* and *Readings in Training and Simulations Vol 2.*

Erin Czerwinski

Erin Czerwinski is the Manager of Learning Engineering for the Open Learning Initiative (OLI) and the Simon Initiative's Community/Product Manager at Carnegie Mellon University (CMU), leading the charge to advance the university's strategic initiative to be the leader in learning science and learning engineering. Erin has deep expertise defining and using learning science methodologies, best practices, and product quality guidelines to deliver impactful learning experiences, with over fifteen years of experience effectively designing, implementing, evaluating, and improving online courses, curricula, and platforms. Erin has also provided curriculum leadership at Western Governors University, and was the Director of Learning Engineering at Acrobatiq, Inc. after serving in a Learning Engineering position with CMU's OLI. She serves on the IEEE Industry Consortium on Learning Engineering Steering Committee and chairs the Maturity Standards for Learning Solutions & Tools Special Interest Group.

Brandt Dargue

Brandt Dargue is a Sr. Systems Engineer and Boeing Associate Technical Fellow specializing in adaptive, personalized, competency-based learning for Boeing Training Solutions. Brandt has spent his 33 years at Boeing researching, designing, developing, integrating, and testing training and performance support solutions for Boeing customers and employees. Brandt's main focus is in automated curation of learning and operational experiences. He is inventor and co-inventor of several patents for adaptive training curation technologies that enable automated performance assessment, adaptive scenarios, intelligent tutoring, and adaptive instruction. These technologies have been applied to several learning experience modalities, including e-learning, classroom instruction, simulations, virtual/augmented environments, and live aircraft. Brandt has served as technical lead, principal investigator, or program manager on numerous government contracts to create adaptive training solutions and to develop/perform the empirical studies to measure their effectiveness.

Chris Dede

Chris Dede is the Timothy E. Wirth Professor in Learning Technologies at Harvard's Graduate School of Education. His fields of scholarship include emerging technologies, policy, and leadership. In 2007, he was honored by Harvard University as an outstanding teacher, and in 2011, he was named a Fellow of the American Educational Research Association. He is currently a member of the OECD 2030 Scientific Committee and an Advisor to the Alliance for the Future of Digital Learning, sponsored by the Mohammed bin Rashid Global Initiative (MBRGI). His co-edited books include: *Scaling Up Success: Lessons Learned from Technology-based Educational Improvement; Digital Teaching Platforms: Customizing Classroom Learning for Each Student; Teacher Learning in the Digital Age: Online Professional Development in STEM Education; Virtual, Augmented, and Mixed Realities in Education; Learning Engineering for Online Education: Theoretical Contexts and Design-Based Examples;* and *The 60-Year Curriculum: New Models for Lifelong Learning in the Digital Economy.*

Diana Delgado

Diana Delgado is an Assistant Professor in the Applied Behavior Analysis Program at the University of Memphis and a Board Certified Behavior Analyst. Dr. Delgado has provided behavioral services to individuals with developmental disabilities and ASD, in home settings, schools and clinics, and she supervises students who are in training to obtain certification. Dr. Delgado has been a professor of behavior analysis at the graduate level for 11 years and is an active contributor to the field through her research and service activities. She has published her research in *Behavior Analysis in Practice, The Psychological Record, Children and Youth Services Review, The Behavior Analyst Today, Mexican Journal of Behavior Analysis,* and also in Latin American journals of psychology including *Conductual, Suma Psicológica,* and *Revista Latinoamericana de Psicología.* Her research focuses in the areas of learning processes in humans, problem solving, and in the application of behavior analysis to problems of social significance.

Tanvi Domadia

Tanvi Domadia is a Learning Engineer at Carnegie Mellon's Open Learning Initiative. She has a background in Computer Science, NGO leadership, game development, and curriculum design. Prior to working at Carnegie Mellon University, she has worked as a Senior Software Engineer at Tata Institute of Social Sciences to develop interactive tools for high school students in rural areas. She has developed educational games in astronomy and math learning for ninth-grade students in India. She has led volunteer operations for conducting storytelling sessions at children's homes with Bookwallah Organization. At OLI, she manages various projects ranging from course development to data-driven course improvement. Tanvi has a Masters in Educational Technology and Applied Learning Sciences from CMU and BE in Computer Science from KJ Somaiya College of Engineering.

Jim Goodell

Jim Goodell is co-author of *Student-Centered Learning: Functional Requirements for Integrated Systems to Optimize Learning* and a thought leader in the world of learning engineering and data standards. He is Director of Innovation at Quality Information Partners, where he helps lead development of the US Department of Education sponsored Common Education Data Standards. He is Chair of the IEEE Learning Technology Standards Committee, chairs the IEEE Industry Consortium on Learning Engineering Competencies, Curriculum, and Credentials SIG, the IEEE Competency Data Standards Workgroup, the Adaptive Instructional Systems Interoperability Workgroup, and serves on the ICICLE Steering Committee. He supports the US Chamber of Commerce Foundation's T3 Innovation Network and co-led development of the Learning and Employment Record (LER) Wrapper Specification. Prior to QIP, he was Executive Vice President at the Center for Educational Leadership and Technology where he led the development of interactive learning technologies and provided information-driven process improvement solutions to state education agencies and school districts throughout the United States.

Scott W. Greenwald

Scott W. Greenwald, PhD, is President and CEO of Three Space Lab, a spatial computing company focusing on learning, collaboration, and communication. He's a PhD alum of the MIT Media Lab, where he wrote a thesis titled *The Equipped Explorer: VR as a Medium for Learning* in 2017 with Prof. Pattie Maes. He's a former Research Scientist at MIT's Materials Research Lab, where he pursued exploratory learning and interactive visualization for crystallography with Prof. Joseph Checkelsky. He's co-founder and chair of the nonprofit Reality Hack, Inc., which co-produces an annual VR/AR hackathon event at MIT. He has co-created numerous VR installations and several live performances using AR and VR technology, where his past and present projects have involved the neuroscience of the retina, improv comedy, immersive narrative for children, crystallography, simulating electrostatics, 3D capture of a string quartet, stories of flight from East Berlin, and contemporary circus. He holds degrees from Northwestern University, the Free University of Berlin, and MIT, and has recently been appointed a Visiting Professor in Design and Computation, a joint program between TU Berlin and UdK Berlin. In his spare time, he practices dance improvisation, contact staff juggling, guitar, and singing.

Andrew J. Hampton

Andrew Hampton is an Assistant Professor of Psychology in the Behavioral Sciences Department at Christian Brothers University. He studied Human Factors/Industrial Organizational Psychology at Wright State University. At the University of Memphis, he served as project manager on a pioneering hybrid tutor, chair of the IEEE Standards Association working group for Adaptive Instructional Systems, and project co-leader for a conversation-based AI for education. He has taught general psychology, writing for psychology, research methods, psychology of film, personality psychology, and advanced statistics. Research interests include technologically mediated communication, psycholinguistics, adaptive educational technology, artificial intelligence, and the ethical implications of AI.

Daniel Jacobs

Daniel Jacobs is currently Director of Data Science at Age of Learning. He has spent over five years working on their industry leading product, *My Math Academy,* which teaches math to young children. He has a long history of working in educational technology, video games and data, and over ten years of professional experience as a software engineer. He has an MS in Electrical Engineering and a BS in Computer System Engineering from Stanford University.

Aaron Kessler

Dr. Aaron Kessler is Assistant Director, Learning Sciences and Teaching for Open Learning at MIT. In his role within the residential education team, he is responsible for working with faculty and course teams in the development and research of online and residential courses that use educational technologies. He serves on the IEEE Industry Consortium on Learning Engineering Steering Committee and chairs the Design for Learning SIG. Prior to his arrival at MIT, Aaron taught high school chemistry, co-developed and supported the implementation of online learning environments and a cognitive tutoring system, and taught pre-service and in-service educators as an assistant professor of educational technology. At the core of all his work is supporting the development of instructional opportunities that provide learners the chance to engage in building deep conceptual understanding of content.

Janet Kolodner

Janet Kolodner is Regents' Professor Emerita of Computing and Cognitive Science in Georgia Institute of Technology's College of Computing and Professor of the Practice at Boston College's Lynch School of Education and Human Development. Her research has addressed issues in learning, memory, and problem solving, both in computers and in people. She pioneered the machine learning method called case-based reasoning, which allows a computer to learn from its experiences, and she used its underlying model to design a project-based approach to education called Learning by Design. She is lead author of a comprehensive middle-school science curriculum, *Project-Based Inquiry Science,* and collaborated on other curriculum design projects. Kolodner was Founding Director of Georgia Tech's EduTech Institute, and she coordinated Georgia Tech's Cognitive Science program for many years. She is founding Editor-in-Chief and Editor-in-Chief Emerita of *The Journal of the Learning Sciences.* She is a co-founder of the International Society for the Learning Sciences and served as its first Executive Officer. Kolodner was a program officer at the US National Science Foundation and led efforts to establish and sustain the Cyberlearning Program (now called SETTL). Currently, she is co-director of Boston College's MA program in Learning Engineering, and she led its development.

Dina Kurzweil

Dr. Kurzweil is the Director of the Education & Technology Innovation (ETI) Support office and an Assistant Professor of Medicine in Health Professions Education at the Uniformed Services University of the Health Sciences. As ETI Director, she provides strategic direction for the ETI, instructional and educational technology support for faculty, supervision of ETI personnel, and management of the ETI office. Prior to that, she worked at the National Defense University providing direction and vision of the instructional team supporting the Center for Educational Technology. Dr. Kurzweil has over twenty-five years of experience leading educational teams focused on effectively designing, implementing, evaluating, and improving courses and curricula in K-12 and higher education environments. She has served on numerous committees and task forces examining a wide range of topics including educational technologies, interprofessional education, professional development for K-12 and higher education faculty, learning management systems, program assessment and evaluation, instructional design, and teaching/faculty support paradigms. Dr. Kurzweil's scholarly interests include a wide variety of issues in learning, teaching, instructional design, faculty development, leadership, teams and educational technology.

Jodi Lis

Jodi Lis is a Senior Learning Advisor at an international nonprofit organization. She has over twenty years experience designing, implementing and monitoring digital learning interventions in workforce development, pre-service education and capacity-building initiatives for the health and education sectors in low-resource environments. She has been a computer teacher at an international school in The Gambia, directed an organization technology to promote the use of technology in education in West Africa and advised digital education programs in primary and secondary schools, teacher training colleges and health training institutions and facilities throughout Africa. She is on the Executive Board of IEEE IC Industry Consortium on Learning Engineering (ICICLE).

Prasad Ram

Dr. Prasad Ram ("Pram") is the Founder, CEO of Gooru. While at Google, he developed the prototype of Gooru Navigator—a GPS for Learning. Gooru since has become an independent nonprofit organization that provides Gooru Navigator with web and mobile applications for students, teachers, parents and school leaders. Students seeking to learn a topic are presented with an adaptive pathway of learning activities and teachers, parents and school leaders obtain real-time actionable insights to personalize interventions. Gooru reaches over 7 million learners through over sixty collaborators. Previously, Pram led Google Books for Education in Mountain View and before that he was the head of Google R&D in India and led projects on Google Maps, News, Language Technologies, Search, and Ads. Pram received the Founders' Award at Google for his work on Google Ads. Prior to joining Google, Pram led engineering at Yahoo! and was a scientist at Xerox Research. Pram has a PhD in Computer Science from UCLA, and a BTech in Computer Science from Indian Institute of Technology-Bombay, India.

Brandt Redd

Brandt Redd is CTO for MatchMaker Education Labs and Secretary to the IEEE Learning Technology Standards Committee. He is a recognized authority in learning technology strategy with expertise in competency-based learning, advanced assessment, and learning data standards. Redd previously served as CIO at the Smarter Balanced Assessment Consortium and, prior to that, as Senior Technology Officer for Education at the Bill & Melinda Gates Foundation. Redd coordinates the EdMatrix.org directory of Learning Tech standards. He helped found three successful startups and is co-inventor of three patents. He has a BS in Computer Science and an MBA from Brigham Young University.

Steve Ritter

Steve Ritter is Founder and Chief Scientist at Carnegie Learning. Dr. Ritter was instrumental in the development and evaluation of the Cognitive Tutors for mathematics. He is the author of numerous papers on the design, architecture and evaluation of Intelligent Tutoring Systems and other advanced educational technology and is recognized as an expert on the design and evaluation of educational technology and on educational analytics. He is lead author of an evaluation that is one of the few to be judged by the US Department of Education's What Works Clearinghouse as meeting their standards without reservations. He has received several awards, including the Best Paper award at the International Conference on Educational Data Mining. Carnegie Learning's mathematics curricula are currently used by over 500,000 students each year.

Bror Saxberg

Bror Saxberg served most recently as the VP of Learning Science at the Chan Zuckerberg Initiative, where he worked on how to bring more evidence-based practices into the learning ecosystem as a whole. He previously served as the Chief Learning Officer at Kaplan, Inc, where he worked to convert Kaplan into a "learning engineering" organization. Before that he served as Senior Vice President and Chief Learning Officer at K12, Inc., where he helped build evidence-based learning for practical use at scale across K-12. Prior to this, he had assignments at Knowledge Universe, Dorling Kindersley, and McKinsey. Saxberg holds a BA in Mathematics and BS in Electrical Engineering from the University of Washington, both received in 1980. He received an MA in Mathematics from Oxford University, and also received his PhD in Electrical Engineering and Computer Science from MIT in 1989 and an MD from Harvard Medical School in 1990.

Sae Schatz

Sae Schatz, PhD, serves as the Director of the Advanced Distributed Learning (ADL) Initiative, a science, technology, and policy program under the Office of the Secretary of Defense in the US Department of Defense. Before joining the government in 2015, Sae worked as an applied human–systems scientist, with an emphasis on human cognition and learning, adaptive systems, learning technologies, performance assessment, and modeling and simulation. Sae has authored numerous peer-reviewed scholarly publications, and she led development of three military textbooks. More recently, she co-edited the book, *Modernizing Learning: Building the Future Learning Ecosystem,* which defines a blueprint for revolutionizing training and education through technology, data, next-generation learning science, and innovation. Sae has worked in defense training and education for over a decade, and she holds a doctorate in Modeling and Simulation from the University of Central Florida.

Jordan Richard Schoenherr

Jordan Richard Schoenherr, PhD, is an Assistant Professor (Department of Psychology, Concordia University), an Adjunct Research Professor in the Department of Psychology and a member of the Institute for Data Science at Carleton University, and a research and ethics consultant. He has published widely in the areas of cognitive psychology, medical education, ethics, and scientific integrity, served on the Executive Board for the International Society for Psychophysics, worked on IEEE Standards Association working group for Adaptive Instructional Systems and Adaptive Instructional Systems Ethics, and was a member of the Alan Turing Institute's AI in Cybersecurity working group. His research interests focus on understanding judgment and decision-making in pure and applied domains including ethics.

Robert Sottilare

Dr. Robert Sottilare is the Director of Learning Sciences at Soar Technology, Inc. (soartech.com) and Chairman of the Board for the not-for-profit Adaptive Instructional Systems (AIS) Consortium (aisconsortium.org), an industry group focused on enhancing the effectiveness of tailored training and educational solutions. He has nearly 40 years of experience as a researcher, developer and evaluator of instructional technology and training systems. Dr. Sottilare received his doctorate in modeling and simulation with a focus on intelligent systems. His experience spans government (US Army and Navy science and technology organizations), industry and academia. His recent research has focused on adaptive instruction including learner and team modeling, automated authoring tools, AI-based real-time instructional management, and evaluation methods for intelligent tutoring systems. At the US Army Research Laboratory, he founded and led the adaptive training science and technology program and is the father of the award-winning Generalized Intelligent Framework for Tutoring (GIFT), an adaptive instructional architecture. Dr. Sottilare is widely published with over 250 technical papers with over 2,500 citations. He is a senior member of the IEEE and founding Chair of the IEEE AIS Working Group and the HCII AIS Conference.

Khanh-Phuong (KP) Thai

Dr. KP Thai is Director of Learning Sciences and Learning Analytics at Age of Learning, Inc. She works on innovative applications of learning sciences, game design, and analytics for advancing early childhood learning with adaptive learning technology. Previously, she was Founder and Chief Learning Scientist of an educational research consultancy that provided research and analytic services to help organizations develop evidence-based coursework, digital learning media, games, and assessments. She also led adaptive system design research as a Senior Learning and Data Scientist at Squirrel AI Learning. KP is co-editor of the *Handbook of Research on Innovative Approaches to Early Childhood Development and School Readiness.* She obtained her PhD in Cognitive Psychology with a minor in Quantitative Methods from University of California, Los Angeles.

Richard Tong

Richard Tong is an experienced technologist, executive, entrepreneur and one of the leading evangelists for global standardization efforts for learning technologies and artificial intelligence. Richard Tong is currently the Chief Architect and General Manager of US Operations, Squirrel AI Learning. He also currently serves as the Chair of IEEE Learning Technology Standards Committee and Chair of IEEE artificial intelligence Standards Committee. Prior to Squirrel AI, he was the Head of Implementation, Greater China Region for Knewton, and Director of Solution Architecture for Amplify Education. He also served as the CTO of Phoenix New Media (NYSE:FENG). On the academic and research front, he has organized conferences such as the AIAED conferences (2018, 2019, 2020), and organized workshops such as multimodal artificial intelligence for education workshops (AIMA4EDU) at the IJCAI 2019, IJCAI 2020, IJCAI 2021, the ed-tech standardization and collaboration workshops at the AIED 2019, AIED 2020 and AIED 2021. He was the workshop co-chair of AIED 2020, industry co-chair of ITS 2021 and AIED 2021 and held several track-chair positions in various AI and EdTech conferences.

JJ Walcutt

Dr. JJ Walcutt is a scientist, innovator, and digital learning engineer who specializes in strategic development and reform across education, military, and government. Her current work focuses on leveraging digital transformation capabilities for optimizing human cognition to drive decision superiority and improved performance across a wide spectrum of programs including neuro-informed military training, data-driven knowledge management, and talent development optimization. Dr. Walcutt also recently served in the US Government as the Director of Innovation at the Advanced Distributed Learning (ADL) Initiative under the Office of the Secretary of Defense and as a Human Innovation Fellow under the Office of Personnel Management. In her role at the Pentagon, Dr. Walcutt focused on promoting the science of learning through the stewardship of policy and her service as a US Delegate to NATO, Partnership for Peace, and as a national and international keynote speaker.